T0092153

Exam Ref MD-102
Microsoft Endpoint
Administrator

Andrew Bettany
Andrew Warren

Exam Ref MD-102 Microsoft Endpoint Administrator

Published with the authorization of Microsoft Corporation by:
Pearson Education, Inc.

ISBN-13: 978-0-13-825493-3
ISBN-10: 0-13-825493-1

Library of Congress Control Number: 2023941325

$PrintCode

TRADEMARKS

Microsoft and the trademarks listed at http://www.microsoft.com on the "Trademarks" webpage are trademarks of the Microsoft group of companies. All other marks are property of their respective owners.

WARNING AND DISCLAIMER

Every effort has been made to make this book as complete and as accurate as possible, but no warranty or fitness is implied. The information provided is on an "as is" basis. The author, the publisher, and Microsoft Corporation shall have neither liability nor responsibility to any person or entity with respect to any loss or damages arising from the information contained in this book or from the use of the programs accompanying it.

SPECIAL SALES

For information about buying this title in bulk quantities, or for special sales opportunities (which may include electronic versions; custom cover designs; and content particular to your business, training goals, marketing focus, or branding interests), please contact our corporate sales department at corpsales@pearsoned.com or (800) 382-3419.

For government sales inquiries, please contact governmentsales@pearsoned.com.

For questions about sales outside the U.S., please contact intlcs@pearson.com.

EDITOR-IN-CHIEF
Brett Bartow

EXECUTIVE EDITOR
Loretta Yates

ASSOCIATE EDITOR
Shourav Bose

DEVELOPMENT EDITOR
Rick Kughen

MANAGING EDITOR
Sandra Schroeder

SENIOR PROJECT EDITOR
Tracey Croom

COPY EDITOR
Rick Kughen

INDEXER
Ken Johnson

PROOFREADER
Barbara Mack

TECHNICAL EDITOR
Tommy B. Kobberøe

EDITORIAL ASSISTANT
Cindy Teeters

COVER DESIGNER
Twist Creative, Seattle

COMPOSITOR
codeMantra

Pearson's Commitment to Diversity, Equity, and Inclusion

Pearson is dedicated to creating bias-free content that reflects the diversity of all learners. We embrace the many dimensions of diversity, including but not limited to race, ethnicity, gender, socioeconomic status, ability, age, sexual orientation, and religious or political beliefs.

Education is a powerful force for equity and change in our world. It has the potential to deliver opportunities that improve lives and enable economic mobility. As we work with authors to create content for every product and service, we acknowledge our responsibility to demonstrate inclusivity and incorporate diverse scholarship so that everyone can achieve their potential through learning. As the world's leading learning company, we have a duty to help drive change and live up to our purpose to help more people create a better life for themselves and to create a better world.

Our ambition is to purposefully contribute to a world where:

- Everyone has an equitable and lifelong opportunity to succeed through learning.
- Our educational products and services are inclusive and represent the rich diversity of learners.
- Our educational content accurately reflects the histories and experiences of the learners we serve.
- Our educational content prompts deeper discussions with learners and motivates them to expand their own learning (and worldview).

While we work hard to present unbiased content, we want to hear from you about any concerns or needs with this Pearson product so that we can investigate and address them.

- Please contact us with concerns about any potential bias at https://www.pearson.com/report-bias.html.

Contents at a glance

Contents

Chapter 3   Manage, maintain, and protect devices 139

Acknowledgments

Thank you to the team at Pearson, who helped make the book production process efficient and painless. I'm dedicating this book to Annette and Tommy for being supportive and encouraging. This book is also for the reader. I hope this book helps you proficiently manage Microsoft Windows within a modern cloud environment. The world of IT changes often, and we should all strive to stay up-to-date and use the most appropriate tools. I hope this book helps you to achieve success!

—ANDREW BETTANY

Procrastination is a writer's constant companion, which is nice, because writing can sometimes be a solitary occupation. But working with a great team helps avoid literary dithering and fosters a community spirit. So, I'd like to thank the editorial folks at Pearson for their help and guidance these last few months. I'd also like to thank Nuala, our dog, for giving me plenty of excuses to get up from my desk and go and see what's happening outside. After all, there's always tomorrow.

—ANDREW WARREN

About the authors

ANDREW BETTANY has been awarded the Microsoft Most Valuable Professional (Windows and Devices for IT) for nine years. In 2020, he joined Microsoft for a couple of years to help the Education team drive cloud skills and now helps students globally with achieving skills and certifications via his Cloud Ready Skills programs. He is a loving dad, IT Geek, training mentor, and consultant, entrepreneur, and author.

Andrew is recognized for his Windows expertise and is the author of many publications, including several Windows exam certification prep guides and Microsoft official training materials. He has created video training materials for LinkedIn Learning and Pluralsight. As a Microsoft Certified Trainer for 18 years, Andrew delivers learning and consultancy to businesses in many technical areas, including Microsoft 365, Azure, and Windows.

Andrew is active on social media and can be found on LinkedIn, Facebook, and Twitter. He lives in a village just outside the beautiful city of York in Yorkshire, England.

ANDREW WARREN, MCT, has been writing for Microsoft for many years, helping to develop its official curriculum of instructor-led training material. He has served as a subject matter expert on many Windows Server courses, was technical lead on several Windows client titles, and was involved in Microsoft 365, Azure, and Intune course development. When not writing about Microsoft technologies, he can be found in the classroom, teaching other IT professionals what they need to know to manage their organization's IT infrastructure.

Introduction

With the Microsoft 365 Certified: Modern Desktop Administrator Associate certification, Microsoft has changed how IT Pro certifications work. Rather than being based on a technology area, they are focused on a specific job role. The Microsoft MD-102: Endpoint Administrator exam provides the foundation of this Microsoft 365 Certified: Modern Desktop Administrator Associate certification.

This book covers every major topic area on the exam but does not cover every exam question. Only the Microsoft exam team has access to the exam questions, and Microsoft regularly adds new questions to the exam, making it impossible to cover specific questions. You should consider this book a supplement to your relevant real-world experience and other study materials. If you encounter a topic in this book that you do not feel completely comfortable with, use the "Need more review?" links you'll find in the text to find more information and take the time to research and study the topic. Great information is available on the Microsoft website at *docs.microsoft.com*.

Organization of this book

This book is organized by the "Skills measured" list published for the exam. The "Skills measured" list is available for each exam on the Microsoft Learn website: *microsoft.com/learn*. Each chapter in this book corresponds to a major topic area in the list, and the technical tasks in each topic area determine a chapter's organization. For example, if an exam covers six major topic areas, the book will contain six chapters.

Preparing for the exam

Microsoft certification exams are a great way to build your resume and let the world know about your level of expertise. Certification exams validate your on-the-job experience and product knowledge. Although there is no substitute for on-the-job experience, preparation through study and hands-on practice can help you prepare for the exam.

We recommend augmenting your exam preparation plan by using a combination of available study materials and courses. For example, you might use the Exam Ref and another study guide for your "at-home" preparation and take a Microsoft Official Curriculum course for the classroom experience. Choose the combination that you think works best for you. Learn more about available classroom training, online courses, and live events at *microsoft.com/learn*.

Note that this Exam Ref is based on publicly available information about the exam and the author's experience. To safeguard the integrity of the exam, authors do not have access to the live exam.

Microsoft certifications

Microsoft certifications distinguish you by proving your command of a broad set of skills and experience with current Microsoft products and technologies. The exams and corresponding certifications are developed to validate your mastery of critical competencies as you design and develop, or implement and support, solutions with Microsoft products and technologies, both on-premises and in the cloud. Certification brings various benefits to the individual, employers, and organizations.

> **MORE INFO**   **ALL MICROSOFT CERTIFICATIONS**
>
> For information about Microsoft certifications, including a full list of available certifications, go to *microsoft.com/learn*.

Access the exam updates chapter and online references

The final chapter of this book, "MD-102 Endpoint Administrator exam updates," will be used to provide information about new content per new exam topics, content that has been removed from the exam objectives, and revised mapping of exam objectives to chapter content. The chapter will be made available from the link below as exam updates are released.

This book contains webpage addresses that the author has recommended you visit for more information. Some of these links can be very long and painstaking to type, so we've shortened them for you to make them easier to visit. We've also compiled them into a single list that readers of the print edition can refer to while they read.

The URLs are organized by chapter and heading. Every time you come across a URL in the book, find the hyperlink in the list to go directly to the webpage.

Download the Exam Updates chapter and the URL list at *MicrosoftPressStore.com/ERMD102/ downloads*.

Errata, updates & book support

We've made every effort to ensure the accuracy of this book and its companion content. You can access updates to this book—in the form of a list of submitted errata and their related corrections—at:

MicrosoftPressStore.com/ERMD102/errata

If you discover an error that is not already listed, please submit it to us at the same page.

For additional book support and information, please visit *MicrosoftPressStore.com/Support*.

Please note that product support for Microsoft software and hardware is not offered through the previous addresses. For help with Microsoft software or hardware, go to *support.microsoft.com*.

Stay in touch

Let's keep the conversation going! We're on Twitter: *twitter.com/MicrosoftPress*.

CHAPTER 1

Deploy Windows client

The MD-102 Windows 11 exam focuses on efficiently deploying Windows 11 with the least administrative effort and using modern tools and technologies. You must understand how to plan and deploy Windows 11 and be able to choose the most appropriate method.

Skills covered in this chapter:

- Skill 1.1: Prepare for a Windows client deployment
- Skill 1.2: Plan and implement a Windows client deployment by using Windows Autopilot
- Skill 1.3: Plan and implement a Windows client deployment by using MDT
- Skill 1.4: Configure remote management

Skill 1.1: Prepare for a Windows client deployment

Windows 11 offers new and exciting methods for organizations to deploy the operating system to users. For many years, enterprises have resisted adopting modern dynamic deployment methods and utilized legacy tools to deploy Windows. On the MD-102 exam, you must understand when the newer methods are used and how to implement them over more traditional methods. By nudging the audience, we can see Microsoft shift the adoption of the new dynamic deployment methods, which will gain traction in the modern workplace.

> **This skill covers how to:**
> - Select a deployment tool based on requirements
> - Choose between migrate and rebuild
> - Choose an imaging and/or provisioning strategy
> - Select a Windows edition based on requirements
> - Implement subscription-based activation

Select a deployment tool based on requirements

Deploying Windows 11 within an enterprise environment should be carefully planned so the delivery has every chance to succeed. This is especially applicable when faced with choosing from numerous tools and methods.

Technologies evolve and modernize, so your deployment process should evolve too. You should follow best practices and current guidance to utilize the productivity advancements to ensure that your deployment is delivered with minimal issues and delivered on schedule.

Windows 11 is released using a continuous delivery model known as Windows as a Service, with a new version of Windows 11 available annually. Therefore, the skills you learn in deploying Windows 11 to your users will be reused again and often.

It is recommended that administrators choose a group of users and deploy Windows 11 into focused pilot projects to test each version of Windows 11 within their organizations before rolling out the operating system to larger cohorts of users.

You must explore each of the available deployment options. These options include technology such as Windows Autopilot, Microsoft Deployment Toolkit (MDT), or Configuration Manager that might be currently used within your organization.

Table 1-1 lists many different methods to deploy and configure Windows 11. You need to understand when to use each deployment method.

TABLE 1-1 Methods for deploying and configuring Windows

Method	Description
Windows Autopilot	Transform an existing Windows 11 installation, join the device to Azure AD, and enroll it into a Mobile Device Management solution to complete the configuration. Deploy Windows 11 on an existing Windows 7, 8.1, or 10 device.
Windows 11 subscription activation	Upgrade the Windows edition seamlessly without requiring intervention or rebooting of the device.
Azure AD / MDM	Cloud-based identity and management solution offering device, app, and security configuration.
Provisioning packages	Small distributable .appx files that securely transform devices to meet organizational requirements.
In-place upgrade	Upgrade an earlier version of Windows to Windows 10 while retaining all apps, user data, and settings.
Bare metal	Deploy Windows 11 to newly built devices or wipe existing devices and deploy fresh Windows 11 images to them.
Refresh (wipe and load)	Re-use existing devices. Retain user state (user data, Windows, and app settings). Wipe devices, deploy Windows 11 images to them, and finally, restore the user state.
Replace	Purchase new devices. Back up the user state from the current device. Transform or wipe a pre-installed Windows 11 installation and restore the user state.

Deployment using dynamic provisioning

Dynamic provisioning uses modern tools, including mobile device management solutions, to deploy devices. Many of these options were unavailable when deploying previous Windows versions using traditional deployment methods. Table 1-2 compares modern dynamic provisioning and traditional deployment methods, which can also incorporate image creation.

TABLE 1-2 Provisioning methods

Dynamic provisioning methods	Traditional deployment methods
Enrollment into Azure Active Directory and Mobile Device Management (such as Microsoft Intune)	On-premises deployment tools using Windows ADK, Windows Deployment Services, Microsoft Deployment Toolkit, or Configuration Manager
Provisioning packages using Windows Configuration Designer	Bare-metal install
Subscription activation	In-place upgrade
Windows Autopilot	Wipe-and-load upgrade

The deployment choices available to an organization might be skewed by its investment in traditional deployment methods and infrastructure. This might include reliance upon on-premises tools and procedures, such as Microsoft Deployment Toolkit (MDT) and Endpoint Configuration Manager. These tools continue to be supported and can be used to support on-premises deployment methods, such as bare metal, refresh, and replace scenarios. You should understand the modern alternatives to the traditional on-premises methods.

Deploying Windows 11 using modern cloud-based deployment and dynamic provisioning methods includes using subscription activation, Windows Autopilot, and Azure Active Directory (Azure AD) join. Ongoing management of Windows 11 is then undertaken using Mobile Device Management (MDM), such as Microsoft Intune.

Dynamic provisioning

You should see a theme throughout this book, which is to recommend an alternative method of provisioning client devices to the traditional approach, which would typically include the following stages:

- Purchase or reprovision a device
- Wipe the device
- Replace the preinstalled operating system with a customized image
- Join an on-premises Active Directory
- Apply Group Policy settings
- Manage apps using Configuration Manager or MDT

With a cloud-based deployment approach, the stages are simplified to the following:

- Purchase or re-provision a device
- Apply a transformation to the preinstalled operating system
- Join Azure AD and enroll in MDM
- Use MDM to configure the device, enforce compliance with corporate policies, and add, remove, and configure apps

There is a significant difference between the two approaches. Dynamic provisioning seeks to avoid needing on-premises infrastructure and resource-intensive reimaging procedures.

Because Windows 11 is updated once a year to a newer version—with each new version supported for a maximum of 24 months (36 months for Enterprise and Education editions)— maintaining customized deployment images can become a costly and burdensome process for the IT department.

The types of transformations that are currently available using dynamic provisioning include the following:

- **Provisioning packages** A provisioning package is created using the Windows Configuration Designer and can send one or more configurations to apps and settings on a device.
- **Subscription Activation** Windows 11 Subscription Activation allows you to automatically upgrade devices from Windows 11 Pro to Windows 11 Enterprise without entering a product key or performing a restart.
- **Azure AD join with automatic MDM enrollment** A device can be joined to Azure AD and automatically enrolled into the organizational MDM solution by having users enter their work or school account details. Once enrolled, MDM will configure the device to the organization's policies.

Provisioning packages

Provisioning packages are still a new method of deploying changes to Windows clients. They are created using the Windows Configuration Designer included in the Windows Assessment and Deployment Kit (Windows ADK). You can also download the standalone Windows Configuration Designer app from the Microsoft Store. The Microsoft Store Windows Configuration Designer app will auto-update to the latest version available.

> **NOTE DOWNLOAD WINDOWS ADK**
>
> You can download the Windows ADK from the Microsoft website at *https://learn.microsoft.com/windows-hardware/get-started/adk-install*. Make sure to download the version of Windows ADK that matches the Windows 11 version you intend to deploy.

Provisioning packages use very small configuration files. These are used to modify existing Windows 11 installations and configure their runtime settings.

A provisioning package can perform a variety of functions, such as:

- Configure the computer name and user accounts
- Add the computer to a domain
- Upgrade the Windows 11 version, such as upgrading Windows 11 Home to Windows 11 Enterprise
- Configure the Windows user interface
- Add additional files or install apps
- Remove installed software
- Configure network connectivity settings
- Install certificates
- Implement security settings
- Reset Windows 11
- Run PowerShell scripts

To create a provisioning package, you should complete the Windows Configuration Designer installation process using either Windows ADK or the Microsoft Store. Once done, you can create and deploy your provisioning packages. Start by opening Windows Configuration Designer. On the **Start page** displayed in Figure 1-1, select the option that best describes the type of provisioning you want. If you're unsure, choose the **Advanced provisioning** tile.

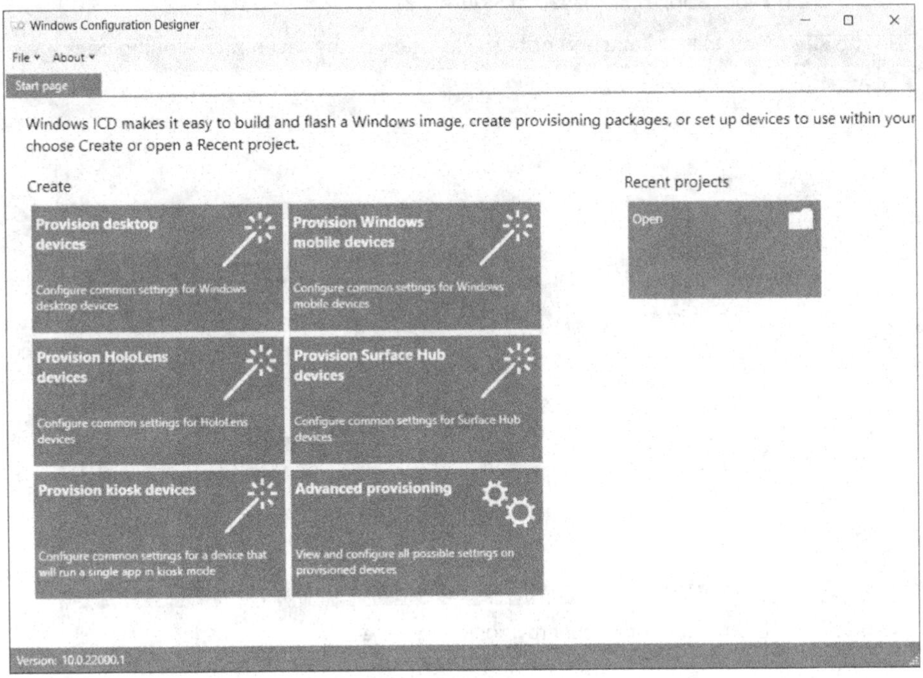

FIGURE 1-1 Creating a new provisioning package

Use the following procedure to create your provisioning package to deploy a universal line of business (LOB) app:

1. Select the **Advanced provisioning** tile.

2. In the **New project** wizard, on the **Enter project details** page, enter the name and a meaningful description for your provisioning package. For example, enter **Deploy LOB App1** and then select **Next**.

3. On the **Choose which settings to view and configure** page, select **All Windows desktop editions,** and select **Next**.

4. On the **Import a provisioning package (optional)** page, select **Finish**. (You can use this option to import settings from a previously configured package that mostly, but not entirely, meets your needs.)

5. On the **Available customizations** page, in **View**, select **All settings**, and then expand **Runtime settings**, as displayed in Figure 1-2.

6. On the **Available customizations** page, in the navigation pane, expand **Universal-AppInstall**, and then select **DeviceContextApp**.

7. In the details pane, in the **PackageFamilyName** text box, enter a name for this collection of apps. For example, enter **LOB App1**.

8. Select the **PackageFamilyName: LOB App1** node.

9. In the **ApplicationFile** text box, select **Browse**. Navigate to and select the .appx file representing your app, as displayed in Figure 1-2.

10. In the **File** menu, select **Save** and note the location of the saved provisioning package file.

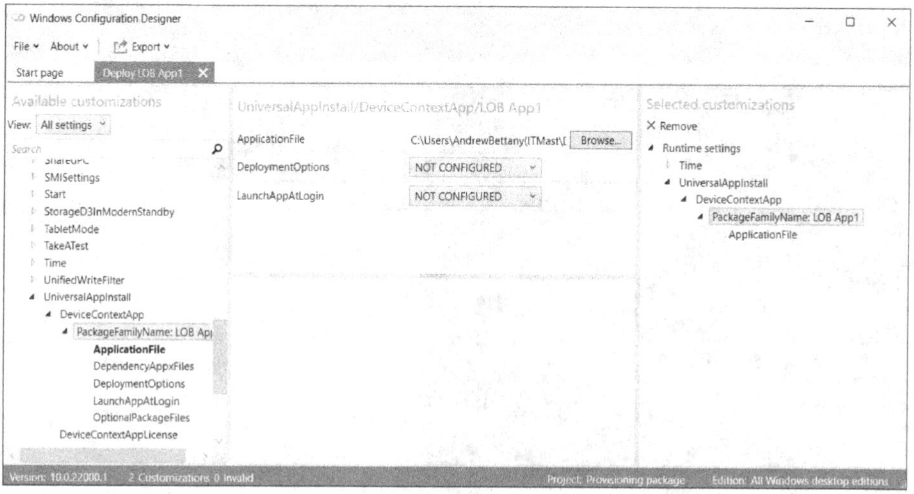

FIGURE 1-2 Available customizations for your provisioning package

You have created a customization for your app and are now ready to deploy this customization by applying the provisioning package.

Apply provisioning packages

To apply a provisioning package, you must start by exporting the package. To export your provisioning package, in the Windows Configuration Designer, use the following procedure:

1. Select the project file from the **Recent Projects** area of the **Start page** or select **File** and locate the project file. (It should use the project's name and have an `.icdproj` file extension.)

2. On the menu bar, select **Export** > **Provisioning package**.

3. In the **Build** wizard, on the **Describe the provisioning package** page, the **Name** box is already complete with the project name. You can now specify the package version number and **Owner** information, such as **IT Admin**. Complete this information and select **Next**.

4. On the **Select security details for the provisioning package** page, choose whether you want to encrypt or sign your package (or both) and then select **Next**. (To digitally sign your package, you must have an appropriate digital certificate that users of your package trust.)

5. On the **Select where to save the provisioning package** page, specify where you want to store the package and then select **Next**.

6. On the **Build the provisioning package** page, select **Build**. Your provisioning package is exported to your specified location.

7. The **All done** page appears. Make a note of the package details and then select **Finish**.

8. You can now apply the package to client devices and run the `.ppkg` file.

Once you have configured the settings within the Windows Configuration Designer, you export the provisioning package to a `.ppkg` file. To secure the `.ppkg` file, you can optionally encrypt the package and digitally sign it. Once signed, only packages that are trusted can be applied on a client computer.

You can deploy the provisioning package to users via email, physical media, or by sharing the file using OneDrive for Business. The settings are applied to the target device by one of the following methods:

- Running the `.ppkg` file
- Adding the provisioning package using the Settings app
- Use the `Add-ProvisioningPackage` Windows PowerShell cmdlet

Provisioning packages can be applied to a device during the first-run experience when a device is first turned on using a USB drive containing the provisioning package or after the out-of-box experience (or "OOBE") has been completed.

NEED MORE REVIEW? **PROVISIONING PACKAGES FOR WINDOWS 11**

To review further details about provisioning packages, refer to the Microsoft website at *https://learn.microsoft.com/en-us/windows/configuration/provisioning-packages/ provisioning-packages*.

Manage and troubleshoot provisioning packages

You have already seen how using provisioning packages as part of your dynamic provisioning of Windows 11 can simplify your deployment processes.

The Windows Configuration Designer tool can be installed from the Microsoft Store as an app, which allows it to be regularly updated. Alternatively, you can install the Windows Configuration Designer tool as part of Windows ADK.

The WCD interface is simple, and common tasks are offered using the available wizards, which can be used to create a provisioning package that can be used in the following environments:

- **Provision desktop devices**   Provides the typical settings for Windows 11 desktop devices.

- **Provision Windows mobile devices**   Provides the typical settings for Windows 11 mobile devices.

- **Provision HoloLens devices**   Provides the typical settings for Windows 11 Holographic devices, such as HoloLens headsets.

- **Provision Surface Hub devices**   Provides the typical settings for Surface Hub devices.

- **Provision kiosk devices**   Provides the typical settings for a device running a single app.

- **Advanced provisioning**   Enables you to view and configure all available settings. Choose this option if you are unsure which specific package type to use.

Most provisioning packages will be aimed at provisioning Windows 11 desktop devices and will use the advanced configuration option because this allows the greatest customization.

Provisioning packages offer administrators a quick and simplified mechanism to configure devices securely. Once created, the settings within a .ppkg file can be viewed using the WCD and edited using the built-in wizards or the advanced editor. When provisioning packages that need to be deployed to remote devices, they can be protected using encryption and signed.

Several usage scenarios for provisioning packages are shown in Table 1-3.

TABLE 1-3 Usage Scenarios for Provisioning Packages

Scenario	Phase	Description
New devices with Windows 11 need to have apps deployed to the devices.	New device	Provisioning packages can be used to deploy apps to devices.
Existing Windows 11 Pro devices need to be upgraded to Windows 11 Enterprise.	Upgrade	Provisioning packages can be used to change the Windows edition by deploying product keys or licenses using the Edition Upgrade settings.
You must update device drivers on Windows 11 devices.	Maintain	Provisioning packages can be used to deploy device drivers to devices.

When using provisioning packages, you might need to troubleshoot them if devices are not configured as expected.

There are several areas on which you can focus your attention when troubleshooting provisioning packages, as follows:

- Configuration errors and missing customizations
- Expired Azure AD Token
- Export errors, including encryption and signing issues
- User issues
- Advanced troubleshooting

If you have deployed the .ppkg file to multiple devices, and they have all failed to process the required changes, then you should first inspect the provisioning package. Locate the project file (with the .icdproj file extension) and open it using the WCD. You should then inspect the settings and confirm that they match your expectations and the design specification or change the documentation for the provisioning package.

If you use the configuration wizard to configure automatic enrollment into Azure AD, you should ensure that the bulk token embedded inside the provisioning package has not expired. By default, this token is set to expire one month after creation, though you can manually set the token expiry date to 180 days after the creation date. If the package is used after the Bulk AAD Token has expired, the package will fail to install. You must edit the package, apply for a new Bulk AAD Token, and re-export the package.

After verifying the customization settings are correct, you should export the package again. Increment the version number to avoid confusion with the package's previous version. Packages with the same versioning number will not be applied to the same target device twice.

If issues are suspected with either the encryption or signing of the package, you can export without these enhancements and redeploy to your test machine to determine whether the issue remains.

For users, devices can be configured by placing the provisioning package on a USB drive and inserting it during the initial OOBE setup phase. Windows Setup should automatically recognize the drive and ask the user if they want to install the provisioning package. If the package is not recognized, check that the file is in the root directory of the USB drive.

You can use the Windows Performance Recorder to perform advanced troubleshooting for provisioning packages on user devices. The Windows Performance Recorder in the Windows Assessment and Deployment Kit (Windows ADK) offers advanced Event Tracing for Windows. The system events recorded by this tool can be analyzed using Windows Performance Analyzer, available from the Windows ADK or Microsoft Store.

Choose between migrate and rebuild

In previous versions of Windows, you could upgrade a device to the latest version of Windows, migrate data from another device to a new device, or perform a clean install. Enterprises have long believed that performing a clean install offers them the most reliable outcome. However, the best practice is to retain the operating system on the device and then transform it or upgrade to the required build of Windows. Microsoft has successfully and consistently applied updates to Windows from one build to a later one; this is now an accepted and trusted process.

Many large enterprises use Microsoft Configuration Manager, a powerful yet complex tool to manage an organization's devices, apps, and upgrades. Configuration Manager (current branch) continues to be supported by Microsoft and can be used to upgrade older operating systems to Windows 11.

Rebuilding new computers

Some organizations prefer to completely rebuild devices before handing them to users. This is typical within smaller organizations with limited resources to create and maintain images and provisioning packages. Many will want to remove bloatware—software added by the vendor. This software can be utilities and software that enhances the user experience, which is favorable. However, third-party software, such as security software or apps, is often included. Most of these apps are preinstalled as trial software and are often unwanted, especially in a corporate environment.

While it is best practice to transform an existing device and re-provision it to the latest version of Windows, it is still common for devices to be formatted and completely rebuilt. By reinstalling Windows, the device must be provisioned with the operating system, drivers, patches, applications, and security measures (such as BitLocker Drive Encryption) before they are handed to users.

Rebuilding a device is a straightforward process, though it can be a manual and time-consuming process. The resources must be reviewed to ensure that the latest drivers and other software are up-to-date and compatible.

Seldom will a newly formatted device that is re-installed be as performant as a device supplied preconfigured by the original equipment manufacturer (OEM). This is because device manufacturers often optimize the computer set up with extra drivers or tweaks to settings not included in the public drivers and software packages. This "secret sauce" can greatly affect the device's speed and battery life.

A new and especially useful option in this new post-COVID world is allowing users to drive the device provisioning process. The user-driven method allows users to join their device into

Azure Active Directory and then allow the automatic mobile device management (MDM) provisioning capabilities to configure and set up the device. The user must enter their Azure Active Directory account and password (called their "work or school account" within Windows 11). The MDM service then configures the device, making it ready for work.

Choose an imaging and/or provisioning strategy

When deploying Windows 11 in your organization, it's important to understand the different ways Windows can be deployed. You have seen the various methods to deploy and configure Windows based on the scenarios you face. You need to evaluate these scenarios, understand each deployment methodology's capabilities and limitations, and decide the most appropriate for your organization.

The key benefit of using an image-based method is that the deployment is completed within one action. The Windows image and configuration settings, apps, and files can be deployed to the device. The device then performs the out-of-box experience (OOBE) process and can be seamlessly enrolled into management. The key downside of this macro image approach is that the image is only up to date when it is built. Subsequent deployments will require the image to be updated and validated, which can outweigh the speed benefits of using an image if several updates and patches are required.

Using provisioning packages to transform a device can apply tailored settings and configurations to a device, including:

- Transform the edition of Windows that is in use.
- Apply configuration and settings to the device, including:
- Security settings
- Device restrictions
- Policies
- WiFi and VPN profiles
- Certificates
- Install apps
- Language packs
- Windows updates
- Enroll the device in a management solution such as Intune

Once the device has been configured, it can then be managed via the management solution for further configuration and ongoing management.

Larger enterprises will choose to use more robust and scalable tools, including one or more of the following:

- Azure Active Directory join and automatic MDM enrollment
- Windows Autopilot
- Microsoft Deployment Toolkit (MDT)
- Microsoft Endpoint Configuration Manager

We will summarize each of these later in this and later chapters. We could devote an entire chapter to each solution, but you only need an overview of MDT and Configuration Manager for the MD-102 exam.

Azure AD Join with automatic MDM enrollment

You can dynamically provision Windows 11 devices using Azure AD and a Mobile Device Management (MDM) solution, such as Microsoft Intune. Once a device is enrolled into management, Microsoft Intune can deploy compliance and corporate security policies to the device in a similar way (but not the same) as Group Policy objects are used within a domain-based environment to configure computers.

MDM can be used to add or remove apps, restrict device features, and more. Through the application of MDM policies, Azure AD can block or allow access to corporate resources or applications based on the status of the device compliance.

To benefit from the cloud-based dynamic provisioning, you need the following requirements:

- Windows 11 Pro or Windows 11 Enterprise
- Azure AD for identity management
- A mobile device management solution, such as Microsoft Intune

User-driven deployments

Most IT deployments are strictly controlled and managed centrally by the IT department. Deploying, managing, and maintaining remote devices can be challenging for organizations. With the new modern provisioning called Windows Autopilot, users can receive a new device directly from an OEM retailer (or central IT) and have the device configured automatically and ready for use.

Central IT will configure device profiles which will then be deployed to the pre-registered devices once the user signs onto the device for the first time. Once authenticated, Windows Autopilot sets up the device, adds it to Azure AD, and enrolls it with Microsoft Intune.

The user is responsible for initiating the Windows Autopilot process. The device will be fully configured and ready for use, typically within an hour. This is especially beneficial for remote salesforce devices where users seldom visit the office. Other use cases include replacement devices shipped directly to the user following loss or damage.

Windows Autopilot deployment overview

We will cover Windows Autopilot in more detail later in this chapter, but it is useful to provide an overview of this new deployment solution here.

Devices deployed by Windows Autopilot can be traditional Windows computers or kiosk devices. Kiosk devices are regular devices dedicated to a specific task, such as a multi-app kiosk device like Surface Go, which displays a messaging app, or the Microsoft Edge browser in a corporate office lobby.

In addition to deploying devices, Autopilot allows you to remotely reset and repurpose devices. Therefore, IT departments can be further optimized and no longer need to process devices themselves—they can ship devices direct to the end user and allow the user to start the deployment configuration remotely. Because Autopilot runs as a cloud service, there's no infrastructure to manage. Administrators can manage and configure devices remotely from the Microsoft Endpoint Manager portal.

Windows Autopilot allows administrators to customize the out-of-the-box experience and reduce the time IT spends deploying and managing devices. Because devices are shipped directly to the end user, rather than via IT, and then transformed "while you wait," there is minimal delay in the deployment, and the user can be productive quickly.

All devices that are to be configured by Autopilot must first be known to the Windows Autopilot service. A hardware hash, or ID, is collected from each device – this can be done within your organization for devices your organization already owns, or your hardware vendor can upload these hardware hashes on your behalf. Windows Autopilot requires Azure AD to provide the cloud identity for the user, and the hardware hash is associated with the cloud device identity. The overview of the Windows Autopilot device provisioning process can be seen in Figure 1-3. The flow diagram shows Windows Autopilot used to configure AAD-joined devices supplied by the hardware vendor directly to the user.

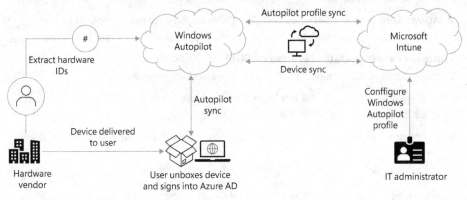

FIGURE 1-3 Windows Autopilot overview

The role of MDT and Configuration Manager

If your organization predominantly manages an on-premises enterprise environment, you'll likely use MDT and possibly Microsoft Endpoint Configuration Manager (previously known as System Center Configuration Manager (SCCM and commonly known as Configuration Manager). These tools enable you to deploy, configure, and manage Windows devices, apps, and drivers within your infrastructure.

You'll also likely be using Configuration Manager to collect data from your devices for inventory, upgrade planning, update status, and many other purposes.

Some organizations might intend to manage a hybrid infrastructure, with devices configured as part of both an on-premises Active Directory forest and enrolled in Intune. In these scenarios, you'll need to consider which device management workloads are best handled by Intune or Configuration Manager.

Implementing MDT as part of your deployment strategy

MDT provides a unified collection of tools and related processes. You can use these tools and processes to implement a complete deployment solution for your on-premises environment.

> **NOTE ZERO-TOUCH INSTALLATION**
>
> You can implement zero-touch (ZTI) deployments by combining MDT with Configuration Manager.

Before you can use MDT, you must ensure your infrastructure meets the following requirements:

- **AD DS**   Provides authentication and joins endpoints to Active Directory during deployment.
- **Windows Server**   Used to host MDT deployment shares and related content.
- **Windows Assessment and Deployment Kit (Windows ADK)**   Provides additional capabilities during deployment.

Optionally, you can also consider integrating MDT with the following additional components:

- **Windows Deployment Services (WDS)**   Enables you to provide network-driven operating system deployment to bare-metal devices. Installed as a Windows Server role.
- **Windows Server Updates Services (WSUS)**   Enables you to manage Windows Updates during deployment. Installed as a Windows Server role.

After installing MDT on your Windows Server, you can use it to support your on-premises deployments. MDT consists of the following key components:

- **Boot images**   These are Window PE images that initiate operating system deployment.

> **NOTE PXE BOOT**
>
> You can start boot images from bare-metal computers using PXE network boot.

- **Operating system images**   These are either full source files or custom images you import into the Workbench. Figure 1-4 displays the Deployment Workbench in MDT; the **Operating Systems** folder is open.
- **Applications**   Enables you to add any apps you want to deploy to devices. MDT supports many app installation formats, including MSI packages, .exe files, and Universal Windows apps.
- **Drivers**   Used to deploy required driver updates to your devices.
- **Packages**   Can be used to deploy packages, such as language packs. Also, packages can be used for Windows updates, although WSUS is usually more appropriate.
- **Task sequences**   Tasks sequences are the collection of actions performed to complete a specific job. You use predefined templates to create your task sequences. Tasks might include Gather, Format and Partition, Inject Drivers, Apply Operating System, and Windows Update.

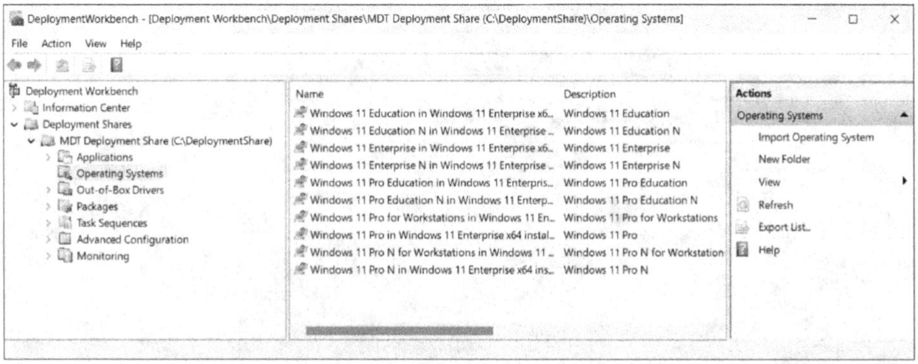

FIGURE 1-4 Adding operating system images in MDT

You must determine whether you can use MDT in your organization's deployment strategy. MDT isn't suitable if all your users' devices are cloud managed and you have little or no on-premises infrastructure. However, in hybrid environments, you'll need to consider using MDT—with or without Configuration Manager—or Intune.

Answering "yes" to all or most of the following questions suggests that MDT would be useful in your organization:

- Are you mostly deploying AD DS–joined devices?
- Do you need to deploy a standard image to your users?
- Will many applications be part of this image?
- Must all devices be the same?
- Will some of your devices be bare metal?

However, if you can answer "yes" to the following questions, you might consider using Windows Autopilot to provision your devices:

- Are you mostly provisioning devices that are NOT AD DS–joined?
- Will most of your devices have dissimilar configurations?
- Do you intend to use Intune to deploy and configure apps?
- Do you want to use Windows Update for Business to deliver Windows 11 updates?
- Might users have a choice about which applications they have?

Implementing Configuration Manager as part of your deployment strategy

Many organizations have relied on Configuration Manager to manage their operating system deployments and act as the core of their device management strategies. Although Configuration Manager, displayed in Figure 1-5, has been around for quite a while, it still plays a critical role, acting as a bridge between traditional and modern management. This is especially true for organizations managing hybrid devices (those joined to Azure AD and AD DS).

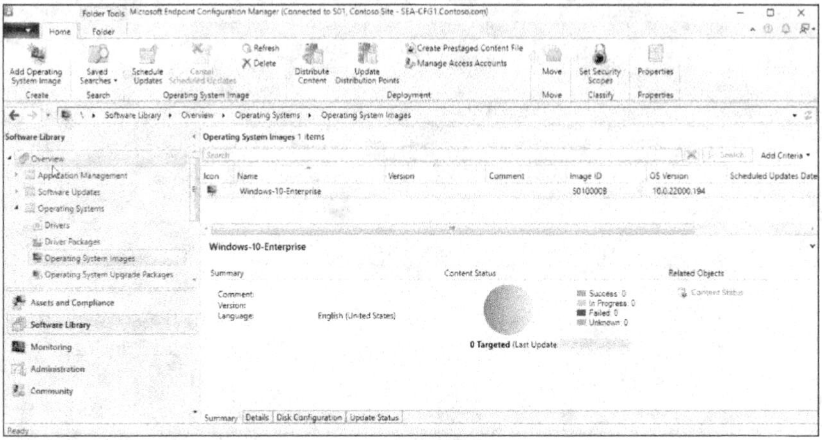

FIGURE 1-5 The Operating System Images node in the Software Library

Configuration Manager offers a wide range of services, including:

- Operating system deployment
- Application management
- Update and servicing management
- Device inventory
- Cloud management capability
- Advanced reporting capability
- Integration with Azure AD
- Integration with Desktop Analytics
- Remote control
- User state migration

The question is, can Configuration Manager help your organization with their Windows 11 deployment strategy, or are MDT or Intune sufficient? Configuration Manager uses boot and operating system images, much like MDT. It also supports capabilities that help deliver upgrade packages, device drivers, and operating system and software updates.

Configuration Manager also uses task sequences to complete a collection of actions. However, Configuration Manager extends these capabilities by supporting schedule-based deployments. This extends MDT's lite-touch (LTI) deployment model to zero-touch installation (ZTI).

Configuration Manager uses task sequences to complete the following typical tasks:

- Deployment of:
  - An operating system to a new or rebuilt device
  - A Windows 11 upgrade
- Capturing an operating system image
- Migrating user state settings

Select a Windows edition based on requirements

When evaluating the Windows edition you will deploy, you should consider the business requirements because not all editions support all features. Editions offering more features will cost more, so you should consider the most appropriate edition to support your needs.

For example, not all Windows editions have the same built-in management features and settings. If you intend to manage devices using mobile device management (MDM) such as Microsoft Intune, you should consider Windows 11 Enterprise, which has full management features. Both Home and Pro editions have fewer management capabilities in Intune.

If your organization's devices are fully working and running supported Windows 10 or Windows 11 devices, Microsoft recommends using an in-place upgrade strategy to deploy Windows 11 to the Windows 10 devices to preserve all the management settings after the upgrade.

Plan upgrade and downgrade paths

If an organization's environment is running fully working and supported Windows 10 and older operating systems, Microsoft recommends using an in-place upgrade strategy to deploy Windows 11 to these devices.

The upgrade process updates the operating system while retaining the apps, user data, and user settings. Utilizing in-place upgrades can offer a low-risk, quick, and reliable method of transforming devices and enabling users to be productive once the upgrade has been completed.

If administrators fear that an existing installation is "old" or not a reliable candidate to upgrade to Windows 11, they could redeploy the legacy operating system—complete with apps, policies, and settings—and then perform the in-place upgrade shortly afterward. Another benefit of using an in-place upgrade approach is that driver and app compatibility issues are minimized.

When planning to deploy Windows 11, you should consider whether your existing version of Windows can be directly upgraded to Windows 11 and whether you can migrate from one version of Windows 11 to a different version of the same release.

When upgrading from one version of Windows to a later version, the upgrade process can preserve personal data, settings, and applications. If you recently upgraded from a previous version of Windows and want to downgrade, you can only downgrade to Windows 10 within 10 days of upgrading when using the built-in rollback process within the Settings app.

In a few situations, you can perform an edition downgrade. In these situations, you should note that all personal data is maintained, though any incompatible applications and settings will be removed.

> **NOTE** **WINDOWS 11 LTSC**
>
> An in-place upgrade from Windows 7, Windows 8.1, or Windows 10 Semi-Annual Channel to Windows 11 Long Term Servicing Channel (LTSC) version is not supported. For more information on Windows 11 LTSC and how it should be used, visit *https://learn.microsoft.com/windows/deployment/update/waas-overview#long-term-servicing-channel*.

Windows upgrade and downgrade paths

You should review the information in Tables 1-4 and 1-5, which shows the various upgrade and downgrade paths available in Windows 10 and 11.

When reviewing the table, use the following key:

- **X** The upgrade path is supported.
- **D** The downgrade path is supported.

TABLE 1-4 Windows 10 Upgrade and Downgrade Paths

Destination Edition							
Starting Edition			**Windows 10 Home**	**Windows 10 Pro**	**Windows 10 Pro Education**	**Windows 10 Education**	**Windows 10 Enterprise**
Windows 7	Starter		X	X	X	X	
	Home Basic		X	X	X	X	
	Home Premium		X	X	X	X	
	Professional		D	X	X	X	X
	Ultimate		D	X	X	X	X
	Enterprise					X	X
Windows 8.1	(Core)		X	X	X	X	
	Connected		X	X	X	X	
	Pro		D	X	X	X	X
	Pro Student		D	X	X	X	X
	Pro WMC		D	X	X	X	X
	Enterprise					X	X
	Embedded Industry						X
	Windows RT						
	Windows Phone 8.1						
Windows 10	Home		X	X	X	X	
	Pro		D	X	X	X	X
	Education			D	D	X	
	Enterprise			D	D	X	X

The upgrade paths for Windows 11, excluding the N editions, are shown in Table 1-5.

TABLE 1-5 Windows 11 Upgrade and Downgrade Paths

Destination Edition							
Starting Edition			Windows 11 Home	Windows 11 Pro	Windows 11 Pro Education	Windows 11 Education	Windows 11 Enterprise
Windows 10	Home			X	X	X	
	Pro				X	X	X
	Education					X	
	Enterprise					X	X
	Pro Education					X	
	Cloud		X		X	X	X
	Core				X	X	X
Windows 11	Home			X	X	X	
	Pro				X	X	X
	Education					X	
	Enterprise					X	X
	Pro Education					X	
	Cloud		X		X	X	X
	Core				X	X	X

> **NOTE WINDOWS 11 EDITION UPGRADE**
>
> The process is quick and easy for organizations performing a supported upgrade from one edition of Windows 11 to another. The new product key can be added to the device and will be upgraded. There are multiple possible variants of the edition upgrade; some require a reboot, and others allow the upgrade without a reboot.

Downgrade paths due to license expiration

Organizations with an expired or expiring volume license agreement can opt to downgrade their edition of Windows 11 to an edition with an active license. Like the options for performing an edition upgrade, if a downgrade path is supported, the user's apps and settings will be available in the downgraded version of Windows 11. In this way, you can continue to use Windows.

Upgrading from Windows 11 in S mode

If you have devices that ship with Windows 11 in S mode, the edition of Windows can be upgraded at any time using the Microsoft Store. Windows 11 in S mode is free and is only available in the Windows 11 Home edition. The switch from S Mode to Windows 11 Home is a one-time switch, and the device cannot be reverted to Windows 11 in S mode without a complete wipe and reload of the operating system. If you have the Pro, Enterprise, or Education editions of Windows 10 in S mode, you'll need to switch out of S mode before the upgrade to Windows 11.

Table 1-6 shows several methods to switch devices out of Windows 11 in S mode.

TABLE 1-6 Windows 11 in S mode switch methods

Tool	Description
Settings app	Unless it's been disabled, this app allows you to configure one device at a time.
Microsoft Store	Unless it's been disabled, the Microsoft Store allows you to configure one device at a time; a Microsoft account is required.
Microsoft Intune	Allows you to configure a group of devices known to Azure AD.

To switch one device at a time, you can use the Settings app and then perform Activation on the device. Alternatively, a user with a Microsoft account can use the Microsoft Store.

Organizations can use the following procedure to switch multiple devices in bulk using Microsoft Intune:

1. Open the **Microsoft Endpoint Manager admin center** and sign in with a Global Administrator account.
2. In the navigation pane, select **Devices**.
3. Select **Configuration profiles**.
4. On the **Configuration profiles** page, select **Create profile**.
5. On the **Create a profile** blade, in the **Platform** list, select **Windows 10 and later**.
6. In the **Profile type** list, select **Templates**, then select **Edition upgrade and mode switch**.
7. Select **Create**.
8. In the **Edition upgrade and mode switch** wizard, on the **Basics** tab, enter a name and description, and then select **Next**.
9. On the **Configuration settings** tab, expand the **Mode switch (Windows Insider only)** list.
10. In the **Switch out of S mode** list, displayed in Figure 1-6, select **Switch**, and then select **Next**.

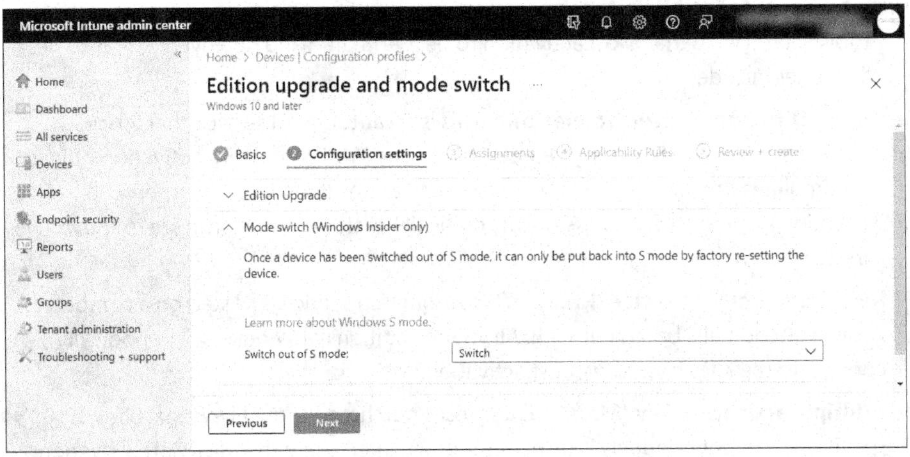

FIGURE 1-6 Select Edition upgrade and mode switch settings

11. On the **Assignments** tab, define the groups to which you want to assign the profile, and then select **Next**.

12. On the **Applicability Rules** tab, define any filtering rules you want to use. These determine specific operating system editions that are affected by the profile. Select **Next**.

13. On the **Review + create** tab, select **Create**. The profile is created.

> **NOTE BLOCK SWITCHING OUT OF WINDOWS 11 IN S MODE**
>
> You can control which devices or users can switch out of Windows 11 in S mode by using Group Policy. Review the GPO at `Device Configuration\Profiles\Windows 11 And Later\ Edition Upgrade And Mode Switch` In Microsoft Intune.

Implement subscription-based activation

Windows 11 requires activation to unlock all the operating system's features and comply with the licensing requirements.

Once activated, Windows 11 devices can:

- Receive updates
- Access all Windows 11 features
- Access support

Several types of activation register the installation of Windows on a device with a stand-alone or corporate Windows 11 product key. The three main methods of activation are:

- Retail
- OEM
- Microsoft Volume Licensing (volume activation)

Organizations with Enterprise Agreements (EA) can use volume activation methods, which provide tools and services that allow activation to be automated and deployed at scale. These tools and services include

- **Active Directory–based activation**   This is an automated service that, once installed, uses Active Directory Directory Services (AD DS) to store activation objects. This simplifies the maintenance of volume activation services for an enterprise. Activation requests are processed automatically as devices authenticate to the Active Directory domain.

- **Key Management Service (KMS)**   This automated service is hosted on a computer within your domain-based network. All volume editions of Windows 11 periodically connect to the KMS host to request activation.

- **Multiple activation key (MAK)**   Enterprises purchase product keys that allow a specific number of Windows 11 devices to be activated using the Microsoft activation servers on the Internet.

All the above enterprise activation methods utilize services found within traditional on-premises, domain-based environments. An alternative activation method is required to meet the needs of devices registered to cloud-based authentication and identity services, such as Azure Active Directory.

Subscription Activation allows your organization's Azure AD tenant to be associated with an existing Enterprise Agreement; all valid devices connected to that tenant will be automatically activated.

Eligible licenses that can use Subscription Activation include

- Windows 11 Enterprise E3 or E5 licenses obtained as part of an Enterprise Agreement
- Devices containing a firmware-embedded activation key
- Windows 11 Enterprise E3 in CSP (Cloud Solution Provider), which is offered as a subscription for small- and medium-sized organizations—from one to hundreds of users

> **NOTE**   **FIRMWARE-EMBEDDED ACTIVATION KEY**
>
> Most OEM-provided devices designed to run Windows 8 or later will have a firmware-embedded key. You can read more information about firmware-embedded activation key licensing on the Microsoft website at *https://learn.microsoft.com/windows/deployment/deploy-enterprise-licenses*.

Organizations must meet the following requirements to implement Subscription Activation:

- Enterprise Agreement or a Microsoft Products and Services Agreement (MPSA) associated with the organization's Azure AD tenant.
- Windows 11 Pro or Windows 11 Enterprise is installed on the devices you want to upgrade.
- Azure AD for identity management.
- All devices are either Azure AD–joined or are members of an AD DS domain synchronized to Azure AD using Azure AD Connect.

If all the requirements are met, when a licensed user signs in using their Azure AD credentials using a device, the operating system switches from Windows 11 Pro to Windows 11 Enterprise, and all Windows 11 Enterprise features are then available. This process takes place without entering a product key and without requiring that users restart their computers.

EXAM TIP

Devices that have been upgraded using Subscription Activation must be able to connect to the Azure AD tenant at least every 90 days to remain licensed. If the Azure AD tenant expires or the user license is unassigned, the device will revert to Windows 11 Pro.

Windows 11 Enterprise Subscription Activation

Using the Subscription activation for Enterprise feature, you can deploy Windows Enterprise to your devices without requiring software license keys. If you have used the Windows 11 Enterprise Subscription Activation to step up from Windows Pro edition to Enterprise or Education edition (or from Windows Pro Education edition to Education edition), you should ensure that the device remains licensed with an *Enterprise Agreement (EA)* or by using a Windows Enterprise E3 or E5 license. Each user that has an enterprise license can upgrade up to 5 devices.

Devices that have been upgraded will attempt to renew licenses about every 30 days. If the license expires, devices will automatically revert to the original edition after the 90-day grace period. For example, if you originally upgraded to Windows 11 Enterprise from Windows 11 Pro, the device will revert to Windows 11 Pro.

If you want to downgrade from Windows 11 Enterprise to Windows 11 Pro for Workstations, Pro Education, or Education editions, you must obtain an additional activation key, which will supersede the original firmware-embedded Windows 11 Pro key.

If an organization uses Windows virtual machines, these can automatically inherit the activation state from the Windows client host. The host computer must meet the following conditions for this feature to be supported:

- Run Windows 10 or Windows 11.
- The user must have a Windows Enterprise E3 or E5 license assigned.
- The Hypervisor platform must be Windows Hyper-V.
- The user signs in to the VM with a local or Azure AD account.

> **NOTE SOFTWARE ACTIVATION CHANGES THE EDITION ONLY**
> Subscription activation doesn't update a device from Windows 10 to Windows 11. Only the edition is updated.

Skill 1.2: Plan and implement a Windows client deployment by using Windows Autopilot

Within a domain-based environment, deploying new devices to users has become increasingly complex. There are many "moving" parts and components, and each needs to work precisely to ensure devices are compliant, secure, and usable. This is partly because of the granular nature of the tooling used to ensure that devices comply with strict organizational security requirements. Windows Autopilot is a solution that radically changes this approach while allowing IT administrators to deploy secure and compliant devices.

You must understand how to plan and implement Windows 11 within an organization using Windows Autopilot. This skill explores the planning, example scenarios, and installation requirements for the application of Windows Autopilot.

> **This skill covers how to:**
> - Configure device registration for Autopilot
> - Create, validate, and assign deployment profiles
> - Set up the Enrolment Status Page (ESP)
> - Deploy Windows devices by using Autopilot
> - Troubleshoot an Autopilot deployment

Configure device registration for Autopilot

Windows Autopilot offers a new method of provisioning Windows 11 within an enterprise. Of course, it is not the only deployment choice, and indeed, there will be scenarios in which using Autopilot would be folly.

You must explore each of the available deployment options for Windows. These options include technology such as MDT or Configuration Manager that might be currently used within your organization. Other methods, such as using Windows Autopilot or Microsoft Intune, might be worth employing to achieve your Windows 11 deployment goals. The MD-102 exam will likely focus on newer, cloud-enabled technologies such as Windows Autopilot or Microsoft Intune.

Table 1-7 lists many Windows deployment and configuration methods. You need to understand when to use each.

TABLE 1-7 Methods for Deploying and Configuring Windows 11

Method	Description
Windows Autopilot	Transform an existing Windows 11 installation, join the device to Azure AD, and enroll it into a Mobile Device Management solution to complete the configuration. Deploy Windows 11 on an existing Windows 7 or 8.1 device.
Windows 11 subscription activation	Upgrade the Windows edition seamlessly without requiring intervention or rebooting of the device.

Method	Description
Azure AD / MDM	Cloud-based identity and management solution offering device, app, and security configuration.
Provisioning packages	Small distributable `.appx` files that securely transform devices to meet organizational requirements.
In-place upgrade	Upgrade an earlier version of Windows to Windows 11 while retaining all apps, user data, and settings.
Bare metal	Deploy Windows 11 to newly built devices or wipe existing devices and deploy fresh Windows 11 images to them.
Refresh (wipe and load)	Reuse existing devices. Retain user state (user data, Windows, and app settings). Wipe devices, deploy Windows 11 images to them, and finally, restore the user state.
Replace	Purchase new devices. Back up the user state from the current device. Transform or wipe a pre-installed Windows 11 installation and restore the user state.

Windows Autopilot deployment scenarios

Windows Autopilot simplifies and automates the customization of the out-of-box experience (OOBE) and seamlessly enrolls your devices into a management solution such as Microsoft Intune. Once enrolled into Microsoft Intune, devices are secured, configured, and further managed. They can also be removed from management or fully wiped should a device be stolen or lost.

Several usage scenarios are currently available with Windows Autopilot, and additional functionality will be added in the future. You should understand the scenarios shown in Table 1-8 that show when you would use Windows Autopilot as part of your Windows 11 deployment strategy.

TABLE 1-8 Windows Autopilot Scenarios

Scenario	Description
Windows Autopilot for existing devices	Deploy Windows 11 on an existing Windows 8.1 device. Requires Configuration Manager Current Branch (1806 or later) to replace the operating system and then allow Windows Autopilot to continue.
Windows Autopilot user-driven mode	Provision Windows 11 on a new Windows 11 device. Devices will be set up by a member of the organization and configured for that person to use.
Windows Autopilot self-deploying mode	Used for transforming Windows 11 devices that will be automatically configured as a kiosk terminal, shared computer, or digital signage device. Can be performed locally by an administrator or via MDM.
Windows Autopilot reset	Used to redeploy a Windows 11 device. The reset process removes personal files, apps, and settings and reapplies a device's original settings. The connection to Azure AD and Microsoft Intune is retained. A user can Sign in to the device using their Azure AD credentials and be productive immediately.

There are clear advantages when comparing Autopilot to traditional on-premises deployment methods, such as imaging.

- Windows images are not required.
- Drivers are included with Windows 11 and are pre-installed on the device.
- No on-premises deployment infrastructure is required (except if using Windows Autopilot for existing devices).

In the next section, you will learn that devices must have a connection to the Internet to use Windows Autopilot. If Internet access is not available for the Windows Autopilot deployment, it will not work, and you will need to select an alternative deployment method.

So long as an organization uses cloud-based services such as Microsoft 365, which includes Azure AD and Microsoft Intune they will be able to benefit from:

- Joining devices to Azure AD automatically
- Auto enrolling your devices into Microsoft Intune
- Lower provisioning costs
- Restricted Administrator account creation during OOBE
- Agile deployment of Windows 11 devices
- Users will be productive more quickly

Windows Autopilot requirements

There are several requirements and prerequisites that you need to put in place before you can use Windows Autopilot with your Windows 11 devices. If your organization already has a Microsoft 365 subscription, then you will already meet the licensing requirements:

Licensing requirements

The following licensing requirements must be met:

- Devices must be preinstalled with Windows 11 Pro, Pro Education, Pro for Workstations, Enterprise, or Education.
- Azure Active Directory Premium P1 or P2.
- Microsoft Intune subscription (or an alternative MDM service).

EXAM TIP

You can use the Microsoft Store for Business to manage Windows Autopilot deployment profiles. You can create a new profile and edit or delete a profile in the Microsoft Store.

Networking configuration

The following network configuration requirements must be met:

- Devices must have access to the Internet.
- Devices must be able to access cloud services used by Windows Autopilot:
  - Using DNS name resolution.
  - Firewall access through port 80 (for HTTP), port 443 (for HTTPS), and port 123 (for UDP and NTP).
- The following URLs must be accessible:
  - *https://go.microsoft.com*
  - *https://login.microsoftonline.com*
  - *https://login.live.com*
  - *https://account.live.com*
  - *https://signup.live.com*
  - *https://licensing.mp.microsoft.com*
  - *https://licensing.md.mp.microsoft.com*
  - *https://ztd.dds.microsoft.com*
  - *https://cs.dds.microsoft.com*
  - *ctldl.windowsupdate.com*
  - *download.windowsupdate.com*

Azure AD configuration prerequisites

The following Azure AD configuration prerequisites must be met:

- Azure AD company branding must be configured.
- Azure AD automatic enrollment must be configured.
- A device must be registered with Azure AD.
- Users must have permission to join devices into Azure AD.

Windows Autopilot configuration

The following Windows Autopilot configuration prerequisites must be met:

- Devices must have their device hardware IDs known by Windows Autopilot.
- Devices must have a Windows Autopilot deployment profile assigned.

Implement pilot deployment

Windows Autopilot is not complex to configure and use, though several services need to work together for your users to see a seamless out-of-box experience. After completing the Windows Autopilot prerequisites, you might want to practice using Windows Autopilot to provision Windows 11 in a test lab using a virtual machine. When using a VM for Autopilot testing, assign at least two processors and 4 GB of memory.

Once you have the basic functionality working, you can explore the available additional features; these features can be used to streamline the deployment process or personalize the experience for the user. These enhancements currently include the following:

- **Device Groups**   Creating device groups with Azure AD allows you to separate devices into logical groupings.
- **Dynamic Groups**   You can use Azure AD Dynamic Groups to simplify device group management. Devices are automatically added to the dynamic group if they meet the group membership criteria outlined in the rules. Dynamic groups are an Azure AD premium feature.
- **Deployment Profiles**   You can create a single default deployment profile for your whole organization or add additional deployment profiles and assign them to device groups.
- **Personalization**   Windows Autopilot allows you to assign a username and a friendly name to a specific device. During OOBE, the friendly name is then shown to the user.
- **Enrollment Status Page**   During Microsoft Intune device enrollment, users can be shown a progress status page. This is configurable.

After configuring your Windows Autopilot processes and successfully provisioning devices in your test lab, you are ready to deploy Windows Autopilot in your production environment. You should follow best practices for any new technology deployment and pilot the processes to a small group of new devices and their users.

The pilot phase of the Windows Autopilot rollout should be closely monitored, and feedback should be sought from all stakeholders. Any problems with the pilot deployment should be thoroughly resolved before proceeding to a larger-scale rollout.

> *NOTE*   **WINDOWS AUTOPILOT ROADMAP**
>
> Windows Autopilot is a comparatively new technology that will likely have additional functionality added frequently. To ensure that you are up to date with the most recent Windows Autopilot features, you should review the reference information on the Microsoft website at *https://learn.microsoft.com/mem/autopilot/windows-autopilot*.

Create, validate, and assign deployment profiles

When using Windows Autopilot, Deployment Profiles customize the OOBE for a device or group of devices. You can create a single default deployment profile of settings for your whole organization or assign additional deployment profiles to device groups.

At the time of this writing, the available profile settings you can configure within a Windows Autopilot deployment profile are shown in Table 1-9.

TABLE 1-9 Windows Autopilot Deployment Profile Settings

Profile setting	Description
Convert all targeted devices to Autopilot	■ Enables you to register all targeted devices to Autopilot if not already registered. The next time registered devices go through the OOBE, they go through the assigned Autopilot scenario.
Deployment mode	■ User-driven devices are devices that are associated with the user enrolling the device. ■ Self-Deploying (preview) devices have no user affinity; an example is a kiosk device.
Join to Azure AD as	■ Azure AD–joined = Cloud-only. ■ Hybrid Azure AD–joined = Cloud and on-premises Windows Server Active Directory.
Microsoft Software License Terms	■ This means that organizations accept the software license terms on behalf of their users.
Privacy settings	■ Organizations can choose not to ask users about Microsoft-related privacy settings during the OOBE process.
Hide change account options	■ Removes the option for users to restart the OOBE process with a different account. (Requires Windows 11 1809 or later.)
User account type	■ Typically, during the OOBE process, a device will automatically be set up with administrator access. This option can be disabled when using Windows Autopilot because you can choose a Standard or Administrator account type.
Allow preprovisioned deployment	■ Enables a partner or IT pro to press the Windows key five times during OOBE to run without user authentication, enroll the device, and provision all system-context apps and settings.
Language (Region)	■ Enables you to select the appropriate regional settings. The keyboard is automatically selected based on this selection unless you choose otherwise. Defaults to Operating System Default.
Automatically configure keyboard	If set to **Yes**, uses the regional selection to choose the keyboard layout.
Apply device name template	Allows you to specify a naming convention to name devices automatically. For example, Contoso-%RAND:3% will generate a device name such as **Contoso-565**.

> **NOTE COMPANY BRANDING IS REQUIRED FOR AUTOPILOT**
>
> You will notice that Autopilot profiles allow you to choose whether a user is presented with the company branding during OOBE. This setting is optional in each profile you create. However, you must configure Azure Active Directory Company Branding.

Use the following procedure to create a deployment profile using Microsoft Intune for a user-driven device that is to be joined to Azure AD:

1. Sign in to the **Microsoft Intune admin center** (*https://endpoint.microsoft.com/*) as a Global Administrator.

2. Select **Devices** > **Enroll devices**, and then select the **Automatic Enrollment** tile.

3. Ensure the **MDM user scope** is not set to **None**.

4. Go back to **Enroll devices**, and select **Deployment Profiles**.

5. Select **Create profile**, and choose **Windows PC**.

6. On the **Create profile** page, on the **Basics** tab, enter a profile name and optional description.

7. Select **Next**, and then, on the **Out-of-box experience (OOBE)** tab, displayed in Figure 1-7, configure the values described in Table 1-9, and then select **Next**.

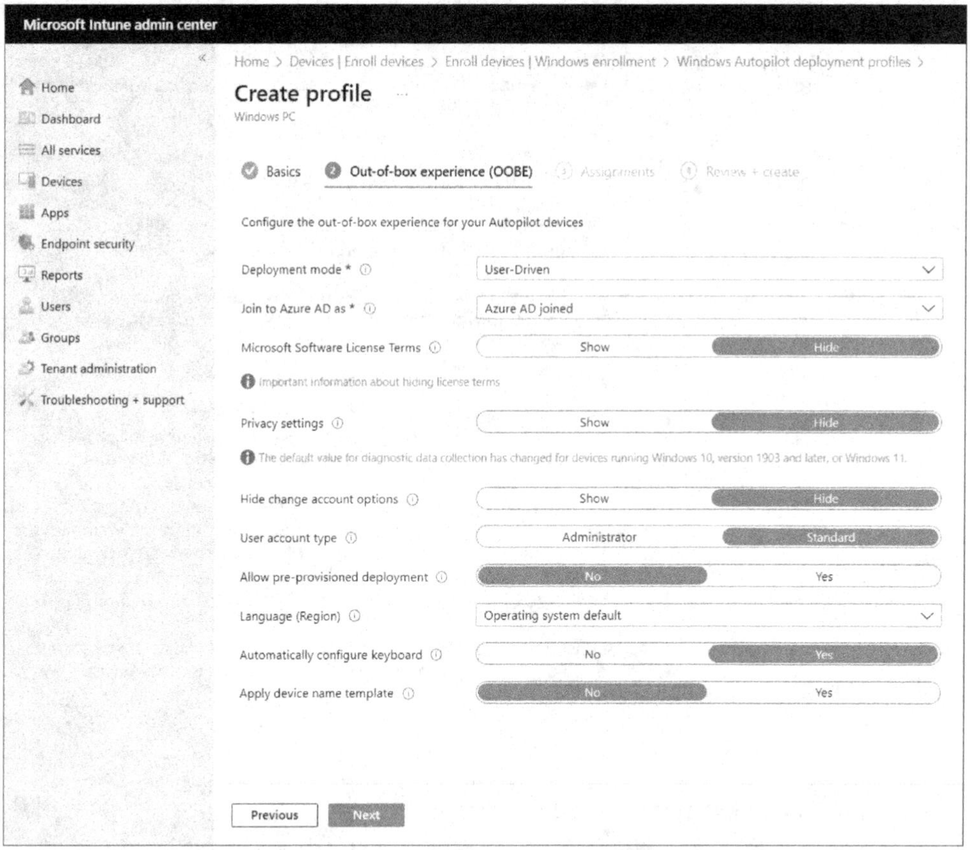

FIGURE 1-7 Creating an Autopilot profile

8. On the **Assignments** page, choose the device groups you want to include or exclude or choose **Add all devices**. Then select **Next**.

9. On the **Review + create** tab, select **Create**.

After you've assigned the profile, devices are allocated to use this profile during the Windows Autopilot deployment process.

> **NOTE** **FORCE AUTOPILOT PROFILE TO BE DOWNLOADED**
>
> If a device has not downloaded an Autopilot profile, you should reboot the device during OOBE to allow the device to retrieve the profile. You can press Shift-F10 to open a command prompt at the start of the OOBE and then enter **shutdown /r /t 0** to restart the device immediately or enter **shutdown /s /t 0** to shut down immediately.

Windows Autopilot uses Azure AD company branding to show custom logos and text during the OOBE Azure AD authentication and join process. You need to have Azure AD Premium licensing to configure company branding. There are three image layouts that you need to configure.

- A square logo; 240 pixels by 240 pixels; PNG or JPG; 10KB or smaller
- A banner logo; 280 pixels by 60 pixels; PNG or JPG; 10KB or smaller
- A background image; 1920 pixels by 1080 pixels; PNG or JPG; 300KB or smaller

To configure your company branding, use these steps.

1. Sign in to the Azure portal or the **Microsoft Entra admin center** using a Global Administrator account for the directory.
2. Under **User experiences**, select **Company branding**.
3. Under **Default Sign-In Experience**, select **Edit**.
4. On the **Basics** blade, upload your images for **Favicon** and **Background image**. You can also configure the **Page background color**.
5. Select **Review & create**.
6. Select **Create**.

Extract device hardware information

The next stage of configuring Windows Autopilot is to extract the device hardware information so that the Autopilot service can recognize devices that will be provisioned using Windows Autopilot.

The device-specific information, which includes hardware device IDs of the devices, needs to be uploaded to one of the following platforms and then synchronized to the Windows Autopilot Deployment Service.

- Microsoft Intune
- Microsoft Store for Business
- OEM Direct API
- Partner Center
- Microsoft 365 Business Premium

You will learn how to upload the device IDs in the next section.

Typically, the hardware vendor that supplied the new devices will upload the device-specific information and associate that information with your organization's Microsoft 365 tenant. If an organization works closely with a Cloud Solution Provider (CSP) partner, then the vendor might pass the file to it for subsequent uploading via the Partner Center.

Alternatively, the vendor can provide you with a list of the required device information in .csv file format so that you can upload the information.

Another useful method is for the organization to extract device-specific information from devices by running a Windows PowerShell script. This is especially useful if you are deploying a small number of devices using Windows Autopilot (for example, in a test lab environment or if you are reusing existing devices).

You can extract the hardware ID (or hardware hash) from any existing device that device is running Windows 11. Use the `Get-WindowsAutoPilotInfo.ps1` PowerShell script, which has been published to the PowerShell Gallery website at *https://www.powershellgallery.com/packages/ Get-WindowsAutoPilotInfo*.

The following script must be run on each computer from an elevated Windows PowerShell prompt:

```
md c:\HWID
Set-Location c:\HWID
Set-ExecutionPolicy Unrestricted
Install-Script -Name Get-WindowsAutoPilotInfo.ps1
Get-WindowsAutoPilotInfo.ps1 -OutputFile DeviceID.csv
```

Once the output file has been created, you can save it to a location such as a USB drive or network share. As discussed in the following section, you must then import the file to your organization's preferred cloud service.

Once you have created the output 8k hash CSV file using the above scripts, rather than manually importing the file to Intune, you can run the following script to automatically connect to Intune and import it to Endpoint Manager's enrolled devices.

```
Get-WindowsAutoPilotInfo.ps1 -online
```

You will need to log in with your Azure AD credentials for Endpoint Manager when prompted. The process can take up to 15 minutes to complete.

Import device hardware information to cloud service

With the hardware ID for each device, you need to import the information into one of the cloud-based administration centers and then synchronize this information to the Windows Autopilot deployment service.

Devices must be known to Azure AD and registered to your tenant before you can provision the devices using Autopilot.

There are several administrative portals that you can use to import the hardware device IDs. However, generally, you'll use one of the following:

- Microsoft Endpoint Manager admin center
- Microsoft Intune admin center
- Microsoft Store for Business

Use the following procedure to add Windows Autopilot devices to a Microsoft 365 tenant by importing a CSV file with its information:

1. Sign in to the **Microsoft Intune admin center** (*https://endpoint.microsoft.com/*) as a Global Administrator.

2. Select **Devices**, select **Enroll devices**, and then under **Windows Autopilot Deployment Program**, select the **Devices** tile.

3. On the **Windows Autopilot Devices** page, select **Import**.

4. On the **Add Autopilot devices** blade, browse to a .csv file containing the hardware IDs of the devices you want to add, and select **Open**.

5. If the imported file displays as correctly formatted, select **Import**. It can take up to 15 minutes to import and process the file contents. On the **Windows Autopilot Devices** page, the banner should indicate that the import is in progress and show the elapsed time.

6. When the import process has been completed, select **Sync** on the menu bar. A banner should indicate that synchronization is in progress. The process might take a few minutes, depending on how many devices are synchronized.

7. Once the sync process has been completed, you will see a notification indicating whether the sync was successful and whether some devices have not been imported. Select **Refresh** to see the new devices added, as Figure 1-8 shows.

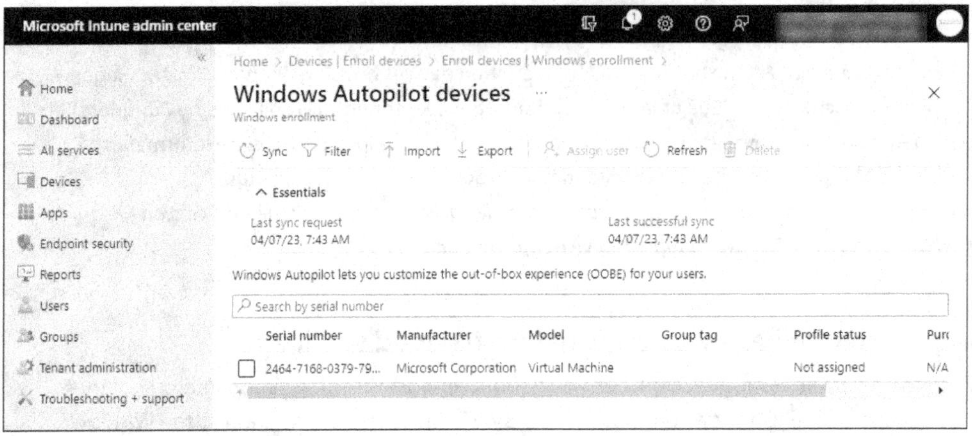

FIGURE 1-8 Importing Windows Autopilot Devices

8.   After you've imported the relevant device IDs, you can optionally assign specific devices to users. On the **Windows Autopilot devices** page, select the device checkbox, and then select **Assign user** on the toolbar.

9.   On the **Select user** blade, choose the appropriate user, and then click **Select**.

10.   On the device ID blade, select **Save**.

Set up the Enrolment Status Page

The Enrolment Status Page (ESP) is useful for the end user as it can show them the status of the configuration of their device. Every device that joins Azure AD during the OOBE phase will have an Enrolment Status Page (ESP) shown. With Windows Autopilot, you can configure this page to show the user progress information and to ensure the device is in the expected state before the user can access the desktop for the first time.

The ESP allows you to set various configurations that apply during a Windows Autopilot deployment. You can use the ESP to interact with the user in the following ways.

- Display the installation progress
- Block device use until the required apps are installed
- Display time limits
- Track the installation status of applications, security policies, certificates, and network connections
- Display troubleshooting operations available and collect troubleshooting logs

Create a new Enrolment Status Page profile

A default Enrollment Status Page policy is created within the Windows enrollment settings, but minimal settings are configured. It carries the lowest priority and will be applied to all users and all devices.

To create a new Enrolment Status Page profile in which you can configure the settings, follow these steps.

1. Sign in to the Microsoft Intune admin center (*https://endpoint.microsoft.com/*) as a Global Administrator.

2. Select **Devices**.

3. Under **By platform**, select **Windows > Windows enrollment > Enrollment Status Page**.

4. Select **Create**.

5. In **Basics**, enter the following properties:

   - **Name:** Name your profile.

   - **Description:** Enter a description for the profile.

6. Select **Next**.

7. In **Settings**, configure the following settings:

   - **Show app and profile configuration progress:** Your options are

     - **No**   The enrollment status page doesn't appear during device OOBE. Select this option if you don't want to show the ESP to users.

     - **Yes**   The enrollment status page appears during device OOBE.

8. When you select **Yes** to **Show app and profile configuration progress**, the following additional settings are available:

   - **Show an error when installation takes longer than specified number of minutes:** The default time-out is 60 minutes. Use this setting to allow more time to install apps on your devices.

   - **Show custom message when time limit or error occur:** Include a message that tells your users who to contact for help. Your options are

     - **No**   The default message is shown to users when an error occurs: "Setup could not be completed. Please try again or contact your support person for help."

     - **Yes**   Your custom message is shown to users when an error occurs. Enter your message in the provided text box.

   - **Turn on log collection and diagnostics page for end users:** The user's logs and diagnostics could aid with troubleshooting, so we recommend turning this on. Your options:

     - **No**   The **Collect logs** button isn't shown to users when an installation error occurs. The Windows Autopilot diagnostics page isn't shown on devices running Windows 11.

     - **Yes**   The **Collect logs** button is shown to users when an installation error occurs. The Windows Autopilot diagnostics page is shown on devices running Windows 11.

- **Only show page to devices provisioned by out-of-box experience (OOBE):** Use this setting to stop the enrollment status page from reappearing to every new user who signs into the device. Your options are
  - **No**   The enrollment status page is shown during the device phase and the out-of-box experience (OOBE).
  - **Yes**   The enrollment status page is shown during the device phase and the OOBE. It is not shown to subsequent users who sign in to the device.
- **Block device use until all apps and profiles are installed:** Your options are
  - **No**   Users can leave the ESP before Intune has finished setting up the device.
  - **Yes**   Users can't leave the ESP until Intune has finished setting up the device. This option unlocks additional settings for this scenario.
- **Allow users to reset device if installation error occurs:** Your options are
  - **No**   The ESP doesn't give users the option to reset their devices when an installation fails.
  - **Yes**   The ESP gives users the option to reset their devices when an installation fails.
- **Allow users to use device if installation error occurs:** Your options are
  - **No**   The ESP doesn't allow users to bypass the ESP when an installation fails.
  - **Yes**   The ESP allows users to bypass the ESP and use their devices when an installation fails.
- **Block device use until these required apps are installed if they are assigned to the user/device:** Your options are
  - **All**   All assigned apps must be installed before users can use their devices.
  - **Selected**   The selected apps must be installed before users can use their devices. Choose **Select apps** to start a *Blocking apps* list. This option unlocks the **Blocking apps** settings.
- **Only fail selected blocking apps in technician phase:** Use this setting with Windows Autopilot pre-provisioned deployments to control how your required apps are prioritized during the technician flow.

9. Select **Next**.

10. In **Assignments**, select the groups, users, or devices that will receive your profile. Optionally, select **Edit filter** to restrict the assignment further.

11. Select **Next**.

12. In **Scope Tags**, assign a tag to limit profile management to specific IT groups defined using a tag.

13. Select **Next**.

14. In **Review + create**, review your settings.

15. Select **Create**. Your changes are saved, and the profile is assigned.

16. The profile will be applied the next time devices check in with Intune. On the **Enrollment Status Page** profile list, the new profile is listed first and assigned a **Priority** of **1**, meaning it will take precedence over the default profile, as shown in Figure 1-9.

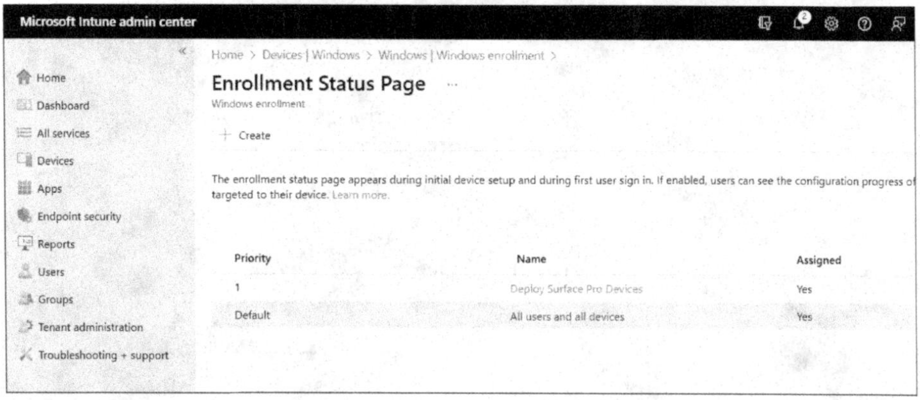

FIGURE 1-9 The Enrollment Status Page profile list

17. If you assign a user or device more than one ESP profile, the profile with the highest priority takes precedence over the other profiles. The profile set to **1** has the highest priority. To modify the priority of a profile, you can assign more than one ESP profile to a user or device. The profile with the highest priority takes precedence over the other profiles. The profile set to **1** has the highest priority. To modify the priority of a profile, follow these steps:

- Hover over the profile in the list with your cursor until you see three vertical dots.
- Drag the profile to the desired position in the list.

Deploy Windows devices by using Autopilot

When you have imported your device hardware IDs, you can deploy Windows 11 using Autopilot to one or more devices. Remember, though, that you're provisioning the devices rather than deploying Windows to them. Your users will start the process when you send them their new computers.

When a user turns on their new computer, it starts the OOBE. The user is prompted to connect the device to a wireless network if the device is not connected automatically.

> **NOTE AUTOPILOT-REQUIRED DEVICES NEED TO BE GENERALIZED**
>
> Devices to be deployed using Windows Autopilot must be in a generalized state. The OEM vendor normally performs this and allows the device to boot into the OOBE when first turned on. Generalized devices have all user and computer-specific information removed. If you want to generalize a Windows computer or VM, you can use the Sysprep utility, which can be found at C:\windows\system32\sysprep\sysprep.exe. Alternatively, in Windows 11, you can use the Reset your PC option in the Settings app.

If you choose to assign a specific device to a particular user, as displayed in Figure 1-10, the next prompt the user receives is to enter their password. If you didn't assign the device to a particular user, the user is prompted for their username and password.

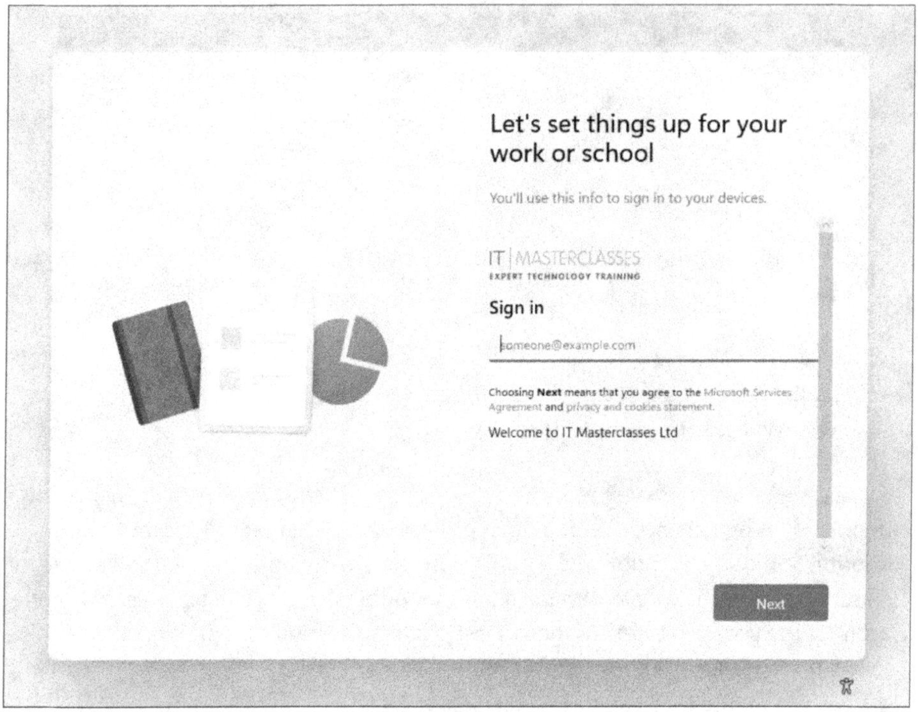

FIGURE 1-10 The Account tab in the OOBE process for an Autopilot device

After they've entered the required credentials, the device is Azure AD joined and enrolled in MDM. Intune then applies the necessary device configuration profiles, compliance and conditional access policies, and other configured settings.

Depending on the settings, the user might be prompted for additional authentication for device verification. This might be a text message with a one-time code or verifying the Azure AD join activity using the Microsoft Authenticator app.

The device is provisioned and passes through three stages—device preparation, device setup, and account setup—to become fully enrolled into Intune, as shown in Figure 1-11. You can select the dropdown to the right of each stage to display the detailed progress. The user desktop displays once the remainder of the OOBE process is completed.

> **NOTE ENROLLMENT STATUS PAGE**
> You can configure the enrollment status page for specific groups. While devices are provisioned during enrollment, you can control what the user sees and whether they can bypass the provisioning and gain early access to their desktop. Provisioning then continues while the user is signed in.

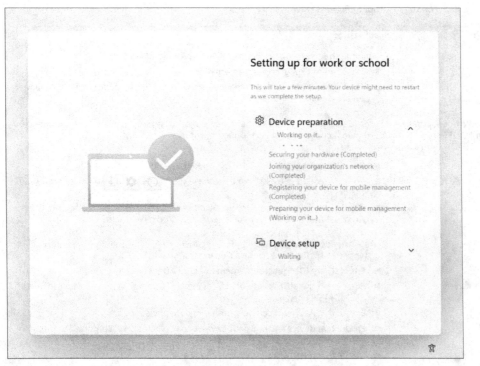

FIGURE 1-11 Autopilot Enrolment Status page displayed during enrollment

Troubleshoot an Autopilot deployment

Before you can resolve an issue with Windows Autopilot, you need to identify in which part of the overall process the problem is occurring. The Windows Autopilot process can be broken down into logical stages:

- **Network connectivity**   Establish an Internet connection and connect to the Windows Autopilot service.
- **Company branding**   Company branding within Azure AD must be configured.
- **Deployment profile and OOBE**   A deployment profile will be delivered to the device to manage the out-of-box experience (or OOBE). The OOBE will be completed using the settings within the deployment profile.
- **Azure AD**   Has Azure AD been configured correctly? For user-driven deployments, users need to enter their Azure AD credentials to join the device to Azure AD.
- **MDM enrollment issues**   After being auto-enrolled into the MDM service, any policies, settings, and apps will be delivered to the device.

The whole process should result in the device being set up, configured, and ready for the user to be productive.

For a summary of possible troubleshooting areas within these stages, review Table 1-10.

TABLE 1-10 Windows Autopilot Process Flow

Process	Troubleshooting
Network connectivity	Ensure that the device can access the Windows Autopilot services. ■ Windows Autopilot requires Internet access. ■ Ensure that specific network requirements are met, including firewall port settings and DNS name resolution.
Deployment profile and OOBE	There are settings in the deployment profile that configure the out-of-box experience. You should focus your troubleshooting on whether ■ The device has received its deployment profile. ■ A deployment profile has been assigned to the device. ■ The device has been assigned the correct deployment profile type; for example, is the device a kiosk? ■ The assigned deployment profile settings are correct; for example, has the Administrator account creation been configured by accident?
Azure AD	Azure AD needs to be configured before deploying devices with Windows Autopilot. Focus your troubleshooting on the following things: ■ Ensure that MDM auto-enrollment in Azure AD is correctly configured. ■ Ensure that the MDM discovery URL is correctly configured, so devices can find the MDM service. ■ Ensure that Azure AD company branding is in place. ■ Ensure that device hardware IDs have been successfully synchronized to the Windows Autopilot deployment service. ■ Ensure that the user has a valid Azure AD account. ■ Ensure that the user has not exceeded the maximum number of devices allowed to be joined to Azure AD. ■ If a third-party MDM solution is being used, make sure it has been correctly authorized in Azure AD.
MDM enrollment issues	In the final stage of the Windows Autopilot process, the device will be enrolled into Mobile Device Management. If MDM fails, then policies, settings, and apps will not be deployed to the device. You should focus your troubleshooting on the following things: ■ The Enrollment Status Page is useful for troubleshooting MDM issues. ■ Has the user been assigned an Enterprise Mobility + Security license? ■ Ensure that users have not exceeded their device enrollment limits.

> *NOTE* **TIME**
>
> If you have ensured that the configuration is correct, then wait—maybe go grab a coffee. Nearly all issues I have experienced, such as the new device not being recognized by the Autopilot service, can be resolved by waiting 15 minutes and rebooting the device. Remember that Autopilot uses the cloud, and Azure AD group membership propagation or device ID synchronization can sometimes take a little longer to update.

Error codes

An error code will be generated when a major issue occurs with Windows Autopilot. Some error codes can be viewed on the device whenever a problem occurs during setup. Also, error codes can be viewed using the Event Trace for Windows tool.

Some common error codes relating to Windows Autopilot are shown in Table 1-11.

TABLE 1-11 Windows Autopilot Error Codes

Error code	Description
0x800705B4	This error is caused by the device being either a virtual machine or not having TPM 2.0; therefore, the device cannot run Autopilot in self-deploying mode.
0x801c03ea	This error means that the device is TPM 2.0 capable but that the TPM still needs to be upgraded from 1.2 to 2.0.
0x801c0003	The error page will report this error code with a message reading, "Something went wrong," which indicates that the Azure AD join failed.
0x80180018	The error page will report this error code with a message reading, "Something went wrong," which indicates the MDM enrollment failed.
0x80070032	When Windows Autopilot Reset is used to prepare existing devices to become business ready, you should confirm that the Windows Recovery Environment (WinRE) is correctly configured and enabled on the device; otherwise, you will get this error. Use the REAgentC.exe tool to enable WinRE.
OOBEIDPS	When using the self-deploying mode, a deployment might fail, and a "Something went wrong" screen will appear. Configure Azure AD company branding to prevent this error from occurring.

When troubleshooting, other sources of information include looking in the Event Viewer for issues relating to the deployment profile settings and the OOBE. The relevant logs are located at

```
Application and Services Logs -> Microsoft -> Windows -> Provisioning-Diagnostics-
Provider -> Autopilot.
```

An example log entry might read, "Autopilot policy name not found."

NEED MORE REVIEW? **REVIEWING EVENT LOG ENTRIES**

If you want to know more about the event log entries related to troubleshooting Autopilot profile settings and OOBE flow, visit the Microsoft website at *https://learn.microsoft.com/mem/autopilot/troubleshooting*.

You can also look in the registry to find evidence of Windows Autopilot failures. The Autopilot deployment service will record information in the registry at this location:

```
HKLM\SOFTWARE\Microsoft\Provisioning\Diagnostics\Autopilot.
```

An example of a problem recorded in the registry would read, "The device has not been registered with Autopilot."

For more advanced troubleshooting, administrators can use the Event Tracing for Windows (ETW) tool to capture detailed information from Autopilot. This will generate trace files, which you can view by using the Windows Performance Analyzer.

> **NOTE SUPPORT CASE FOR WINDOWS AUTOPILOT**
>
> If you have an issue you cannot resolve, you can obtain help by contacting Microsoft Support. Because you will have Azure AD premium and other subscriptions, you are entitled to Microsoft Support. You view the options to open a support case for Windows Autopilot at *https:// learn.microsoft.com/mem/autopilot/autopilot-support*.

Skill 1.3: Plan and implement a Windows client deployment by using MDT

Microsoft Deployment Toolkit (MDT) is a deployment tool used by many medium and large-sized organizations to provide zero-touch installation (ZTI) deployments in on-premises infrastructures. When combined with Microsoft Endpoint Configuration Manager, you can implement ZTI deployments. In this skill, you'll learn what you need to know about when and how to use MDT to deploy Windows 11 in your organization.

> **This skill covers how to:**
>
> - Plan and implement an MDT deployment infrastructure
> - Create, manage, and deploy images
> - Monitor and troubleshoot a deployment
> - Plan and configure user state migration

Plan and implement an MDT deployment infrastructure

Most enterprise organizations have used image-based deployment for many years. Both MDT and Configuration Manager rely on images and build a device in layers or task sequences deployed onto a device over the network. When working with images, you must determine whether you want to use a default or custom image to deploy the Windows operating system.

- **Default image**   A default image results from performing a standard installation of Windows 11 on a computer using default values. A default image, install.wim, is provided in the Sources folder on Windows 11 ISO. When using default images, remember that
    - You don't need to create the image.
    - You must apply settings and apps separately after the deployment of the image.

- Updates to applications don't affect the image.
- The same image can be used throughout the organization.
- End-to-end deployment time is longer than with custom images because you must perform deployment tasks after the image application.
- **Custom image** A custom image contains additional components, such as drivers and apps, and specific settings and customizations relevant to the organization. When using custom images, remember that
    - You'll need to create and maintain the image.
    - You can include all required apps and settings in the image.
    - You might need to maintain multiple images to manage the needs of your different departments.
    - Updates to applications require you to update the image.
    - End-to-end deployment time can be faster.

> **NOTE   THIN VERSUS THICK**
>
> Images containing only an operating system are often referred to as *thin images*, while those that contain many apps are called *thick images*. Most organizations use thin images because they require less ongoing maintenance. A thick image is more comprehensive and requires less action post-deployment, but the image needs to be maintained with the latest software patches and updates.

MDT supports two types of images:

- **Boot images** These are used to start the deployment process. It's typical for computers targeted for deployment with MDT to have no installed operating system. This is known as bare-metal deployment. The boot image can be accessed from a USB thumb drive, ISO file, or a Pre-Boot Execution Environment (PXE) server (such as Windows Deployment Services). When you deploy MDT, you'll also install Windows ADK, including standard boot images for both x86 and x64 architectures.
- **Operating system images** You'll use the deployment workbench to create and manage your operating system images. As mentioned, you can use either a default or custom image, depending on your requirements.

Create and manage images

Before you can do anything else, you'll need to create your images. The starting point is called a reference image. The reference image is the standard operating system you'll deliver to your users. You'll have to consider what you want to add to the image, such as drivers, apps, or specific configurations.

Create a reference image

After determining what will be included in the image, you'll need to create it. Use the following top-level procedure:

1. On a reference computer, install Windows 11 Enterprise 21H2.
2. Apply any Windows updates.
3. Add any drivers, apps, or other required software.
4. Apply any app updates.
5. Configure any installed apps or software as needed.
6. Using the Sysprep.exe tool, generalize the image.

EXAM TIP

You use the Sysprep.exe app to generalize your image. It's located in the C:\Windows\ System32\Sysprep\ folder and requires administrator-level privileges to reset your operating system, ready for OOBE.

7. Capture the generalized image.
8. Store the captured image in a location accessible to MDT.

In addition to your operating system image, you'll also need a boot image. Typically, you'll use the boot image provided on an installation Windows 11 ISO that matches the edition to be deployed.

At the time of writing, Microsoft has not updated the Microsoft Deployment Toolkit to support Windows 11 Enterprise 22H2. It's incompatible with MDT build 6.3.8456.1000 since the new version no longer contains the x86 version of WinPE that MDT uses. Therefore, you should ensure your reference environment contains the following software:

- Windows ADK for Windows 11 21H2 (Windows 11 Enterprise 22H2 is not supported). The required version of the adksetup.exe is 10.1.22000.1. See *https://go.microsoft.com/ fwlink/?linkid=2165884*.

- Microsoft Deployment Toolkit, Build 6.3.8456.1000. See *https://www.microsoft.com/ download/details.aspx?id=54259*.

- WinPE Addon for Windows ADK for Windows 11 21H2. See *https://go.microsoft.com/ fwlink/?linkid=2166133*.

> **NOTE** **WINDOWS 11 IS NETWORK-HUNGRY**
>
> During the build and capture phases and creating a Windows 11 reference image, Windows 11 is very active over the network while updating its native applications via the Internet. This is known for breaking Sysprep. If possible, you should disable Internet access during these stages.

Add the images to MDT

After you've created any required images, the next step is to add the images to MDT. Before you can add images, you'll need to create a deployment share. Use the following procedure:

1. Open the **Deployment Workbench**.
2. Select the **Deployment Shares** folder.
3. Right-click Deployment Shares and then select **New Deployment Share**.
4. Complete the New Deployment Share Wizard by providing:
   - A local path on the MDT server for the share.
   - A share name, such as **Deployment Share$**.
   - A description.
   - The following options can be configured to control the deployment experience when images are created within MDT:
     - **Ask if a computer backup should be performed.**
     - **Ask for a product key.**
     - **Ask to set the local Administrator password.**
     - **Ask if an image should be captured.**
     - **Ask if BitLocker should be enabled.**
5. You can add your images to the deployment share when you've created the deployment share.

To add an operating system image, use the following procedure:

1. Expand your deployment share and select **Operating Systems**.
2. Right-click **Operating Systems** and then select **Import Operating System**.
3. Complete the **Import Operating System Wizard**, displayed in Figure 1-12, by entering the following information:
   - Choose OS Type and select **Full set of source files**, **Custom image file**, or **Windows Deployment Services images**.
   - Choose **Source** to enter your image's source location.
   - Choose **WDS Server** to add a WDS server name if you're using a Windows Deployment Services image.
   - Choose **Destination** to add a destination directory name.

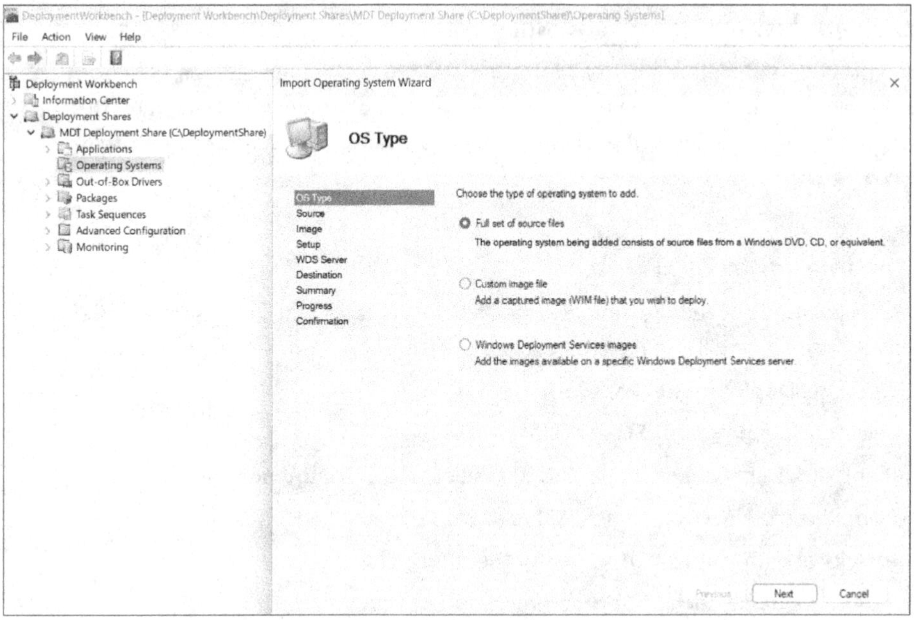

FIGURE 1-12 Choosing the operating system image type

Manage application and driver deployment

You can use MDT to deploy and manage apps and drivers. To add applications, use the following procedure:

1. In your deployment share, select and then right-click **Applications**.

2. Select **New Application**.

3. Complete the New Application Wizard by entering the following information:

   - Choose between **Application with source files, Application without source files or elsewhere on the network**, or **Application bundle.**

   - The details for the app, including **Publisher**, **Application Name**, **Version**, and **Language**.

   - The **Source** (where the files are for the app) and the **Destination** (the name by which the app is known).

   - Any command line details needed to install the app. For example, for XML Notepad, the command line would typically be **xmlnotepad.msi /q**.

> **EXAM TIP**
>
> If you want to deploy many apps, consider using a Windows PowerShell script to acceler-ate the process. You'll need to import the Windows PowerShell snap-in (Microsoft.BDD. SnapIn), which can be located at *https://learn.microsoft.com/en-us/mem/configmgr/mdt/ samples-guide#LoadMDTSnapIn.*

Installing drivers is similar. Follow these steps:

1. Select and then right-click the **Out-of-Box Drivers** folder.

2. Select **Import Drivers.**

3. Specify the folder location for the drivers you want to import.

Create task sequences

After you've added all the required images, apps, and drivers, you must create task sequences to apply these to target computers. Task sequences are the collection of actions performed to complete a specific job, such as deploying Windows 11 and related apps to a target computer.

You use predefined templates to create your task sequences. Tasks typically include:

- **Gather**   This task reads required configuration information from a deployment server.
- **Format and Partition**   This task prepares the target hard disk for the operating system you're deploying.
- **Inject Drivers**   This task obtains the required drivers for a target computer and downloads them from a driver repository.
- **Apply Operating System**   This task deploys the appropriate operating system image.
- **Windows Update**   This task connects to a WSUS server and retrieves updates to apply to the target computer.

To create a task sequence, use the following procedure:

1. In your deployment share, right-click **Task Sequences**.

2. Select **New Task Sequence**.

3. Complete the **New Task Sequence Wizard** by entering the following information:

   - A **Task sequence ID** and **Task sequence name**. These identify the task sequence, which is displayed with the optional **Task sequence comments** by the deployment wizard during deployment.
   - Choose a template. You can choose between **Sysprep and Capture**, **Standard Client Task Sequence**, **Standard Client Upgrade Task Sequence**, **Post OS Installation Task Sequence**, and many others.
   - Choose the **Operating Systems** image.
   - If necessary, enter a product key.
   - Enter a user's **Full Name**, **Organization**, web browser home page, and local administrator account password.

After creating the task sequence, you'll need to configure its settings. The procedure will vary based on what the task sequence does. But for example, to complete the process of configuring an operating system deployment task sequence, use the following procedure:

1. In your deployment share, in the **Task Sequences** folder, right-click your task sequence, and select **Properties**.

2. Select the **Task Sequences** tab, displayed in Figure 1-13.

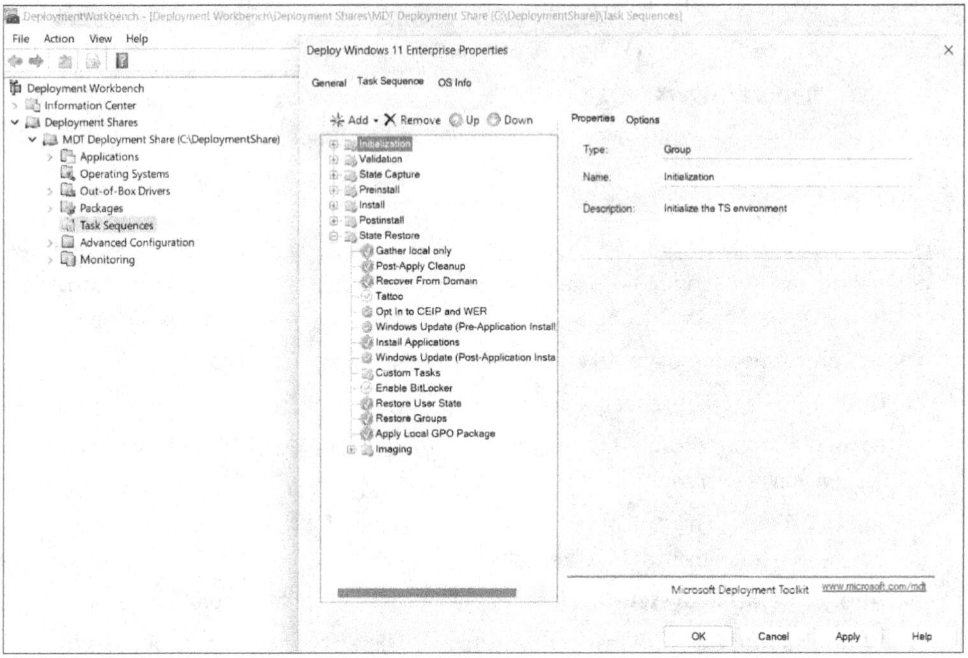

FIGURE 1-13 Reviewing the Task Sequences details

3. Verify and modify any required settings.

   The final step before deployment is configuring the deployment share properties and related Windows PE settings. Use the following procedure:

   1. Right-click your deployment share and select **Properties**.

   2. On the **General** tab, verify the **Platforms Supported** (x86 and x64).

   3. Optionally, select the **Enable multicast for this deployment share** checkbox. This is only available if you've deployed a Windows Deployment Services role in your environment.

   4. On the **Rules** tab, review the contents of the displayed `CustomSettings.ini` file. These were defined in the initial task sequence creation.

   5. Review the settings for creating a Windows PE boot disk on the **Windows PE** tab. Remember to review the settings for your platform by selecting either **x86** or **x64** from the **Platform** list.

   6. On the **Windows PE** tab, beneath the **Platform** list, select the **Features** tab and review and revise the required settings. These options determine additional features.

   7. Select **OK**, and if you made any changes, right-click your deployment share, and select **Update Deployment Share**. Complete the wizard to refresh the settings in your deployment share.

Deploy images

After creating and configuring your task sequences, you're ready to deploy your images. All you need to do is start the required computers, which should start using the MDT PE. Then use the following procedure to apply the image and deploy Windows 11. Note that steps might vary based on your specific configuration options.

1. Turn on your target computer.
2. The **Microsoft Deployment Toolkit** deployment wizard starts.
3. As displayed in Figure 1-14, select **Run the Deployment Wizard to install a new Operating System**.

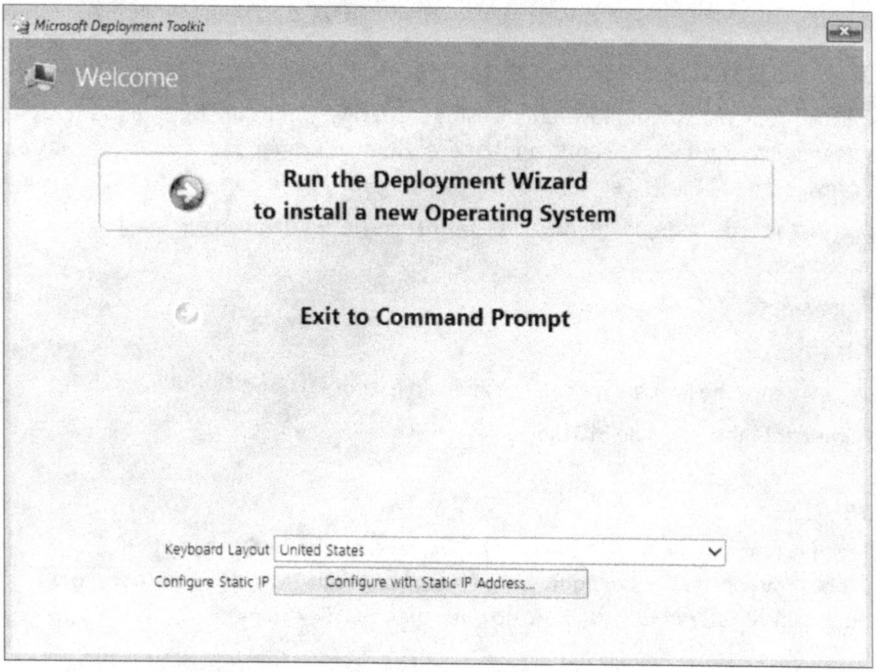

FIGURE 1-14 Deploying Windows 11 using an MDT task sequence

4. Enter your **Username**, **Password**, and **Domain**, and select **OK**.
5. On the **Task Sequence** page, select the appropriate task sequence and select Next.
6. On the **Computer Details** page, review the generated computer name, and then select either **Join a domain** or **Join a workgroup**. For the domain option, enter the **Domain to join**, **Organizational Unit**, and credentials to join (**Username**, **Password**, and **Domain**). Select **Next**.
7. Complete the **Windows Deployment Wizard** by entering the following information:
   - Choose whether to move user data and settings from a previous version of Windows.
   - Choose whether to restore user data.

- Specify the **Language Settings** and **Time Settings**.
- Select any apps you want to deploy.

8. When you've completed the required settings, select **Begin**. Your operating system and selected apps are deployed.

NEED MORE REVIEW?   **DEPLOY A WINDOWS IMAGE USING MDT**

To review further details about deploying images with MDT, refer to the Microsoft website at *https://learn.microsoft.com/windows/deployment/deploy-windows-mdt/deploy-a-windows-10-image-using-mdt*. This page relates to Windows 10.

Monitor and troubleshoot a deployment

If you experience problems with deployment by using MDT, review the configuration settings for your deployment share. If you're confident that everything is properly configured, then you can consider reviewing MDT logs. Each MDT script automatically generates logs.

Depending on the type of deployment you're performing, after deployment, the log files are moved to either:

- %WINDIR%\SMSOSD
- %WINDIR%\TEMP\SMSOSD

For LTI deployments, the logs are moved to %WINDIR%\TEMP\DeploymentLogs.

Table 1-12 describes the available MDT logs.

EXAM TIP

The MDT log file format is designed to be read by CMTrace, one of the Configuration Manager tools. You will need to configure .log files to open with CMTrace because the tool isn't automatically registered with Windows to open the .log file extension.

TABLE 1-12 MDT logs

Log	Description
BDD.log	Copied to a network location at the end of the deployment. You must specify the SLShare property in the Customsettings.ini file to create this log.
LiteTouch.log	Created during LTI deployments and stored in the %WINDIR%\TEMP\DeploymentLogs folder.
Scriptname*.log	Created by each MDT script. The log name is the same as the script name.
SMSTS.log	Created by the Task Sequencer. Describes all Task Sequencer transactions. Stored in %TEMP%, %WINDIR%\System32\ccm\logs, C:_SMSTaskSequence or C:\SMSTSLog, depending on your specific deployment scenario.

Log	Description
Wizard.log	Created and updated by the deployment wizards.
WPEinit.log	Created during the Windows PE initialization process. This log is useful for trouble-shooting errors encountered when starting Windows PE.
Deployment-Workbench_*id*.log	Created in the %temp% folder when you add the /debug switch when you start the Deployment Workbench.

When you investigate the logs, you'll want to identify any errors. There are numerous error codes with specific meanings. For example, error codes 5201, 5203, and 5205 all mean that a connection to the deployment share could not be made, and deployment cannot proceed.

NEED MORE REVIEW? **ERROR CODES AND THEIR DESCRIPTION**

To review further details about error codes with MDT, refer to the Microsoft website at *https://learn.microsoft.com troubleshoot/mem/configmgr/mdt/troubleshooting-reference# table-1-error-codes-and-their-description*.

NEED MORE REVIEW? **TROUBLESHOOTING REFERENCE FOR MDT**

To review further details about troubleshooting MDT, refer to the Microsoft website at *https://learn.microsoft.com/troubleshoot/mem/configmgr/mdt/troubleshooting-reference*.

Plan and configure user state migration

Users are at the heart of every organization, and data is seldom held on a device. Users often invest a lot of time and effort in configuring their Windows environment. This can include customizing their apps, such as developing templates and toolbars.

Losing app data and personalized settings can significantly affect the productivity and even the morale of users. By migrating their Windows and app settings, you will likely reduce the number of help desk calls and avoid user downtime required to customize their desktops and find missing files.

Most user data is contained in a profile, and the user folders are synchronized to a cloud-based location by using a solution such as Enterprise State Roaming in Azure Active Directory.

When devices contain data, you might want to transfer or migrate that data to a new device. Microsoft supports this migration process using the Windows Assessment and Deployment Kit (Windows ADK) tools. These tools and processes require specialist knowledge and often add significant time and cost to the rollout project.

Preserving user state data

When you upgrade to Windows 11, unless you perform an in-place upgrade, you might overlook the migration of the user's app data and Windows settings.

You should aim to migrate user settings, which are often contained in their user profiles, during your Windows 11 deployment project.

Following are the two traditional methods of upgrading to Windows 11 that don't involve an in-place upgrade:

- **Side-by-side migration**   This type of migration is used when the source and destination computers for the upgrade are different machines. You install a new computer with Windows 11 and then migrate the data and user settings from the computer running the older operating system to the new computer.

- **Wipe-and-load migration**   In this scenario, the source and destination computers are the same. You back up the user data and settings to an external location and then install Windows 11 on the user's existing computer. Afterward, you restore user data and settings.

User State Migration Tool

You can automate much of the user profile migration process for large-scale deployments by using deployment automation tools, such as Configuration Manager or the Microsoft Deployment Toolkit (MDT). Both solutions use the User State Migration Tool (USMT), part of the Windows ADK.

> *NOTE* **DOWNLOAD WINDOWS ADK**
>
> You can download the Windows ADK from the Microsoft website at *https://docs.microsoft.com/en-us/windows-hardware/get-started/adk-install.*

For smaller migrations, you can use USMT directly from the command line to capture user accounts, user files, operating system settings, and application settings; you can then migrate the captured settings to a new Windows installation.

Although quite dated, USMT has received several updates, which make it more secure and usable. It is available as a command line tool. The features include

- **Size estimation of the migration stores**   Allows you to gauge the amount of storage you will need to perform a data capture for a targeted Windows device.

- **Encryption of the migration stores**   This protects the information stored in the user's profile, reducing the risk of data being compromised while being stored.

- **Hard links to the migration store**   This is useful for PC refresh scenarios that do not involve the reformatting of the primary Windows partition. Using a hard-link migration store with USMT allows the restore process to come from the same local partition, significantly increasing transfer performance.

- **Perform offline migrations**   You can run migrations from within a Windows Preinstallation Environment (WinPE). You can also perform migrations from the data stored in Windows.old directories.

You perform a user state migration in two phases as follows:

1. Settings and data are captured (collected) from the source and stored in a secure migration store using the ScanState tool.

2. Captured settings and data are restored to the destination computer using the LoadState tool.

Also, USMT can be scripted to enhance efficiency, and it can be customized with settings and rules using migration XML files:

- `MigApp.xml`

- `MigDocs.xml`

- `MigUser.xml`

- Custom XML files that you can create

The types of data that USMT can capture and migrate are shown in Table 1-13.

TABLE 1-13 Data Types Accessible by USMT

Data type	Example	Description
User accounts, user settings, and user data	My Documents, My Video, My Music, My Pictures, Desktop files, Start menu, Quick Launch settings, and Favorites	Local and domain-based user accounts. Folders from each user profile.
Shared user data	Shared Documents, Shared Video, Shared Music, Shared Desktop files, Shared Pictures, Shared Start menu, and Shared Favorites	Folders from the Public profiles.
Files, folders, and settings	Files, folders, and Registry keys	USMT searches fixed drives, collecting files with any file name extensions, folders, and Registry keys defined in the configuration XML file.
NTFS permissions	Access control lists (ACLs)	USMT can migrate the ACL information for specified files and folders.
Operating system components	Mapped network drives, network printers, folder options, EFS files, users' personal certificates, and Internet Explorer settings	USMT migrates most standard operating system settings.
Supported applications settings	Microsoft Office, Skype, Google Chrome, Adobe Acrobat Reader, Apple iTunes, and more	USMT will migrate settings for many applications, which can be specified in the MigApp.xml file. The version of each application must match the source and destination computers. With Microsoft Office, USMT allows migration of the settings from an earlier version of an Office application.

As shown in Table 1-13, the list of settings that can be migrated is quite extensive. However, the following settings cannot be migrated with USMT:

- Local printers and hardware-related settings
- Device drivers
- Passwords
- Customized icons for shortcuts
- Shared folder permissions
- Files and settings if the operating systems have different languages installed

USMT comprises several command-line tools and configuration files, which use XML files to store customizations. The USMT components are described in Table 1-14.

TABLE 1-14 USMT Components

Component	Description
ScanState.exe	Scans a source computer, collects files and settings, and writes them to a migration store. (The store file can be password protected and can be compressed and encrypted if required. You cannot use the /nocompress option with the /encrypt option.) You can turn off the default compression with the /nocompress option.
LoadState.exe	Migrates the files and settings from the migration store to the destination computer.
USMTUtils.exe	Used to compress, encrypt, and validate the migration store files.
Migration XML files	MigApp.xml, MigUser.xml, or MigDocs.xml files, and custom XML files that USMT uses to configure the process.
Config.xml	Used with the /genconfig option to exclude data from a migration.
Component manifests	Controls which operating system settings are to be migrated. These manifests are specific to the operating system and are not modifiable.

Use the following steps to initiate the collection of the files and settings from the source computer and back up the settings and files to a network share:

1. Ensure you have a backup of the source computer.
2. Close all applications.
3. Using an account with administrative privileges, run ScanState, using the following command:

   ```
   ScanState \\remotelocation\migration\mystore /config:config.xml / i:migdocs.xml
   /:migapp.xml /v:13 /l:scan.log
   ```

4. Run UsmtUtils with the /verify switch to ensure that the migration store is not corrupted; use the command

   ```
   UsmtUtils /verify C:\mystore\storename.img
   ```

5. On the destination computer running Windows 11, you need to install any applications on the source computer and close any open applications.

6. Run the LoadState command, specifying the same .xml files and network share location that you used when you ran ScanState; use the following command:

    ```
    LoadState \\remotelocation\migration\ /config:config.xml / i:migdocs.xml
    /i:migapp.xml /v:13 /l:load.log
    ```

7. Once completed, restart the device, and verify that the settings successfully migrated.

Skill 1.4: Configure remote management

Users are at the heart of most organizations, and keeping them productive is key to a successful business. Support personnel can remotely administer computers within their organization to help address user issues. In addition to telephone and chat support, you can use various tools to see what the users see and even take control of their interfaces.

You need to understand the different utilities you can use to securely troubleshoot your hardware while also securely managing and supporting it. This skill will explore the various tools and utilities available to manage your devices remotely.

> **This skill covers how to:**
> - Configure Remote Help in Intune
> - Configure Remote Desktop on a Windows client
> - Configure the Windows Admin Center
> - Configure PowerShell remoting and Windows Remote Management (WinRM)

Configure Remote Help in Intune

Remote Help is a new cloud-based solution that help desk operators can use to remotely and securely connect to a user's device. Connections use role-based access controls to ensure that support staff (helpers) can securely access (sharers) devices and that proper Azure Active Directory (Azure AD) trusts are established for the Remote Help sessions.

Support users are classed as helpers, and users that receive remote help are referred to as sharers. Helpers can view the sharer's device's display, and if permitted by the sharer, they can take full control to make configurations directly or take actions on the device.

Remote Help uses Intune role-based access controls (RBAC) to set the level of access that a helper is permitted. Through RBAC, administrators can determine which users can provide help and the level of help they can provide. Both devices enrolled and not enrolled with Intune can use the Remote Help app. For devices enrolled in management, the app can the deployed by Intune. The Remote Help app supports the capabilities shown in Table 1-15.

TABLE 1-15 Remote Help capabilities

Capability	Description
Remote Help capabilities and requirements	Remote Help is disabled by default. Remote Help can be enabled tenant-wide. Once enabled, Remote Help is available to users authenticated in the tenant.
Use Remote Help with unenrolled devices	Disabled by default, you can choose to allow help to devices that aren't enrolled with Intune.
Requires Organization login	To use Remote Help, both the helper and the sharer must sign in with an Azure AD account from your organization. You can't use Remote Help to help users outside of your organization.
Compliance Warnings	A compliance warning will be displayed if a device is not compliant with its assigned policies. This warning doesn't block access, but helpers should know the risk of using sensitive data during the session.
Role-based access control	Admins can set RBAC rules that determine the scope of a helper's access and define the range of actions they can do while providing help. Includes view only and being able to run elevated privileges while helping.
Elevation of privilege	A helper with the correct RBAC permissions can accept the UAC prompt on the sharer's machine to enter credentials to achieve administrative permissions.
Monitor active Remote Help sessions, and view details about past sessions	You can view reports detailing active and prior sessions in the Microsoft Intune admin center.

Prerequisites and network considerations

Remote Help is included in the Intune licensing and requires both the helper and sharer to install the Remote Help app for Windows. You can find the complete list of license requirements and network requirements here.

- Intune subscription
- Remote Help add-on license or an Intune Suite license for helpers and sharers
- Windows 11 (or Windows 10)
- The Remote Help app for Windows available from *aka.ms/downloadremotehelp*
- Remote Help is available within the same tenant only
- Remote Help uses port 443(HTTPS) and connects to the Remote Assistance Service by using the Remote Desktop Protocol (RDP)
- Traffic is encrypted with TLS 1.2

> **NOTE   REMOTE HELP TRIAL**
>
> Remote Help is free for 90 days with up to 250 trial users. One trial is allowed for each organization. See *https://learn.microsoft.com/mem/intune/fundamentals/intune-add-ons*.

Data collected during the Remote Help session logs are stored on Microsoft servers for 30 days and then deleted. These logs provide the data visible in the history shown in the Microsoft Intune admin center. Microsoft Remote Help session logs do not record actions or keystrokes. Each device will record errors and elevation of privilege actions within the event view.

Administrators should ensure that both the helper and sharer can reach the network endpoints using port 443, as shown in Table 1-16.

TABLE 1-16 Remote Help network endpoints

Domain/name	Description
*.aria.microsoft.com	Used for accessibility features within the app.
*.events.data.microsoft.com	Microsoft Telemetry Service.
*.monitor.azure.com	Required for telemetry and remote service initialization.
*.support.services.microsoft.com	Primary endpoint used for the Remote Help application.
*.trouter.skype.com	Used for Azure Communication Service for chat and connection between parties.
*.aadcdn.msauth.net	Required for logging in to the application (AAD).
*.aadcdn.msftauth.net	Required for logging in to the application (AAD).
*.edge.skype.com	Used for Azure Communication Service for chat and connection between parties.
*.graph.microsoft.com	Used for connecting to the Microsoft Graph service.
*.login.microsoftonline.com	Required for Microsoft login service. Might not be available in preview in all markets or for all localizations.
*.remoteassistanceprodacs.communication.azure.com	Used for Azure Communication Service for chat and connection between parties.
Allow list for Microsoft Edge endpoints. See *https://learn.microsoft.com/ en-us/deployedge/microsoft-edge-security-endpoints*.	The app uses Edge WebView2 browser control. This article lists the domain URLs that should be added to the allow list to ensure communications through firewalls and other security mechanisms.

Deploy Remote Help as a Win32 app

Individuals can install the latest version of Remote Help direct from Microsoft at *aka.ms/ downloadremotehelp*. Alternatively, administrators can deploy Remote Help as a Win32 app via Intune.

To add Remote Help as a Win32 app, you must first repackage the `remotehelpinstaller.exe` as a `.intunewin file`. This then changes the file to become a valid Win32 app file that can be deployed with Intune.

NEED MORE REVIEW? **PREPARE A WIN32 APP**

You can find the guidance on how to prepare a Win32 app here: *https://learn.microsoft.com/mem/intune/apps/apps-win32-prepare.*

Once you have repackaged Remote Help as an `.intunewin` file, use the following procedure to upload and deploy Remote Help to Intune.

1. Sign in as Global Administrator to the Microsoft Intune admin center portal at *https://endpoint.microsoft.com/.*
2. On the left navigation bar, select **Apps**, then select **All apps**.
3. On the **All apps** blade, select **Add**.
4. On the **Select app type** blade, select **Windows app (Win32)** and select **Select**.
5. On the **Add App** blade, select **Select app package file** and locate the **remotehelpinstaller.intunewin** file you've previously prepared. Verify that the details are populated correctly and then select **OK**, as shown in Figure 1-15.

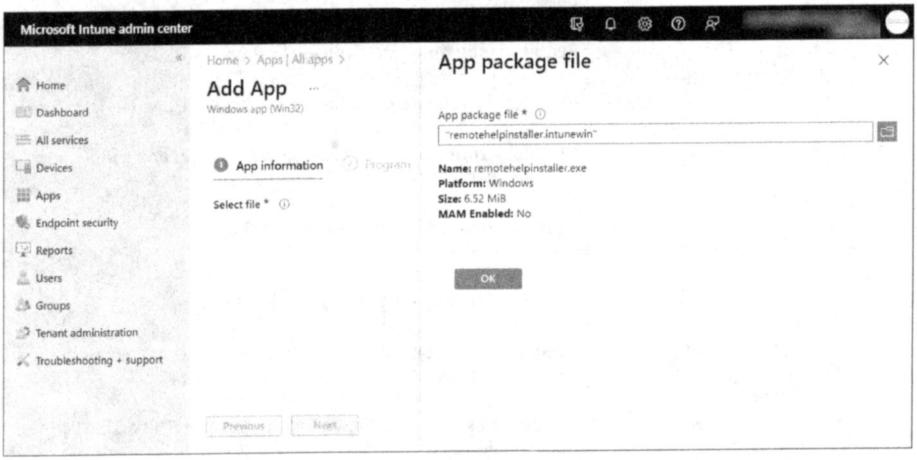

FIGURE 1-15 Adding Windows App (Win32) packaged file to Intune

6. On the **App information** page, add the details for your app. Some of the values on this page might be automatically filled in if your app automatically supplied them.
   - **Name** Enter the app's name as you want it to appear in the company portal.
   - **Description** Enter the description of the app. The description appears in the company portal.
   - **Publisher** Enter the name of the publisher of the app.
   - **Category** Select one or more of the built-in app categories or a category you created.
   - **Show this as a featured app in the Company Portal** Display the app prominently on the main page of the company portal when users browse for apps.

- **Information URL**   Optionally, enter a website's URL containing information about this app.

- **Privacy URL**   Optionally, enter the URL of a website that contains privacy information for this app.

- **Developer**   Optionally, enter the name of the app developer.

- **Owner**   Optionally, enter a name for the owner of this app, such as the **HR department**.

- **Notes**   Enter any notes you want to associate with this app.

- **Logo**   Upload an icon that's associated with the app. The app displays this icon when users browse through the company portal.

7. Select **Next** to display the **Program** page.

8. On the **Program** page, configure the app installation and removal commands for the app using the following options:

    - For `Install command line`, specify `remotehelpinstaller.exe /quiet acceptTerms=1`

    - For `Uninstall command line`, specify `remotehelpinstaller.exe /uninstall /quiet acceptTerms=1`

9. The other details on the **Program** page are optional. Select **Next**, and on the **Requirements** page, configure the **Operating system architecture** to **32-bit** and **64-bit**, and set the **Minimum operating system** to **Windows 11 21H2**. Ignore the remaining options. Select **Next.**

10. On the **Detection rules** page, under **Rules format**, select **Manually Configure detection rules**, and then select **Add** to open the **Detection rule** pane. Configure the following options:

    - For **Rule type**, select **File.**

    - For **Path**, specify **C:\Program Files\Remote Help**

    - For **File or folder**, specify **RemoteHelp.exe.**

    - For **Detection method**, select **String (version)**

    - For **Operator**, select **Greater than or equal to**

    - For **Value**, specify the version of Remote Help you are deploying. For example, **10.0.22467.1000**

    - Leave **Associated with a 32-bit app on 64-bit clients** set to **No**

11. Select **OK** to close the blade, then select **Next.**

12. On the **Dependencies** and **Supersedence** pages, click **Next.**

13. On the **Assignments** page, select an applicable device group or device groups that should install the Remote Help app and select **Next.**

14. On the **Review + create** page, review the configuration and select **Create.**

15. Intune will upload the app file and prepare the Remote Help app for deployment and installation on applicable devices. The Remote Help app might take up to an hour to upload, depending on your Internet bandwidth.

Once uploaded, the app will be automatically distributed and installed on all devices assigned to the app.

> **NEED MORE REVIEW?** **DISTRIBUTE REMOTE HELP USING INTUNE**
>
> **You can find the guidance on distributing Remote Help using Intune at** *https://learn.microsoft.com/en-us/mem/intune/fundamentals/remote-help.*

Configure Remote Help within Intune

Once the Remote App is added to your tenant, you must configure your tenant to support Remote Help using the following steps.

Enable Remote Help

1. Sign in as Global Administrator to the Microsoft Intune admin center portal at *https://endpoint.microsoft.com/.*
2. On the left navigation bar, select **Tenant administration**, and then select **Remote Help**.
3. On the **Settings** tab, select **Configure** and implement these settings:
   1. Set **Enable Remote Help** to **Enabled** to allow the use of remote help. By default, this setting is **Disabled**.
   2. Set **Allow Remote Help to unenrolled devices** to **Enabled** if you want to allow this option. By default, this setting is **Disabled**.
   3. Set **Disable chat** to **Yes** to remove the chat functionality in the Remote Help app. By default, chat is enabled, and this setting is set to **No**.
4. Select **Save**.

Configure permissions for Remote Help

You will need to ensure that your support team is assigned the **Help Desk Operator** role. This role has the following Intune RBAC permissions to manage the use of the Remote Help app.

- **Category** Select the **Remote Help** app.
- **Permissions**
  - **Take full control** Select **Yes** or **No**.
  - **Elevation** Select **Yes** or **No**.
  - **View screen** Select **Yes** or **No**.

By default, the built-in **Help Desk Operator** role sets all these permissions to **Yes**, as shown in Figure 1-16.

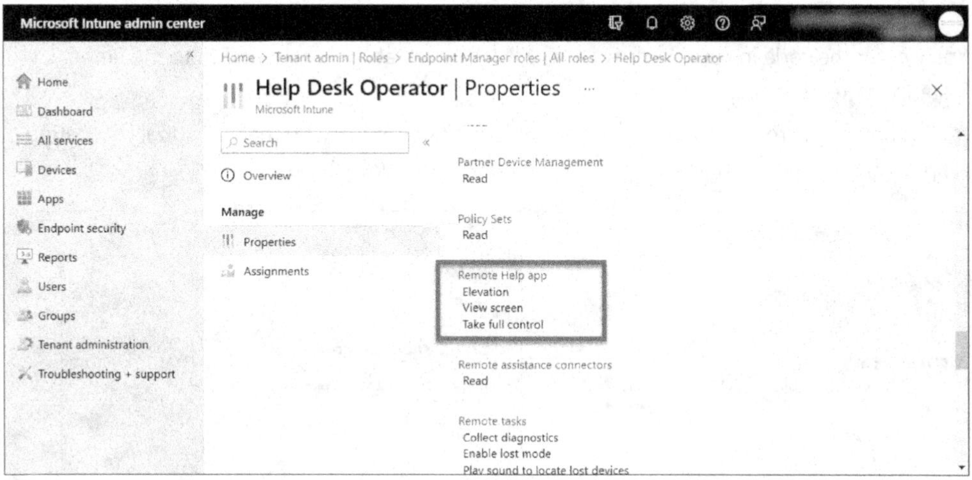

FIGURE 1-16 The Help Desk Operator RBAC settings

ASSIGN USER TO ROLES

After reviewing or creating the custom RBAC roles you can assign users and groups to those roles so that they can use Remote Help.

1. Sign in as Global Administrator to the Microsoft Intune admin center portal at *https://endpoint.microsoft.com/*.

2. On the left navigation bar, select **Tenant administration**, and then select **Roles.**

3. On the **All roles** page, select **Help Desk Operator**.

4. Select **Assignments**, then select **+Assign** to open **Add Role Assignment**.

5. On the *Basics* page, enter an **Assignment name** and optional **Assignment description**, and then select **Next**.

6. On the **Admin Groups** page, select the group that contains the users you want to give the permissions to. Choose **Next**.

7. On the **Scope Groups** page, choose a group containing the users/devices that the member above will be allowed to manage. You also can choose all users or all devices. Choose **Next** to continue.

8. On the **Review + create** page, and then select **Create**. The new assignment is displayed in the list of assignments.

How to use Remote Help

The use of Remote Help depends on whether you're requesting help or providing help. To request help, you must contact your support staff to request assistance using a call, chat, email, or other method. On the first opening of the Remote App tool, you will be required to accept the privacy policy.

As the sharer, you will be provided a security code from the support individual assisting you. You'll enter the code in your Remote Help instance to establish a connection to the helper's instance of Remote Help.

The helper will request a security code, which will be shared with the individual requesting help. Both the sharer and helper screens are shown in Figure 1-17.

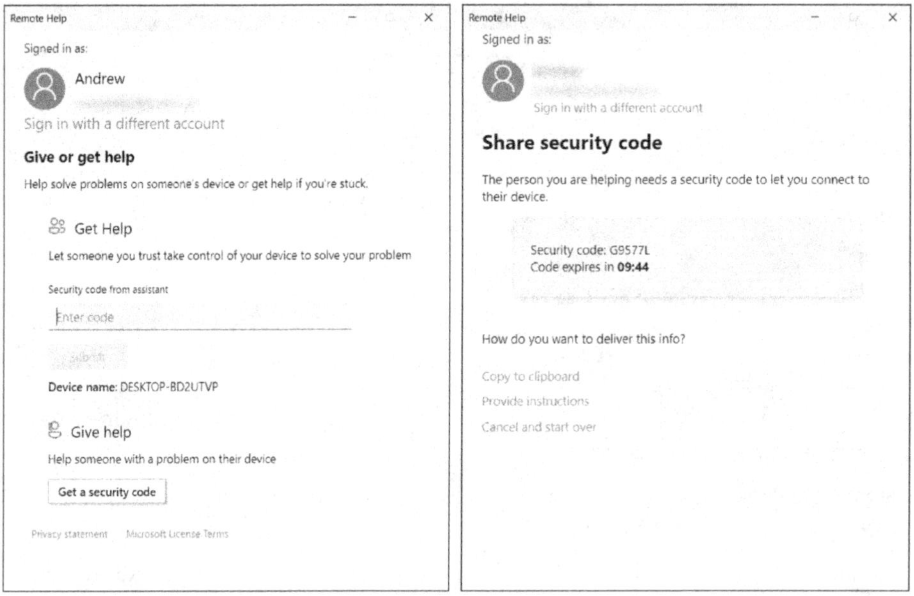

FIGURE 1-17 Remote Help sharer and helper screens

As a sharer, you will enter the security code from the helper, and the helper can request a session with full control of your device or choose only screen sharing. The code expires in 10 minutes; if not used, you must generate a new code. Once the code has been entered, the connection is established.

After you have opened a remote session, you can use the toolbar across the top of the display to perform the following actions:

- **Select Monitor**   Enables you to select a remote screen to review or interact with.
- **Laser Pointer**   Allows you to draw a laser pointer on the screen.
  - **Pen**   Provides you with the ability to write on the screen.
  - **Actual Size**   Enables you to resize the screen output to the actual size.
- **Toggle Chat**   Turns on (or off) the chat window where you can provide instructions to the remote user.
  - **Restart**   If the session uses **Full Control**, this option is enabled. Allows the helper to initiate a restart of the remote computer.
  - **Task Manager**   If the session uses **Full Control**, this option is enabled. Enables Task Manager on the remote computer, as shown in Figure 1-18.

- **Reconnect** If the session uses **Full Control**, this option is enabled and reconnects your session.

- **Leave** Terminates the session.

The remote session will time out after a period of inactivity, or you can end it once you have finished helping the remote user.

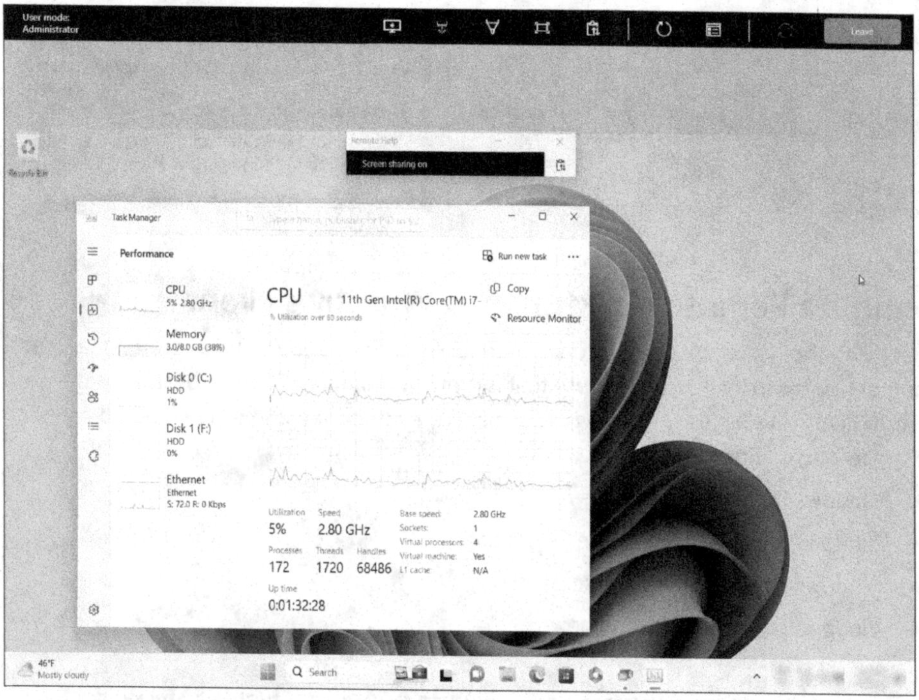

FIGURE 1-18 Remote Help sharer and helper screens

Monitoring, reports, and logging

You can monitor Remote Help from within the Microsoft Intune admin canter. Use the following steps to view active sessions or a history of sessions.

1. Sign in as Global Administrator to the Microsoft Intune admin center portal at *https://endpoint.microsoft.com/*.

2. On the left navigation bar, select **Tenant administration**, and then select **Remote Help**.

3. On the **Monitor** tab, you can view a count of active sessions and historical data about past sessions.

4. On the **Remote Help sessions** tab, you'll see the records of past sessions, including the following data.

   - The helper (**Provider ID**) and sharer (**Recipient ID**) of each session

   - The device that received assistance

   - The start and end times of the Remote session

You can access the Remote Help log files for the installation process and those created during Remote Help sessions. The Remote Help logs are available, as shown in Table 1-17.

TABLE 1-17 Remote Help Logs

Log file	Location	Description
Remote_help_*_Quick-Assist_Win10_x64.msi.log Remote_help_*.log	`C:\Users\<username>\AppData\Local\Temp`	■ Installation of Remote Help. ■ The * in the log file name represents the date and time stamp of when the log was created.
RemoteHelp	Event Viewer > Application and Services > Microsoft > Windows	■ Operational logs. ■ When using Remote Help, operational details are logged in the Windows Event Viewer.
*.monitor.azure.com	Azure Monitor	■ Required for telemetry and remote service initialization.

Configure Remote Desktop on a Windows client

Remote Desktop is a secure remote connection tool that allows you to take control of a remote computer's keyboard, video, and mouse that is running Windows. The Microsoft Remote Desktop client is available for Windows, iOS, macOS, and Android and can be used to connect to the following editions of Windows.

- Windows 11 Pro and Enterprise
- Windows 10 Pro and Enterprise
- Windows 8.1 Pro and Enterprise
- Windows Server 2012 R2 and newer

> **NOTE** **REMOTE DESKTOP CONNECTIONS TO WINDOWS HOME EDITIONS ARE NOT SUPPORTED**
>
> You can't connect to computers running a Home edition (like Windows 11 Home) using Remote Desktop.

Unlike the Remote Help app, which offers a helper/sharer support model, the Remote Desktop tool does not require a user to be available on the remote computer. The remote computer can be accessed via Remote Desktop if the following conditions are met.

- The remote computer is turned on and connected to the network.
- The correct credentials are provided to access the remote computer.
- The device allows connections via Remote Desktop.
- The device is running a supported Windows edition.
- Traffic is allowed to access ports TCP 3389 and UDP port 3389.

Once Remote Desktop has successfully connected to the device, it will remain locked on the local PC, and any actions performed remotely will not be visible on the monitor attached to the remote computer.

Remote Desktop uses Remote Desktop Protocol (RDP) which provides the secure data connection. The Remote Desktop client is available as a native Windows (MSTSC.exe) client, a web-based version, and an app available in the Microsoft Store. You can also obtain an app that runs on Android, iOS, and macOS.

The Remote Desktop client is built into Windows and allows you to create connections to Remote Desktop Session Host servers or other remote computers. Using the MSTSC.exe file, you can create and edit an existing Remote Desktop Connection (.rdp) configuration file.

A version of Remote Desktop has been available in Windows and Windows Server since Windows XP onwards. It uses the proprietary Remote Desktop Connection (RDC) Terminal Services client (mstsc.exe), which has been improved over the years. Windows 11 Remote Desktop features include:

- Remote Desktop sessions presented in a full-screen or windowed mode
- RDP core performance enhancements
- True multimonitor support with smart sizing (up to 16 monitors)
- Direct 2D and Direct 3D 10.1 application support
- Bidirectional audio support
- Supports multifactor authentication for remote connections
- Multimedia and Media Foundation support
- Remote FX user enhancements for RDP

> **NOTE   NOT ALL REMOTE DESKTOP CLIENT APPS ARE EQUAL**
>
> Not all Remote Desktop apps offer the same level of functionality. The most feature-rich experience is using the Remote Desktop version built into Windows 11. To review the list of features for each client, review this resource: *https://learn.microsoft.com/windows-server/ remote/remote-desktop-services/clients/remote-desktop-features*.

Enable Remote Desktop

Remote Desktop can be configured using the Remote Desktop options under Settings on Windows 11. By enabling the Remote Desktop feature, you allow access to your PC from a remote device. Because this provides remote access to your device, you need administrator-level privileges to turn this feature on.

You can also download a separate downloadable app for earlier versions of Windows.

To configure your PC for remote access, follow these steps.

1. On the device you want to connect to, select **Start** and then select **Settings.**
2. Select **System**, then select **Remote Desktop**.
3. Use the slider to enable Remote Desktop, as shown in Figure 1-19.
4. As needed, add users who can connect remotely by clicking **Select who can remotely access this PC** within the **Remote Desktop Users** section. Members of the Administrators group automatically have access.

5. Note the PC name shown in the **PC Name** section because you'll need this to configure the Remote Desktop client.

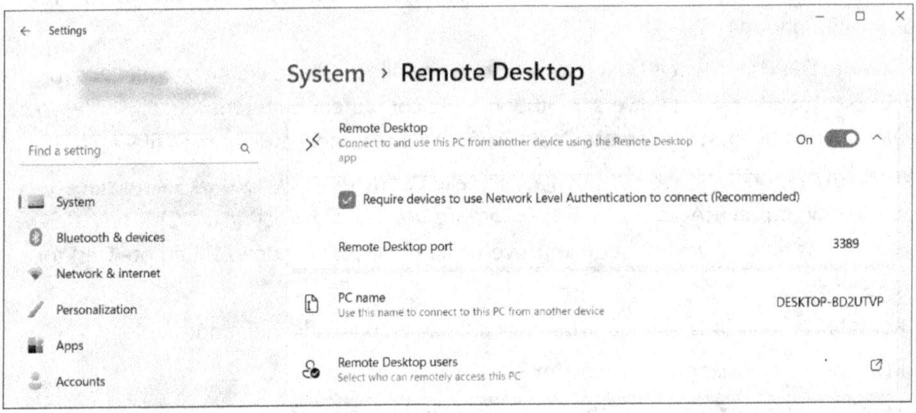

FIGURE 1-19 Enable Remote Help within Settings

Creating and editing Remote Desktop connections

To create a Remote Desktop connection, from **Start**, select **Remote Desktop Connection**. You must then specify the computer that you want to connect to. Use either a NETBIOS computer name or an IP address, as shown in Figure 1-20.

You can choose to securely save the credentials within the RDP connection file.

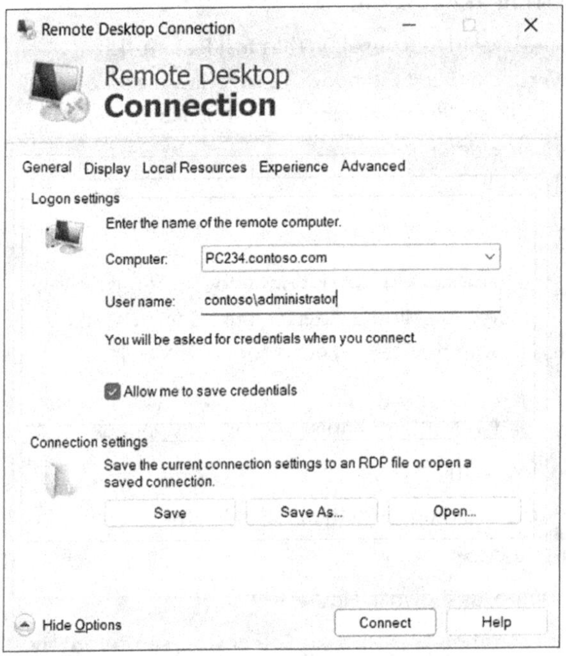

FIGURE 1-20 Configure Remote Desktop Settings

When the Remote Desktop connection tries to connect with the remote computer, you will be prompted to provide login credentials. If the credentials are correct, the connection is secured and completed. You can save your configuration to an RDP file for subsequent use. Upon successful connection, the remote machine's desktop will be locked. The remote connection will be terminated if a local user logs in to the computer.

You can configure additional connection settings using the options in Table 1-18. These are beneficial if you want to connect via a low-bandwidth connection or want to access local resources such as remote audio, clipboard data, files, printers, and other plug-and-play devices. If you are considering taking the MD-102 exam, ensure you review the new features added to the Remote Desktop Connection settings, such as redirecting remote cameras.

TABLE 1-18 Configurable Remote Desktop Connection options

Tab	Settings
General	<ul><li>Logon Settings:<ul><li>Computer</li><li>Username</li><li>Allow Me to Save Credentials</li><li>Connection Settings:</li><li>Save</li><li>Save As</li><li>Open</li></ul></li></ul>
Display	<ul><li>Display Configuration:<ul><li>Small > Large</li><li>Use All My Monitors For The Remote</li><li>Session</li></ul></li><li>Colors:<ul><li>Choose The Color Depth Of The Remote</li><li>Session</li><li>Display The Connection Bar When I Use Full Screen</li></ul></li></ul>
Local Resources	<ul><li>Remote Audio Settings</li><li>Remote Audio Playback:<ul><li>Play On This Computer</li><li>Do Not Play</li><li>Play On Remote Computer</li></ul></li><li>Remote Audio Recording:<ul><li>Record From This Computer</li><li>Do Not Record</li></ul></li><li>Keyboard, Apply Windows Key Combinations:<ul><li>Only When Using The Full Screen</li><li>On This Computer</li><li>On The Remote Computer</li></ul></li></ul>

Tab	Settings
	<ul><li>Local Devices And Resources:<ul><li>Printers</li><li>Clipboard</li><li>Smart Cards or Windows Hello For Business</li><li>WebAuthn (Windows Hello Or Security Keys)</li><li>Ports</li><li>Location</li><li>Drives</li><li>Video Capture Devices</li><li>Other Supported Plug And Play (Pnp) Devices</li></ul></li></ul>
Experience	<ul><li>Performance:<ul><li>Modem (56 kbps)</li><li>Low-Speed Broadband (256 Kbps–2 Mbps)</li><li>Satellite (2 Mbps–16 Mbps With High</li><li>Latency)</li><li>High-Speed Broadband (2mbps–10 Mbps)</li><li>Wan (10 Mpbs Or Higher With High Latency)</li><li>Lan (10 Mbps Or Higher)</li><li>Detect Connection Quality Automatically</li><li>Persistent Bitmap Caching</li><li>Reconnect If The Connection Is Dropped</li></ul></li></ul>
Advanced	<ul><li>Server Authentication, If Server Authentication Fails:<ul><li>Connect And Don't Warn Me</li><li>Warn Me</li><li>Do Not Connect</li></ul></li><li>Connect From Anywhere:</li><li>Connection Settings:<ul><li>Automatically Detect RD Gateway Server</li><li>Settings</li><li>Use These RD Gateway Server Settings</li><li>Do Not Use An RD Gateway Server</li></ul></li><li>Log-on Settings:<ul><li>Username</li><li>Use My RD Gateway Credentials For The Remote Computer</li></ul></li></ul>

Customizing Remote Desktop settings from the command line

You can open the Remote Desktop Connection app by running Mstsc.exe from the command line or the Windows Run dialog box. The Mstsc.exe command also enables administrators to open the tool with several parameters configured. The default firewall port that Remote Desktop uses is 3389, which must allow RDP traffic through for Remote Desktop to work.

If an administrator changes the firewall port for RDP traffic, the revised port number must be specified in the command-line tool Mstsc.exe when opening the application.

Each user's `default.rdp` file is stored as a hidden file in the user's Documents folder. The syntax for `mstsc` is as follows:

```
Mstsc [<connection file>] [/v:<server[:port]>] [/admin]
[/f[fullscreen]] [/w:<width>]
[/h:<height>] [/public] | [/span] [/multimon] [/edit
"connection file"]
[/restrictedAdmin] [/remoteGuard] [/prompt] [/shadow:sessionID>
[/control]
[/noConsentPrompt]] [/?]
```

The list of command-line parameters for Remote Desktop Connection is shown in Table 1-19.

TABLE 1-19 Command-line parameters for Remote Desktop Connection

Parameter	Description
<connection file>	Specifies the name of an RDP file for the connection.
/v: <Server[:<Port>]	Specifies the remote computer to which you want to connect.
/g:<gateway>	Specifies the RD Gateway server to use for the connection. This parameter is only read if the endpoint PC is specified with /v.
/admin	This parameter is used to connect you to a session to administer a Remote Desktop Session Host server (the RD Session Host role service must be installed on the remote server).
/edit <"connection file">	Opens the specified RDP file for editing.
/f	Starts Remote Desktop Connection in full-screen mode.
/w: <Width>	Specifies the width of the Remote Desktop window.
/h: <Height>	Specifies the height of the Remote Desktop window.
/l	Enumerates the monitor attached to the local PC and the ID associated with each monitor. The monitor ID can populate the selected monitor's RDP file setting.
/public	Runs the Remote Desktop in public mode, where passwords and bitmaps are not cached.
/span	This enables the Remote Desktop width and height to be matched with the local virtual desktop, spanning across multiple monitors if necessary.
/multimon	Configures the Remote Desktop session monitor layout to render it identical to the client configuration.
/restrictedAdmin	Connects to the remote PC or server in Restricted Administration mode, which prevents login credentials from being sent to the remote PC or server. Functionality and/or compatibility might be impacted because the connection is made as a local administrator.
/remoteGuard	Utilizes Remote Guard to protect the connection. No credentials are sent to the remote device; however, full access is provided.
/shadow:<sessionID>	Allows you to specify the SessionID to which you want to connect.
/control	Allows control of the remote session.

Parameter	Description
/prompt	Prompts you for your credentials when you connect to the remote PC.
/noConsentPrompt	Allows the connection to continue without user consent.
/?	Lists the available parameters.

Troubleshooting Remote Desktop Connections

Remote Desktop is a powerful tool for administrators to manage PCs and servers within the enterprise. Some common problems encountered when connecting to a remote PC using Remote Desktop, and their resolution, are listed in Table 1-20.

TABLE 1-20 Troubleshooting Remote Desktop Connections

Problem	Possible resolution
The remote PC can't be found.	■ Make sure you have the correct PC name. ■ Try using the IP address of the remote PC.
There's a problem with the network.	■ Ensure that the router is turned on (home networks only). ■ Make sure that the Ethernet cable is plugged into your network adapter (wired networks only). ■ See that the wireless switch on the PC is turned on (devices using wireless networks only). ■ Make sure your network adapter is functional.
The Remote Desktop port might be blocked by a firewall.	■ Contact your system administrator to check that Remote Desktop is not blocked. ■ Allow the Remote Desktop application through Windows Firewall. ■ Make sure the port for Remote Desktop (usually 3389) is open.
Remote connections might not be set up on the remote PC	■ In the System Properties dialog box, under Remote Desktop, select the Allow Remote Connections To This Computer button.
The remote PC might only enable PCs that have Network Level Authentication set up to connect.	■ Upgrade to Windows 10 or later, which supports Network Level Authentication.

Configure the Windows Admin Center

The Windows Admin Center is a free web-based management console that you can use to manage remote servers, computers, and services, including virtual machines hosted in Microsoft Azure. Windows Admin Center has two core components that enable you to manage remote devices and services:

- **Gateway** Enables you to manage servers through Windows PowerShell Remoting and WMI using WinRM.
- **Web server** Enables management through standard HTTPS communications.

Windows Admin Center Installation

To use Windows Admin Center, you must first download the current version from the Microsoft Download website at *https://aka.ms.downloadWAC*.

After downloading, run the **Windows Admin Center msi** installation program. Then use the following procedure to complete the setup:

1. In the Windows Admin Center Setup Wizard, accept the software license and select **Next**.

2. On the **Install Windows Admin Center on Windows 10** page, select **Next**.

3. On the **Send diagnostic data to Microsoft** screen, choose **Required diagnostic data** or **Required and optional diagnostic data** and select **Next**.

4. On the **Use Microsoft Update to help keep your computer secure and up-to-date** page choose one of the two options then select **Next**.

5. On the **Install Windows Admin Center** page, select **Next**.

6. On the **Installing Windows Admin Center** page, select a port for the Windows Admin Center site, enter a suitable TCP port, and select **Next**. The default port is 6516. This port is used to communicate with the Windows Admin Center.

7. Select the **Allow Windows Admin Center to modify this machine's trusted hosts settings** checkbox if you want to manage computers that are not part of your AD DS forest. See more information about authentication in the next section.

8. Select **Install**. Accept the User Access Control (UAC) prompt.

9. When you see the prompt, select **Finish**.

10. After installation, launch the Windows Admin Center. You are prompted for a certificate when you run Windows Admin Center for the first time. Select the **Windows Admin Center Client** certificate, as displayed in Figure 1-21, and select **OK**.

Select a certificate for authentication	✕
Site localhost:6516 needs your credentials:	

> 🗔 **Windows Admin Center Client**
> Windows Admin Center Client CA

Certificate information   OK   Cancel

FIGURE 1-21 Windows Admin Center certificate

11. Accept the UAC prompt to allow the Windows Admin Center Client to change your device.

Authentication

You must authenticate with the remote computer if you connect to remote computers, either with Windows Admin Center or Windows PowerShell remoting (covered in the next skill). If your two computers are part of the same AD DS forest, Kerberos authentication automatically occurs. However, if you connect to computers in a different forest or non-domain-joined computers, you must configure the TrustedHosts settings to allow the devices to communicate securely.

If you accept the defaults, then the TrustedHosts are set to be automatically configured. However, if you want to manage these settings manually, you do so by using Windows Power-Shell using these steps.

1. Open an elevated **Windows PowerShell** prompt.

2. Run the following command.

   ```
   Set-Item WSMan:localhost\Client\TrustedHosts -Value 'svr1.Contoso.com'
   ```

3. When prompted, enter **Y** to confirm the change.

4. For each device you want to manage, run the preceding command, remembering to change the computer name specified in the value parameter.

5. You can also use a wildcard to enable connectivity to any computer. Run the following command.

   ```
   Set-Item WSMan:\localhost\Client\TrustedHosts -Value '*'
   ```

Using Windows Admin Center

After you have set up Windows Admin Center, you can start managing computers. The first step is to add computers to the available connections. Use the following procedure.

1. In the console, select **Add**.

2. On the **Add or create resources** blade, select the type of resource.

3. Choose between **Servers, Windows PCs, Server Clusters**, or **Azure VMs**. In this case, in the Windows PCs section, select **Add**.

4. On the **Connection tags** blade, in the **Computer** name box, enter the name of the remote computer. Windows Admin Center will search for the device and declare that it has been found. Select **Add**.

5. Windows Admin Center now updates to include the newly added computer.

6. Select it from the **All connections** list to connect to a remote computer, as shown in Figure 1-22. All computers to be managed remotely should have the Remote Management service configured and running. (This uses the `winrm quickconfig` command, as you will learn later in this chapter.)

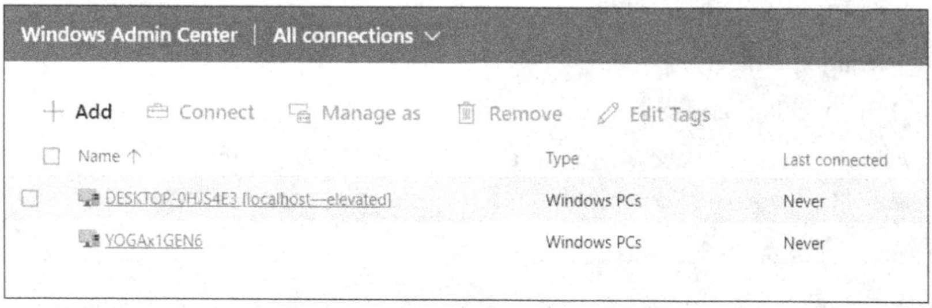

FIGURE 1-22 Windows Admin Center All Connections list

You can then use the navigation pane on the left to select a specific management component. The system overview is displayed in Figure 1-23.

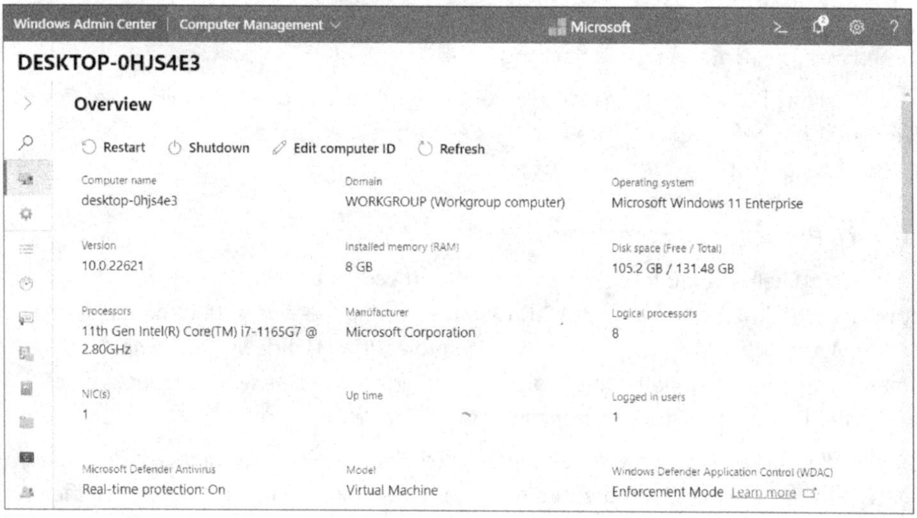

FIGURE 1-23 Connecting to a remote computer using the Windows Admin Center

You can manage many aspects of a remote computer, including the following.

- Restart or shut down the computer.
- Edit the computer ID.
- Add or remove apps and features.
- Review installed certificates.
- Review the event logs.
- Navigate the file system and manage shared resources.
- Review and configure network and firewall settings.
- Gather performance-related data.
- Configure the registry.
- Manage scheduled tasks.

- Manage services and storage.
- Certificate management.
- Manage virtual machines and switches.

The Windows Admin Center also allows you to run scripts directly from the tool through the web-based PowerShell console. The PowerShell symbol >_ is displayed in the top-right corner of Figure 1-23.

Configure PowerShell remoting and Windows Remote Management (WinRM)

Using Windows PowerShell cmdlets can sometimes seem daunting if you are unfamiliar with PowerShell. PowerShell offers a convenient and quick way of configuring many machines faster than a graphical tool. In addition, you can use Windows PowerShell to complete frequently performed management tasks using scripting.

Using Windows PowerShell to manage remote computers is referred to as *Windows Power-Shell remoting*, but before you can use Windows PowerShell remoting, you must know how to enable and configure it.

Configure PowerShell remoting

Windows PowerShell is ubiquitous across the Microsoft ecosystem. You can configure both Windows and Windows Servers and use PowerShell to configure Microsoft Exchange, Micro-soft Teams, Azure Active Directory, and more. Therefore, using Windows PowerShell to per-form management tasks on both local and remote computers makes sense because you can transfer those skills to other management and administration situations.

Many cmdlets in Windows PowerShell can be used with a -ComputerName parameter; doing so makes using the command remotely no more complex than specifying the name of the computer you want to run the command against. For example, you can run the following command to determine the IP configuration of a computer named LON-CL1.

```
Get-NetIPConfiguration -computername LON-CL1
```

However, not all cmdlets accept the -ComputerName parameter, and for these, you must enable and configure Windows PowerShell remoting and effectively run the command on the device itself. Windows PowerShell remoting enables you to connect to one or several remote computers, execute one or more cmdlets or scripts on those remote computers, and return the results to your local computer.

Although Windows PowerShell remoting is enabled by default on Windows Server, you must manually enable it on Windows 11 and earlier versions of Windows. To do this, complete the following procedures:

If necessary, you will need to start the Windows Remote Management service. You must also enable Windows Remote Management through the Windows Defender Firewall.

You can do this by running the `winrm quickconfig` command at an elevated Command Prompt. When prompted, select **Y** and **Enter** twice, as shown in Figure 1-24.

```
Administrator: Windows PowerShell                                    —    □    ✕
Copyright (C) Microsoft Corporation. All rights reserved.

Install the latest PowerShell for new features and improvements! https://aka.ms/P
SWindows

PS C:\Windows\system32> winrm quickconfig
WinRM is not set up to receive requests on this machine.
The following changes must be made:

Start the WinRM service.
Set the WinRM service type to delayed auto start.

Make these changes [y/n]? y

WinRM has been updated to receive requests.

WinRM service type changed successfully.
WinRM service started.
WinRM is not set up to allow remote access to this machine for management.
The following changes must be made:

Enable the WinRM firewall exception.
Configure LocalAccountTokenFilterPolicy to grant administrative rights remotely t
o local users.

Make these changes [y/n]? y

WinRM has been updated for remote management.

WinRM firewall exception enabled.
Configured LocalAccountTokenFilterPolicy to grant administrative rights remotely
to local users.
PS C:\Windows\system32>
```

FIGURE 1-24 Enabling Windows Remote Management

> **NOTE** **WINRM QUICKCONFIG AND THE PUBLIC NETWORK LOCATION PROFILE**
>
> If one of your network connections is assigned the Public network location profile, this command fails, and you must manually configure the Windows Defender Firewall exceptions. Alternatively, you can run the enable- `PSremoting -force` cmdlet from an elevated Windows PowerShell window to enable Windows PowerShell remoting.

EXAM TIP

Windows Remote Management uses HTTP. By default, both Windows Remote Management and Windows PowerShell remoting uses TCP port 5985 for incoming unencrypted communications and TCP port 5986 for incoming encrypted communications.

Once you run the `winrm quickconfig` command, the WinRM service is switched on. The same effect can be achieved by issuing the `Enable- PSRemoting -Force` command. Note this is a one-time command; it will change the WinRM service startup type to automatic and add exceptions for WinRM ports (TCP 5985 and 5986) to the Microsoft Defender Firewall's list of exceptions.

To check that the WinRM settings on the computer are configured correctly, run the command:

```
winrm e winrm/config/listener
```

The command displays the current WinRM listener settings and shows the service enabled, as shown in Figure 1-25. If you want to list the complete configuration of the WinRM service, you can use this command.

```
winrm get winrm/config
```

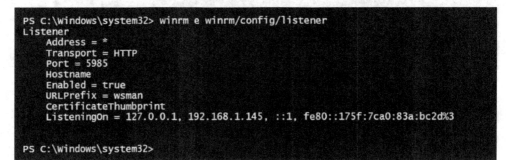

FIGURE 1-25 Checking WinRM Settings

Using Windows PowerShell to manage remote computers

After enabling Windows PowerShell remoting, you can use Windows PowerShell cmdlets and scripts to manage the remote computer in virtually the same way you manage local computers. However, you must first establish a connection with the remote computer.

After establishing a connection, you can run any PowerShell cmdlets or scripts against the remote machine. When you connect to the remote computer and run a remote command against it, the command is transmitted across the network and runs on the remote computer. The results are sent back to your local computer and displayed in your Windows PowerShell window.

One way to establish a remote connection and run a command is to use the `invoke-command` cmdlet. You can also use the `invoke-command` cmdlet to establish a temporary remote connection. For example, the following command retrieves the contents of the system event log from the remote computer LON-CL1.

```
Invoke-Command -ComputerName LON-CL1 -ScriptBlock {Get-EventLog-log system}
```

If you intend to run several cmdlets or more complex scripts, it is useful to establish a persistent connection to the remote computer. Use the `New-PSSession` cmdlet to do this. For example

```
$s = New-PSSession -ComputerName LON-CL1
```

You can now use the `Enter-PSSession` command to establish the persistent connection:

```
Enter-PSSession $s
```

You will now have a Windows PowerShell prompt that looks like this.

```
[LON-CL1]: PS C:\>
```

Any commands that you run in this session run on the LON-CL1 computer. The session remains active until you close with the `exit-PSSession` command.

You can also use these commands to establish remote connections with multiple computers. For example, use the following command to connect simultaneously to computers called LON-CL1 and LON-CL2.

```
$s = New-PSSession -ComputerName LON-CL1, LON-CL2
```

Next, run the remote Windows PowerShell cmdlets against the new session.

```
Invoke-Command -Session $s -ScriptBlock { Get-EventLog -logsystem }
```

You can run any Windows PowerShell command remotely in this way.

Chapter summary

- Dynamic provisioning methods include using Azure AD, Mobile Device Management, provisioning packages, subscription Activation, and Windows Autopilot.
- Dynamic provisioning methods seek to transform an existing Windows 11 installation, rather than replace or upgrade it.
- Provisioning packages are created using the Windows Configuration Designer, part of Windows ADK or as an app from the Microsoft Store.
- Windows Autopilot allows you to automate the out-of-box experience and seamlessly enroll devices directly into MDM.
- All Windows 11 editions are licensed to use Windows Autopilot and require Azure AD and an MDM solution such as Intune.
- The Windows Autopilot Enrollment Status Page allows users to view the progress status page during the device setup.
- Device vendors can extract and register devices with the Windows Autopilot service, or you can use the `Get-WindowsAutoPilotInfo.ps1` PowerShell cmdlet to extract the hardware ID for your existing devices.
- You cannot downgrade from any edition of Windows 11 to Windows 7, 8, or 8.1. You can downgrade from one edition of Windows 11 to another edition of Windows 11.
- Windows 11 in S mode can be switched to another valid edition of Windows 11 at any time using the Microsoft Store.
- You should migrate user profiles and settings whenever possible to reduce user impact.

- Enterprises can securely extract, store, and restore the user state using the User State Migration Tool.

- MDT uses task sequences to process activities to deploy Windows 11 to your devices.

- MDT provides LTI deployments. Combining Configuration Manager with MDT enables you to implement ZTI deployments.

- The Deployment Workbench is the primary interface you'll use to manage your deployments with MDT.

- Always use the latest version of Windows ADK.

- You can choose from several management tools to perform remote management.

- Remote Help requires an Intune license for both helpers and sharers.

- If the Remote Help connection is not established within 10 minutes, the code will expire and must be regenerated.

- Remote Desktop connection provides a rich user experience for managing servers and computers remotely.

- The Windows Admin Center provides a web-based management console for managing remote servers and computers.

- To configure and enable remote management settings, you must ensure the Windows Firewall configuration allows the connections.

- Windows PowerShell remoting enables you to remotely manage any Windows 11–based computer with Windows PowerShell.

Thought experiment

In these thought experiments, demonstrate your skills and knowledge of the topics covered in this chapter. You can find the answers to these thought experiments in the next section.

Scenario 1

Contoso has 2,000 workstations currently running Windows 8.1 Pro. The company plans to perform an in-place upgrade to Windows 11 Enterprise. Most of the users work at the head office, though about 50 staff members work remotely. Your staff already uses Office 365 Pro Plus, and you are considering purchasing a Microsoft 365 Enterprise subscription.

As a consultant for Contoso, answer the following questions:

1. Is an in-place upgrade a suitable method of deploying Windows 11?

2. Your manager is concerned that moving to the cloud will be problematic and involve additional purchase costs and workload to configure Azure Active Directory for your users. How should you advise your manager?

3. Management has been given the green light to proceed with the rollout of Microsoft 365 Enterprise to all Contoso staff. You want to ensure staff can still use their application

settings following the rollout of Microsoft 365. What single resource can you use to migrate user and application settings?

4. The devices within your research and development lab require access to a secure wireless network, which will be implemented simultaneously with the upgrade rollout. You must deploy the network WiFi settings to the R&D team devices with minimal effort. How will you deploy the settings?

Scenario 2

Contoso has 50 remote workers spread across the county. The remote workers will receive new Surface devices to replace their old laptops. You decide the vendor will ship the devices directly to the users rather than have them pick them up during their next visit to the head office. You have planned to deploy the devices using Windows Autopilot.

Answer the following questions for your manager:

1. How will the devices be recognized as belonging to Contoso if the IT department has not first configured them?

2. How will the remote users know to trust the device and that it belongs to Contoso if it is shipped direct from the vendor?

3. How will the user know that the device configuration is progressing, and can the user bypass the device configuration?

4. How will the device be secured per Contoso corporate security and compliance policies?

Scenario 3

Your organization is expanding and runs a mixture of operating systems on its devices, including Windows 7 and Windows 10 Pro. The company wants all the devices running on a single common operating system, Windows 11 Pro.

Answer the following questions for your manager:

1. Some devices were purchased with Windows 11 in S mode. How can the company upgrade Windows 11 in S mode devices to Windows 11 Pro?

2. Your manager asks if the Windows 7 devices can be upgraded directly to Windows 11 Pro or whether they should be replaced.

3. You want to reduce the impact on users during the rollout of Windows 11 Pro. What deployment approach would you recommend that retains all user and application settings wherever possible and involves the least amount of downtime for users?

Scenario 4

Adatum Corporation has deployed Microsoft 365 and Microsoft Intune. Many of your users work in small branch offices—some work from home with work laptops. It is important for you to be able to manage these users' computers remotely. As a consultant for Adatum, answer the following questions about remote management in the Adatum organization:

1. One of your users phones the help desk, requiring assistance with an application. They need to know how to perform a grammar check with Microsoft Word. They are not very experienced, and despite your best efforts and explanation of how the process works, they are still confused. What remote management tool might you consider using in this situation?

2. Another user calls the help desk. They've lost a file and need you to locate and restore it to their desktop. They're due to leave the office for a conference this afternoon, and they tell you that's the best time for you to resolve the issue. What remote management tool would you use?

3. You try to connect to this user's computer later that afternoon, but despite knowing that the necessary Windows Firewall settings are configured, you cannot connect. Why?

4. You want to use Windows PowerShell remoting. You try to connect to a remote machine but are unsuccessful. What steps must you perform on the remote machine before Windows PowerShell remoting can work?

Thought experiment answers

This section provides the solutions for the tasks included in the Thought Experiments section.

Scenario 1

1. Yes. An in-place upgrade is supported and recommended by Microsoft.

2. You should advise your manager that Contoso already uses Azure Active Directory because AAD is included in Office 365 ProPlus, which is already deployed. There will be minimal additional workload and no additional costs beyond the planned expenditure.

3. User State Migration Tool (USMT), included with Windows ADK, provides tools to migrate line-of-business application settings. You need to provide a custom MigApp.xml file for ScanState and LoadState to use, which will define application settings that are not migrated by default.

4. By creating a provisioning package in the Windows Configuration Designer, such as the built-in Provision Desktop Devices wizard, you can deploy WiFi settings to devices easily and quickly.

Scenario 2

1. The vendor will extract and register the device hardware ID directly with the Windows Autopilot service, which will be tied to the Contoso Azure AD tenant.

2. After the initial startup, the remote user will be presented with a login screen that offers Contoso company branding. This branding (which is mandatory) has been configured within the Contoso Azure AD portal.

3. The Enrollment Status Page can be configured to be shown during the device configuration phase. This allows the user to see a visual status of how the configuration is progressing. You can prevent the device from being used during the configuration phase by configuring the Block Device Use Until All Apps And Profiles Are Installed setting in the Enrollment Status Page settings.

4. The device will be automatically joined to Azure AD once the remote user enters their Azure AD credentials. It will then be auto-enrolled into Microsoft Intune, and all Contoso policies will be configured and automatically applied.

Scenario 3

1. The devices can be individually upgraded using the Microsoft Store or using the Settings app. If the business uses Microsoft Intune, this could also be used to configure a group of devices if they are also known to Azure AD.

2. Windows 7 devices cannot be directly upgraded to Windows 11. However, if the Windows 7 PC meets the hardware requirements for Windows 11, you can perform a clean install or upgrade from Windows 7 to Windows 10 and then upgrade to Windows 11. You might find that the hardware is incompatible and must replace the device.

3. You should recommend an in-place upgrade from Windows 10 to Windows 11 Pro because this will retain all user and application settings. An enterprise deployment solution would be to use USMT to back up and restore user and application settings. USMT would be more time-consuming and unnecessary because, with an in-place upgrade, the user will retain the same device, and the current Windows 10 operating system can be upgraded directly to Windows 11 Pro.

Scenario 4

1. Because Adatum has Microsoft Intune, you can use Remote Help. With this tool, you can demonstrate how to perform the grammar check. You could take remote control of the user's computer and show them the procedure.

2. Remote Desktop is the most suitable tool. Remote Desktop requires no invitations and does not require the remote user to assist you in connecting. You need to ask the user to leave the computer switched on.

3. You most likely can't connect because Remote Desktop users must be specifically granted access to RDP, in addition to the Windows Firewall configuration changes and the device being left switched on.

4. You must start the Windows Remote Management service and reconfigure the Windows Firewall, and then Windows PowerShell remoting must be enabled. You can perform these steps by running `winrm quickconfig` or `enable-PSremoting`.

CHAPTER 2

Manage identity and compliance

Two of the most important elements of your IT infrastructure are identity and device compliance. Identity provides knowledge of who somebody or something is, while compliance enables you to determine the overall health of a device. By implementing these two technologies, you can improve your organization's overall security and help protect your organizational data. Compliance policies, especially when implemented with conditional access, are an important part of the MD-102 exam.

Skills covered in this chapter:

- Skill 2.1: Manage identity
- Skill 2.2: Implement compliance policies for all supported device platforms by using Intune

Skill 2.1: Manage identity

Identity services provide authentication and authorization to help protect your organizational resources and data. Over the years, Microsoft has implemented several such identity services: Active Directory Domain Services (AD DS), Azure Active Directory (Azure AD), and Azure AD Domain Services. The MD-102 exam primarily covers content that relates to Azure AD.

> **This skill covers how to:**
> - Implement user authentication on Windows devices, including Windows Hello for Business, passwordless, and tokens
> - Manage role-based access control (RBAC) for Intune
> - Register devices in and join devices to Azure AD
> - Implement the Intune Connector for Active Directory
> - Manage the membership of local groups on Windows devices
> - Implement and manage Local Administrative Passwords Solution (LAPS) for Azure AD

Overview of identity solutions

Before we get into the specific content covered in the exam, it's perhaps worth reviewing these identity providers. There are two identity providers you must be familiar with in the Endpoint Administrator role:

- **AD DS** Windows Server role used to support identity in on-premises environments
- **Azure AD** Cloud-based identity solution used to provide single sign-on (SSO) for cloud apps such as Microsoft 365 and Azure

A third identity provider, Azure AD Domain Services, is a managed Azure service that provides an identity solution that closely resembles the behavior of AD DS but runs in the cloud without needing Windows server computers configured as domain controllers. This identity solution is out of this course's scope.

> **NEED MORE REVIEW?** **IMPLEMENT HYBRID IDENTITY WITH WINDOWS SERVER**
>
> For more information about Azure AD Domain Services, refer to the Microsoft Learn website at *https://learn.microsoft.com/training/modules/implement-hybrid-identity-windows-server*.

Active Directory Domain Services

Detailed knowledge of Windows Server and AD DS is outside the scope of the MD-102 exam. However, it's probably worth at least discussing the fundamentals of AD DS to help put Azure AD into context.

AD DS, commonly referred to as either Windows Active Directory or just Active Directory, is a role of associated services installed on Windows Servers. Windows Server installed with the AD DS role is a complex environment that has benefitted organizations for more than 20 years and has many legacy components necessary to support AD feature backward compatibility. AD DS has the following features:

- Hierarchical and granular and based on the X.500 standard.
- Implements Lightweight Directory Access Protocol (LDAP) for managing directory objects.
- Administrative ability is defined by group membership.
- Objects are stored in containers called organizational units (OUs) that represent the structure of your organization, as shown in Figure 2-1.
- Group Policy manages the administration of objects, as indicated in Figure 2-1.
- Kerberos protocol is primarily used for AD DS authentication.
- Computer objects represent computers that join an Active Directory domain.

> **NOTE** **JOINING AN AD DS DOMAIN**
>
> Only computers running the Windows operating system can be domain-joined.

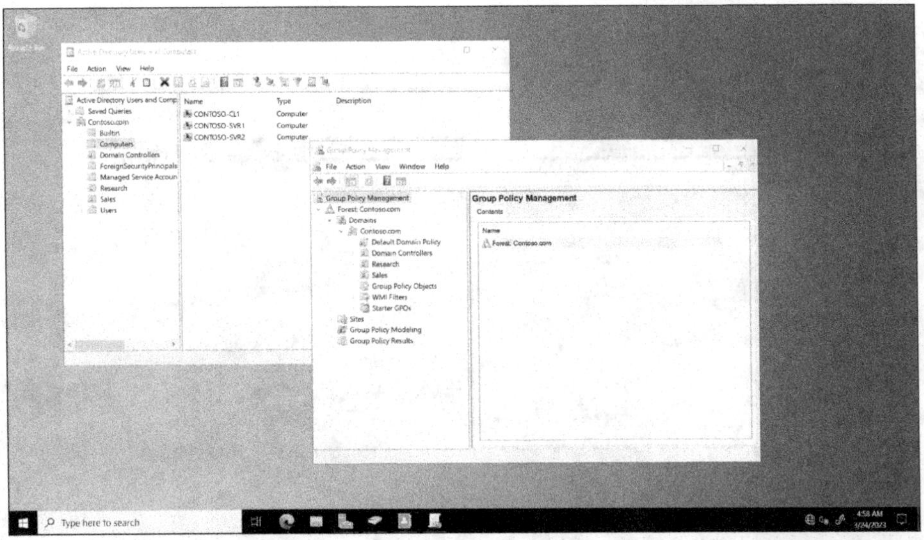

FIGURE 2-1 Management tools on an Active Directory domain controller

Azure Active Directory

Microsoft provides each cloud-based services subscriber, such as Microsoft 365, an instance of Azure AD (a tenant). Organizations can choose to add additional subscriptions, such as Microsoft Azure, and use the same Azure AD tenant for authentication and authorization. Alternatively, organizations can implement a separate Azure AD tenant for each subscribed service or app.

When you subscribe to a cloud service, like Microsoft 365, you can select a specific edition of Azure AD. The free version of Azure AD provides capabilities useful to most organizations; however, paid Azure AD Premium editions are also available, adding capabilities more relevant to large organizations.

It's important not to think of Azure AD as Active Directory in the cloud; instead, it's an entirely different authentication and authorization solution designed to support the cloud environment, unlike AD DS. Azure AD has the following features:

- Is flat, with no container hierarchy
- Provides for less fine-grained administrative control
- Uses role-based access control (RBAC)
- Supports administration management with profiles and group assignments
- Relies on Security Assertion Markup Language (SAML) and Open Authorization (OAuth)

When working with devices, you can add devices to Azure AD that are running a variety of operating systems, including

- Android
- iOS

- Linux
- macOS
- Windows 10 and newer

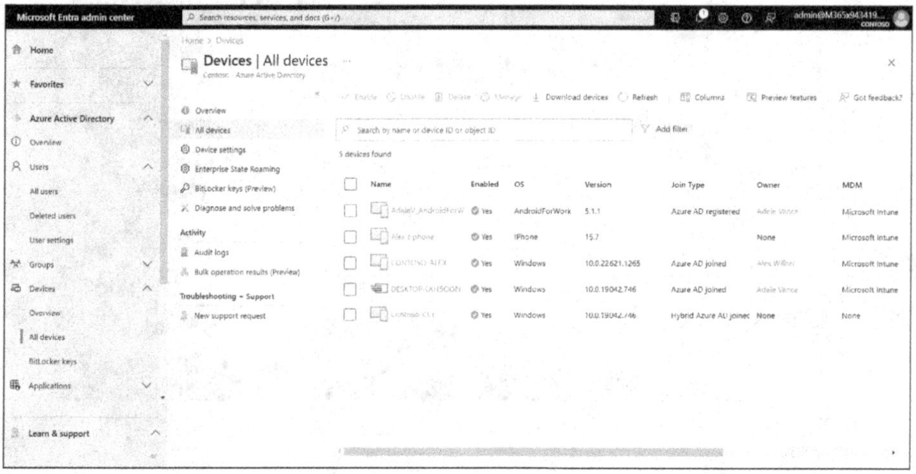

FIGURE 2-2 The Microsoft Entra admin center displaying the Azure Active Directory | All devices folder.

Implement user authentication on Windows devices, including Windows Hello for Business, passwordless, and tokens

You can sign in to your Windows 11 computer by using a variety of user accounts, depending on the configuration of your computer. The following list describes these account types:

- **Microsoft account**   A consumer Microsoft account, often with an Outlook.com or Hotmail.com suffix.
- **Microsoft 365 account**   An Azure AD account, usually called a Work or School account. Typically has an organizational suffix, such as Contoso.com. When a user adds a Work or School account to their device, they sign in using those account details, all services and apps accessed by the user automatically use the account to authenticate; this provides for cloud-based SSO.

EXAM TIP

By default, all Azure AD accounts are configured with a default tenant domain suffix. This default suffix is created when you obtain your Microsoft 365 subscription and always ends with .onmicrosoft.com. When configuring your Azure AD tenant, you typically add a custom domain name, such as Contoso.com, that your organization owns. Users can then sign in using either the custom domain suffix or the default domain suffix, although users find it easier and more logical to use the custom domain suffix.

- **Domain account** An AD DS account. If a computer is AD DS domain-joined, then a user can sign in at their computer using a domain account. When a user signs in using a domain account, all services and apps accessed by the user automatically use the account to authenticate; this provides for AD DS forest-wide SSO.

- **Local account** A computer user account. Typically, Windows 11 computers have local user and group accounts. A user might sign in using a local account when the computer belongs to them rather than the organization they work for. When users sign in using local accounts, they must configure the organizational account for each app or service they want to connect to. For example, they must add a Work or School account as part of a Microsoft Outlook profile to connect to Exchange Online.

Most users are probably familiar with signing in using a username and password. While that's acceptable and fairly common, Microsoft has added support for different authentication methods in Windows 11. These methods are designed to improve the sign-in experience and help make it more secure.

Understand multifactor authentication

Traditional computer authentication is based on users providing a name and password. This enables an authentication authority to validate the exchange and grant access. Although password-based authentication is acceptable in many circumstances, Windows 11 provides a number of additional more secure methods for users to authenticate with their devices, including multifactor authentication (sometimes referred to as two-factor authentication).

Multifactor authentication is based on the principle that users who want to authenticate must have two (or more) things to identify themselves:

- Know something (such as a password)
- Have something (such as a security token)
- Be something (such as fingerprints or biometrics)

For example, a user might know a password, have a security token (in the form of a digital certificate), and be able to prove who they are with biometrics, such as fingerprints or facial recognition.

EXPLORE BIOMETRICS

Biometrics, such as a fingerprint, provides more secure and often more convenient methods for identifying and verifying users and administrators. Windows 11 includes native support for biometrics through the Windows Biometric Framework (WBF), and when used as part of a multifactor authentication plan, biometrics is increasingly replacing passwords in modern workplaces.

Biometric information is obtained from the individual and stored as a biometric sample which is then securely saved in a template and mapped to a specific user. You can use a fingerprint reader to capture a person's fingerprint. (You "enroll" the user when configuring this.) Also, you can use a person's face, retina, or even voice. The Windows Biometric service can also be extended to include behavioral traits, such as body gait and typing rhythm.

Windows includes several Group Policy settings related to biometrics, as shown in Figure 2-3, that you can use to allow or block biometrics from your devices. You can find Group Policy Objects here: `Computer Configuration\Administrative Templates\Windows Components\Biometrics`.

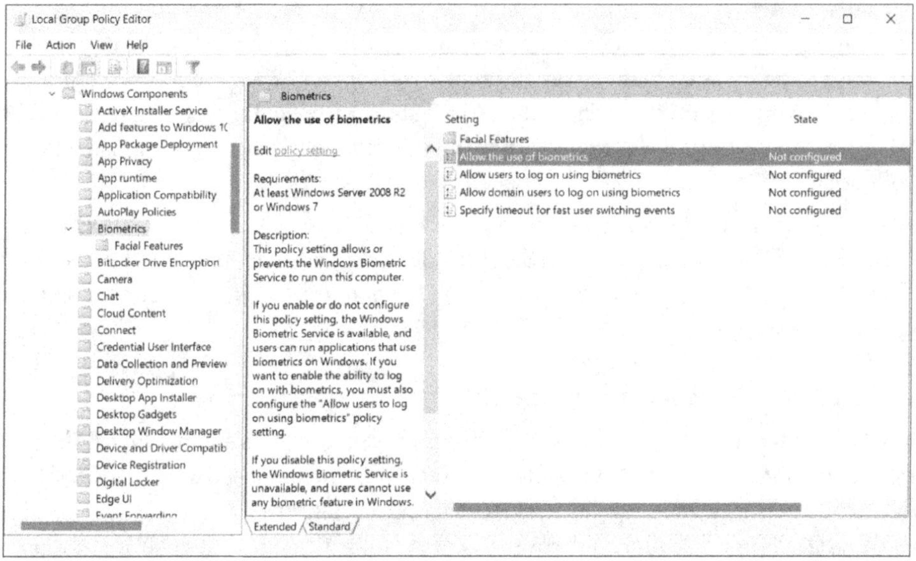

FIGURE 2-3 Biometrics Group Policy settings

Configure Windows Hello and Windows Hello for Business

Windows Hello is a two-factor biometric authentication mechanism built into Windows 11, and it is unique to the device on which it is set up. Windows Hello enables users to unlock their devices using facial recognition, fingerprint scanning, or a PIN.

Windows Hello for Business is the enterprise implementation of Windows Hello and enables users to authenticate to an AD DS or Azure AD account, and it allows them to access network resources. Administrators can configure Windows Hello for Business using Group Policy or mobile device management (MDM) policy and use asymmetric (public/private key) or certificate-based authentication.

Windows Hello provides the following benefits:

- Strong passwords can be difficult to remember, and users often reuse them on multiple sites, reducing security. Windows Hello enables them to authenticate using their biometric data.

- Passwords are vulnerable to replay attacks, and server breaches can expose password-based credentials.

- Passwords offer less security because users can inadvertently expose their passwords because of phishing attacks.

- Windows Hello helps protect against credential theft. Because a malicious person must have both the device and the biometric information or PIN, it becomes more difficult to hack the authentication process.

- Windows Hello can be used both in cloud-only and hybrid deployment scenarios.

- Windows Hello signs you into your devices much faster than when using a password.

To implement Windows Hello, your devices must have the appropriate hardware. For example, facial recognition requires using special cameras that see infrared (IR) light. These can be external cameras or cameras incorporated into the device. The cameras can reliably distinguish between a photograph and a living person. For fingerprint recognition, your devices must be equipped with fingerprint readers, which can be external or integrated into laptops or USB keyboards.

> **NOTE LEGACY FINGERPRINT READERS**
> If you have previously experienced poor reliability from legacy fingerprint readers, you should review the current generation of sensors, which offer significantly better reliability and are less error-prone.

After you have installed the necessary hardware devices, you can set up Windows Hello by opening **Settings**, selecting **Accounts**, and then, on the **Sign-In Options** page, under the **Ways to sign in** heading, reviewing the options for facial or fingerprint recognition. You can still configure a PIN or use a Security key if you do not have Windows Hello–supported hardware.

To configure Windows Hello for facial recognition, follow these steps:

1. Open **Settings** and select **Accounts**.
2. On the **Accounts** page, select **Sign-In Options**.
3. Under the **Ways to sign in** heading, select **Facial recognition (Windows Hello)**.
4. Click **Set up**, and when prompted, click **Get started**.
5. Enter your PIN or password to verify your identity.
6. Allow Windows Hello to capture your facial features, as shown in Figure 2-4.
7. After completion, you are presented with an **All Set!** Message, indicating that you can close the dialog.

Users can use Windows Hello for a convenient and secure sign-in method tied to the device on which it is set up.

For Enterprises that want to enable Windows Hello, they can configure and manage Windows Hello for Business. Windows Hello for Business uses key-based or certificate-based authentication for users by using Group Policy or mobile device management (MDM) policy or a mixture of both methods.

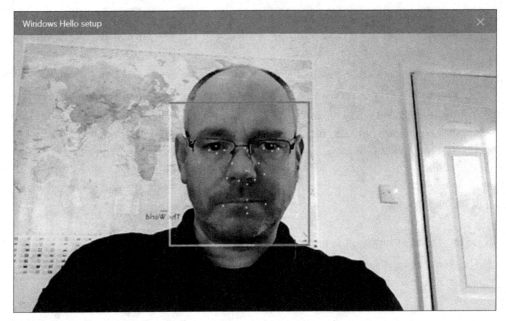

FIGURE 2-4 Configuring Windows Hello

NEED MORE REVIEW? **WINDOWS HELLO BIOMETRICS IN THE ENTERPRISE**

To review further details about using Windows Hello in the enterprise, refer to the Micro-soft website at *https://docs.microsoft.com/windows/access-protection/hello-for-business/hello-biometrics-in-enterprise.*

CONFIGURE PIN

To avoid authentication with passwords, Microsoft provides an authentication method that uses a PIN. When you set up Windows Hello, you're asked to create a PIN first. This PIN enables you to sign in using the PIN as an alternative when you can't use your preferred biometric because of an injury or because the sensor is unavailable or not working properly. The PIN provides the same level of protection as Windows Hello.

Windows Hello PIN provides secure authentication without sending a password to an authenticating authority, such as Azure AD or an AD DS domain controller. Windows Hello for Business provides enterprises with compliance with the new FIDO 2.0 (Fast ID Online) frame-work for end-to-end multifactor authentication.

A user cannot use a PIN alone (known as a convenience PIN) within a domain environment. Figure 2-5 shows that the PIN settings are known as the Windows Hello PIN. A user must first configure Windows Hello and already be signed in using a local account, a domain account, a Microsoft account, or an Azure AD account. The user can then set up PIN authentication asso-ciated with the credential for the account.

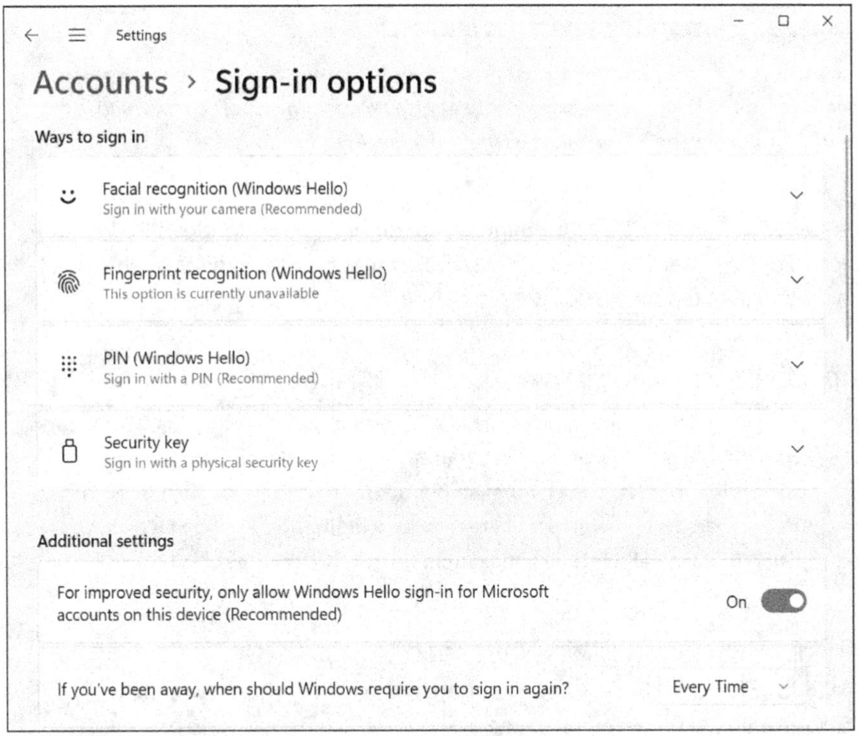

FIGURE 2-5 Configuring Windows Hello PIN

After a user has completed the registration process, Windows Hello for Business generates a new public-private key pair on the device known as a *protector key*. If installed in the device, the Trusted Platform Module (TPM) generates and stores this protector key; if the device does not have a TPM, Windows encrypts the protector key and stores it on the file system. Windows Hello for Business also generates an administrative key to reset credentials if necessary.

> **NOTE PAIRING OF CREDENTIALS AND DEVICES**
>
> Windows Hello for Business pairs a specific device and a user credential. Consequently, the PIN chosen by the user is associated only with the signed-in account and that specific device.

The user now has a PIN *gesture* defined on the device and an associated protector key for that PIN gesture. The user can now securely sign in to his device using the PIN and then add support for a biometric gesture as an alternative to the PIN. The *gesture* can be facial recognition, iris scanning, or fingerprint recognition, depending on the available device hardware. When a user adds a biometric gesture, it follows the same basic sequence mentioned in the previous section. The user authenticates to the system using the PIN and then registers the new biometric. Windows generates a unique key pair and stores it securely. The user can then sign in using the PIN or a biometric gesture.

You can use MDM policies or GPOs to configure your organization's Windows Hello for Business settings. For example, you can configure a policy that enables or disables the use of biometrics on devices affected by the policy.

USING GROUP POLICY TO CONFIGURE WINDOWS HELLO FOR BUSINESS

To configure Windows Hello for Business in your on-premises organization, you use the appropriate GPOs within the following location:

```
Computer Configuration\Policies\Administrative Templates\Windows Components\
Windows Hello for Business
```

To configure PIN complexity with Windows 11 (with and without Windows Hello for Business), you can use the eight PIN Complexity Group Policy settings, which allow you to control PIN creation and management.

You can deploy these policy settings to computers or users. If you deploy settings to both, then the user policy settings have precedence over computer policy settings, and GPO conflict resolution is based on the last applied policy. The policy settings included are:

- Require digits
- Require lowercase letters
- Maximum PIN length
- Minimum PIN length
- Expiration
- History
- Require special characters
- Require uppercase letters

In Windows 11, the PIN complexity Group Policy settings are located at: Administrative Templates\System\PIN Complexity (under both the **Computer** and **User Configuration** nodes).

If your organization is not using Windows Hello for Business, you can still use the option to set a Convenience PIN. A Convenience PIN is very different from a Windows Hello for Business PIN because it is merely a wrapper for the user's domain password. This means that the user's password is cached and substituted by Windows when signing in with a Convenience PIN.

The option to allow a Convenience PIN is disabled by default for domain-joined clients. To enable this feature, enable the **Turn On Convenience PIN Sign-In GPO** value located at `Computer Configuration\Administrative Templates\System\Logon`.

USING INTUNE TO CONFIGURE WINDOWS HELLO FOR BUSINESS

To configure the required Windows Hello for Business settings using Intune, open the Microsoft Intune admin center and then create a device configuration profile with the **Identity protection** type. Use the following procedure:

1. In the Microsoft Intune admin center, select **Devices** > **Windows** and click **Configuration Profiles**.
2. Click **Create profile**, select **Windows 10 and later**, and then select **Identity protection** from the list of templates.
3. Click **Create**, and then on the **Basics** tab, provide a name and description. Click **Next**.
4. On the **Configuration settings** tab, enable the **Configure Windows Hello for Business** setting.
5. As shown in Figure 2-6, you can configure the required settings described earlier. Click **Next**.
6. On the **Assignments** tab, assign the policy to the desired group, click **Next**, and then complete the wizard to complete the profile configuration.

You can also achieve the same result by using an Account protection policy in Endpoint security. Account protection policies support the configuration of the following:

- Local user group membership
- Local admin password solution (LAPS)
- Account protection

Choose **Account protection**. You can then follow a similar wizard-driven procedure to configure Windows Hello for Business settings.

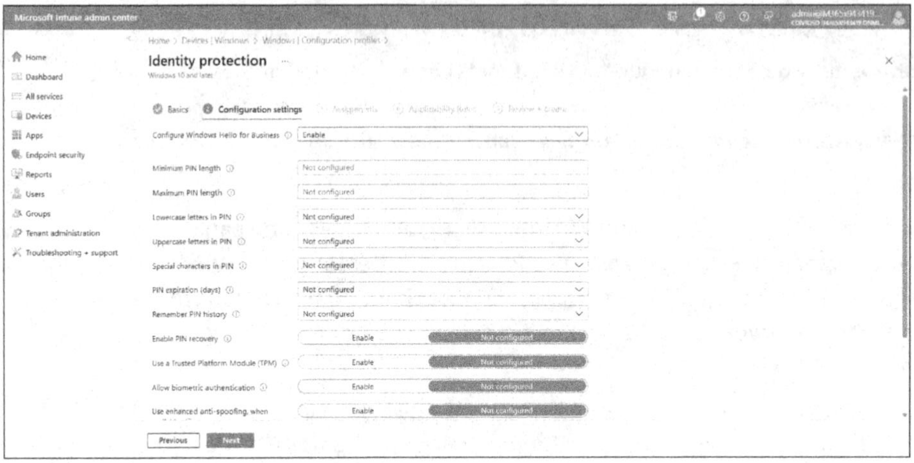

FIGURE 2-6 Enabling Windows Hello for Business with Intune

Manage RBAC for Intune

In Windows Server and Windows 11, users are assigned administrative ability through group membership. Typically, built-in groups are used to support this process. For example, to enable a user to perform server management tasks, you can add their user account to the Server Operators local group. Because the Server Operators local group has been automatically assigned numerous management abilities, a user added to that group inherits the abilities of that group. This process is referred to as group-based security.

In Intune, a different process is used; this process is called role-based access control. Although you can use RBAC to assign management and administrative permissions in Intune, RBAC is usually managed in Azure AD. Although your job function might not entail configuring RBAC in Azure AD, it's probably worth reviewing some of the available settings.

Configuring RBAC in Azure AD

There are numerous built-in roles in Azure AD. You can rely solely on these roles and, for many situations, they'll provide you with the necessary management delegation you likely need. However, you can also create custom roles; these are roles for which you define the management permissions to suit your specific organizational requirements.

You use the Microsoft Entra admin center or the Azure Active Directory admin center to manage and assign roles.

> **NOTE MICROSOFT ENTRA OR AZURE ACTIVE DIRECTORY ADMIN CENTER**
>
> You can use either of these management consoles to perform Azure AD management and administration tasks. However, because Microsoft Entra is the newer administrative console, we focus on that throughout this book.

In Microsoft Entra, expand **Azure Active Directory** in the navigation pane, then expand **Roles & admins**. Select the **Roles & admins** node, as displayed in Figure 2-7.

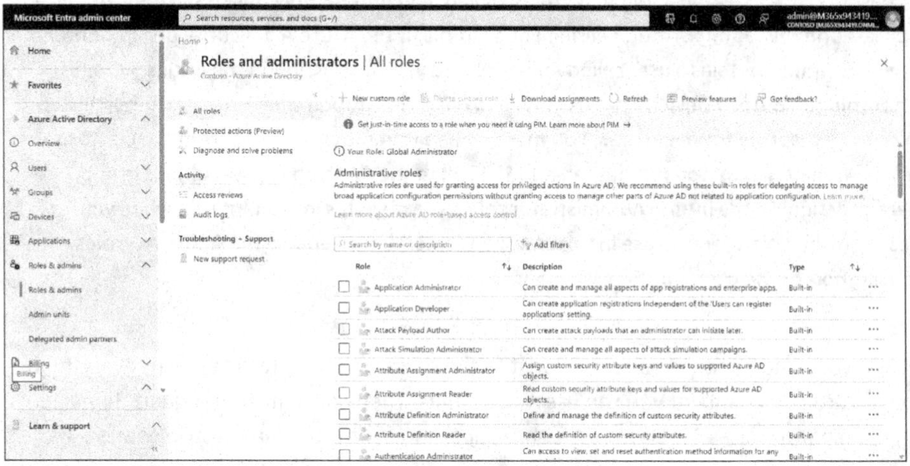

FIGURE 2-7 Reviewing RBAC roles in Microsoft Entra

You can search for a specific role and then review who has that role assigned. For example, in the search box, enter **Intune** and then select the **Intune Administrator** role from the returned list.

On the **Assignments** tab, you can review and modify role-holders. To add an assignment, use the following procedure:

1. Click **Add assignments**.

2. Click the **No member selected** link.

3. In the **Select a member** pane, select a user or group to which you want to assign the role. Click **Next**.

4. You can now choose between the following options:

   ■ **Eligible** Means that the user can exercise the permissions of the assigned role. You can then make the assignment permanently eligible or define a time range. When a user is eligible for a role, a designated administrator must confirm their use of that role when the user attempts to exercise their administrative permissions.

   ■ **Active** Means the user can immediately exercise the administrative permissions associated with the assigned role.

> *NOTE* **PRIVILEGED IDENTITY MANAGEMENT**
>
> The choice between Eligible and Active is only possible when "Privileged Identity Management (PIM)" is activated in the Azure subscription.

5. Click **Assign**.

> ***NOTE*** **ASSIGN ROLES TO GROUPS**
>
> It's best practice to assign a role to a group—even if it contains only one user. This is because it makes ongoing administration easier. For example, if the Azure AD security group **Contoso Device Admins** contains a user called `AndrewW`, and you have assigned the Intune Administrator role to Contoso Device Admins, `AndrewW` has that through their group membership. To remove that role from `AndrewW`, you merely need to remove `AndrewW` from the Contoso Device Admins group. You might then add `SallyM` to the Contoso Device Admins group, thereby assigning the Intune Administrator role to `SallyM`. It's important that when you create groups you intend to use in this way, you remember to enable the **Azure AD roles can be assigned to the group** option.

When you assign a role, you can assign it to the entire directory (which means everything in your Azure AD tenant), or you can use Admin units. These are similar to organizational units (OUs) in an on-premises AD DS infrastructure, allowing for a more targeted delegation of admin permissions.

You define the scope of the role when you add a user or group to the role. That's to say, you select the **Scope type** option on the **Add assignments** page, as displayed in Figure 2-8. You can then select either **Directory** (the default) or **Administrative unit**. You must then choose the appropriate admin unit.

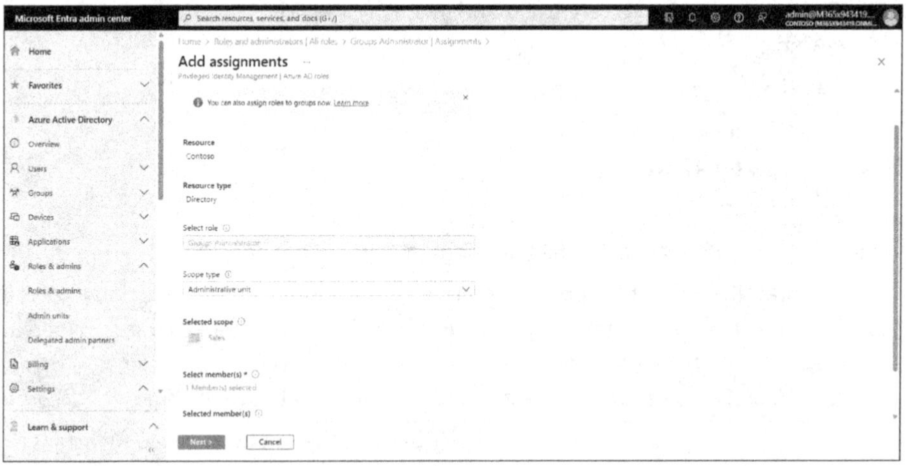

FIGURE 2-8 Scoping the application of a role

As an Endpoint Administrator, your job role entails performing device management and related tasks. In Azure AD, there are a number of relevant RBAC roles for administrative tasks in Microsoft Intune. These are:

- **Intune Administrator** Role holders can manage all aspects of Microsoft Intune.
- **Azure AD Joined Local Administrator** Users assigned to this role are added to the local administrators group on Azure AD-joined devices.

- **Cloud Device Administrator** Users with this role have limited device management capabilities, including enabling, disabling, and deleting devices.

Configuring RBAC in Intune

Although you'll typically manage roles and role assignments in Microsoft Entra, you can also manage these roles directly in Intune. Or, more accurately, you can manage role assignments in Intune. To review or change role assignments using the Microsoft Intune admin center, use the following procedure:

1. Select the appropriate user account.
2. On the user details page, select **Assigned roles** in the navigation pane.
3. Review or update the assigned roles as shown in Figure 2-9.

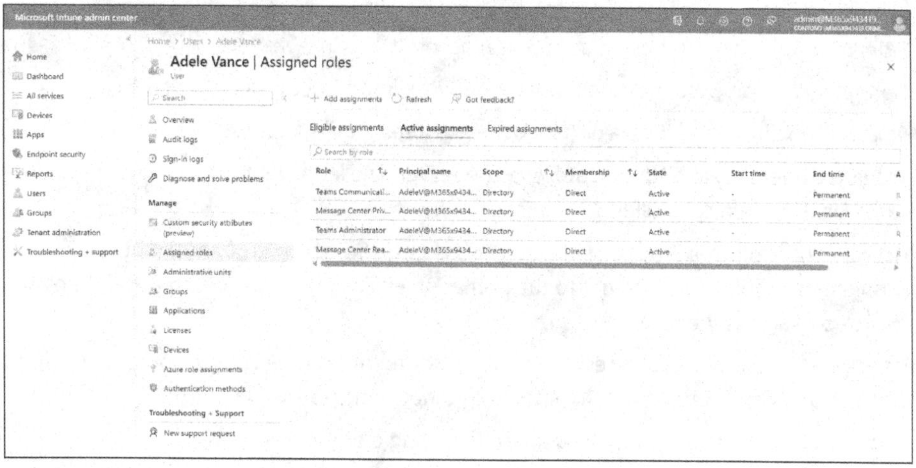

FIGURE 2-9 Updating role assignments in Intune

Register devices in and join devices to Azure AD

Microsoft designed Windows 11 to be remotely managed using cloud-based tools, such as Microsoft Intune. As more organizations migrate to the cloud, you must understand how to configure your users' devices to register them in Azure AD.

In this section, you'll learn how to register a device so a workplace or school with cloud-based services can manage it. You'll learn how to enable device registration and join devices to Azure AD.

Understand device management

When joining devices to an on-premises domain environment, the types of devices you can join to the domain are quite restrictive; devices, for example, must be running a supported operating system. This means that any users that have devices running Windows 11 Home editions cannot join the company's on-premises domain.

However, Azure AD is less restrictive in this respect; you can add to Azure AD almost any tablet, laptop, smartphone, and desktop computer running various operating systems. When you enable users to add their devices to Azure AD, you will manage their enrolled devices using an MDM solution, such as Microsoft Intune, which enables you to manage and provision your users' devices.

You can connect your devices to Azure AD in one of two ways. These are:

- Registering a device to Azure AD
- Joining a device to Azure AD

To understand these options, it's worth considering an on-premises scenario. Suppose you want to connect a computer to a workplace file server. Let's assume your computer is configured in a workgroup—a standalone configuration. You'll perform the following procedure:

1. Sign in to your computer using a local user account.
2. Connect your computer to the corporate network infrastructure.
3. Open File Explorer and map a network drive to a target file server shared folder.
4. Provide credentials to authenticate with the server. These credentials are in AD DS and stored in a domain controller.
5. Access your mailbox in your organization's Exchange Server by creating an Outlook profile that enables connectivity to the Exchange environment, including the credentials required to access the mailbox.

The process is decentralized and requires manual configuration to access resources in your corporate environment. Contrast that to a domain-joined workstation:

1. You sign in to the domain-joined workstation using a domain account.
2. You map a network drive to a file server. The server uses your existing credentials to authenticate you.
3. You open Outlook. Your Exchange Server mailbox server uses your existing credentials to authenticate you.

Using domain-joined devices has enabled SSO, ensuring all apps can be accessed using the signed-in credentials. This is very convenient for the user.

In some ways, you can consider an Azure AD–registered Windows 11 computer to be functionally equivalent to an on-premises, workgroup-configured computer. The user signs in using a local account and then uses a work or school account to access cloud apps and services, having to provide the credentials each time they connect to a new app or service.

Similarly, an Azure AD-joined device behaves much like a computer joined to an AD DS domain. The user signs in with their work or school account, and then all apps and services use these credentials thereafter, providing a better user experience.

Let's examine these two options more closely.

AZURE AD–REGISTERED DEVICES

Windows devices can be registered with Azure AD or joined to Azure AD. Other operating systems, such as iOS, Linux, macOS, and Android, can only be registered.

Generally, corporately owned devices running Windows should be Azure AD-joined, whereas users' own devices running Windows should be registered with Azure AD.

EXAM TIP

Remember, ONLY Windows devices can be joined to Azure AD.

After a user registers or joins their device with Azure AD, it is "known" to Azure AD, and information about the device is stored in Azure AD. Effectively, the device is given an identity with Azure AD. You can then create conditional access policies to determine whether access to resources from your users' devices will be granted.

Azure AD–registered devices enable users to use personally owned devices to access your organization's resources in a controlled manner. Azure AD supports Bring Your Own Device (BYOD) scenarios for multiple devices, including Windows 11, iOS, Android, and macOS.

With an Azure AD–registered device, the user gains access to resources using a work or school Azure AD account at the time they access the resources. All corporate data and apps are kept completely separate from the personal data and apps on the device. If the personal computer, tablet, or phone that is registered with Azure AD doesn't meet your corporate standards for security and compliance—for example, if a device is not running a supported version of the operating system or has been rooted— the access to the resource is denied.

The main reasons for implementing device registration are

- Enabling access to corporate resources from nondomain–joined or personally owned devices.
- Enabling SSO for specific apps and/or resources managed by Azure AD.

After you enable device registration, users can register and enroll their devices in your organizational tenant. After they have enrolled their devices

- Enrolled devices are associated with a specific user account in Azure AD.
- A device object is created in Azure AD to represent the physical device and its associated user account.
- A user certificate is installed on the user's device.

AZURE AD–JOINED DEVICE

Joining a Windows 11 device to Azure AD is similar to registering a device with Azure AD, but it enables enhanced management capabilities. After a device has been joined to Azure AD, the local state of a device changes to enable your users to sign into the device using the work or school account instead of a local account.

An enterprise typically joins its owned devices to the Azure AD to allow for cloud-based management of the devices and to grant access to corporate apps and resources.

Organizations of any size can deploy Azure AD Join. Azure AD Join works well in a cloud-only (no on-premises infrastructure) environment. When Azure AD Join is implemented in a hybrid environment, users can access both cloud and on-premises apps and resources.

Azure AD–joined devices enable your users to access the following benefits:

- **SSO** Enables users simplified access to Azure-managed SaaS apps, services, and work resources.

- **Enterprise-compliant roaming** User settings can be roamed across joined devices using their Azure AD–joined devices (without the need to sign in using a Microsoft account).

- **Windows Hello** Devices can be secured using the enterprise features of Windows Hello.

- **Restriction of access** Devices can only access apps that meet the organizational compliance policy.

- **Seamless access to on-premises resources** Hybrid Azure AD–joined devices can access on-premises resources when connected to the domain network.

Organizations that already have Microsoft 365 or other SaaS apps integrated with Azure AD have the necessary components in place to have devices managed in Azure AD instead of being managed in Active Directory.

Enable device management

Device management requires configuration to ensure that when your users attempt device registration (register or join), the process doesn't fail. By default, the setting is enabled, allowing all Windows 11 devices with valid credentials to be managed by your Azure AD.

Typically, you'll use Microsoft Entra to configure the required settings. Use the following procedure to verify and, where necessary, update the settings:

1. Open the Microsoft Entra admin center.

2. Under **Azure Active Directory** in the navigation pane, select **Devices**, and then click **Overview**.

3. On the **Devices | Overview** page, click **Device settings**.

4. As shown in Figure 2-10, enable the **Users may join devices to Azure AD** setting. You can choose **All** to allow all users to perform this task, or you can choose **Selected** and choose which users can perform this task.

5. If necessary, also enable **Users may register their devices with Azure AD**.

6. Enable the Require Multi-Factor Authentication to register or join devices with Azure AD setting for additional security. However, you must ensure that users' accounts are configured with the necessary settings for MFA.

7. Finally, click the **Manage Additional local administrators on all Azure AD joined devices** link to add specified users as local administrators on joined devices. Any users you add are assigned to the Azure AD Joined Device Local Administrator role. This

setting ensures that a cloud user is always added as a local admin on all your organization's devices.

8. You can also enable the **Azure AD Local Administrator Password Solution (LAPS)** setting for any new devices.

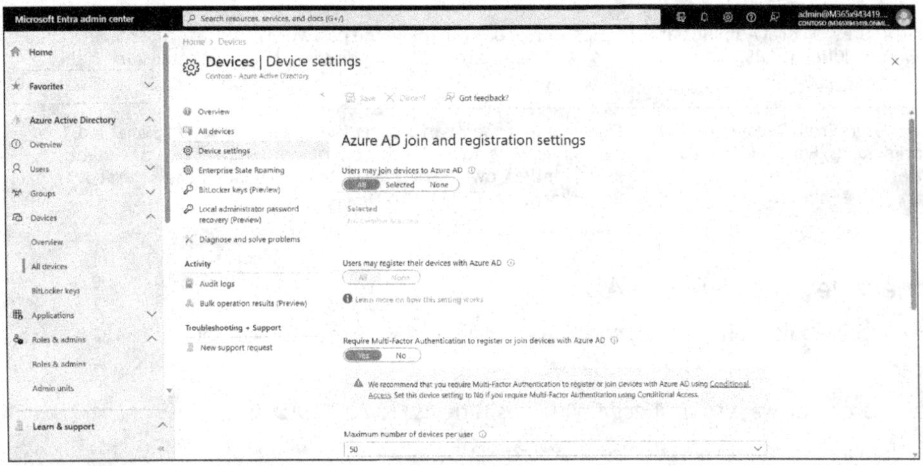

FIGURE 2-10 Configuring the settings for Azure AD registration or join

On the **Device settings** page, you can fine-tune the process of registering and joining devices by configuring the device settings, as shown in Table 2-1.

TABLE 2-1 Azure AD device configuration settings

Device setting	Description
Users May Join Devices To Azure AD	Allows you to select users that can join Windows 11 devices to Azure AD. The default is All.
Users May Register Their Devices With Azure AD	Allows devices to be registered with Azure AD by users. Options include: ■ **None:** Prevents devices from being registered with Azure AD. ■ **ALL:** Automatically configured if Enrollment with Microsoft Intune or Mobile Device Management (MDM) for Office 365 is configured as they require Device Registration.
Require Multi-Factor Authentication To Register Or Join Devices With Azure AD	Determines whether users are required to use multifactor authentication factor to join their devices to Azure AD. This setting only applies to Azure AD Join on Windows 11 and BYOD registration for Windows 11, iOS, and Android. This setting does not apply to hybrid Azure AD–joined devices, Azure AD–joined VMs in Azure, and Azure AD–joined devices using Windows Autopilot self-deployment mode. The default setting is **No**.
Maximum Number Of Devices Per User	Restricts the number of devices per user. Once this quota is reached, they cannot add devices until one or more existing devices are removed. The device quota is across both Azure AD–joined and Azure AD–registered devices. By default, all users can have a maximum of 50 devices in Azure AD.

Device setting	Description
Manage Additional Local Administrators On All Azure AD Joined Devices	Enables you to assign the users that are granted local administrator rights on a device and added to the Device Administrators role in Azure AD. By default, global administrators in Azure AD and device owners are granted local administrator rights. Requires an Azure AD Premium license.
Enable Azure AD Local Administrator Password Solution (LAPS)	Helps you securely manage the passwords of local accounts on joined devices. Defaults to **No**. This is discussed in more detail later in this chapter.
Restrict Users From Recovering The BitLocker Key(s) For Their Owned Devices	Determines if users can recover their BitLocker key(s). If enabled, the setting restricts non-admins from being able to access the BitLocker key(s) for their own devices. Selecting **No** enables users to recover their BitLocker key(s). Defaults to **No**.

Connect devices to Azure AD

Once the prerequisites have been configured to allow device registration service to take place, you can connect devices to Azure AD.

There are three ways to connect a Windows 11 device to Azure AD as follows:

- Join a new Windows 11 device to Azure AD
- Join an existing Windows 11 device to Azure AD
- Register devices to Azure AD

In this section, you'll learn the steps required to connect Windows 11 to Azure AD.

JOIN A NEW WINDOWS 11 DEVICE TO AZURE AD

In this method, you take a new Windows 11 device and join the device to Azure AD during the first-run experience.

> **NOTE** **OUT-OF-BOX-EXPERIENCE**
>
> The "first-run experience" is more usually known as the "out-of-box experience" (OOBE). OOBE runs when you start a computer for the first time, and a series of questions is displayed before you are presented with the Windows desktop.

The device could have been previously prepared using an enterprise deployment method, or it could have been distributed by the original equipment manufacturer (OEM) directly to your employees.

If the device is running either Windows 11 Professional or Windows 11 Enterprise, OOBE presents the setup process for company-owned devices.

To join a new Windows 11 device to Azure AD during OOBE, use the following steps:

1. Start the new device and allow the setup process to begin.
2. When prompted, on the **Is this the right country or region?** page, select your country or region, and click **Yes**.

3. On the **Is this the right keyboard layout or input method?** page, select the appropriate keyboard layout, and click **Yes**.

4. When prompted, if you want to add an additional keyboard layout, follow the steps to do so. Otherwise, click **Skip**.

5. Your computer checks for updates.

6. If prompted, review and **Accept** the License Agreement.

7. On the **Let's set things up for your work or school** page, as shown in Figure 2-11, in the **Sign in** box, enter your organizational user account and click **Next**.

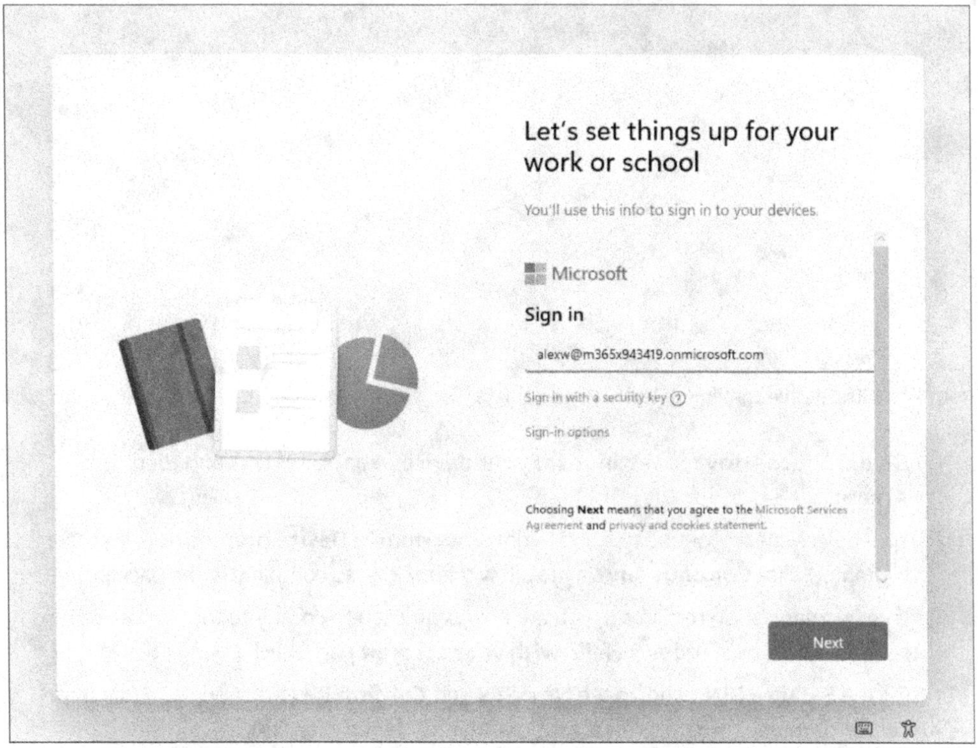

FIGURE 2-11 Joining a device to Azure AD during OOBE

8. When prompted, enter your password and click **Sign in**.

9. If your account requires it, you are prompted to identify yourself with MFA. This is configured at the organizational level but requires your user account to be configured.

10. The **Enrollment Status Page**, if configured, displays, as shown in Figure 2-12, guiding users during the device enrollment process.

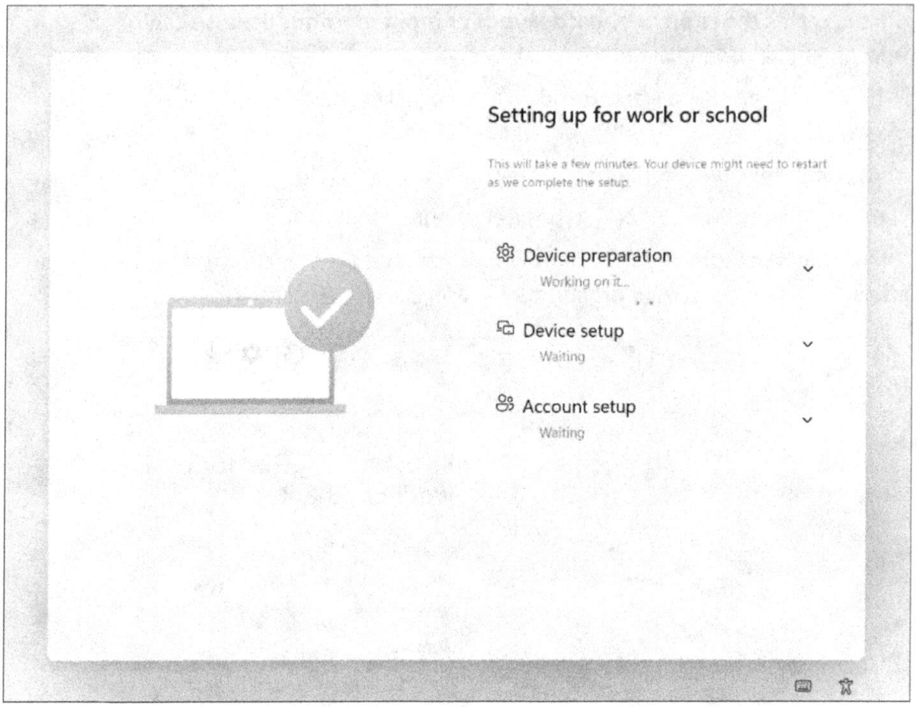

FIGURE 2-12 The device Enrollment Status Page displays

11. On the **Choose privacy settings for your device** page, click **Next** and then click **Accept.**

12. Your device checks for updates and might now return to **Device preparation**. You can, if prompted, click **Continue anyway** to allow this process to complete in the background.

13. If your organization requires it, you are now prompted to complete the Windows Hello setup. At the **Use Windows Hello with your account** page, click **OK**.

14. On the **Set up a PIN** page, in the **New PIN** and **Confirm PIN** boxes, enter a PIN that conforms to your organizational requirements and then click **OK**.

15. Click **OK**, and then you should be automatically signed in to the device, joined to your organization or school Azure AD tenant, and presented with the desktop.

JOIN AN EXISTING WINDOWS 11 DEVICE TO AZURE AD

In this method, we will join an existing Windows 11 device to Azure AD. You can join a Windows 11 device to Azure AD at any time. Use the following procedure to join the device:

1. Open the **Settings App** and then select **Accounts**.

2. In **Accounts**, select the **Access work or school** tab.

3. Select **Connect**.

4. On the **Set up a work or education account** page, under **Alternative actions**, select **Join this device to Azure Active Directory**, as shown in Figure 2-13.

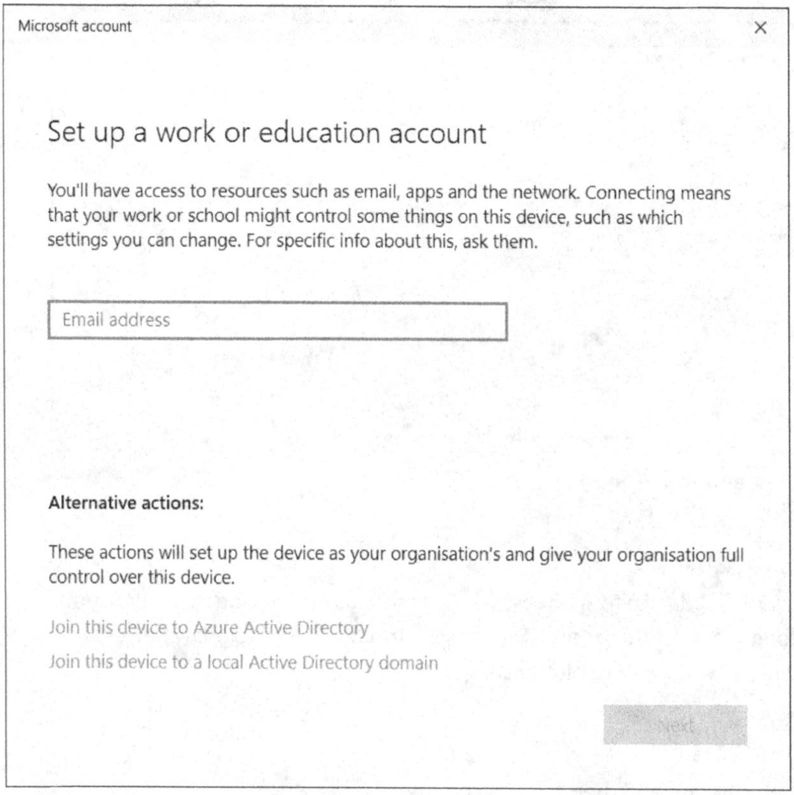

Set up a work or education account

You'll have access to resources such as email, apps and the network. Connecting means that your work or school might control some things on this device, such as which settings you can change. For specific info about this, ask them.

Email address

Alternative actions:

These actions will set up the device as your organisation's and give your organisation full control over this device.

Join this device to Azure Active Directory

Join this device to a local Active Directory domain

Next

FIGURE 2-13 Joining a device to Azure AD

5. Enter your organizational email address on the **Microsoft account** page and select **Next**.

6. On the **Enter password** page, enter your password and click **Sign In**.

7. If prompted, confirm your identity with MFA.

8. On the **Make sure this is your organization** page, confirm that the details on screen are correct and select **Join**.

9. On the **You're all ready!** page, click **Done**.

10. To verify that your device is connected to your organization or school, your Azure AD email address will be listed under the **Connect** button, indicating that it is connected to Azure AD.

If you have access to Microsoft Entra admin center, then you can validate that the device is joined to Azure AD by following these steps:

1. Open Microsoft Entra, and in the navigation pane, expand **Azure Active Directory**.

2. Expand **Devices** and then click **All Devices**.

3. Verify that the device is listed as shown in Figure 2-14.

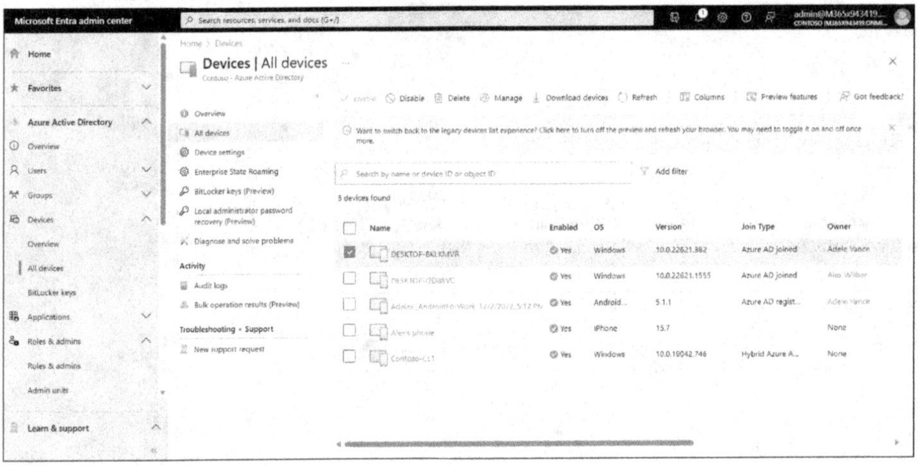

FIGURE 2-14 Viewing All devices in Azure AD

REGISTER DEVICES TO AZURE AD

You connect a Windows 11 device to Azure Active Directory using the Add Work or School Account feature found in the Settings app. Device registration is used to allow devices to be known by both Azure AD and MDM solutions.

In this method, we will register an existing Windows 11 device to Azure AD. Use the following procedure to register the device:

1. Open the Settings app and then select **Accounts**.
2. In **Accounts**, click **Access work or school**.
3. Select **Connect**.
4. On the **Set up a work or school account** page, enter your work or education email address, click **Next**, and complete the wizard.

To verify that a device is registered to your organization or school Azure AD tenant, users can use these steps:

1. Open **Settings**, then select **Accounts**.
2. In **Accounts**, click **Access work or school**.
3. Verify that your organization or school's Azure AD email address is listed on the **Access work or school** page under the **Connect** button.

> **NOTE REGISTER BYO DEVICES TO AZURE AD**
>
> You can register a personally owned device with Azure AD using the Set Up A Work Or Education Account wizard. Personal devices are then known to Azure AD but are not fully managed by the organization.

DEVICE MANAGEMENT TASKS

After devices have been registered or joined to Azure AD, they appear in the All Devices section of the Microsoft Entra admin center list. Devices managed by another management authority, such as Microsoft Intune, are also listed. You can search using the device name or device ID to locate a device.

When you have located a device, you can perform additional device management tasks, including:

- **Disable** Disables access for all user accounts within your tenant on the disabled device. Once disabled, you can enable a device when necessary.
- **Delete** Removes the devices from Azure AD.
- **Manage** Enables you to manage some aspects of the selected device(s). Selecting **Manage** for devices opens the **Managed Devices** page and displays the **All devices** page from Intune. From here, you can perform standard Intune device management tasks, including:
  - **Retire, wipe, and delete**
  - **Remote lock and restart**
  - **Sync**
  - **Fresh Start or Autopilot Reset**
  - **BitLocker key rotation**
  - **Establish a remote assistance session**

> **NOTE MANAGEMENT OPTIONS VARY**
>
> The management options available depend on whether the device is enrolled in Intune, which is typical for Azure AD–joined devices. In addition, the operating system of the target device determines available options.

Implement the Intune Connector for Active Directory

Many organizations undertake a gradual migration to the cloud. This means that for a period of time—possibly an extended period of time—an organization's devices might exist within the on-premises environment and the cloud. More specifically, devices will be joined to both AD DS and Azure AD. When a device is both AD DS– and Azure AD–joined, it is referred to as an Azure AD Hybrid–joined device.

There are two ways to Azure AD Hybrid-join your Windows devices:

- For existing AD DS devices, configure synchronization with Azure AD using either:
  - Azure AD Connect Sync
  - Azure AD Cloud Sync
- For new devices, configure an appropriate Windows Autopilot profile that uses the **Hybrid Azure AD joined** option and use the Intune Connector for Active Directory to create the required on-premises objects.

Synchronizing with Azure AD

You must select one of two methods to synchronize your organization's devices with Azure AD. These are:

- **Azure AD Connect Sync**   Requires that you download and install the Azure AD Connect program on an AD DS domain-joined server computer. Once configured, the on-premises Azure AD Connect application manages the synchronization process. If you need to change the synchronization settings, run the Azure AD Connect application and choose the appropriate configuration option on the on-premises server.

- **Azure AD Cloud Sync**   Requires that you deploy and configure a sync agent on an on-premises server computer. However, you then configure the required settings in Microsoft Entra. It is the cloud sync service that drives the synchronization process.

To review or configure either of these, open the Microsoft Entra admin center and then follow these steps:

1. In the navigation pane, expand **Hybrid management**.
2. Select **Azure AD Connect**.
3. Then select either **Cloud Sync** or **Connect Sync** from the navigation pane.

Whichever option you choose, you can synchronize various object types, including

- User accounts
- Group accounts
- Devices
- Passwords

In addition, depending on settings configured in Azure AD, you can also synchronize

- Password writeback
- Group writeback
- Device writeback

> *NOTE* **SYNCHRONIZING PASSWORDS**
>
> A significant benefit of synchronizing passwords is that users can then access both on-premises and cloud apps and resources using the same account and password. In order to enable password writeback, you'll also need to enable a feature called Self-Service Password Reset (SSPR) in Azure AD.

To enable device synchronization, which in turn enables Hybrid Azure AD joined devices, use the following procedure with Azure AD Connect Sync:

1. In Azure AD Connect, click **Configure**.
2. On the **Additional tasks** page, click **Configure device options** and then click **Next**.
3. On the **Overview** page, review the descriptive text and then click **Next**.

4. When prompted, provide a user's credentials holding the Global Administrator role in your Azure AD tenant. Click **Next**.

5. On the **Device options** page, as shown in Figure 2-15, select **Configure Hybrid Azure AD join** and click **Next**.

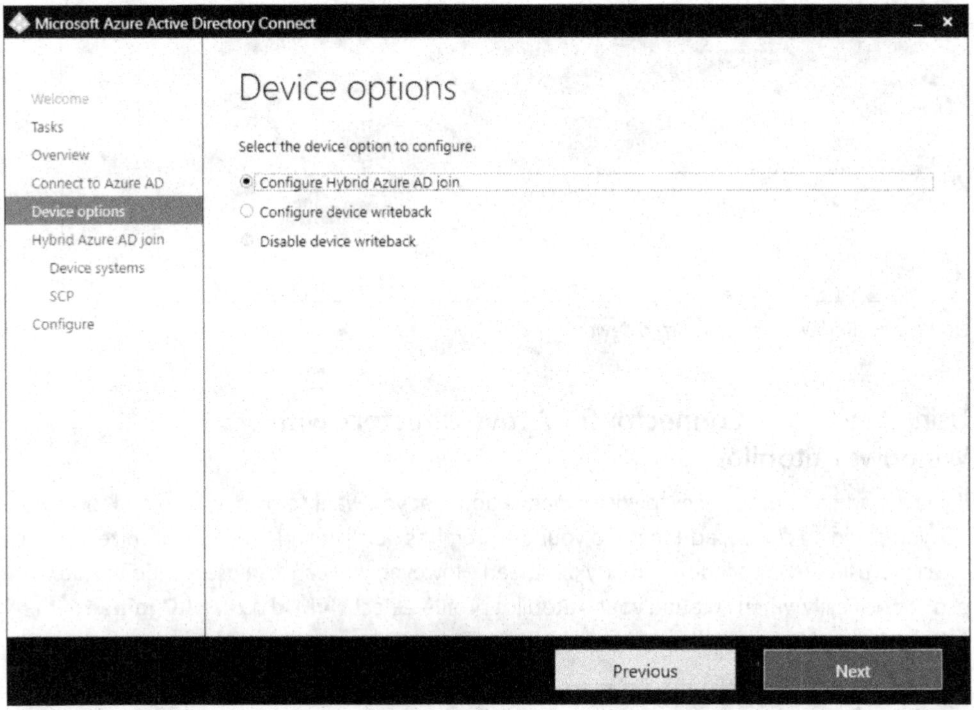

FIGURE 2-15 Configuring device options for Azure AD Connect Sync

6. On the **Device operating system** page, select **Windows 10 or later domain-joined devices** and click **Next**.

7. On the **SCP configuration** page, select the AD DS forest you want to synchronize from. Click **Add**.

8. In the **Windows Security** dialog, enter the credentials for a user in your forest with Enterprise Admin privileges and click **OK**. Click **Next**.

9. When prompted, on the **Ready to configure** page, click **Configure**.

10. When the process is complete, exit the Azure AD Connect Sync application.

To review synchronized devices, open Microsoft Entra admin center, and then:

1. Expand **Devices** and then click **All Devices**.

2. Review the list of devices. Any synced devices are indicated with the **Hybrid Azure AD joined** join type, as displayed in Figure 2-16.

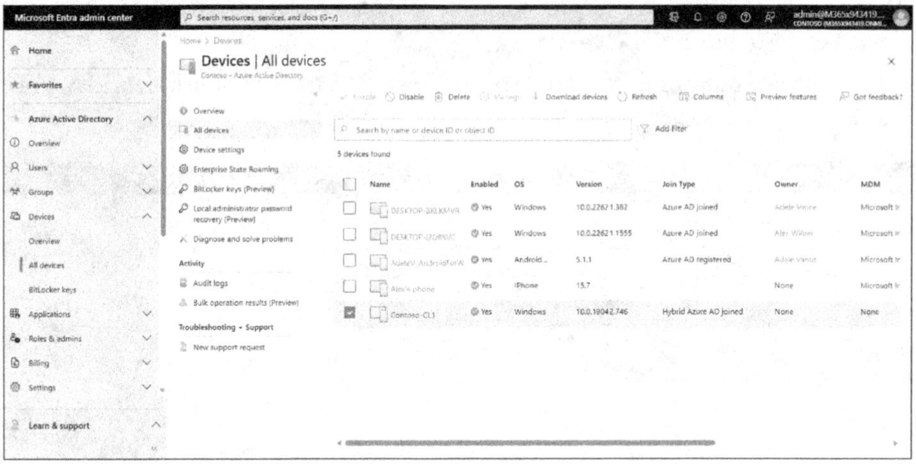

FIGURE 2-16 Reviewing synchronized devices

Using the Intune Connector for Active Directory with Windows Autopilot

If you are adding new devices to your organization that you want to be hybrid joined to Azure AD, you could, of course, add them to your on-premises domain and then synchronize them to the cloud using the procedure already discussed. However, you can also use Windows Autopilot. Specifically, when creating your Autopilot profile, select **Hybrid Azure AD joined** in the **Join to Azure AD as** dropdown, as displayed in Figure 2-17.

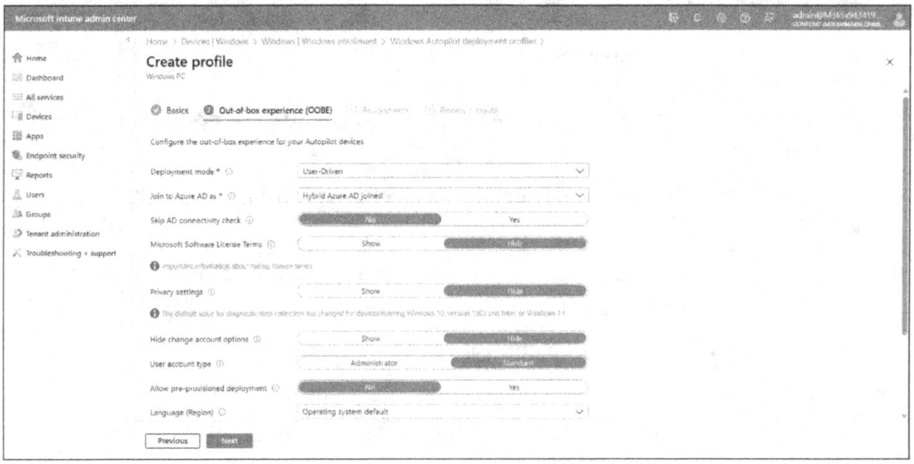

FIGURE 2-17 Enabling hybrid Azure AD join using Windows Autopilot

After you have configured the other settings in your profile, go ahead and assign it in the usual way. However, for the process to be successful, there must be a means for Intune to create the required objects in your AD DS environment. This requires the configuration of the Intune Connector for Active Directory.

To enable this connector, in the Microsoft Intune admin center, perform the following high-level procedure:

1. Select **Devices** from the navigation pane.
2. Select **Windows** and then select **Windows enrollment**.
3. On the **Windows | Windows enrollment** page, under the **Windows Autopilot Deployment Program** heading, click **Intune Connector for Active Directory**.
4. On the **Intune Connector for Active Directory** page, click **Add**.
5. Click the link to **Download the on-premises Intune Connector for Active Directory**.
6. Copy the downloaded file to an on-premises server that is domain-joined.
7. Run the downloaded file on the server. Accept the license terms and conditions, and then click **Install**.
8. When prompted, click **Configure Now**.
9. Sign in when prompted using a user account in Azure AD with Global administrator or Intune administrator role credentials.
10. Return to the Microsoft Intune admin center and verify that the connector you installed is listed and its status is active, as shown in Figure 2-18.

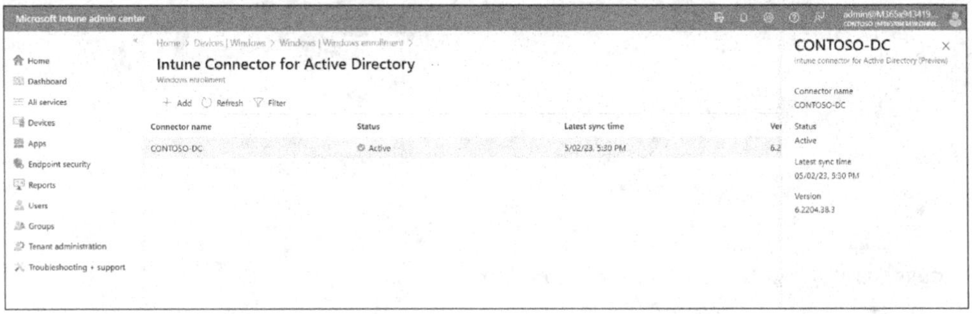

FIGURE 2-18 Reviewing the status of the Intune Connector for Active Directory

It only remains for you to upload your new computers' device IDs and assign the previously created Autopilot profile as usual.

NEED MORE REVIEW? **DEPLOY HYBRID AZURE AD-JOINED DEVICES BY USING INTUNE AND WINDOWS AUTOPILOT**

For more information about configuring Intune and Autopilot for hybrid join, refer to the Microsoft Learn website at *https://learn.microsoft.com/mem/autopilot/windows-autopilot-hybrid*.

Manage the membership of local groups on Windows devices

There are numerous built-in groups with Windows 11 that provide an easy way for users to be granted the same permissions and rights as other group members. Assigning permissions to groups is usually more efficient than applying them to individual users.

You use the Computer Management console or, if you are an administrator, you can create a custom Microsoft Management Console (MMC) and add the **Local Users and Groups** snap-in as shown in Figure 2-19 to create and manage local groups.

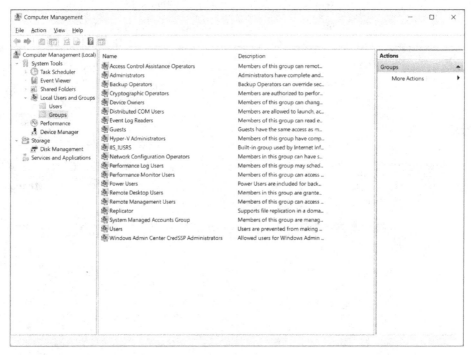

FIGURE 2-19 Windows 11 Local Users and Groups snap-in

In Figure 2-19, you can see the default built-in local groups (such as **Administrators** and **Device Owners**) and a description for each. These built-in groups already have the necessary associated permissions to accomplish specific administration or management tasks.

If you select the **Users** or **Administrators** groups, you should see members you recognize. Members of **Administrators** have complete and unrestricted access to the computer, whereas members of **Users** cannot make accidental or intentional system-wide changes, but they can run most applications that have already been installed on a device.

Built-in local groups

You can add your own groups, change group membership, rename groups, and delete groups (although you cannot remove built-in groups). However, it is best practice to use the built-in groups wherever possible because these already have the appropriate permissions and are familiar to other administrators.

Some built-in local groups are special groups that Windows 11 system requires (and cannot be managed). Some of the following local groups created on Windows 11 devices are shown in Table 2-2.

TABLE 2-2 Built-in Local Groups

Local group	Description
Access Control Assistance Operators	Members of this group can remotely query authorization attributes and permissions for resources on the computer.
Administrators	The Administrators group has full permissions and privileges on a Windows 11 device. Members can manage all the objects on the computer. The Administrator and initial user accounts are members of the Administrators local group.
Backup Operators	Backup Operators group members have permission to back up and restore the file system regardless of any NTFS permissions. Backup Operators can access the file system only through the Backup utility.
Cryptographic Operators	The Cryptographic Operators group has access to perform cryptographic operations on the computer.
Device Owners	Members of this group can change system-wide settings to the computer.
Distributed COM Users	The Distributed COM Users group can launch and run Distributed COM objects on the computer.
Event Log Readers	Event Log Readers group members can read the event log on the local computer.
Guests	The Guests group has very limited access to the computer. Administrators usually disable guest access because it can pose a potential security risk; instead, most administrators prefer to create specific users. By default, the Guest user account is a member of the Guests local group.
Hyper-V Administrators	Members of this group have complete and unrestricted access to all features of Hyper-V if this feature has been installed.
IIS_IUSRS	The IIS_IUSRS group is used by Internet Information Services (IIS). By default, the NT AUTHORITY\IUSR user account, used by IIS, is a member of the IIS_IUSRS group.
Network Configuration Operators	Members can manage the computer's network configuration.
Performance Log Users	The Performance Log Users group can access and schedule the logging of performance counters and create and manage trace counters on a device.
Performance Monitor Users	Members can access and view performance counter information on a device. Members of this group can access performance counters both locally and remotely.
Power Users	The Power Users group is included in Windows 11 for backward compatibility only. Power Users was used on Windows XP computers and granted members limited administrative rights.

Local group	Description
Remote Desktop Users	Members can log on remotely using the Remote Desktop service.
Remote Management Users	Members of this group can access WMI resources over management protocols (such as WS-Management via the Windows Remote Management service). This applies only to WMI namespaces that grant access to the user.
Replicator	The Replicator group supports directory replication, which is a feature used by domain controllers.
System Managed Accounts Group	The system manages members of this group.
Users	The Users group is used for end users who require very limited system access. On a fresh copy of Windows 11, members of the Users group cannot compromise the operating system or program files. By default, all users created on a device, except Guest users, are members of the Users local group.

In Table 2-2, you saw that Administrators group members have full permissions and privileges on a Windows 11 device. A member of the Administrators local group can perform many administrative functions, including the following:

- Access any data on the computer
- Assign and manage user rights
- Back up and restore all data
- Configure audit policies
- Configure password policies
- Configure services
- Create administrative accounts
- Create administrative shares
- Increase and manage disk quotas
- Install and configure hardware device drivers
- Install applications that modify the Windows system files
- Install the operating system
- Install Windows updates, service packs, and hotfixes
- Manage disk properties, including formatting hard drives
- Manage security logs
- Modify groups and accounts that other users have created
- Modify systemwide environment variables
- Perform a system restore
- Re-enable locked-out and disabled user accounts

- Remotely access the registry
- Remotely shut down the system
- Stop or start any service
- Upgrade the operating system

Create and delete groups

Only members of the Administrators group can manage users and groups. When creating a new group, the group name must be unique on the local computer and cannot be the same as a local username on the computer.

You should make the group name descriptive, and wherever possible, you should include a description of the new group's function. Group names can have up to 256 characters in length and include alphanumeric characters, including spaces, but the backslash (\) character is not allowed.

To create a new group, follow these steps:

1. Right-click **Start** and select **Computer Management**.
2. Open the **Local Users and Groups** console.
3. Right-click the **Groups** folder and select **New Group** from the context menu.
4. In the **New Group** dialog, enter the group name. (Optionally, you can enter a description for this group.)
5. To add group members, select the **Add** button.
6. In the **Select Users** dialog, type the username, then select **OK**.
7. In the **New Group** dialog, you will see that the user has been added to the group.
8. To create the new group, select the **Create** button.

To delete a group from the **Local Users and Groups** console in **Computer Management**, right-click the group name and choose **Delete** from the context menu. You will see a warning that deleting a group cannot be undone, and you should select the **Yes** button to confirm the deletion of the group. When a group is deleted, all permissions assignments specified for the group will be lost.

Special identity groups

Several special identity groups (sometimes known as special groups) are used by the system or by administrators for resource allocation. Membership in special groups is automatic, based on criteria, and you cannot manage special groups through the **Local Users and Groups** console. Table 2-3 describes the special identity groups built into Windows 11.

TABLE 2-3 Built-in Special Identity Groups

Special identity group	Description
Anonymous Logon	When a user accesses the computer through an anonymous logon, such as via special accounts created for anonymous access to Windows 11 services, they become members of the Anonymous Logon group.
Authenticated Users	This is a useful group because it includes all users who access Windows 11 using a valid username and password.
Batch	This group includes users who log on as batch job operators to run a batch job.
Creator Owner	The creator owner is the account that created or took ownership of an object, such as a file, folder, printer, or print job. Members of the Creator Owner group have special administrator-level permissions to the resources over which they have ownership.
Dialup	This group includes users who log on to the network from a dial-up connection.
Everyone	This group includes anyone accessing the computer, including all users—Guest accounts and all users within a domain or trusted domains. Members of the Anonymous Logon group are not included in the Everyone group.
Interactive	This group includes all users who use the computer's resources locally and those who are not using the computer's resources remotely via a network connection.
Network	This group includes users who access the computer's resources over a network connection.
Service	This group includes users who sign in as a user account used to run a service.
System	When Windows 11 needs to access internal functions, it can perform actions as a system user. The process accessed by the operating system becomes a member of the System group.
Terminal Server User	This group includes users who log on through Terminal Server applications.

Using Intune to manage local group memberships

In an on-premises domain, it's usual for the domain administrator to want to manage group membership on domain-joined computers. In a cloud context, it's also desirable for administrators to be able to manage the membership of groups on Azure AD joined computers. To manage local group memberships on Azure AD joined computers, you use Intune. Specifically, you create an Account protection policy in Endpoint Security settings.

Use the following procedure:

1. Open the Microsoft Intune admin center.

2. In the navigation pane, select **Endpoint security** and click **Account protection**.

3. In the details pane, click **Create Policy**.

4. On the **Create a profile** page, in the **Platform** list, select **Windows 10 and later**.

5. In the **Profile** list, select **Local user group membership**.

6. Click **Create**.

7. In the **Create profile** wizard, enter a name on the **Basics** tab and click **Next**.

8. On the **Configuration** settings tab, displayed in Figure 2-20, select the local group in the dropdown, and then configure the required settings. For example, choose **Administrators**, select **Add (update)**, and choose the required users or groups you want to add from your Azure AD tenant.

9. Click **Next**, and configure any scope tags.

10. Click **Next** and then assign the policy to the appropriate device group.

11. Click **Next** and then click **Create**.

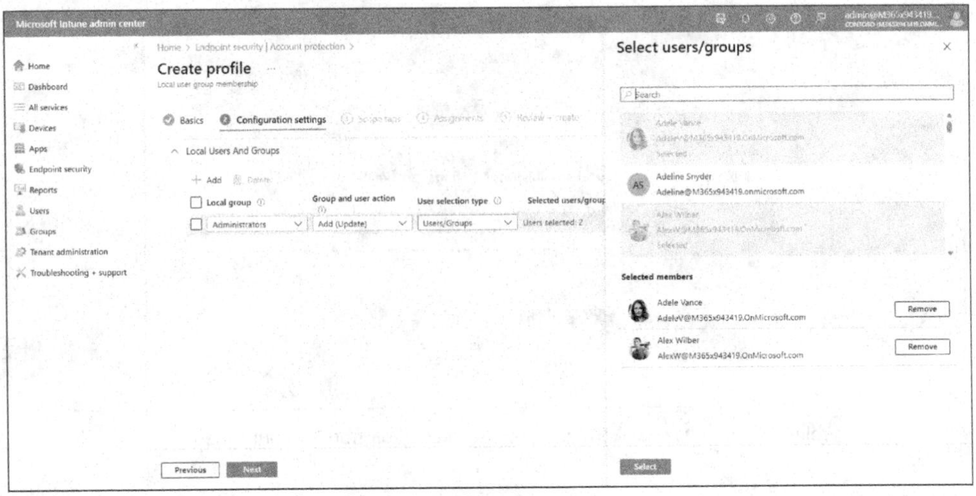

FIGURE 2-20 Adding Azure AD users to local groups

Implement and manage LAPS for Azure AD

Password management for administrator accounts on AD DS or Azure AD–joined computers is a significant problem for Windows administrators. Implementing Local Administrator Password Solution (LAPS) is one solution.

LAPS enables you to secure and help protect your Windows devices' local admin passwords. Features include the ability to back up passwords and auto-rotate passwords. You must configure two related settings to enable and use LAPS in your Azure AD tenant:

- Enable LAPS in Microsoft Entra
- Configure LAPS using Intune

Enabling LAPS in Microsoft Entra

Before you can implement LAPS, you must enable it within your Azure AD tenant. You do this using the Microsoft Entra admin center. Use the following procedure:

1. Open Microsoft Entra admin center.

2. Expand **Azure Active Directory** in the navigation pane.

3. Expand **Devices** and then select **All devices**.

4. Click **Device settings**.

5. Under the **Local administrator settings** heading, as shown in Figure 2-21, turn on the **Enable Azure AD Local Administrator Password Solution (LAPS)** setting.

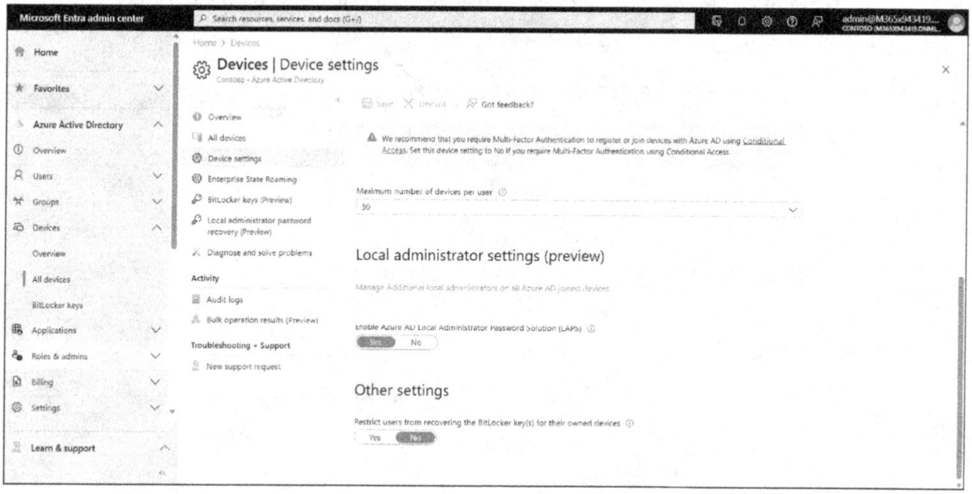

FIGURE 2-21 Enabling Azure AD Local Administrator Password Solution for your tenant

Configuring LAPS using Intune

The next step is to create an account protection policy in Intune. Use the following procedure:

1. Open the Microsoft Intune admin center.

2. In the navigation pane, select **Endpoint security** and click **Account protection**.

3. In the details pane, click **Create Policy**.

4. On the **Create a profile** page, in the **Platform** list, select **Windows 10 and later**.

5. In the **Profile** list, select **Local admin password solution (LAPS)**.

6. Click **Create**.

7. In the **Create profile** wizard, enter a name on the **Basics** tab and click **Next**.

8. Configure the desired settings on the **Configuration settings** tab, as shown in Figure 2-22.

9. Click **Next**, and configure any scope tags.

10. Click **Next** and then assign the policy to the appropriate device group.

11. Click **Next** and then click **Create**.

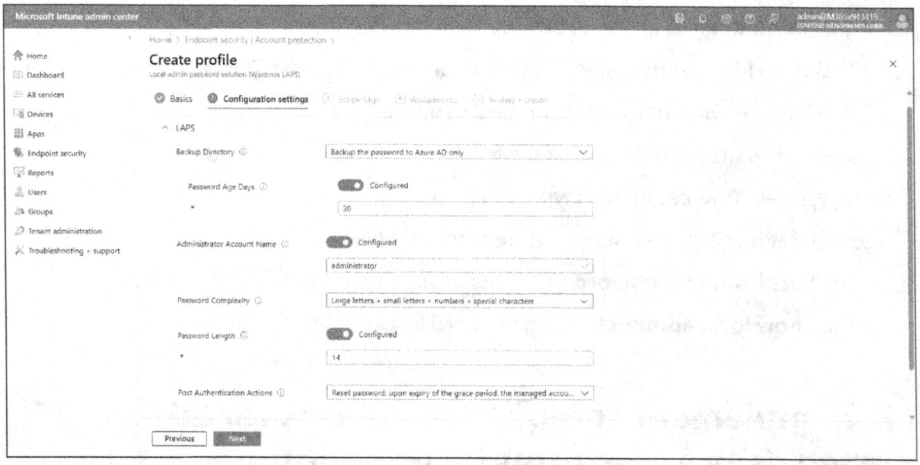

FIGURE 2-22 Configuring a local admin password solution in Intune

When you create your policy, there are numerous settings you can configure, as described in Table 2-4.

TABLE 2-4 LAPS account protection policy configuration settings

Setting	Description
Backup directory	Defines whether and where you'll back up admin passwords. You can disable this feature or target AD DS or Azure AD as the backup location.
Password age days	Determines how old passwords are permitted to be before rotation. If not configured manually, this setting defaults to 30 days. Minimum and maximum configurable values are 1 to 365 days.
Administrator account name	Enables you to target the local administrative account by its name. If not specified, the system searches for the well-known SID of the built-in administrator account and targets that account.
Password complexity	Enables you to define the complexity rules for the managed account's password, including options such as uppercase, lowercase, numbers, and special characters in various combinations.
Password length	Defines the managed password length. Defaults to 14 but can be any value between 8 and 64 characters.
Post authentication actions	Specifies what LAPS does to the target account after successful authentication. Available options are **Reset password**, **Reset password and logoff**, and **Reset password and restart the computer**.
Post authentication delay	Determines how long LAPS waits before performing the previously defined post-authentication action. Defaults to 24 hours.

After configuring the desired settings for your tenant, you will almost certainly want to review the configured computers' administrator account passwords. You can do this in the Microsoft Entra admin center:

1. Navigate to **All devices** and select the appropriate device.
2. On the **Device | Properties** page, click the **Local administrator password recovery** tab.
3. Click the **Show local administrator password** link.

You can also review the password using the Microsoft Intune admin center:

1. In Intune, select **Devices** in the navigation pane.
2. Select **All devices** and then select the appropriate device.
3. Click the **Local admin password** tab in the navigation pane.
4. Click the **Show local administrator password** link.

Skill 2.2: Implement compliance policies for all supported device platforms by using Intune

After you start managing Windows 11 devices using Microsoft Intune, you'll want to implement conditional access to provide granular access control for your corporate resources. These resources can include data contained in controlled applications, such as Exchange Online. Intune works with Azure AD to actively check the status of enrolled devices against your policies each time a resource such as corporate email is accessed.

With Microsoft Intune, you can stipulate the necessary compliance checks that Azure AD will perform on enrolled devices. Deploying compliance policies allows devices to be allowed or denied access to your corporate resources. In addition, when used with Azure AD Conditional Access policies, you can determine precisely when those resources are accessible. Therefore, you must understand how to plan, implement, and manage them to meet organizational security requirements.

This skill covers how to:

- Specify compliance policies to meet requirements
- Manage notifications for compliance policies
- Implement compliance policies
- Monitor device compliance
- Troubleshoot compliance policies
- Implement Conditional Access policies that require a compliance status

Specify compliance policies to meet requirements

Many organizations are regulated and must comply with laws and regulations, such as those shown in Table 2-5. To remain compliant, administrators must configure and manage devices and any data on them per corporate security and compliance requirements. Modern management enables administrators to control devices and restrict their use when accessing corporate data.

TABLE 2-5 Regulations and compliance

Regulation	Region	Requirement
HIPAA (Health Insurance Portability and Accountability Act of 1996)	USA	User isn't prompted to MFA.
Sarbanes–Oxley Act	USA	The Chief Financial Officer (CFO) and Chief Executive Officer (CEO) have joint responsibility for the financial data. Administrators must keep financial data secure and free from tampering, theft, and deletion.
Gramm–Leach–Bliley Act	USA	Responsibility for security lies within the entire board of directors. While not legally bound, IT administrators will be delegated the implementation and management of IT security.
GDPR (General Data Protection Regulation)	EU	Regardless of location, all enterprises must adhere to EU privacy laws relating to any person living in the EU.

Using Microsoft Intune, you can define compliance policies. After you have created compliance policies, you can assign them to enrolled devices and device groups.

Each time a device attempts to access corporate resources, such as a SharePoint Site or corporate email client, its policy is evaluated, and its compliance status is determined. Only compliant devices are granted access to the resources.

> **NOTE REQUIRES AZURE AD PREMIUM**
>
> Organizations must have Azure AD Premium P1 or P2 licenses, and each device requires an Intune license to use compliance policies.

The following device platforms can be managed using compliance policies once they have been enrolled into Intune:

- Android and Android Enterprise
- iOS and iPadOS
- Linux
- macOS
- Windows 10 and later
- Windows 8.1 and later

When considering how your organization will achieve compliance, you might want to review the features available and support for compliance policies. Each compliance policy within Intune is platform-specific, and the actual compliance policy settings available will vary depending on the settings the platform vendor exposes to the MDM framework. For example, BitLocker encryption is only available on Windows devices, and Google Play Protect is available only on Android.

EXAM TIP

Make sure you understand the different compliance features that can be selected for each operating system.

Some of the more commonly used device compliance settings that you can implement include:

- **Require a password to access devices**   For example, a PIN or password.
- **Local data encryption**   BitLocker encryption or other boot protection such as Secure Boot.
- **Is the device jailbroken or rooted?**   Often, a device that has been jailbroken or rooted will be more vulnerable to malware attacks.
- **Minimum operating system version required**   Prevents outdated software, which may be more vulnerable to malware attacks.
- **Maximum operating system version allowed**   Prevents software that has not been tested or approved for corporate use from being used.
- **Protected Against Malware Threats**   Requires the device to have an antimalware solution enabled, signatures are up to date, or real-time protection is enabled.

Configuring compliance policy settings

Before configuring and assigning your compliance policies, you must define your organization's initial compliance policy settings. These define how compliance is determined on devices without a compliance policy. Configurable settings, displayed in Figure 2-23, are:

- **Mark devices with no compliance policy assigned as**   If set to Compliant, this setting effectively turns off compliance in your organization.

NOTE CAUTION

It's important to remember that if you mark devices as noncompliant by default before you start creating and assigning compliance policies, and a conditional access policy exists that requires compliance, you have effectively denied access to all devices in your organization to resources being protected by the conditional access policy. Be careful. Depending on the conditional access policy settings, you can lock yourself out of the Intune admin center.

- **Enhanced jailbreak detection**   Rooted devices pose a serious potential security risk. Selecting this option helps mitigate those risks.
- **Compliance status validity period**   Devices that fail to report their compliance policy status within the defined period are treated as noncompliant.

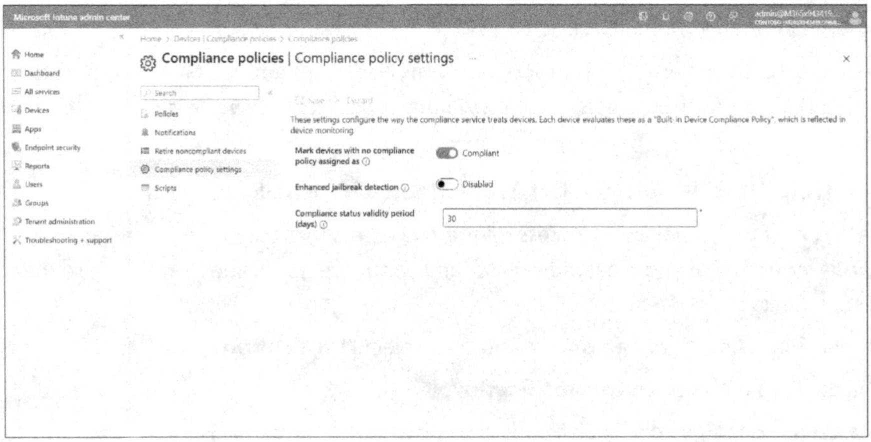

FIGURE 2-23 Configuring the initial compliance policy settings

Configuring scripts

You can use discovery scripts to help define custom compliance settings. Both Linux and Windows operating systems are supported. You deploy the script to devices in order to determine custom compliance settings, and then you can define those settings in a compliance policy for those platforms.

The first step is to add the scripts. You do this through the Scripts tab in Compliance Policies, as shown in Figure 2-24. For Windows scripts, you can determine whether the script:

- Runs in the context of the currently signed-in user
- Requires a signature check
- Runs in the 64-bit PowerShell host

After you've added your discovery scripts, you can leverage them when you create a compliance policy (see Figure 2-24).

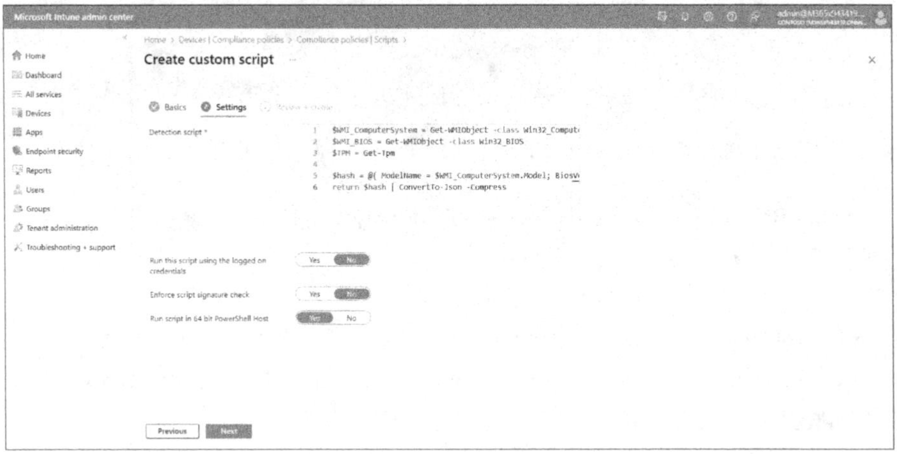

FIGURE 2-24 Adding a compliance script for Windows devices

NEED MORE REVIEW? COMPLIANCE SCRIPTS

For more information about using scripts for custom compliance settings, refer to the Microsoft Learn website at _https://learn.microsoft.com/mem/intune/protect/compliance-custom-script_.

Manage notifications for compliance policies

An important part of the compliance process is informing users that their devices are non-compliant. This requires that you create templates and configure notification settings. Use the following procedure:

1. In Intune, open **Compliance policies** and then select **Notifications**.
2. In the details pane, click **Create notification**.
3. In the **Create notification** wizard, enter a name on the **Basics** tab, as shown in Figure 2-25. Then configure the following, and click **Next**:
   - **Email header – Include company logo**
   - **Email footer – Include company name**
   - **Email footer – Include contact information**
   - **Company Portal Website Link**

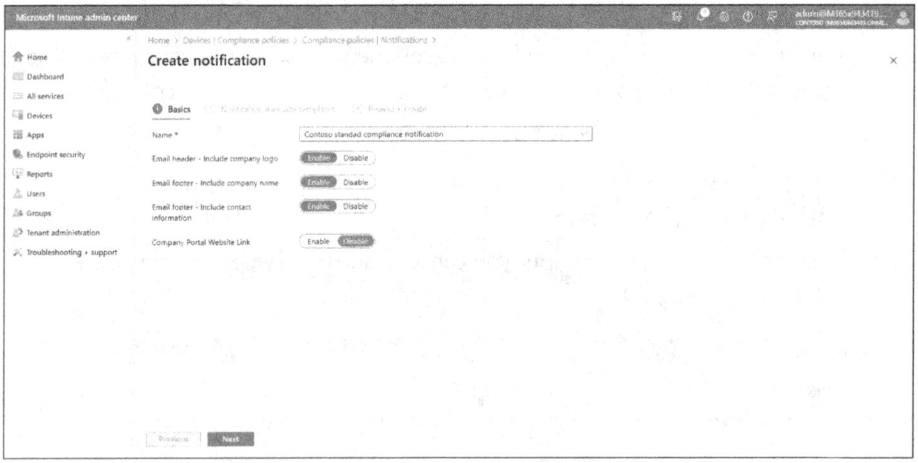

FIGURE 2-25 Configuring a compliance notification

4. On the **Notification message templates** tab, displayed in Figure 2-26, configure the following settings:
   - **Select a locale** This determines the language used in the notification.
   - **Enter a subject** This determines the email subject displayed in the user's mailbox.
   - **Enter a message** This is the text displayed in the notification email body text.
   - **Is default** Select this template as the default if desired.

5. If desired, add additional templates. When you have all the required templates, click **Next**.

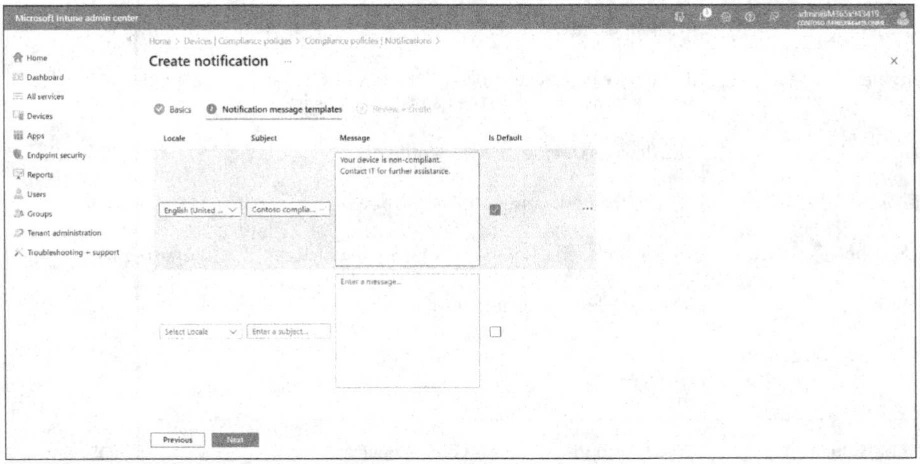

FIGURE 2-26 Configuring message template settings

6. On the **Review + create**, verify your settings and then click **Create**.

After creating the template, you can test the notification by selecting the template and clicking **Send preview email**.

Implement device compliance policies

Device compliance policies can be used with or without conditional access policies and achieve the following outcomes:

- **With conditional access** Devices in compliance can access corporate resources. Devices that are not compliant are blocked from accessing corporate resources.
- **Without conditional access** Effectively, these policies evaluate the compliance status of a device only. Used alone, there are no access restrictions to corporate resources because of a compliance policy.

You can use compliance policies without conditional access policies to evaluate the status of your devices. You can report information relating to device platform characteristics, such as:

- The number of devices that do not have compliance policies
- The number of devices that are not encrypted
- Whether devices are jailbroken or rooted
- Threat agent status

A list of the device attributes that can be reported is shown in Table 2-6.

TABLE 2-6 Device data available in Microsoft Intune

Detail	Description	Platform
Name	The name of the device.	Windows, iOS
Management Name	The device name used only in the console. Changing this name won't change the name on the device.	Windows, iOS
UDID	The device's Unique Device identifier.	Windows, iOS
Intune Device ID	A GUID that uniquely identifies the device.	Windows, iOS
Serial Number	The device's serial number from the manufacturer.	Windows, iOS
Shared Device	If Yes, the device is shared by more than one user.	Windows, iOS
User Approved Enrollment	If Yes, then the device has user-approved enrollment, which lets admins manage certain security settings on the device.	Windows, iOS
Operating System	The operating system used on the device.	Windows, iOS
Operating System Version	The version of the operating system on the device.	Windows, iOS
Operating System Language	The language set for the operating system on the device.	Windows, iOS
Total Storage Space	The total storage space on the device (in gigabytes).	Windows, iOS
Free Storage Space	The unused storage space on the device (in gigabytes).	Windows, iOS
IMEI	The device's International Mobile Equipment Identity.	Windows, iOS, Android
MEID	The device's mobile equipment identifier.	Windows, iOS, Android
Manufacturer	The manufacturer of the device.	Windows, iOS, Android
Model	The model of the device.	Windows, iOS, Android
Phone Number	The phone number assigned to the device.	Windows, iOS, Android
Subscribe Carrier	The device's wireless carrier.	Windows, iOS, Android
Cellular Technology	The radio system used by the device.	Windows, iOS, Android
Wi-Fi MAC	The device's Media Access Control address.	Windows, iOS, Android
ICCID	The Integrated Circuit Card Identifier is a SIM card's unique identification number.	Windows, iOS, Android

Detail	Description	Platform
Enrolled Date	The date and time the device was enrolled in Intune.	Windows, iOS, Android
Last Contact	The date and time the device last connected to Intune.	Windows, iOS, Android
Activation Lock Bypass Code	The code that can be used to bypass the activation lock.	Windows, iOS, Android
Azure AD Registered	If Yes, the device is registered with Azure Directory.	Windows, iOS, Android
Compliance	The device's compliance state.	Windows, iOS, Android
EAS Activated	If Yes, then the device is synchronized with an Exchange mailbox.	Windows, iOS, Android
EAS Activation ID	The device's Exchange ActiveSync identifier.	Windows, iOS, Android
Supervised	If Yes, administrators have enhanced control over the device.	Windows, iOS, Android
Encrypted	If Yes, the data stored on the device is encrypted.	Windows, iOS, Android

Create a device compliance policy

After configuring compliance policy settings defaults, notifications, and scripts, it's time to create your compliance policies. Perform these steps to create a compliance policy that requires enrolled Android devices to enter a password of a specific length before access is granted to corporate resources:

1. Open **Microsoft Intune admin center** as a global administrator.
2. Select **Devices**, and then under **Policy**, click **Compliance policies**.
3. On the **Compliance policies** page, click **Create Policy**.
4. In the **Create a policy** window, under **Platform**, select **Android device administrator** and select **Create**.
5. On the **Android compliance policy** page, on the **Basics** tab, enter a name, add a description, and select **Next**.
6. On the **Compliance settings** tab, modify your required settings and then select **System Security**.
7. In the **System Security** area, click **Require** for the **Require a password to unlock mobile devices** option.
8. Select **At least numeric** for the **Required password type** option, as shown in Figure 2-27.
9. Enter **6** in the **Minimum password length** dialog.
10. Review the remaining security settings, and then click **Next** twice.

11. On the **Assignments** tab, choose the Android device or device group to assign the policy to, click **Select**, and then select **Next**.

12. Select **Create** to create the policy.

When you've successfully created the compliance policy and assigned it, the policy will appear in your list of device-compliance policies.

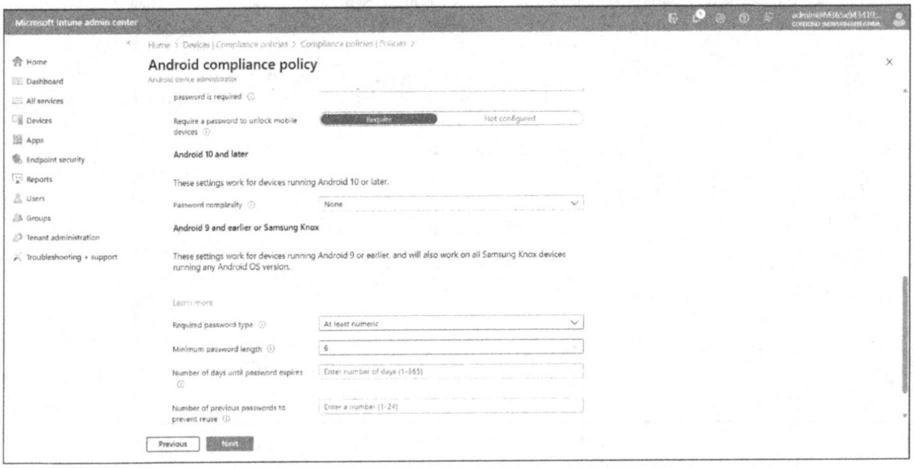

FIGURE 2-27 Configure Android Compliance Policy

Actions for noncompliant devices

An unenrolled device attempting to access corporate resources is deemed noncompliant, and access is blocked. If a user subsequently enrolls the device in Intune and re-attempts to access corporate resources, the Intune compliance policies are evaluated again, and the device might not be granted access based on the current policies in place.

The outcome for noncompliant but enrolled devices is typically to block access to company resources. However, you can configure actions for noncompliance as follows:

- **Mark device noncompliant** The noncompliant device can be allowed access to company resources if it is made compliant within a specified grace period. After the grace period has expired, noncompliant devices are blocked. Alternatively, the grace period can be set to zero, and the action will take effect immediately. Note that this is enabled by default and configured for immediate effect.

- **Send email to end user** You can customize an email notification sent to the user. You can customize the recipients, subject, and message body. Also, you can add a company logo and contact information. Lastly, you can add instructions for making the device compliant.

- **Add device to retire list** Noncompliant devices are added to a retirement list for administrator review and action.

As shown in Figure 2-28, you configure noncompliant actions when creating your compliance policy by using the **Actions for noncompliance** tab settings.

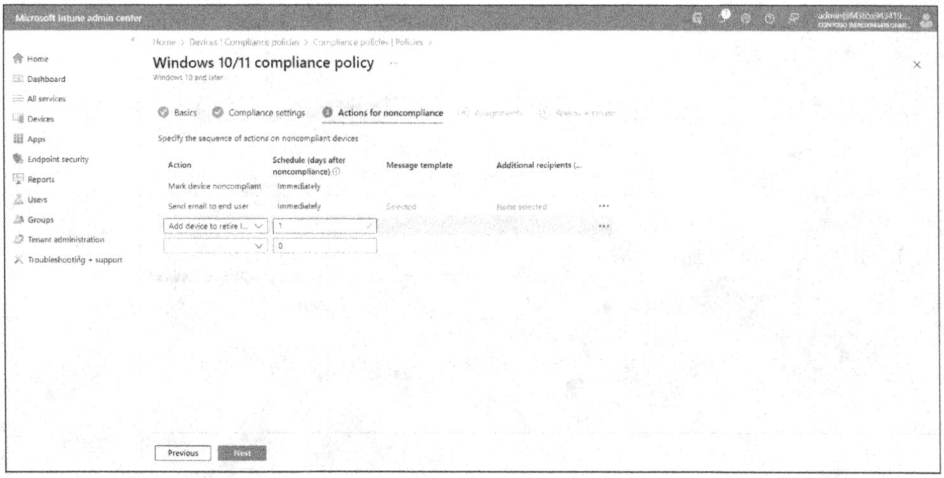

FIGURE 2-28 Configure actions for noncompliance.

Monitor device compliance

It's important to understand the compliance state of your devices. You can access this information through Intune in several places:

- The Microsoft Intune admin center's **Home** page displays device compliance warnings.
- The **Compliance status** tab of the **Devices | Overview** page, shown in Figure 2-29,
  displays a summary of compliance, including devices that are:
  - Compliant
  - In grace period
  - Not evaluated
  - Noncompliant

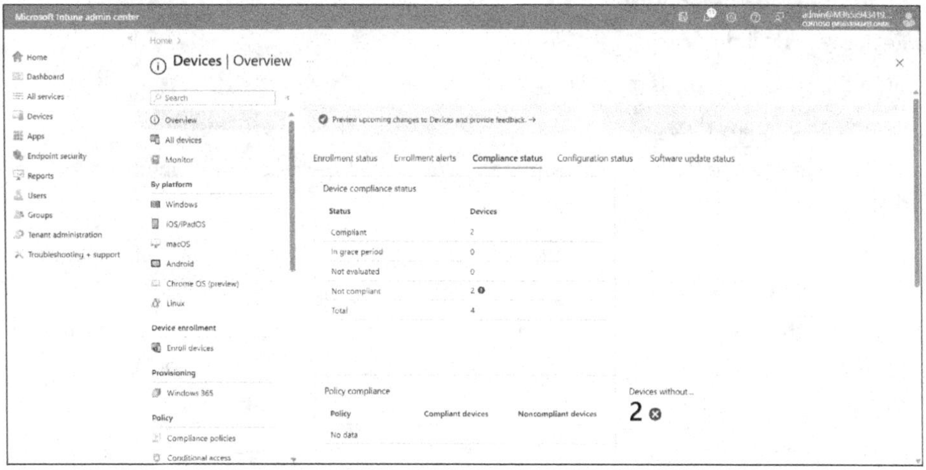

FIGURE 2-29 Reviewing device compliance

- Intune's **Reports** page. Under **Device management**, select **Device compliance**, as shown in Figure 2-30.

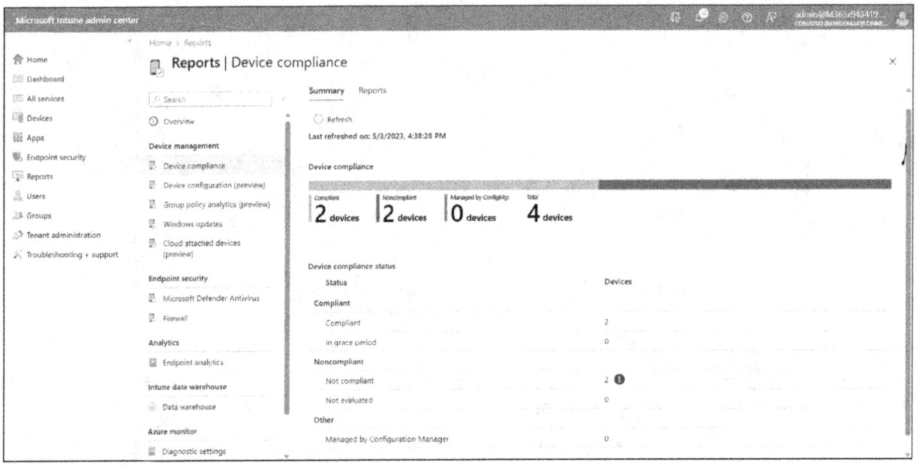

FIGURE 2-30 Reviewing device compliance reports

- The **Retire noncompliant devices** page on the **Compliance policies | Policies** page.

Reviewing the retire list for noncompliant devices

If devices are noncompliant, and your compliance policy configures an action for noncompliant devices to move them to the retire list, you must review the list periodically. You can do this from the **Compliance policies** folder in Intune; select **Retire noncompliant devices**.

Noncompliant devices are listed; choose one of the following actions:

- **Clear all devices retire state**
- **Retire all devices**
- **Clear selected devices retire state**
- **Retire selected devices**

A retirement action performs the following on a device:

- Removes company data
- Removes the device from the management scope of Intune (effectively unenrolls the device)

Troubleshoot compliance policies

Most problems with compliance policies relate to devices being marked as noncompliant when you were expecting otherwise. This is often an issue that relates to the incorrect configuration of:

- The compliance policy
- The device configuration profiles that are being applied might be expected to bring the devices into compliance

If you experience such problems, review the compliance policies and device configuration profiles. (We'll be talking about configuration profiles in the next chapter).

It's also important to understand how Intune applies and refreshes compliance policies. A compliance status will be determined whenever a device has a compliance policy assigned, as shown in Table 2-7.

TABLE 2-7 Compliance policy status

Status	Severity
Unknown	1
NotApplicable	2
Compliant	3
InGracePeriod	4
NonCompliant	5
Error	6

Notice that the severity increases when the device is in an error state or is noncompliant. The severity is reported to Microsoft Intune and used to determine access to organizational data.

When a device has multiple policies assigned, the device may have different compliance statuses. In these situations, Intune assigns a single resulting compliance status based on the highest severity level of all the policies assigned to that device.

> **NOTE WHEN POLICIES CONFLICT**
>
> If a device has two policies applied—one compliant, and the other noncompliant—the resulting device status will be noncompliant.

Devices connect to Intune periodically, and the compliance status is checked. The refresh cycle is the same as configuration profiles and can be found in Table 2-8. If a device has been recently enrolled, the compliance check-in runs more frequently during this initial period.

TABLE 2-8 Compliance policy refresh cycle

Platform	Initial check-in frequency	Ongoing refresh cycle
iOS/iPadOS	Every 15 minutes for 1 hour, and then every 8 hours	8 hours
macOS	Every 15 minutes for 1 hour, and then every 8 hours	8 hours
Android	Every 3 minutes for 15 minutes, followed by every 15 minutes for 2 hours, and then every 8 hours	8 hours

Platform	Initial check-in frequency	Ongoing refresh cycle
Windows 11 (enrolled as a device)	Every 3 minutes for 15 minutes, followed by every 15 minutes for 2 hours, and then every 8 hours	8 hours
Windows 8.1	Every 5 minutes for 15 minutes, followed by every 15 minutes for 2 hours, and then every 8 hours	8 hours

If users open the **Company Portal** app on their devices, they can immediately sync the device to check for new or updated policies. The Company Portal app also shows the compliance status of the managed device. For scenarios that include urgent compliance actions, such as **Wipe, Lock, Passcode Reset, New App Deployment, New Profile Deployment**, or **New Policy Deployment**, Intune immediately notifies the devices to perform a sync.

Implement Conditional Access policies that require a compliance status

Azure AD Conditional Access policies enable you to determine whether a user can connect their device to organizational apps and resources. Conditional access policies work alongside compliance policies. A condition is used to check if a device is compliant with something, such as whether the device is encrypted. If the device passes the compliance check, the action within the conditional access policy, such as accessing a particular app, is allowed.

When you create a conditional access policy, you must define and configure a number of properties. These fall into two sections:

- **Assignments** Determines who the policy targets.
- **Access controls** Determines whether the policy targets are blocked access, granted access, or granted access with additional conditions.

Within assignments, you must configure the following:

- **Name** Enter a name to identify the policy.
- **Users** These are the users or groups the policy targets. You can select options such as **All users** or **Specific users and groups**. If you choose the latter, you can select guests or external users, users with a specific RBAC role, or you can choose specific users or groups by name.
- **Cloud apps or actions** You can target all cloud apps or specific cloud apps. You can also target user actions or authentication contexts.
- **Conditions** These include user risk, sign-in risk, device platforms, locations, and client apps. You can define one, several, or all these to accurately target what are user is trying to do and from which device.

Within access controls, you must configure the following:

- **Grant** Choose between blocking access, allowing access, and allowing access with additional requirements. These additional requirements include
  - **Require MFA**
  - **Require authentication strength**

- **Require device to be marked as compliant**
- **Require Hybrid Azure AD–joined device**
- **Require approved client app**
- **Require app protection policy**

NOTE **CHOOSE ONE OR ALL**

When you define these controls, you can choose whether to require one or all of the selected controls.

- **Session** Enables you to control access based on session controls to enable limited experiences within specific cloud apps. These session controls include:
  - **Sign-in frequency**
  - **Persistent browser session**
  - **Use Conditional Access App Control**

Finally, you must choose whether to make your policy active by turning it on, leaving it off, or enabling it in reporting mode only.

To create a conditional access policy that requires device compliance, use the following procedure:

1. Open **Microsoft Intune admin center** (although you can also use Microsoft Entra).
2. In the navigation pane, select **Devices** and then click **Conditional access**.
3. On the **Conditional Access | Overview** page, click **Policies**.
4. On the **Conditional Access | Policies** page, click **New policy**.
5. On the **New** page, enter a **Name** for your policy.
6. Under **Users**, click **0 users and groups selected**. Then, as shown in Figure 2-31, select the appropriate users, groups, or role holders.

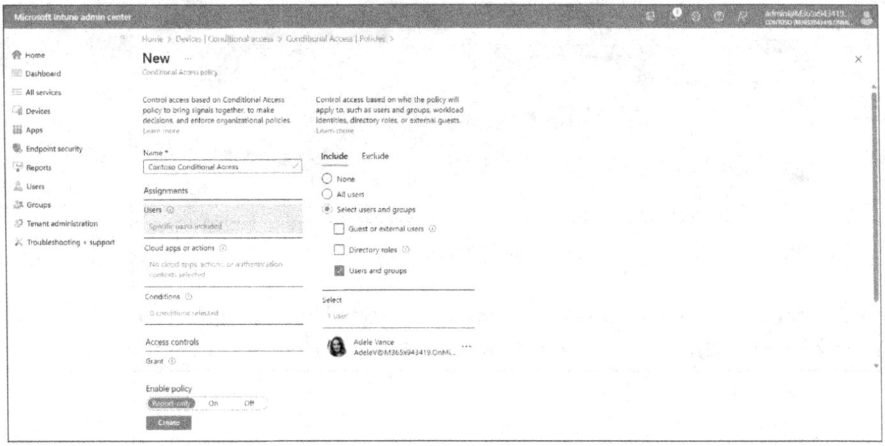

FIGURE 2-31 Selecting the target users for a conditional access policy

7. Under **Cloud apps or actions**, click **No cloud apps, actions, or authentication contexts selected**. Then, as shown in Figure 2-32, select the appropriate apps or actions.

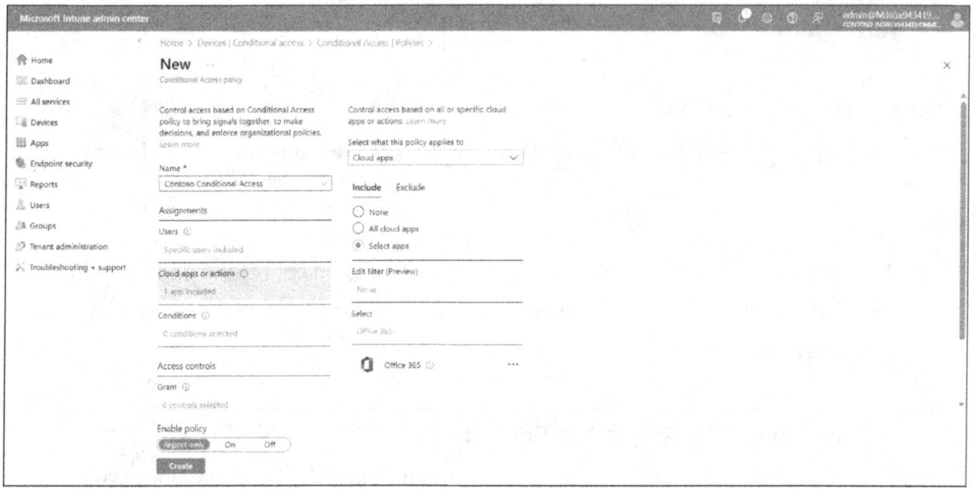

FIGURE 2-32 Defining the cloud apps or actions for a conditional access policy

8. Under **Conditions**, click **0 conditions selected**, and then define the necessary conditions, as displayed in Figure 2-33.

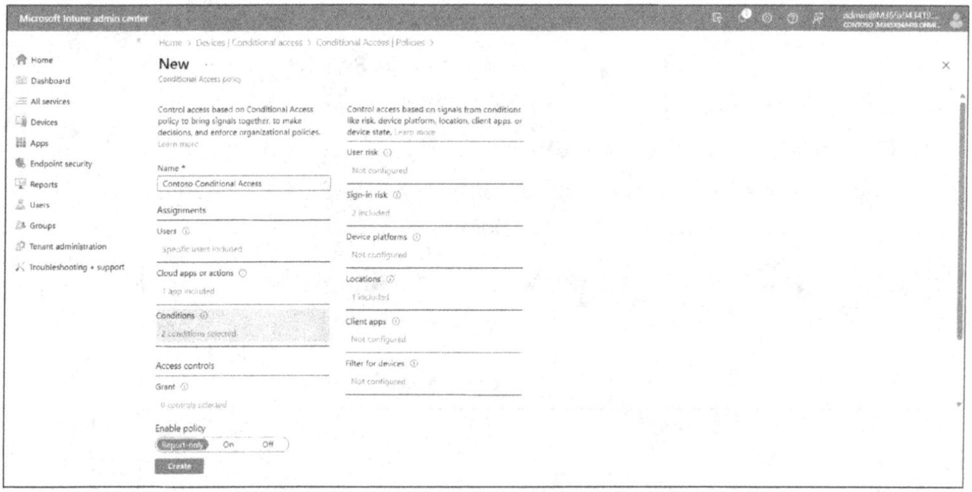

FIGURE 2-33 Defining the conditions for your conditional access policy

9. Then, under **Grant**, click **0 controls selected**. For compliance, as displayed in Figure 2-34, click **Grant access**, and then select **Require device to be marked as compliant**. Click **Select**.

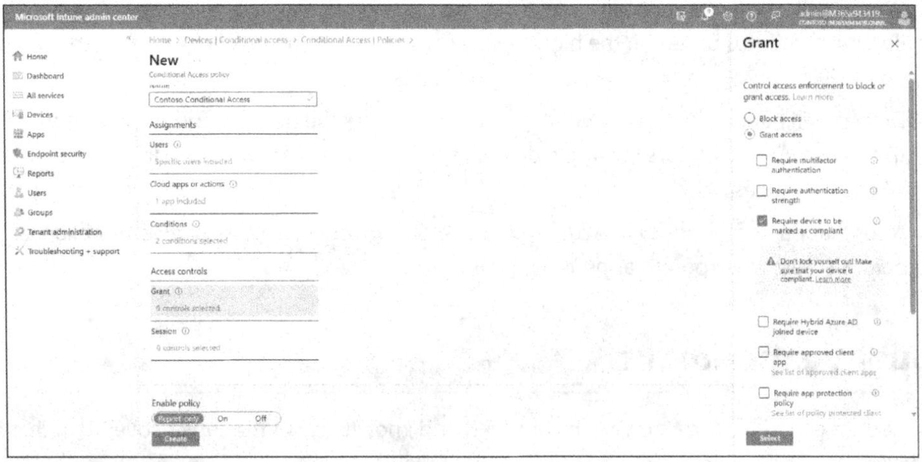

FIGURE 2-34 Determining access with your conditional access policy

10. Finally, if you're ready to enable the policy, select the **On** button beneath the **Enable policy** heading and click **Create**.

> **NOTE** **DON'T LOCK YOURSELF OUT**
> Creating restrictive policies in conditional access for the Global Administrator account requires caution. Ensure you don't configure settings that result in you locking yourself out.

Chapter summary

- Windows computers can be Azure AD-joined or Azure AD-registered. However, other operating systems can only be registered.
- You can configure Windows Hello for Business settings using either GPOs or Microsoft Intune.
- You create custom RBAC roles in Microsoft Entra but can assign roles in Microsoft Entra or Microsoft Intune.
- The Intune Connector for Active Directory enables Windows Autopilot to access AD DS to create computer objects to support hybrid join scenarios.
- LAPS enables you to manage your Windows devices' local administrator passwords. You use Intune to configure the settings using an Account protection policy.
- Compliance policies ensure devices meet compliance requirements, such as being encrypted, not being jailbroken, and using a password for device access.
- Noncompliant devices can be blocked from accessing resources or offered help to become compliant.

- When multiple device compliance policies are assigned to a device, Intune calculates a compliance status based on the highest severity level of all the policies assigned to the device.

- Devices will periodically check with Intune to determine the device's compliance status; this will be every six hours for Apple devices and every eight hours for Android and Windows devices.

- A conditional access policy in Azure AD can be configured to require device compliance before access to corporate apps and data is granted.

Thought experiment

In this thought experiment, demonstrate your skills and knowledge of the topics covered in this chapter. You can find the answers in the section that follows.

Scenario 1

Contoso has a significant on-premises infrastructure. However, their IT department is in the process of planning the migration to the Microsoft cloud. For a significant period, Contoso's computer needed to be hybrid-joined.

As an IT consultant for Contoso, answer the following questions:

1. How can staff in the IT department enable the hybrid joining of existing computers? What would IT staff need to do?

2. How can newly purchased computers be hybrid-joined? What would IT staff need to do?

Scenario 2

Contoso operates in a highly regulated industry. They also work with international customers and have offices worldwide, including in Europe. Contoso utilizes Microsoft 365 Enterprise E5 licensing across all devices.

As an IT consultant for Contoso, answer the following questions:

1. What regulations should Contoso review to ensure compliance?

2. What mechanisms should Contoso deploy on enrolled devices to ensure that data is always safeguarded?

3. What measures are available to Contoso if a user tries to access corporate resources from a noncompliant device?

4. Management wants the accounting staff to access the payroll and other confidential financial-related information from within the physical accounting department. How should you implement this requirement?

Thought experiment answers

This section contains the solution to the thought experiment. Each answer explains why the answer choice is correct.

Scenario 1

1. IT staff have two choices for the hybrid joining of existing computers. They could implement Azure AD Cloud Sync or Azure AD Connect Sync. With Azure AD Cloud Sync, an agent is installed on an on-premises computer. Then, synchronization settings are configured and managed in Intune. With Azure AD Connect Sync, the Azure AD Connect program is downloaded and installed on an on-premises server computer. Then, synchronization settings are configured and managed within the Azure AD Connect program in the on-premises context.

2. Newly purchased computers can be hybrid joined by using Windows Autopilot. The IT staff must create an Autopilot profile using the Hybrid Azure AD–joined setting. Next, the IT staff must deploy and configure the Intune Connector for Active Directory.

Scenario 2

1. Contoso should review these regulations: HIPAA (Health Insurance Portability and Accountability Act of 1996), Sarbanes Oxley Act, Gramm Leach Bliley Act, and GDPR (General Data Protection Regulation).

2. Answers may vary. Control of devices can be implemented by using device Compliance Policies to control devices and restrict their usage when accessing corporate data. Specific device compliance policies, such as device encryption, could also be implemented.

3. IT should configure email notifications sent to the user to inform them that the device is attempting to use a noncompliant device to access corporate data. This notification can contain instructions guiding the user on what steps they should take to bring the device into compliance. IT could also implement conditional access policies that require compliance; such a policy could block access from noncompliant devices.

4. IT can configure a network location-based compliance policy to ensure that the accounting devices can only access corporate data from specific network IP addresses.

CHAPTER 3

Manage, maintain, and protect devices

A critical part of an endpoint administrator's job is managing, maintaining, and protecting their users' devices. As an endpoint administrator, you can use several Windows 11 components and Microsoft Intune features to manage your organization's devices.

MDM enables the administration of remote mobile devices across multiple platforms. Microsoft Intune supports MDM for managing remote mobile devices. However, before managing devices, you must enroll them in Intune. After enrolling devices, you can perform various management tasks using Intune on your mobile devices, as shown in Table 3-1.

TABLE 3-1 Management tasks

Category	Details
App management	<ul><li>App deployment</li><li>App configuration</li><li>App restrictions</li><li>Mobile application management</li></ul>
Device security and configuration	<ul><li>Configuration profiles</li><li>Password management</li><li>Remote wipe and lock</li><li>Custom policies</li></ul>
Company resource access	<ul><li>VPN profiles</li><li>Wi-Fi profiles</li><li>Email profiles</li><li>Certificate profiles</li><li>Conditional access policies</li></ul>
Inventory and reporting	<ul><li>Hardware inventory</li><li>Application inventory</li><li>Reporting</li></ul>
Endpoint protection	<ul><li>Microsoft Defender Application Guard</li><li>Microsoft Defender Credential Guard</li><li>Microsoft Defender Exploit Guard</li><li>Windows Defender Application ControlWindows Defender Firewall</li><li>Microsoft Defender SmartScreen</li><li>BitLocker Encryption</li><li>Windows Security Center</li><li>Microsoft Defender for Endpoint</li><li>Windows Information Protection</li></ul>

This chapter explores many of those management tasks.

Skills covered in this chapter:

- Skill 3.1: Manage the device lifecycle in Intune
- Skill 3.2: Manage device configuration for all supported device platforms by using Intune
- Skill 3.3: Monitor devices
- Skill 3.4: Manage device updates for all supported device platforms by using Intune
- Skill 3.5: Implement endpoint protection for all supported device platforms

Skill 3.1: Manage the device lifecycle in Intune

In an organization, computers operate within the context of a device lifecycle. This lifecycle consists of a number of stages. Typically, you purchase new devices, deploy operating systems to those devices, and then add the devices to the scope of a management system.

Thereafter, you'll use the management system to configure those devices, including deploying apps and updates to them. The management system can provide reporting capabilities and potentially the ability to provide remote help to users of the devices. When the computers can no longer run the required operating system and apps, the devices are retired and removed from the management scope.

You might use Endpoint Configuration Manager to manage this device lifecycle in an on-premises context. In the cloud, you use Microsoft Intune.

> **This skill covers how to:**
> - Configure enrollment settings
> - Configure automatic and bulk enrollment, including Windows, Apple, and Android
> - Enroll devices
> - Configure policy sets
> - Restart, retire, or wipe devices

Configure enrollment settings in Microsoft Intune

You enable MDM for devices by enrolling them. Currently, Microsoft Intune supports the following device types for enrollment:

- Apple iOS 14.0 and newer
- Apple iPadOS 14.0 and newer

- macOS 11.0 and newer
- Linux (Ubuntu Desktop 22.04 with GNOME interface or newer)
- Android 8.0 (and newer)
- Android Enterprise
- Android open source project devices (AOSP)
- Windows 10/11
- Windows 10/11 on Windows 365
- Windows 10 LTSC
- Windows 10 Teams
- Surface Hub

The enrollment process is different for each platform, and each platform has a specific set of requirements, as described in Table 3-2.

TABLE 3-2 Enrollment requirements

Device platform	Enrollment requirements
- Apple iOS and iPadOS - Apple macOS	Obtain an Apple Push Notification service certificate. This enables Microsoft Intune to communicate securely with iOS devices. Download each device's Microsoft Intune Company Portal app from the Apple store.
- Android - Android Enterprise	Download each device's Microsoft Intune Company Portal app from the Google Play store.
- Windows 10/11 - Windows 10/11 on Windows 365 - Windows 10 LTSC - Windows 10 Teams - Surface Hub	There are no special requirements, and Direct enrollment is usually possible in the following ways: - During out-the-box-experience (OOBE) on a new computer - With Windows Autopilot - Following a sign-in to a connected app, such as Microsoft Teams - Manually via the Settings app

For Windows devices, there is an existing trust relationship between the device operating system and Intune; therefore, you can configure and enable automatic enrollment. The following list provides a high-level explanation of the enrollment process for each platform:

- **Windows 11**   If users sign in to the device using their corporate credentials, their account is added to Azure Active Directory (Azure AD), and the device is then managed with Intune.

- **iOS/iPadOS and macOS**   An MDM Push certificate is required for Intune to manage iOS/iPadOS and macOS devices. Install the Company Portal app from the Apple Store, open the app, and follow the Enrollment wizard.

- **iOS/iPadOS Company-owned devices**   For bulk enrollments, you can use the following methods:
  - Apple's Device Enrollment Program (DEP)
  - Apple School Manager
  - Apple Configurator Setup Assistant enrollment
  - Apple Configurator direct enrollment
  - Intune Device Enrollment Manager account
- **Android devices**   Users must enroll their devices by downloading the Intune Company Portal app from Google Play.

> *NOTE*   **ANNUAL CERTIFICATE RENEWAL**
>
> The Apple MDM push certificate is valid for one year and must be renewed annually to maintain iOS and macOS device management. Enrolled Apple devices cannot be contacted or managed if your certificate expires.

To enable Device Enrollment, select **Devices** in the Microsoft Intune admin center's navigation pane, and then select **Enroll Devices**, as shown in Figure 3-1.

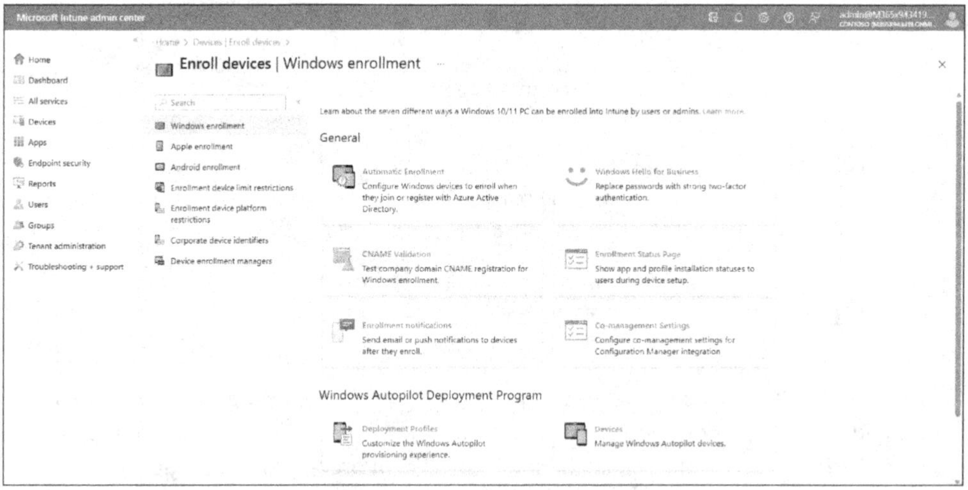

FIGURE 3-1 Configuring Device Enrollment

You can then select from the available options in the navigation pane of the **Enroll Devices** blade. These options are described in Table 3-3.

TABLE 3-3 Enrollment Configuration options

Option	Description
Windows Enrollment	From this blade, you can access the following settings to configure Windows Device Enrollment: ■ **Automatic Enrollment** Configure Windows devices to enroll automatically when they join or register with Azure AD. ■ **Windows Hello For Business** Replace passwords with two-factor authentication. ■ **CNAME Validation** Verify that your company's custom domain name registration is successful. ■ **Enrollment Status Page** Configure the app and profile installation status to users during their device setup. ■ **Enrollment Notifications** Configure email and push notifications to be sent to users after they enroll. ■ **Co-management Settings** Configure co-management settings to integrate with on-premises Configuration Manager. ■ **Deployment Profiles** Configure how provisioning works with Windows Autopilot. ■ **Devices** Manage and configure devices deployed through Windows Autopilot. ■ **Intune Connector for Active Directory** Configure the behavior of enrolled hybrid Azure AD–joined devices.
Apple Enrollment	From this node, you can configure the Apple MDM Push Certificate. You can also configure bulk enrollment methods for iOS devices.
Android Enrollment	By default, all Android devices can be enrolled as conventional devices. Link your Managed Google Play account to Intune from this blade. You can also configure Android Enrollment Profiles: ■ Personally-owned Devices With Work Profile ■ Corporate-Owned Dedicated Devices ■ Corporate-Owned, Fully Managed User Devices ■ Corporate-Owned Devices With Work Profile
Enrollment device limit restrictions	You can create device platform restrictions to determine which operating system versions are permitted. A default device platform restriction, assigned to **All Users**, allows users to enroll any device platform. You can modify this default restriction (but you cannot delete it) or create additional restrictions. Again, a device must comply with the highest-priority platform restriction assigned to its user.
Enrollment device platform restrictions	You can create device platform restrictions to determine which operating system versions are permitted. A default device platform restriction, assigned to **All Users**, allows users to enroll any device platform. You can modify this default restriction (but you cannot delete it) or create additional restrictions. Again, a device must comply with the highest-priority platform restriction assigned to its user.
Corporate Device Identifiers	You can enter (or upload) Device Identifiers for corporate-owned devices. The identifier might be an IMEI number or a serial number (for Android, iOS, and macOS only).
Device Enrollment Managers	Add one or more users with the ability to enroll multiple devices.

There are a number of other settings that relate to enrollment. These are described in Table 3-4.

TABLE 3-4 Other enrollment settings

Terms and Conditions	■ You can access terms and conditions from the Tenant Administration node in Intune.
	■ Create and configure Terms And Conditions statements for enrolled devices. These are messages users see during Device Enrollment.
	■ It's possible to configure multiple terms and conditions and assign them to different groups, such as your organization's departments.
Device Categories	■ You can access device categories from the Devices node in Intune. You can then create Device Categories from which users must choose during Device Enrollment. You can filter reports and create Azure Active Directory device groups based on Device Categories.
	■ Be aware that the user is able to select any of the categories you define, and there's no way to verify that the user has selected a suitable and accurate category. However, you can change the selected device category in the device properties in Intune.

Typically, you'll configure the following settings to help your users enroll their devices:

■ Azure AD company branding and Azure AD device settings

■ Terms and conditions

■ Enrollment restrictions

■ Device categories

■ Configure device identifiers

■ Enrollment managers

Configure Azure AD company branding and Azure AD device settings

Users need to be able to easily identify the organization to which they're connecting their devices during enrollment. If you configure company branding, users can review graphics and text displayed during enrollment, enabling this identification.

To configure company branding, in the Microsoft Entra admin center, perform the following procedure:

1. Expand **Azure Active Directory** in the navigation pane.

2. Click **Show more**, and then expand **User experiences**.

3. Click **Company branding**.

4. On the **Default sign-in** tab, click **Edit**.

5. In the **Edit default sign-in experience** wizard shown in Figure 3-2, click through the tabs to define the graphics and text displayed when users sign in to enroll their devices.

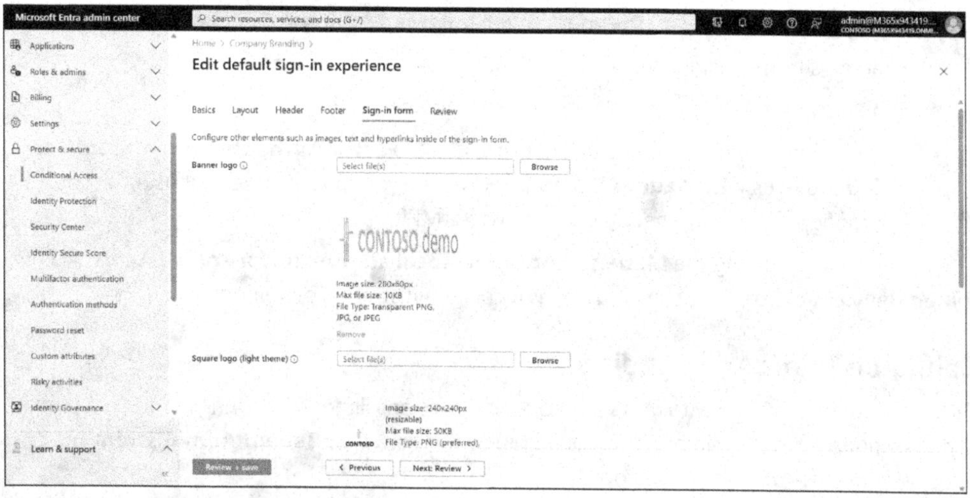

FIGURE 3-2 Configuring Device Enrollment

In addition, it's usual for Windows computers to use automatic enrollment. This process requires several Azure AD settings to be configured before users start enrolling their devices. To configure these settings, in the Microsoft Entra admin center, perform the following procedure:

1. Expand **Azure Active Directory** in the navigation pane.
2. Expand **Devices**, and select **All devices**.
3. Click **Device settings** and ensure that the Azure AD join and registration settings are enabled, as shown in Figure 3-3.

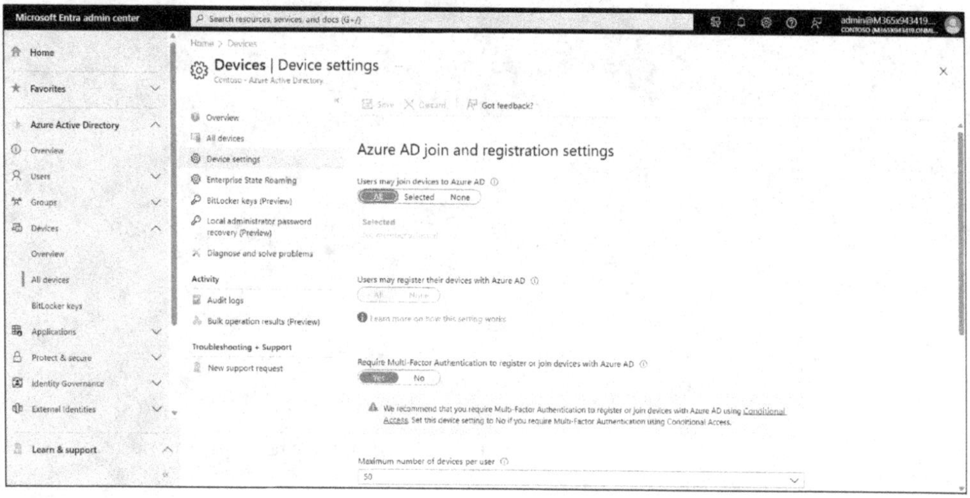

FIGURE 3-3 Enabling Azure AD join and register

In most situations, you'll want to configure the following settings:

- Enable Users may join devices to Azure AD
- Enable Users may register their devices with Azure AD
- For additional security, enable the **Require Multi-Factor Authentication to register or join devices with Azure AD** setting. However, you must ensure that users' accounts are configured with the necessary settings for MFA.

Also, consider selecting the **Manage Additional local administrators on all Azure AD joined devices** link to add specified users as local administrators on joined devices.

Configure Terms And Conditions

Terms and conditions display to users during their device enrollment. To configure custom terms and conditions, from the Microsoft Intune admin center, select the **Tenant Administration** node, and then use the following procedure:

1. Select **Terms and conditions**, and click **Create** on the **Terms and conditions** blade.
2. On the **Tenant admin | Terms and conditions** page, enter a name in the **Name** box.
3. In the **Description** box, enter a meaningful description and select **Next**.
4. On the **Terms** tab in Figure 3-4, enter a title in the **Title** box that displays to users that review your terms and conditions. Then enter the **Terms and conditions** and a **Summary of terms**. Then select **Next**.

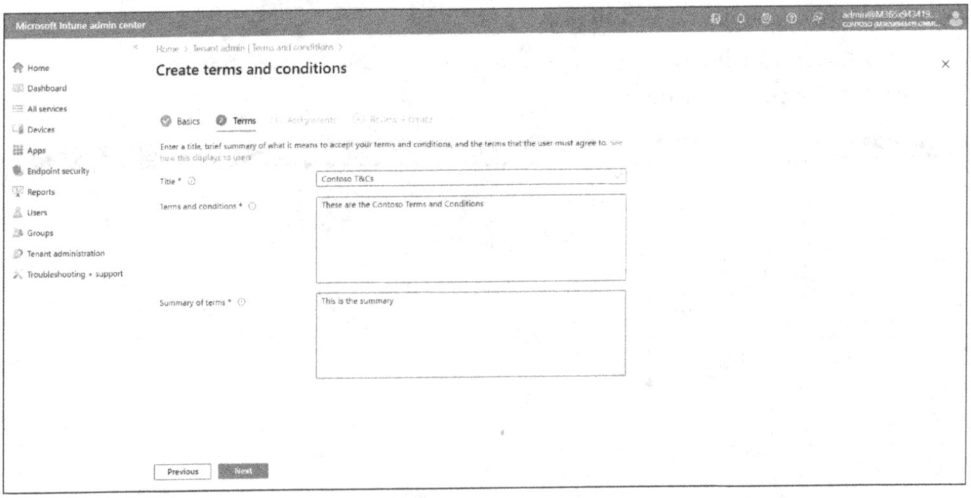

FIGURE 3-4 Defining terms and conditions for enrolling devices

5. On the **Assignments** tab, configure the groups to whom the terms and conditions should be assigned and select **Next**.
6. On the **Review + Create** tab, select **Save**.

Your terms and conditions will now display during enrollment.

Configure Enrollment Restrictions

Enrollment Restrictions determine the number and types of devices users can enroll to Intune. To configure Enrollment device limit restrictions, open the Microsoft Intune admin center and use the following procedure:

1. In the navigation pane, select **Devices** > **Enroll devices**.
2. Select **Enrollment device limit restrictions**, as shown in Figure 3-5.
3. Click **Create restriction**.
4. In the **Create restriction** wizard, enter a **Name** and **Description** and click **Next**.
5. In the **Device limit** dropdown, select the relevant number (between 1 and 15) and click **Next**.
6. Select optional scope tags from the **Scope** tab, and then select **Next**.
7. On the **Assignments** tab, assign the restriction as usual and select **Next**.
8. On the **Review + create** tab, select **Create**.

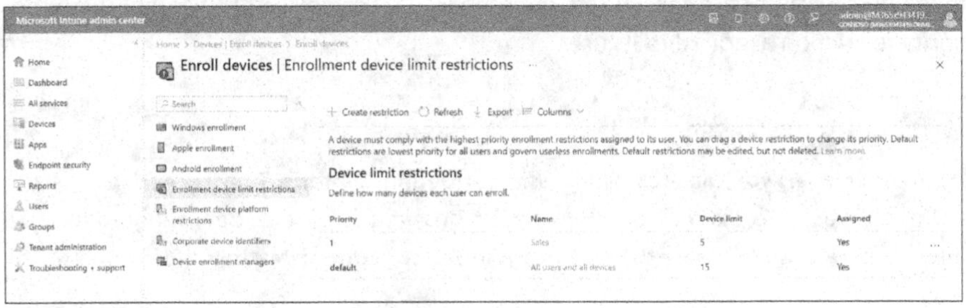

FIGURE 3-5 Reviewing enrollment device limit restrictions

To create a device platform restriction, use the following procedure:

1. In the navigation pane, select **Devices** > **Enroll devices**.
2. Select **Enrollment device platform restrictions**.
3. Select the appropriate tab:
   - Android restrictions
   - Windows restrictions
   - MacOS restrictions
   - iOS restrictions
4. Click **Create restriction**.
5. In the **Create restriction** wizard, enter a **Name** and **Description** and click **Next**.
6. On the **Platform settings** tab shown in Figure 3-6, configure the following, and click **Next**:
   - **MDM** Choose **Allow** or **Block**.
   - **Allow min/max range** Enter the operating system version numbers for the platform selected.
   - **Personally owned devices** Choose **Allow** or **Block**.

7. On the **Scope** tab, select optional scope tags, and then select **Next**.

8. On the **Assignments** tab, assign the restriction as usual, and then select **Next**.

9. On the **Review + create** tab, select **Create**.

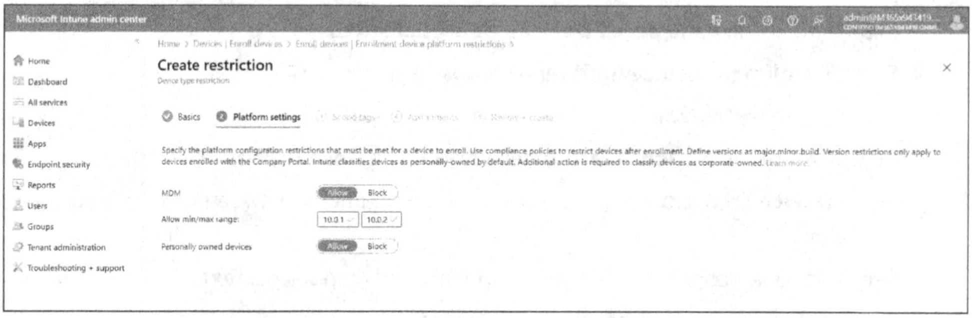

FIGURE 3-6 Configuring a Windows platform restriction

When multiple restrictions are configured, remember that the device must comply with the highest priority restriction assigned to its user.

> **NOTE WHAT ARE SCOPE TAGS?**
>
> Scope tags are text labels you can create and assign throughout Intune. They're used in conjunction with role-based access control. They can also be very useful to target configuration settings more accurately. You create the scope tags in **Tenant administration** under **Roles > Scope** tags.

Configure Device Categories

Categories help you when you are using reporting tools. Users select a suitable category during enrollment. To configure device categories, from the Microsoft Intune admin center, select the **Devices** node, and then use the following procedure:

1. On the **Devices** blade, select **Device categories**.

2. Select **Create device category**.

3. On the **Create device category** blade, enter a suitable name in the **Name** box.

4. In the **Description** box, enter a meaningful description of your category.

5. Select **Next**, and on the **Scope** tab, enter any scope tags and select **Next**.

6. On the **Review + create** tab, select **Create**.

After you have created all the appropriate **Device categories**, as shown in Figure 3-7, users must select from the listed categories when they enroll devices. You can modify the device category for an enrolled device from the **Properties** page in the device details for a selected device.

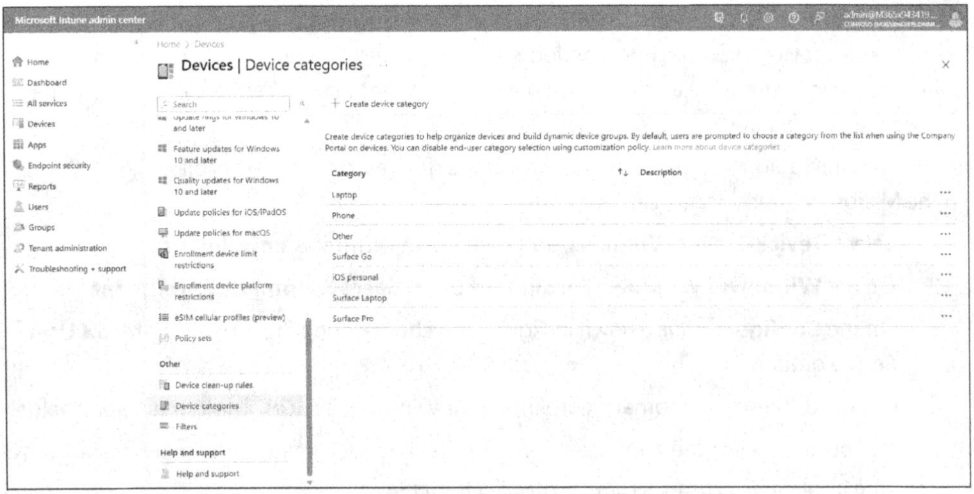

FIGURE 3-7 Defining device categories

You can also use these categories to create dynamic groups in Azure AD. Dynamic groups have a membership based on the result of a query. For example, you could create a dynamic group called "Kiosk device" that had a membership based on the result of the following query:

```
device.deviceCategory -eq "Kiosk device"
```

Configure Device Identifiers

Device identifiers enable you to identify specific devices as being corporate-owned devices. This is done by entering the serial number or IMEI into Intune. To configure device identifiers, from the Microsoft Intune admin center, select the **Devices** node and use the following procedure:

1. Select **Enroll devices** and then select **Corporate device identifiers**.
2. Select **Add** and select either **Upload CSV file** or **Enter manually**.
3. If you select **Upload CSV file**, specify the identifier type (choose between **Serial Number** or **IMEI**) in the CSV file. Browse to the CSV file location, select the CSV file for upload, and select **Add**.
4. If you choose to manually enter the identifiers, for each identifier, select the type (choose between **Serial Number** or **IMEI**), enter the identifier and details information for each device, and select **Add**.

Configure automatic and bulk enrollment

After configuring Device Enrollment settings, you must enable Device Enrollment before you can start enrolling devices. Precisely what you must do varies depending on the device types you want to be able to enroll.

Windows automatic enrollment

For Windows devices, you can now configure automatic enrollment if desired. For non-Windows devices, there are additional preparation steps required. These are described in the subsequent procedures.

To configure automatic enrollment for Windows devices, complete the following procedure in the Microsoft Intune admin center:

1. Select **Devices**, select **Windows**, and then select **Windows enrollment**.

2. On the **Windows | Windows Enrollment** page, select **Automatic Enrollment**.

3. On the **Configure** page, shown in Figure 3-8, choose one of the following **MDM User Scope** options:

    - **None**   Prevent automatic enrollment for Windows devices. This is the default value.

    - **Some**   Specify the appropriate groups that have automatic enrollment permissions.

    - **All**   Enable all users to automatically enroll their devices.

4. If you selected **Some**, then click the **No groups selected** link. Browse and select the necessary groups that will have automatic enrollment privileges.

5. Click **Save**.

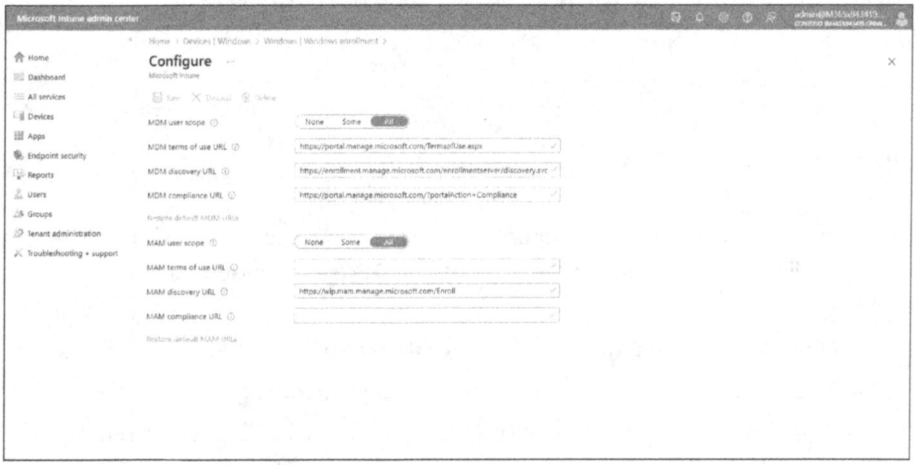

FIGURE 3-8 Enabling automatic Windows enrollment

Bulk enrollment

If you want to enroll a large number of devices in an enterprise scenario, you can use a device enrollment manager (DEM) account in Microsoft Intune. The DEM is a special account in Microsoft Intune that allows you to enroll up to 1,000 devices. (Standard users can manage and enroll up to 15 devices.) For security reasons, the DEM user should not also be an Intune administrator. Each enrolled device requires a single Intune license. By default, no device enrollment account user is present in Microsoft Intune.

Typically, these DEM accounts might be IT personnel. To configure enrollment managers, from the Microsoft Intune admin center, select the **Device enrollment** node and use the following procedure:

1. From the **Enroll devices** page in Intune, click **Device enrollment managers**.

2. Click **Add**, and then enter the email address of the enrollment managers you want to specify and click **Add**.

The complete list of **Device enrollment managers** is displayed, as shown in Figure 3-9.

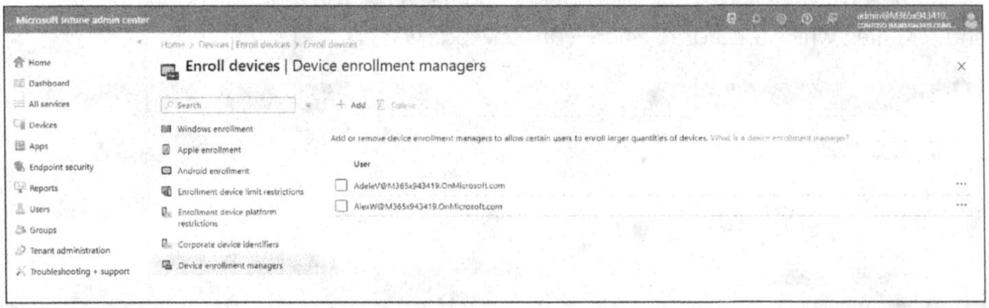

FIGURE 3-9 Defining Device Enrollment Managers

NEED MORE REVIEW?   ENROLL DEVICES USING DEVICE ENROLLMENT MANAGER

For more information on the DEM in Microsoft Intune—together with example scenarios and limitations of devices that are enrolled with a DEM account—visit *https://learn.microsoft.com/ mem/intune/enrollment/device-enrollment-manager-enroll*.

Another possible solution to bulk enrolment is to create and distribute a provisioning package. You use the Windows Configuration Designer, part of the Windows Assessment and Deployment Kit (Windows ADK). You can download Windows ADK from Microsoft and install it on a workstation in IT.

NOTE   WINDOWS ADK DOWNLOAD

Ensure that you download the appropriate version of the Windows ADK for your version of Windows—specifically, the version installed on your management workstation.

Use the following procedure to create a provisioning package for enrollment:

1. Open **Windows Configuration Designer**, and on the home page, select the **Provision desktop devices** tile.

2. In the New Project wizard, on the **Enter project details** page, enter a **Name**, and, optionally, a **Description**.

3. Click **Finish**. A new tab in Windows Configuration Designer opens.

4. On the new tab, enter the required information on the **Set up device** and **Set up network** pages.

5. Then, on the **Account management** page, in the **Manage organization/school accounts** section, select **Enroll in Azure AD**.

6. Select **Get Bulk Token**. You are prompted to sign in to Microsoft 365. Enter a device enrollment manager's credentials.

7. On the **Account management** page displayed in Figure 3-10, click **Next**.

8. Configure any desired settings on the **Add applications** and **Add certificates** pages, and then on the **Finish** page, select **Create**.

You can now distribute and install the provisioning package. You must distribute the .PPKG and .CAT files, which are stored where your package was created.

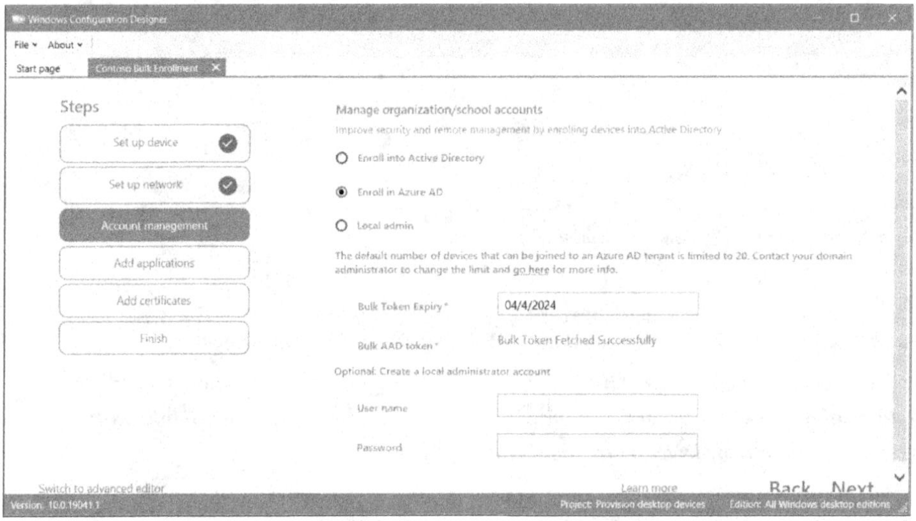

FIGURE 3-10 Performing bulk enrollment

Enroll devices

For individual computers, there are several ways to enroll devices, depending on the device's operating system and state. These are described in this section.

Enroll Windows devices

There are several different ways to enroll devices in Intune. These are:

- **Add a work or school account** Use this method to register the device with Azure AD or join the device to Azure AD. If you have an Azure AD Premium subscription and you have enabled Windows Automatic Enrollment, this method also enrolls the device in Intune. This method is user-initiated.

- **Enroll only in device management** Select this option if you want to enroll your device(s) in Intune only, without registering or joining to Azure AD. This might be appropriate if your organization does not have an Azure AD premium subscription. This method is user-initiated.

- **Azure AD join during OOBE**   This method is very similar in terms of the end result to what happens when you perform an Add a work or school account procedure. However, the process is launched and managed during the device's initial setup; this initial setup is referred to as out-of-box experience (OOBE). This is a user-initiated method.

- **Azure AD join using Windows Autopilot**   This enrollment method works similarly to the preceding method; however, using Windows Autopilot enables you to partially or completely automate the OOBE process for your users. Again, the process is launched and managed through OOBE; your Windows Autopilot settings will determine the precise level of user interaction. You can choose between user-driven mode and self-deploying; these options are configured as part of the Windows Autopilot deployment profile. This is the preferred method of enrolling using OOBE because it is a more managed approach. However, it assumes that your organization has an Azure AD premium subscription and that you have enabled Windows Automatic Enrollment.

- **Enroll in MDM only using a device enrollment manager**   This method is similar to adding a work or school account method, as described above. However, rather than use a standard user account to enroll in your organization's MDM, you use a Device Enrollment Manager Account, which can enroll up to 1,000 devices.

- **Azure AD Join using bulk enrollment**   This method enables you to use provisioning packages to enroll a large number of devices. You create a provisioning package using Windows Configuration Designer and apply it either during OOBE or by distributing and running the package after a device has completed its initial setup process.

The following sections discuss some of these methods in more detail.

Add a work or school account

To enroll a Windows device using this method, use the following procedure:

1. Enable Windows Automatic Enrollment for all users or an appropriate group to whom the designated account (used in step 6) belongs.

2. Sign in to your Windows 11 computer and open **Settings**.

3. Select **Accounts**.

4. Select the **Access work or school** tab.

5. Click **Connect**.

6. On the **Set up a work or school account** page, perform one of the following actions:

   - **To register the device with Azure AD and enroll the device in Intune**   In the **Microsoft Account** dialog shown in Figure 3-11, type the organizational email address in the **Email Address** box and select **Next**.

   - **To join the device to Azure AD and enroll the device in Intune**   In the Microsoft Account dialog, select Join this device to Azure Active Directory. Then, enter the organizational email address in the Sign in dialog and select Next.

7. When prompted, enter the user's password, and select **Sign In**.

8. If prompted, set up additional account verification options, such as a text message confirmation.

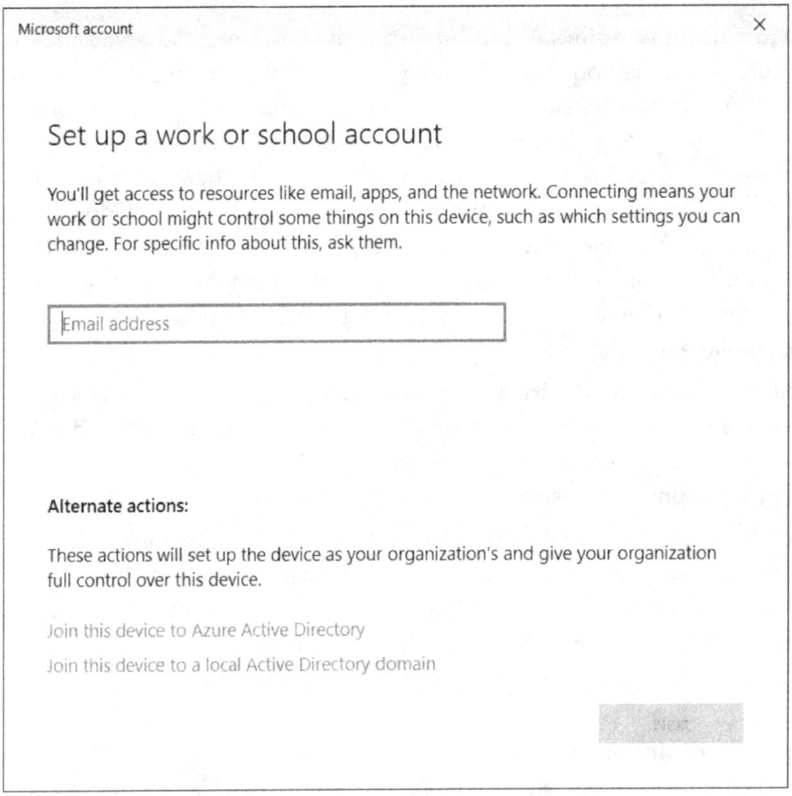

FIGURE 3-11 Enrolling a Windows 11 device with a work or school account

9. If configured, your **Terms and Conditions** are displayed. Select **Accept**.

10. If configured, your user is prompted to select a device category.

11. In the **Make sure this is your organization** dialog, click **Join**.

12. Your device is registered with/joined to your organization and enrolled in Intune. Click **Done** when prompted.

You can verify that the device is properly registered and enrolled from the Microsoft Entra admin center. Use the following procedure:

1. Sign in as Global Administrator and navigate to the **Devices | All devices** node.

2. The new device should be listed. The **Join Type** will be either **Azure AD joined** or **Azure AD registered**, as shown in Figure 3-12, depending on the option you selected during enrollment. The **MDM** column should display **Microsoft Intune** if the device is enrolled in Intune.

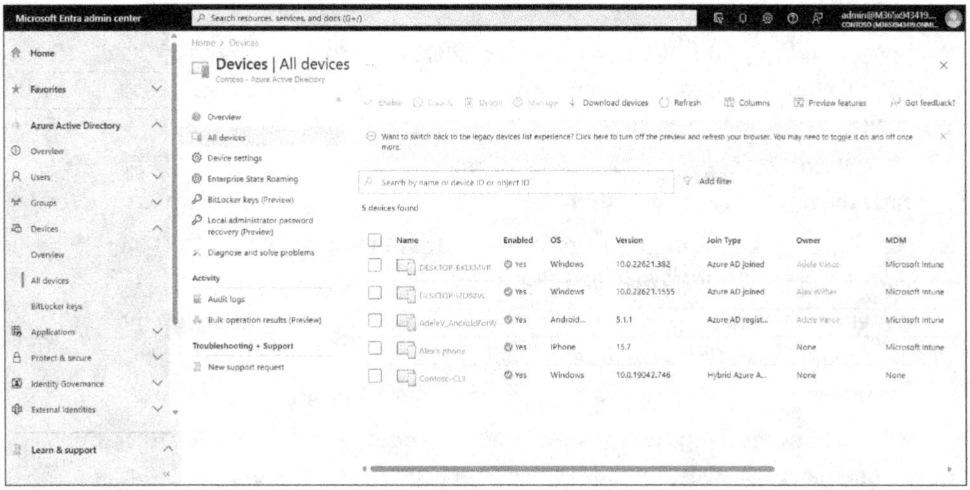

FIGURE 3-12 Verifying the presence of the newly enrolled device

You can also review the device information using the Microsoft Intune admin center.

Enroll in MDM only

If you want to enroll a Windows device using this method, use the following procedure:

1. Enable Windows Automatic Enrollment for all users or an appropriate group to whom the designated account (used in step 6) belongs.

2. Sign in to your Windows 11 computer and open **Settings**.

3. Select **Accounts**.

4. Select the **Access work or school** tab.

5. Select **Enroll only in device management**.

6. In the **Microsoft account** window, enter the organizational email account.

7. The **Connecting to a service** window opens. Enter the user's password and select **Sign in**.

8. In the **Setting up your device** window, select **Got it**. Your device is enrolled in Intune.

You can verify that the device is properly enrolled from the Microsoft Intune admin center. Use the following procedure:

1. Sign in as Global Administrator and navigate to the **Devices** node.

2. Select **All Devices**. The new device should be listed.

Azure AD Join during OOBE

If the device is running either Windows 11 Professional or Windows 11 Enterprise, OOBE presents the setup process for company-owned devices. To enroll a Windows device using this method, use the following procedure:

1. Start the new device and allow the setup process to begin. When prompted, on the **Is this the right country or region?** page, select your country or region, and click **Yes**.

2. On the **Is this the right keyboard layout or input method?** page, select the appropriate keyboard layout, and click **Yes**.

3. When prompted, if you want to add an additional keyboard layout, follow the steps to do so. Otherwise, click **Skip**. Your computer checks for updates.

4. If prompted, review the License Agreement and click **Accept**.

5. On the **Let's set things up for your work or school** page shown in Figure 3-13, enter your organizational user account in the **Sign in** box and click **Next**.

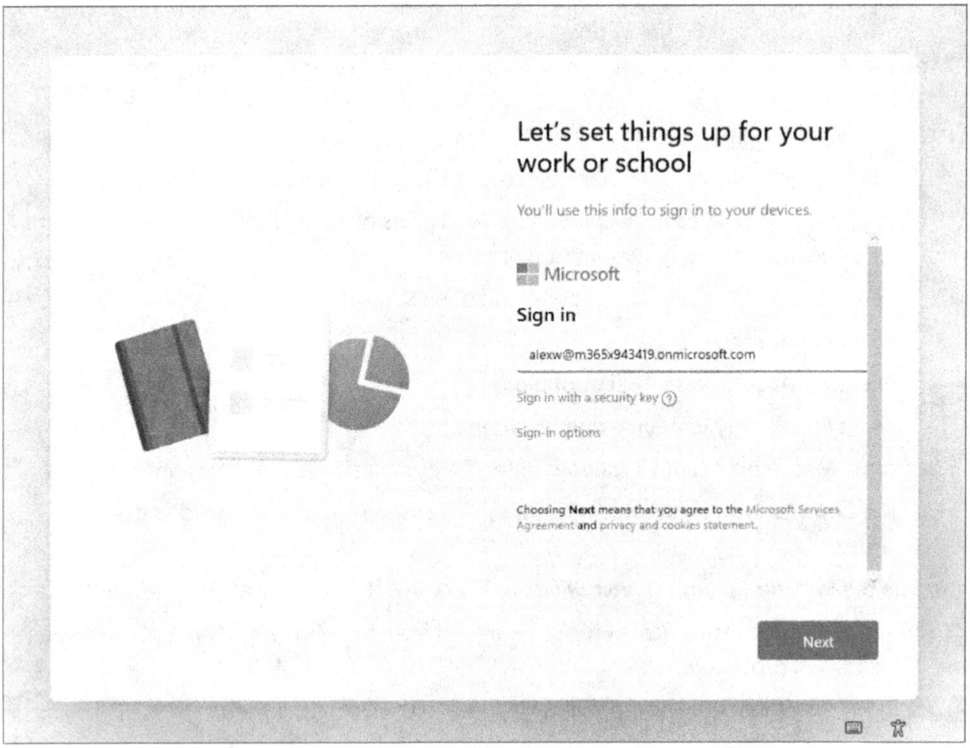

FIGURE 3-13 Joining a device to Azure AD during OOBE

6. When prompted, enter your password and click **Sign in**.

7. If your account requires it, you are prompted to identify yourself with MFA. This is configured at the organizational level but requires your user account to be configured.

8. If configured, the **Enrollment Status Page** is displayed, guiding users during device enrollment.

9. On the **Choose privacy settings for your device** page, click **Next** and then click **Accept**.

10. Your device checks for updates and might now return to the Device preparation stage. You can, if prompted, click **Continue anyway** to allow this process to complete in the background.

11. If your organization requires it, you are now prompted to complete the Windows Hello setup. At the **Use Windows Hello with your account** page, click **OK**.

12. On the **Set up a PIN** page, in the **New PIN** and **Confirm PIN** boxes, enter a PIN that conforms to your organizational requirements and then click **OK**.

13. Click **OK**. You should be automatically signed in to the device, joined to your organization or school Azure AD tenant, and presented with the desktop.

You can review the enrolled device using the Microsoft Entra or Microsoft Intune admin centers. Assuming you have an Azure AD Premium subscription and have enabled Windows Automatic Enrollment for Intune, the device's **Join Type** should be **Azure AD Joined**, and its MDM should be **Microsoft Intune**.

Azure AD Join using Windows Autopilot in user-driven deployment mode

To enroll a Windows device using this method, use the following procedure:

1. Open the Microsoft Intune admin center and sign in with a Global Administrator account.

2. Select **Devices**, select **Windows**, and then select **Windows Enrollment**.

3. Select and enable **Automatic Enrollment**.

4. Under the **Windows Autopilot Deployment Program** heading, select **Devices**.

5. Complete the procedure discussed in Chapter 1, "Deploy and upgrade operating systems" (Skill 1.2: Plan and implement Windows 11 by using Windows Autopilot) to upload the device IDs for your organization's new Windows devices.

6. On the Windows Enrollment blade, under the **Windows Autopilot Deployment Program** heading, select **Deployment Profiles**.

7. Complete the procedure discussed in Chapter 1, "Deploy Windows client" (Skill 1.2: Plan and implement a Windows client deployment by using Windows Autopilot) to create and configure the necessary Windows Autopilot profiles. When configuring your profile, choose between **User-Driven** and **Self-Deploying**, as shown in Figure 3-14. With the former, users see a configurable number of setup screens during OOBE setup. With the latter, the users see no setup screens during OOBE because the process is completely automated.

8. Assign the profile.

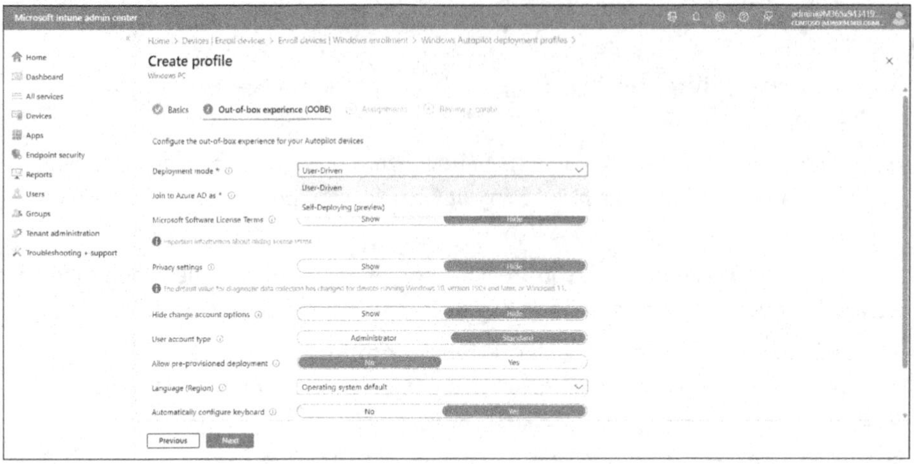

FIGURE 3-14 Configuring a Windows Autopilot deployment profile

9. When you have created, configured, and assigned the necessary Windows Autopilot deployment profiles, turn on the new Windows device(s).

10. The OOBE starts and guides the user through configuring their device. The details vary based on how you have set up your Windows Autopilot deployment profiles. In User-Driven mode, the user(s) will see a customized sign-in screen. Enter the required account information, and the setup will continue and complete according to the Windows Autopilot profile settings.

After deployment, use the Microsoft Entra admin center to view the enrolled device. The device's **Join Type** should be **Azure AD joined**, and its **MDM** should be **Microsoft Intune**.

Enroll non-Windows devices

Enrolling non-Windows devices uses a similar approach. Let's examine the process for Android and iOS.

ENROLL ANDROID DEVICES

To enroll Android devices, use the following procedure:

1. On the Android device, open the **Google Play** store.

2. Search for and install the **Intune Company Portal** app.

3. Launch the **Intune Company Portal** app.

4. Click **Sign In** and then sign in using the appropriate user account from your Microsoft 365 subscription.

5. Follow any instructions given in the portal; these will vary based on the configured settings in Intune. Typically, you are asked to accept new settings on your device. Click **Continue** on each screen to proceed through setup and enrollment.

6. Finally, you are asked to activate the device administrator. Click **Activate**. Your device is registered.

7. If configured, you are asked to define a device category. Select **Done**.

8. When the process is complete, select **Done**.

After deployment, use the Microsoft Entra admin center to view the enrolled device. The device's **Join Type** should be **Azure AD registered**, and its **MDM** should be **Microsoft Intune**. You should be able to see the operating system listed in the **OS column** as **Android**.

ENROLL IOS DEVICES

Enrolling iOS devices, such as iPhones, is a similar process to that used for Android. However, there is one additional step. You must first configure and deploy an Apple MDM Push certificate. Use the following procedure to complete this step:

1. Open the Microsoft Intune admin center.

2. In the navigation pane, select **Devices**, select **iOS/iPadOS**, and then select **iOS/iPadOS enrollment**.

3. Click **Apple MDM Push certificate**.

4. On the **Configure MDM Push Certificate** page, select the **I grant Microsoft permission to send both user and device information to Apple** check box.

5. Click the **Download your CSR** link. When prompted, select **Save** to save the **IntuneCSR.csr** file to your local Downloads folder.

6. Click the **Create your MDM push certificate** link. A new Edge browser tab opens. Sign in using an Apple ID. A verification code is usually sent to one of your Apple devices. Enter the code in the browser window.

7. Select **Create a Certificate**.

8. Accept the **Terms of Use**, and then select **Accept**.

9. Select **Choose File**, and browse to locate the IntuneCSR.csr you downloaded from Intune earlier. Upload this file.

10. Select **Download** to download the Apple Push Certificate. It has a .PEM file extension.

EXAM TIP

Remember that the certificate signing request file has a .CSR extension and is uploaded to Apple, while the Apple Push Certificate has a .PEM extension and is downloaded before being installed in Intune.

---

11. In the Microsoft Intune admin center, switch to the browser tab, and in the **Apple ID** box, enter the Apple ID used to create your Apple MDM push certificate.

12. Browse and locate the Apple MDM push certificate you just downloaded.

13. Select **Upload**.

After you have completed the process, use the following procedure to enroll an iOS device:

1. Sign in to the **Apple Store** on the Apple device.

2. Search for and install the **Intune Company Portal** app.

3. Launch the **Intune Company Portal** app.

4. Click **Sign In** and then sign in using the appropriate user account from your Microsoft 365 subscription.

5. Follow any instructions given in the portal; these will vary based on the configured settings in Intune.

After deployment, use the Microsoft Entra admin center to view the enrolled device. The device's **Join Type** should be **Azure AD registered**, and its **MDM** should be **Microsoft Intune**. You should be able to see the operating system listed in the **OS** column as **iPhone or iPad**.

Configure policy sets

As an on-premises administrator working with Active Directory Domain Services (AD DS), you are probably familiar with using Group Policy Objects (GPOs) to configure your devices. One aspect of using GPOs is that it's possible to use a single GPO linked to an organizational unit (OU) that contains many settings.

For example, you might create a GPO to configure device settings in the Research department, including security settings, application deployment, desktop configuration, and so on.

However, with Intune, you cannot create a single configuration profile that contains settings that will configure these different device configuration aspects; at least, not yet. But you can create the required device configuration profiles, application deployment settings, and so on, and use a policy set to assign these various elements in a single step.

> **NOTE** **CONFIGURATION PROFILES**
>
> We'll be talking about configuration profiles later in this chapter.

You can assign the following elements to your devices by using a policy set:

- Apps
- App configuration policies
- App protection policies
- Device configuration profiles
- Device compliance policies
- Windows autopilot deployment profiles
- Enrollment status page

To create policy sets, start by creating the required elements from the preceding list, but don't assign them. Then, use the following procedure.

1. Create an Azure AD security group that contains the devices you want to target with your policy set.

2. In the Microsoft Intune admin center, navigate to **Devices** and then select **Policy sets** in the navigation pane.

3. On the **Policy sets** page, click **Policy sets**.

4. Click **Create**, and then, on the **Create a policy set** page, on the **Basics** tab, enter a **Policy set name** and **Description** and click **Next: Application management >**.

5. Select the appropriate apps, app configuration policies, and app protection policies, and then click **Next: Device management >**.

> **NOTE APPLICATION MANAGEMENT**
>
> We'll be talking about application management in the next chapter.

6. On the **Device management** page shown in Figure 3-15, select the appropriate device configuration profiles and compliance policies, and then click **Next: Device enrollment**.

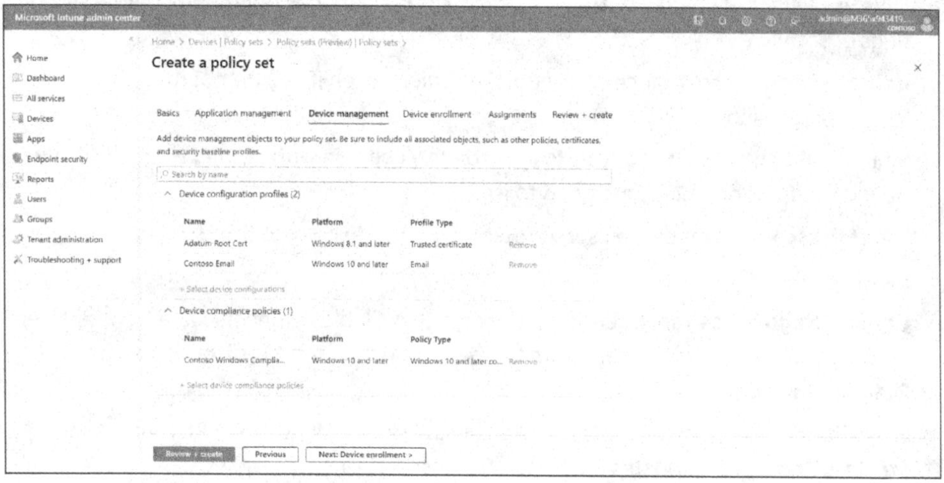

FIGURE 3-15 Configuring the device management settings in a policy set

7. On the **Device enrollment** page, select any Windows Autopilot deployment profiles and enrollment status pages and then click **Next: Assignments**.

8. Select the group you previously created on the **Assignments** page and then click **Next: Review + create**.

> **NOTE DON'T MIX OPERATING SYSTEMS**
>
> When you add profiles and policies to the policy set, selecting profiles and policies for different operating systems is possible. However, avoid this because it's likely that your group will target devices of a specific operating system.

9. Review the information on the **Review + create** tab and click **Create**.

Restart, retire, or wipe devices

You can perform several actions on your organization's enrolled devices, as shown in Figure 3-16. For computers installed with Windows 11, these actions are:

- **Retire** Initiates device retirement. When you choose to retire a device, only company data is removed. Intune also no longer manages the device and can no longer access corporate resources and data. You cannot access company data from devices that are joined to Azure AD.

- **Wipe** Wipes a device. This action performs a factory reset on the device. This removes both company and user data. When you choose Wipe, you can choose additional options:
    - **Wipe device, but keep enrollment state and associated user account**
    - **Wipe device, and continue to wipe even if device loses power**

- **Delete** Removes the device from Microsoft Intune but does not modify device settings or software.

- **Remote Lock** Forces a lock on supported devices, even if you do not have the device in your possession.

- **Sync** Forces the selected device to immediately check in with Intune and receive any pending actions or policies assigned to it.

- **Reset Passcode** Forces the user to reset the passcode on supported devices.

- **Restart** Restarts the remote device.

- **Collect Diagnostics** Instructs Intune to collect available diagnostic data from selected devices. You can access the data from Intune by selecting the **Monitor** > **Device Diagnostics node**.

- **Fresh Start** Removes any apps that were installed on a Windows 11 PC running the Creators Update and updates the PC to the latest version of Windows.

- **Autopilot Reset** Removes personal files, apps, and settings. Resets Windows devices and applies the original management settings from Azure AD and Intune.

- **Quick Scan** Runs a quick malware scan on the selected device.

- **Full Scan** Runs a full malware scan on the selected device.

- **Update Windows Defender Security Intelligence** Initiates an update of malware definitions for the device.

- **Rotate Local Admin Password** Rotates the local admin password on the target device according to Local Admin Password Solution (LAPS) policy settings. Requires that you have already enabled and configured LAPS.

- **BitLocker Key Rotation** Removes all BitLocker encryption keys on the device. A single key is then escrowed to the identity provider (Azure AD or AD DS).

- **Rename Device** Changes the name of the selected device.

- **New Remote Assistance Session**   Enables remote access to the target device, assuming you have added the Remote Help feature to Intune and that the target device has a user with a Microsoft Intune Remote Help license.
- **Locate Device**   Helps you locate lost or stolen devices.

The available actions depend on the type of device and whether the device is personal or corporately owned.

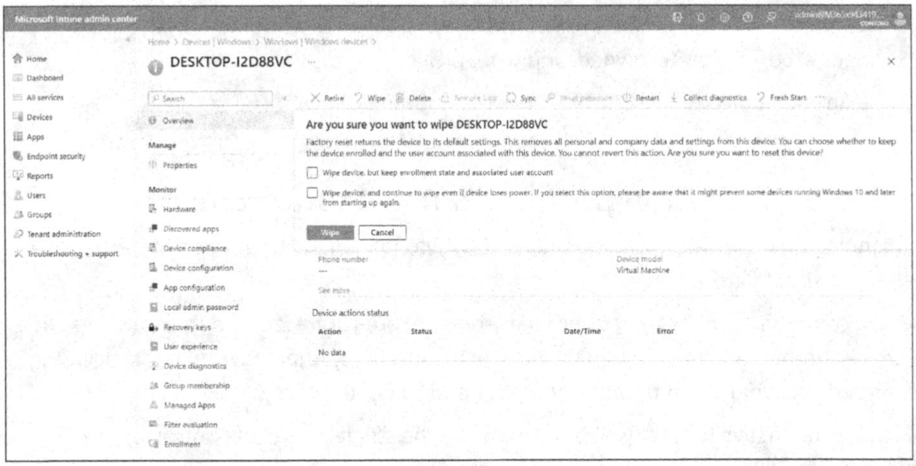

FIGURE 3-16 Preparing to wipe a Windows device in Intune

EXAM TIP

Ensure you are familiar with the actions you can perform on all supported operating systems.

Skill 3.2: Manage device configuration for all supported device platforms by using Intune

You can implement mobile device management (MDM) functionality using Microsoft Intune or a more limited extent, with Basic Mobility and Security for Microsoft 365. In addition to managing settings on iOS and Android mobile devices, MDM allows you to configure policies that control settings on any Windows 11 device, such as desktop PCs and laptops.

You can now manage devices from the cloud using an MDM solution such as Intune. By removing the traditional domain-based constraints often imposed on devices, MDM enables you to implement new management and device functionality. You must understand how to manage devices enrolled in Azure AD and Intune. Also, you must understand how to plan and use profiles and policies to configure devices, control user access, and set device settings to comply with company security and compliance policy.

Specify configuration profiles to meet requirements

When planning how your organization will use MDM to manage your devices, there are several areas that you should include in your scope.

The two common elements of modern management are your users and their device(s). In a traditional environment, you retain full control of a user's computing environment, including the user's desktop, using Configuration Manager and/or Group Policy.

This can be restrictive for the user, but it provides the strictest level of control for the administrator. Using Intune, a similar level of control is possible. Also, the cloud-based nature of Intune can be especially useful for devices that are beyond the management scope of Group Policy, such as in the following scenarios:

- Devices that are not domain members
- Smartphones
- Windows 11 devices that are joined to Azure AD only
- Devices that are used entirely remotely and without access to VPN solutions

Intune provides excellent features for managing devices that connect to your corporate data, enabling you to remain compliant with your corporate security and compliance requirements. All enrolled devices can be forced to comply with your defined device configuration profiles.

Microsoft Intune allows you to manage your devices using an MDM solution that includes settings and features that you can enable or disable on various mobile devices. The full list of platforms supported by Intune through device enrollment is as follows:

- Apple
  - Apple iOS 14.0 and newer
  - Apple iPadOS 14.0 and newer
  - macOS 11.0 and newer

- Google
  - Android 8.0 (and newer)
  - Android Enterprise
  - Android open source project devices (AOSP)
- Microsoft
  - Windows 10/11
  - Windows 10/11 on Windows 365
  - Windows 10 LTSC
  - Windows 10 Teams
- Surface Hub
- Other
- Linux (Ubuntu Desktop 20=2.04 or newer)

Because of the variety of platforms and devices, not all settings and features can be configured on every device platform. You should review the settings and features you can add to a configuration profile for the different devices and platforms you use—or plan to use—in your organization.

The number and scope of the built-in device settings supported by Intune continues to grow as more organizations provide feedback to Microsoft requesting additional support for new scenarios. For each new Windows client version, new MDM functionality will be added to the built-in MDM client to reflect new features that ship with that version of Windows 11.

You can also use Open Mobile Alliance Uniform Resource Identifier (OMA-URI) profiles. Known as custom profiles, these enable you to create and use device settings and features that aren't natively built into Intune. If a setting or feature is supported on devices in your organization, you should be able to create a custom profile that sets the same feature for every device by using OMA-URI settings.

Available profile types

Table 3-5 describes the available profile types. It's important to note that not all profile types are supported by every operating system.

TABLE 3-5 Commonly used Intune device-configuration profiles

Profile	Description
Email	Manages Exchange ActiveSync settings on devices.
Device restrictions	Prevent device usage, such as disabling the built-in camera, connecting to Bluetooth devices, or using cellular data.
Wi-Fi	Allows you to manage wireless network settings for users and devices. In Windows 11, managing settings for users allows them to connect to corporate Wi-Fi without having to configure the connection manually. Instead, users can import a configuration previously exported from another device.

Profile	Description
Administrative templates	Allows you to manage hundreds of settings for Microsoft Edge, OneDrive, Remote Desktop, Word, Excel, and other Microsoft Office programs for Windows 11 devices. Administrative templates provide a simplified view of settings similar to Group Policy for Windows 11.
Kiosk	Allows you to configure a device to run one or multiple apps, such as a web browser. This feature supports Windows 11, and kiosk settings are also available as device restrictions for Android, Android Enterprise, and iOS devices.
VPN	Configures VPN settings for devices. This feature supports: ■ Android ■ Android Enterprise ■ iOS ■ macOS ■ Windows 8.1 ■ Windows 10 and later
Education	Configures options for the Take a Test app in Windows 11. iOS uses the iOS Classroom app.
Certificates	Allows you to configure trust and other certificates used for Wi-Fi, VPN, and email profiles.
Edition upgrade	Allows you to permit users to upgrade some versions of Windows 11.
Endpoint protection	Configures settings for BitLocker and Windows Defender.
Custom profile	Custom settings allow administrators to assign device settings not built into Intune. These use the Open Mobile Alliance Uniform Resource Identifier (OMA-URI) values for Android and Windows devices. For iOS devices, you can import a configuration file you created in the Apple Configurator or Apple Profile Manager.

Profile Types Common Across Platforms

A number of profile types are available across all platforms. These are:

■ Device restrictions

■ Email

■ PKCS certificate

■ PKCS imported certificate

■ SCEP certificate

■ Trusted certificate

■ VPN

■ Wi-Fi

Device profiles available for Windows

Perhaps unsurprisingly, the support for Windows client configuration is very extensive. The available Windows profile types are shown below:

■ Administrative templates

■ Custom

■ Delivery optimization

■ Device firmware configuration interface

- Device restrictions
- Device restrictions (Windows 10 Team)
- Domain join
- Edition upgrade and mode switch
- Email
- Endpoint protection
- Identity protection
- Imported Administrative templates (Preview)
- Kiosk
- Microsoft Defender for Endpoint (Desktop devices running Windows 10 or later)

- Network boundary
- PKCS certificate
- PKCS imported certificate
- SCEP certificate
- Trusted certificate
- Secure assessment (Education)
- Shared multi-user device
- VPN
- Wi-Fi
- Windows health monitoring
- Wired network

Device profiles available for iOS and iPadOS

There are quite a large number of profiles for Apple devices. Table 3-6 lists the available profile types for iOS and macOS.

TABLE 3-6 Intune device-configuration profiles for iOS and macOS

iOS	macOS
Custom	Custom
Derived credential	Device features
Device features	Device restrictions
Device restrictions	Endpoint protection
Edition upgrade and mode switch	Extensions
Email	PKCS certificate
PKCS certificate	PKCS imported certificate
PKCS imported certificate	SCEP certificate
SCEP certificate	Trusted certificate
Trusted certificate	Preference file
Secure assessment (Education)	VPN
VPN	Wi-Fi
Wi-Fi	Wired network

Device profiles available for Android

Table 3-7 lists the available profile types for fully managed corporate Android Enterprise devices and personally-owned work devices running Android.

TABLE 3-7 Intune device-configuration profiles for Android

Fully-managed corporate	Personally-owned work
Derived credential	Custom
Device restrictions	Device restrictions
PKCS certificate	Email
PKCS imported certificate	PKCS certificate
SCEP certificate	PKCS imported certificate
Trusted certificate	SCEP certificate
VPN	Trusted certificate
Wi-Fi	VPN
	Wi-Fi

Implement configuration profiles

A device configuration profile enables you to add and configure settings that you can then deploy to devices enrolled in management within your organization. After the device receives the device configuration profile, the features and settings are applied automatically.

For example, to create a device profile for Windows 11 devices that will configure device restrictions that enforce the **Apps from store only** setting for enrolled Windows devices, use the following procedure:

1. Sign in to the Microsoft Intune admin center as a Global Administratoristrator.
2. Select **Devices**, and then under **Policy**, click **Configuration profiles**.
3. On the **Device | Configuration profiles** page, click **Create profile**.
4. On the **Create a profile** page, under **Platform**, select **Windows 10 and later**, and under **Profile type**, select **Templates**.
5. Under **Template name**, select **Device restrictions** and click **Create**.
6. On the **Device restrictions** page, enter the following properties:
   - **Name**   Enter a descriptive name for the profile.
   - **Description**   Enter a description for the profile.
7. Click **Next**.
8. On the **Configuration settings** tab, expand **App store**.
9. In the **Apps from store only** list, select **Store Only**, as shown in Figure 3-17, and click **Next**.
10. On the **Assignments** tab, assign the policy to users, devices, or groups and then click **Next**.
11. On the **Applicability Rules** tab, review the settings and then click **Next**.
12. On the **Review + create** tab, review the summary and then click **Create**.

The device configuration profile policy is created and is shown in the configuration profiles list.

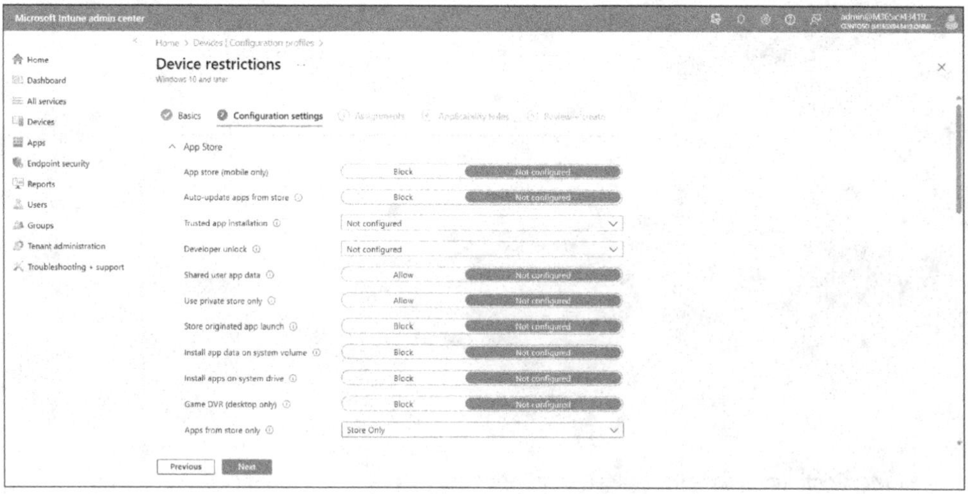

FIGURE 3-17 Creating a device restrictions device configuration profile

> **NOTE   REMEMBER POLICY SETS**
>
> By using policy sets, you can simplify the process of assigning multiple policies to the same collection of users or devices.

Deploy Administrative Template Profiles

In addition to using built-in configuration and custom profiles, Windows 11 allows you to expand the current set of built-in policies using Administrative Templates, as shown in Figure 3-18. The Administrative Templates use Group Policy ADMX-backed policies and allow administrators to implement GPO settings via Intune for both user and device targets. The current functionality adds hundreds of popular settings to Intune.

To create a template for a Windows 11 device using an administrative template, use these steps:

1.   In the **Microsoft Intune admin center**, select **Devices**, and then under **Policy**, click **Configuration profiles**.

2.   On the **Configuration profiles** page, click **Create profile**.

3.   On the **Create a profile** page, under **Platform**, select **Windows 10 and later**, and under **Profile type**, select **Templates**.

4.   Under **Template name**, select **Administrative templates** and click **Create**.

5.   On the **Create profile** page, on the **Basics** tab, enter a **Name** and **Description** and click **Next**.

6.   On the **Configuration settings** tab, displayed in Figure 3-18, use the search bar at the top to search for a setting or select a setting folder name to reveal the settings available.

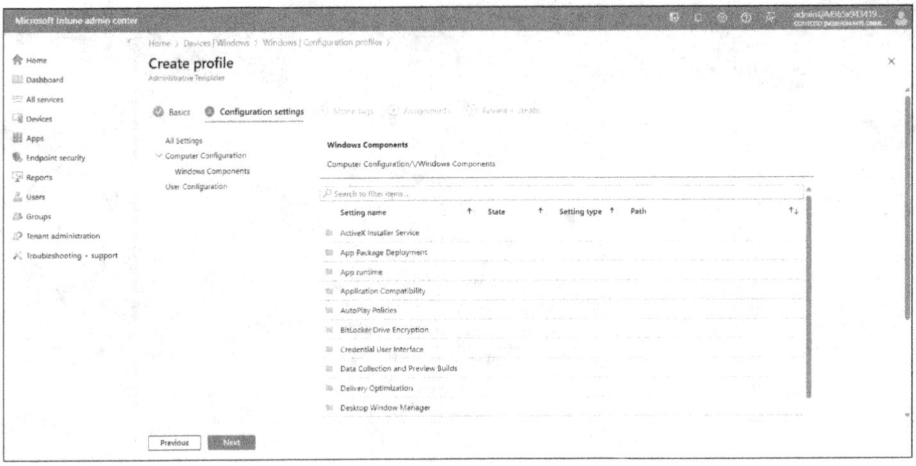

FIGURE 3-18 Configuring an administrative template-based configuration profile

7. Select a setting such as **Allow users to connect remotely by using Remote Desktop Services**. Choose **Enabled** or **Disabled** or leave the setting as **Not configured** (default), as shown in Figure 3-19, and select **OK**.

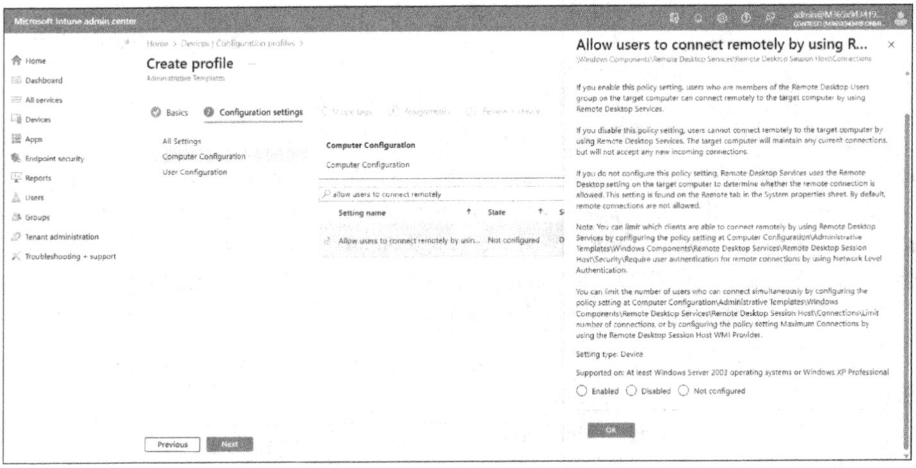

FIGURE 3-19 Configuring a setting in an administrative template-based configuration profile

8. Under **Configuration settings**, click **Next**.

9. On the **Scope tags** blade, allocate scope tags as required and click **Next**.

10. On the **Assignments** blade, assign the policy to users, devices, or groups and then click **Next**.

11. On the **Review + create** blade, review the summary and click **Create**.

The device configuration profile policy is saved and is shown in the configuration profiles list. For the Administrative Template Profile to be applied to an enrolled device, you need to assign the profile to users or devices using Azure AD groups.

> ***NEED MORE REVIEW?*** **UNDERSTANDING ADMX-BACKED POLICIES**
>
> If you want to know how to use ADMX-backed policies, use this Microsoft website: *https://learn.microsoft.com/windows/client-management/understanding-admx-backed-policies.*

IMPORTING ADMX FILES

If you cannot find the specific setting that you want, you can try importing an ADMX file to incorporate more recent settings into the Administrative Template profile. To do this, use the following guidance:

1. Search online for the ADMX file you need and then download the file(s).
2. On the **Configuration profiles** page in Intune, select the **Import ADMX** tab, and then click **Import**.
3. As shown in Figure 3-20, browse for and locate the required ADMX file(s).

For example, if you want to use an administrative template profile that doesn't contain some recent Windows 11 or Office 2021 settings, you can download the appropriate ADMX files and upload them to Intune (ingesting). You'll then find those settings in your administrative templates profiles.

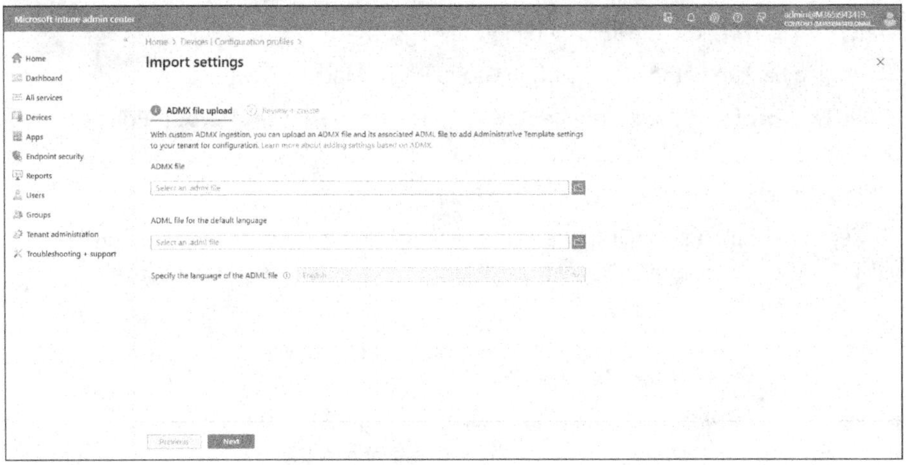

FIGURE 3-20 Importing ADMX files for administrative templates

Migrating from Group Policy

Many administrators for Intune are likely to have a background in managing devices in on-premises environments by using GPOs. By using administrative template-based configuration profiles, you can benefit from a familiar interface and values with the same name and configuration options.

But Microsoft provides a number of other GPO-friendly features in Intune. For example, you can use the Group Policy analytics feature to determine which of your current GPO's settings are directly supported by Intune configuration profiles. As shown in Figure 3-21, you can review a report identifying which of your GPOs have 100 percent support in Intune, where they aren't supported, and which settings you might want to work around (perhaps by using custom profiles).

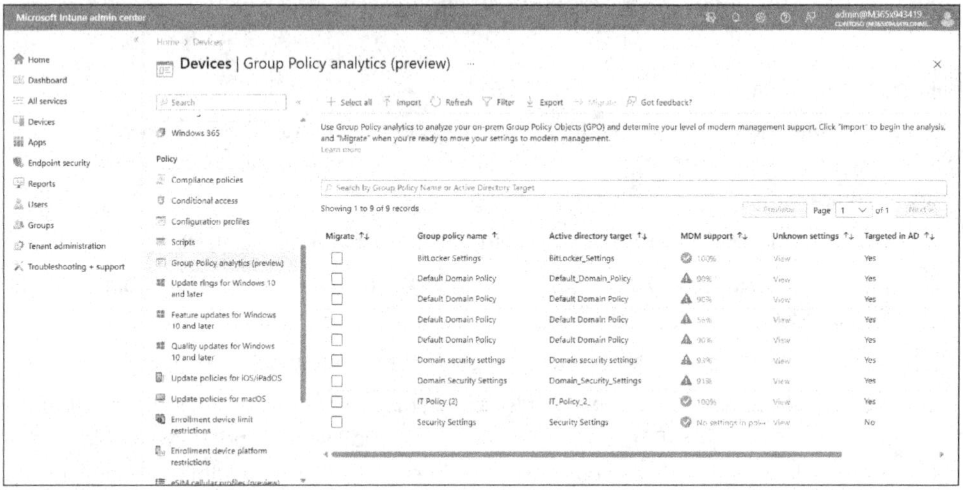

FIGURE 3-21 Reviewing GPO support in Intune with Group Policy analytics

To analyze your GPOs, use the following high-level guidance:

1. Perform a backup of the target GPO in Group Policy Management.

2. Open **Microsoft Intune admin center** and navigate to **Devices | Group Policy analytics**.

3. Upload the exported `GPReport.xml` file to Intune.

4. Review the results. For GPOs that contain settings not 100 percent supported by Intune, click the **View** link in the **Unknown settings** column and review the guidance.

> **NEED MORE REVIEW?** **ANALYZE YOUR ON-PREMISES GPOS USING GROUP POLICY ANALYTICS IN MICROSOFT INTUNE**
>
> If you want to know how to use Group Policy analytics, use this Microsoft website: *https://learn.microsoft.com/mem/intune/configuration/group-policy-analytics*.

Deploy PowerShell scripts in Intune

For Windows 11 devices, you can upload PowerShell scripts in Intune, which can then be run on Windows 11 devices. Intune includes a management extension, which facilitates adding PowerShell scripts.

Deployment of PowerShell scripts using Intune is supported for all enrolled Windows 11 devices that are Azure AD–joined, Hybrid Azure AD domain–joined, or co-managed. The Intune management extension has the prerequisites outlined in Table 3-8.

TABLE 3-8 Intune management extension prerequisites

Requirement	Prerequisite
Windows 11 version	■ Windows 11 Pro, Enterprise, or Education. ■ If the device is enrolled using bulk auto-enrollment.
Directory joined devices	■ Allows Hybrid Azure AD-joined and on-premises Active Directory–joined devices. ■ Azure AD–registered devices.
Devices enrolled in Intune	■ Devices enrolled in a group policy (GPO). ■ Devices enroll in Intune via auto-enrollment. ■ Users enroll their devices using their Azure AD accounts. ■ Co-managed devices that use Configuration Manager and Intune.

When you run a PowerShell script using Intune, there are three script settings, as described in Table 3-9.

TABLE 3-9 PowerShell script runtime settings

Setting	Description
Run This Script Using The Logged-On Credentials	By default, the script will run in the system context. Optionally, this can be modified to run the script with the user's credentials on the device.
Enforce Script Signature Check	By default, the signature check is not enforced. If there is a requirement for the script to be signed, you can choose to enforce the signature check, and a trusted publisher must sign the script.
Run Script In 64-Bit PowerShell Host	By default, the script is run in a 32-bit PowerShell host. Optionally, you can run the script in a 64-bit PowerShell host on a 64-bit client.

For example, you can create a PowerShell script that installs a Win32 app to your Windows 11 device. This scenario involves these high-level steps:

1. Write a PowerShell script to install a Win32 app.
2. Upload the script to Intune as a Device Configuration profile.
3. Configure the script runtime settings.
4. Assign the script to an Azure AD group of users or devices.
5. The script runs on the assigned group.
6. You can then use Intune to monitor the run status of your script.

To create a PowerShell script policy, use these steps.

1. Open Microsoft Intune admin center.
2. Select **Devices**, and then under **Policy**, click **Scripts.**
3. On the **Devices | Scripts** page, click **Add**, and select **Windows 10 and later**. Note that you can also create scripts for Linux and macOS.

4. On the **Add PowerShell script** page, enter the following properties on the **Basics** tab:

- **Name**   Enter a descriptive name for the script.
- **Description**   Enter a description for the script.

5. Click **Next**.

6. On the **Script settings** tab, shown in Figure 3-22, enter the following properties:

- **Script location**   Browse to the PowerShell script. The script must be less than 200 KB (ASCII).
- **Run this script using the logged on credentials**   Select **Yes** to run the script with the user's credentials on the device, or choose **No** (default) to run the script in the system context.
- **Enforce script signature check**   Select Yes or No (default).
- **Run script in 64 bit PowerShell Host**   Select **Yes** to run the script in a 64-bit PowerShell host or select **No** (default) to run the script in a 32-bit PowerShell host.

7. Click **Next**.

8. On the **Assignments** blade, assign the policy to users, devices, or groups and then click **Next**.

9. On the **Review + add** blade, review the summary and click **Create**.

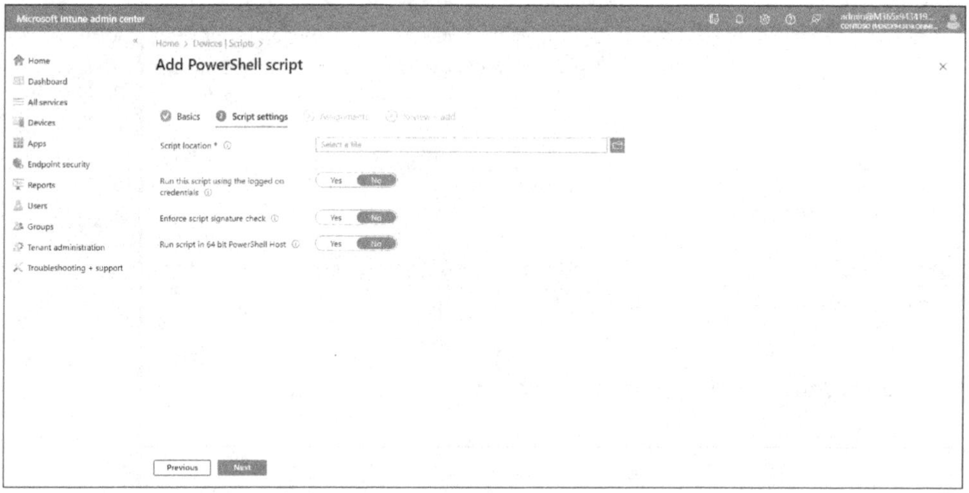

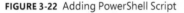

FIGURE 3-22 Adding PowerShell Script

After you have uploaded a PowerShell script to Intune, the management extension client checks with Intune for any new PowerShell scripts or changes; this check is done once every hour and after every reboot. After the PowerShell script has been executed on a targeted device, the PowerShell script is not executed again unless there's a change in the script or policy.

Assigning device profiles

For a device profile to be applied to an enrolled device, you need to assign the profile to users or devices using Azure AD groups. To assign a device profile, use the following procedure:

1. Open the Microsoft Intune admin center.

2. Select **Devices**, and under **Policy**, select **Configuration profiles**.

3. Select the profile that you want to assign or modify the existing assignment.

4. On the profile properties page, next to Assignments, click **Edit**.

5. On the **Assignments** page, update the assignments as needed. You can choose:

   ■ **Add groups**, and then select specific groups to which to assign the profile

   ■ **Add all users**, which results in all supported and enrolled devices of all users being assigned the profile

   ■ **Add all devices**, which results in all supported and enrolled devices being assigned the profile

6. Click **Review + save** and then click **Save**.

You can also exclude groups from policy assignment by using the **Exclude** tab. Care should be taken to ensure that the assignment outcome is as desired.

Implementing Scope tags

When you create Intune configuration profiles and policies, and after you add the settings, you can also add a scope tag to the profile. Scope tags are used to assign and filter policies to specific groups, such as your marketing team or sales employees.

You can also use scope tags to give admins the right access level and visibility to objects in Intune. In this scenario, you combine Azure AD role-based access control (RBAC) and scope tags. The role determines what access admins have to which objects, and the scope tags determine which objects admins can see.

To add a scope tag to a policy, you must have already created the tag. To add a scope tag, use these steps:

1. Open the Microsoft Intune admin center.

2. Select **Tenant administration**, and then select **Roles.**

3. On the **All Roles** page, select **Scope tags** and then click **Create**.

4. On the **Basics** tab, provide a **Name** and optional **Description** and click **Next**.

5. On the **Assignments** page, choose the groups containing the devices to which you want to assign this scope tag. Click **Next**.

6. On the **Review + create** page, review the settings and then choose **Create**. The **Scope tag** is created and appears in the list of **Scope tags.**

TO ADD A SCOPE TAG TO A CONFIGURATION PROFILE

After you have created one or more scope tags, you can add them to your device configuration profile using these steps:

1. In the **Microsoft Intune admin center**, select **Devices**.

2. Under **Policy**, select **Configuration profiles**.

3. Click the link for the relevant profile.

4. On the **Device configuration profiles** page for your profile, next to **Scope tags**, select **Edit**.

5. You can now choose to remove the **Scope tags** or modify the tags by clicking the **Select scope tags**.

6. On the **Select tags** blade, under **Name**, choose the scope tag(s) you want to add to the profile, as shown in Figure 3-23.

7. Click **Select**.

8. On the **Device configuration profile** page for your profile, click **Review + save**, and then click **Save**.

FIGURE 3-23 Add Scope Tags

The Intune Service Administrator and Global Administrator roles have full admin access to all Intune features, regardless of the configured scope tags.

Monitor and troubleshoot configuration profiles

It's important to understand whether profiles are being correctly assigned and applied. It's also important to be aware of conflicts with configuration profiles that contain mismatched or over-lapping settings. Intune provides numerous ways to review and troubleshoot the application of configuration profiles on your organization's devices.

Monitoring and troubleshooting the application of profiles

When you sign in to the Microsoft Intune admin center, you can access your Dashboard from the navigation pane. This contains a summary of device enrollment, device compliance, and device configuration, among other things.

You can quickly review enrollment, compliance, and configuration issues from the dashboard by selecting the relevant tile, as shown in Figure 3-24.

FIGURE 3-24 Reviewing devices on the Intune dashboard

For example, selecting the **Device configuration** tile redirects the console to the **Assignment failures** page in **Devices | Monitor**. From the **Monitor** page, you can review the following configuration-related data:

- Assignment status
- Assignment failures
- Devices with restricted apps
- Encryption report
- Certificates

For example, as displayed in Figure 3-25, two device assignment failures are displayed.

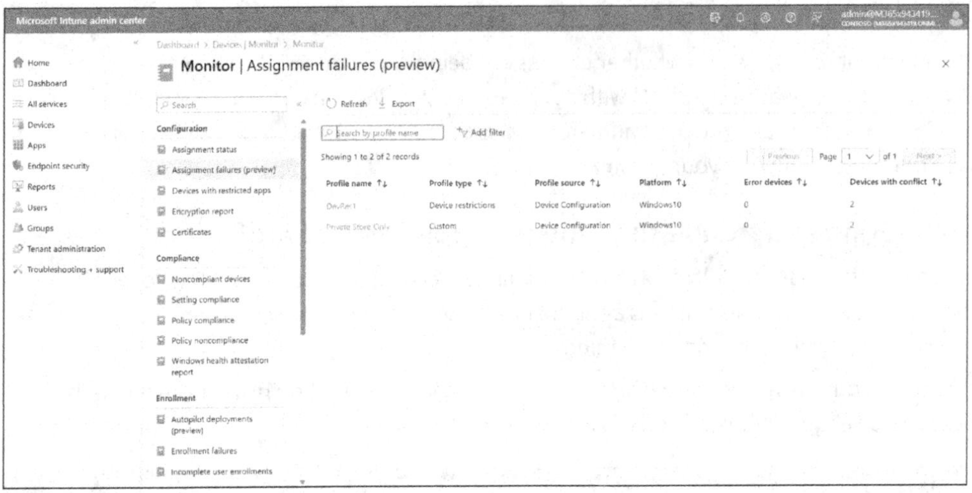

FIGURE 3-25 Reviewing assignment failures

In this instance, the reason for the failure is identified as being a conflict. For further details, an administrator can click the **Profile name** link to find out more, as shown in Figure 3-26.

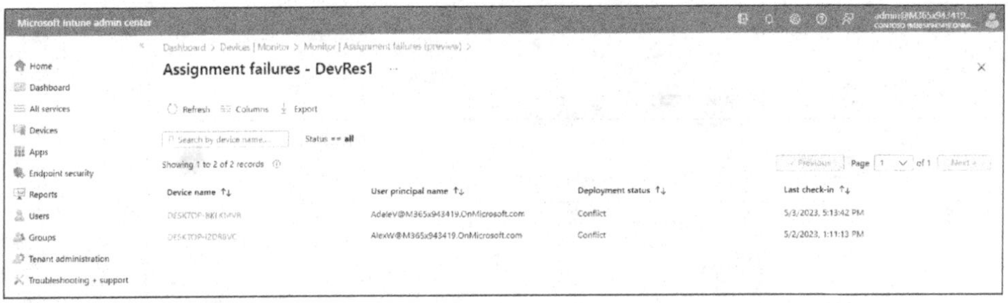

FIGURE 3-26 Reviewing a conflicting profile

Further analysis is possible by clicking through the provided links. For example, clicking the Intune link for a particular computer in conflict identifies the setting in conflict, as shown in Figure 3-27.

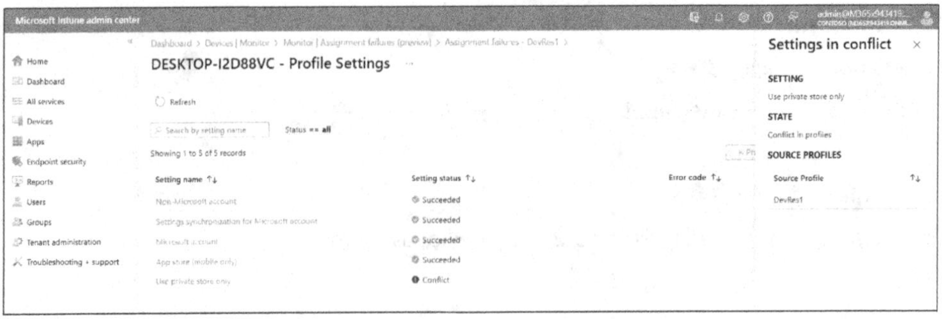

FIGURE 3-27 Determining the cause of the conflict

Selecting the Setting name that is in conflict provides additional information. After that, it's a question of reviewing the policies in conflict and adjusting assignments or the settings being configured.

You can also review the assignment status of a configuration profile from the **Devices | Configuration profiles** page in Intune. Select the target profile, and then on the **Summary** page, review the details, as shown in Figure 3-28.

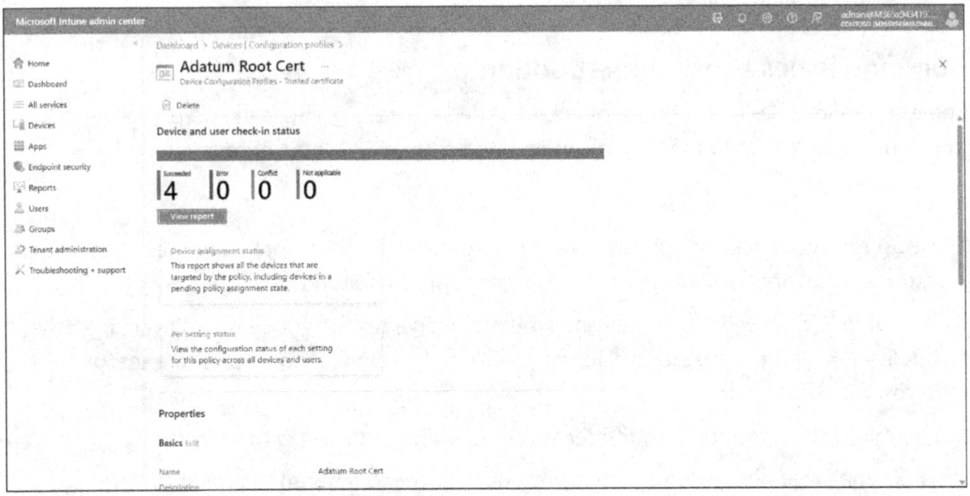

FIGURE 3-28 Reviewing the assignment status of a profile

From this page, you can review

- Device and user check-in details
- Access a report (see Figure 3-29)

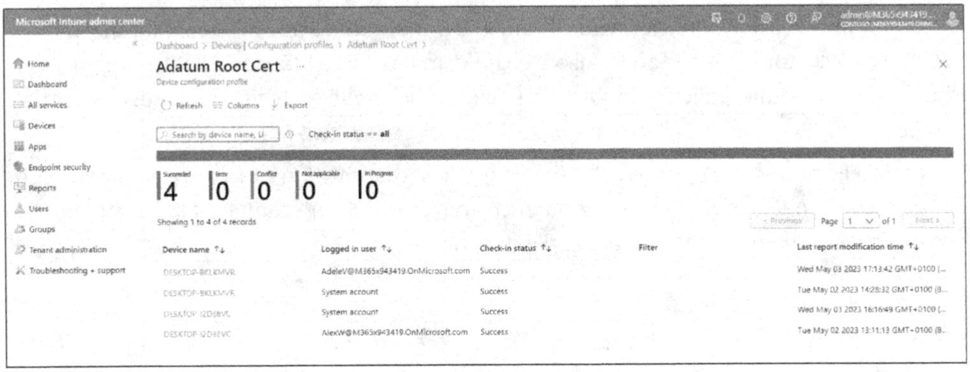

FIGURE 3-29 Reviewing a configuration profile assignment report

- Device assignment status
- User assignment status

- Links to review or edit the following:
  - Basics
  - Assignments
  - Scope tags
  - Configuration settings
  - Applicability rules

Common issues and troubleshooting

Some common issues and resolutions you might encounter with policies and profiles with Intune relate to configuration profile conflicts and Azure AD–Intune enrollment.

CONFIGURATION PROFILE CONFLICTS

The most restrictive value is applied when two profile settings are applied to the same device. Any settings that are the same in each policy are applied as configured.

If a policy is deployed to a device and is active when a second policy is deployed, then the first policy takes precedence, and it will stay applied. Any conflicting settings are set to the most restrictive values.

You might also consider how different types of policies interact with each other.

- Compliance policy settings have precedence over configuration profile settings.
- If a compliance policy includes the same setting found in another compliance policy, then the most restrictive compliance policy setting will be applied.
- If a configuration policy setting conflicts with a setting in another configuration policy, the conflict will be displayed in Intune. You will need to manually resolve the conflict.

CUSTOM PROFILE CONFLICTS

If you configure custom policies, you should know that Intune doesn't evaluate the payload of a custom Open Mobile Alliance Uniform Resource Identifier (OMA-URI) policy. Intune will deliver the policy without referencing other policies, which can cause potential conflicts.

You should therefore confirm that the configured settings within a custom policy don't conflict with compliance, configuration, or other custom policies. For example, if iOS custom policy settings conflict, then the settings are applied randomly.

POLICY REFRESH CYCLE TIMES

You might need to troubleshoot the client if Intune profiles or policies are not being applied to a specific device or PowerShell scripts deployed by Intune are not being run. You should first reboot the device by holding down the Shift key and selecting **Shutdown from Start**. After rebooting the device, the Intune client built into Windows 11 should check whether any changes or new policies are available.

You should allow devices time after rebooting to sync to Intune and receive any changes. Sometimes, the sync can take several minutes to complete, so you might need to be patient. The refresh cycle for device configuration policies can be found in Table 3-10. The application and refresh cycle for device configuration profiles is the same as the compliance profiles.

TABLE 3-10 Configuration profile policy refresh cycle

Platform	Initial estimated check-in frequency	Ongoing refresh cycle
iOS	Every 15 minutes for 6 hours, and then every 8 hours	About every 8 hours
macOS	Every 15 minutes for 6 hours, and then every 8 hours	About every 8 hours
Android	Every 3 minutes for 15 minutes; every 15 minutes for 2 hours; and then every 8 hours	About every 8 hours
Windows 10 or later (enrolled as a device)	Every 3 minutes for 15 minutes; every 15 minutes for 2 hours; and then every 8 hours	About every 8 hours
Windows 8.1 or later	Every 5 minutes for 15 minutes; every 15 minutes for 2 hours; and then about every 8 hours	About every 8 hours

You can, of course, manually sync your configuration profiles from the Microsoft Intune admin center and the device itself.

ENROLLMENT ISSUES

Devices don't receive policies or profiles if the device is not auto-enrolled in Azure AD and Intune. To confirm that a device is auto-enrolled, perform these steps:

1. On the client device, open the **Settings** app.
2. Click **Accounts**.
3. Under **Accounts**, click **Access work or school**.
4. Select the joined account and click **Info**.
5. Under **Advanced Diagnostic Report**, click **Create report**.
6. When prompted, click **Export**. The **MDMDiagReport** will be exported to the following location: C:\Users\Public\Documents\MDMdiagnostics.
7. Open the **MDMDiagReport** in a web browser and locate the **Enrolled Configuration Sources and target resources** section.
8. If you cannot find the MDMDeviceWithAAD property, the device is not auto-enrolled and must be enrolled to receive policies.

Using the Intune troubleshooting portal

You can also use the Microsoft Intune admin center troubleshooting portal to help users at your company review user information and user enrollment issues, as shown in Figure 3-30.

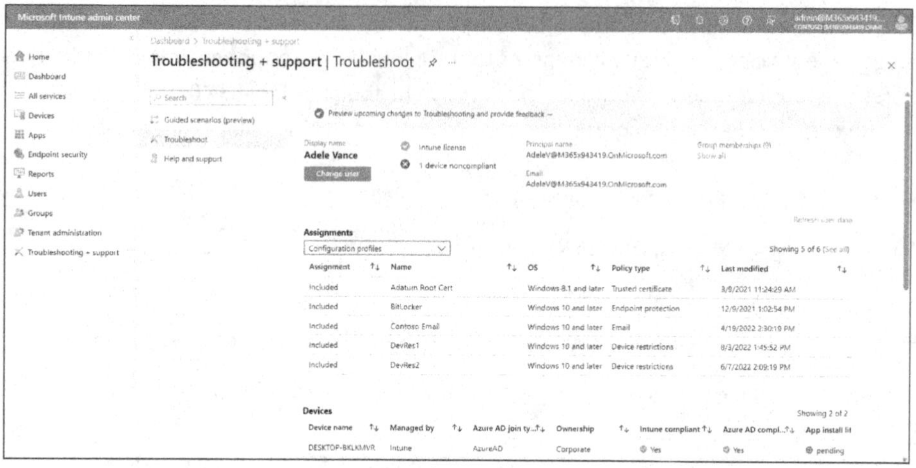

FIGURE 3-30 Troubleshooting Intune user issues

Intune can report the following data, including:

- User status
- Assignments
- Compliance issues
- Device not responding
- Device not getting VPN or Wi-Fi settings
- App installation failure

To access the portal to allow you to troubleshoot user issues in Intune, use the following steps.

1. Open Microsoft Intune admin center as (at least) a help desk operator.
2. Select **Troubleshooting + support** from the navigation pane.
3. Select the appropriate user.
4. Review the user information shown in the **Troubleshooting + support** page, as described in Table 3-11.

TABLE 3-11 Troubleshooting + support information summary

Name	Description
Account status	Shows the status of the current Intune tenant as **Active** or **Inactive**. A green checkmark indicates a valid active Intune status.
User selection	Select the user to review. Click **Change user** to choose a new user.
User status	Displays the status of the user's Intune license, the number of devices, and each device's compliance. A green checkmark indicates a valid Intune license. Any compliance issues will be listed below the Intune status with a cross within a red circle.

Name	Description
User-specific information	Use the **Assignments** dropdown to select the details to review the status for each of the following areas: ■ Client apps ■ Compliance policies ■ Configuration policies ■ App protection policies ■ Update rings for Windows 10 and later ■ PowerShell scripts ■ Enrollment restrictions
Group membership	Shows the current Azure AD groups the selected user is a member of.
Devices	Displays a list of the user's devices and detailed information about each, such as ownership, MDM, compliance state, app installation, operating system, and last check-in date and time.

Configure and implement Windows kiosk mode

You can use Kiosk mode to support the deployment of computers running the Windows operating system that are used as public devices. For example, you could use kiosk mode to

- Run an app enabling guests to sign in to your organization at reception or security
- Run as a public computer with a web browser to enable guest access to the Internet.

Whatever reason you might have for deploying kiosk devices, there are essentially three ways to configure them:

- **Single computer using Settings**   In this situation, you use the **Accounts** page in the **Settings** app to configure Kiosk mode.
- **Multiple computers using a provisioning package**   To support this scenario, you use Windows Configuration Designer to create a provisioning package for a Kiosk computer. You then distribute and apply this package.
- **Multiple computers using Intune**   You can create a configuration profile in Intune that enables and configures the necessary settings for Kiosk mode.

Single computer using Settings

To configure a computer as a kiosk, sign in as a local administrator and then complete the following procedure:

1. Open **Settings** and then select **Accounts**.
2. Select **Other users**.
3. Click **Get started** in the **Set up a kiosk** section.
4. In the **Create an account** dialog, enter the account name that will be used for signing in while in kiosk mode. You can also select an existing account. Click **Next**.
5. On the **Choose a kiosk app** page, browse and select one of the installed apps displayed and then click **Next**.

6. If you chose a web browser, then on the **How will this kiosk be used?** page, choose either:

   - As a digital sign or interactive display

   - As a public browser

7. On the **Enter your website's URL** page, enter the **URL** and click **Next**.

8. On the **You're done!** page, click **Close**.

NOTE REMOVING THE KIOSK

If you want to disable kiosk mode, in **Settings**, in Accounts, on the **Other users** page, click the **Active** link in **Set up a kiosk**. Then click **Remove kiosk**.

While setting up a single computer like this might occasionally be useful, you'll likely want to use a bulk provisioning method.

Multiple computers using a provisioning package

To configure computers as kiosks using a provisioning package, use the following procedure:

1. On a management workstation with Windows ADK installed, open **Windows Configuration Designer**.

2. On the **Start page** tab, click the **Provision kiosk devices** tab.

3. In the **New project** wizard, enter a **Name** and **Description** and click **Finish**.

4. On the newly opened tab (which has the same name as the name you just provided), complete the wizard to define the following properties as necessary:

   - Set up device

   - Set up network

   - Account management

   - Add applications

   - Add certificates

5. Then, on the **Configure kiosk account and app** tab, shown in Figure 3-31, define the following:

   - User name for the kiosk account that will be created

   - Password for the new user

   - Enable auto sign-in if desired

   - The user name that will be used for the kiosk (the same as the previously defined account)

   - The app type and its AUMID (Application User Model ID)

> ***NOTE*** **WHAT IS THE AUMID?**
>
> **To determine the AUMID for an app, use the `Get-Startapps` PowerShell cmdlet using the `-name` property, such as `Get-Startapps -Name Edge`. Then paste the returned ID into the Enter the AUMID for the app text box.**

6. Click **Next**, and on the **Configure kiosk common settings** page, define the following, as needed:
   - Set tablet mode
   - Customize user experience
   - Configure power settings
7. Click **Next**, and then on the **Finish** tab, click **Create**.

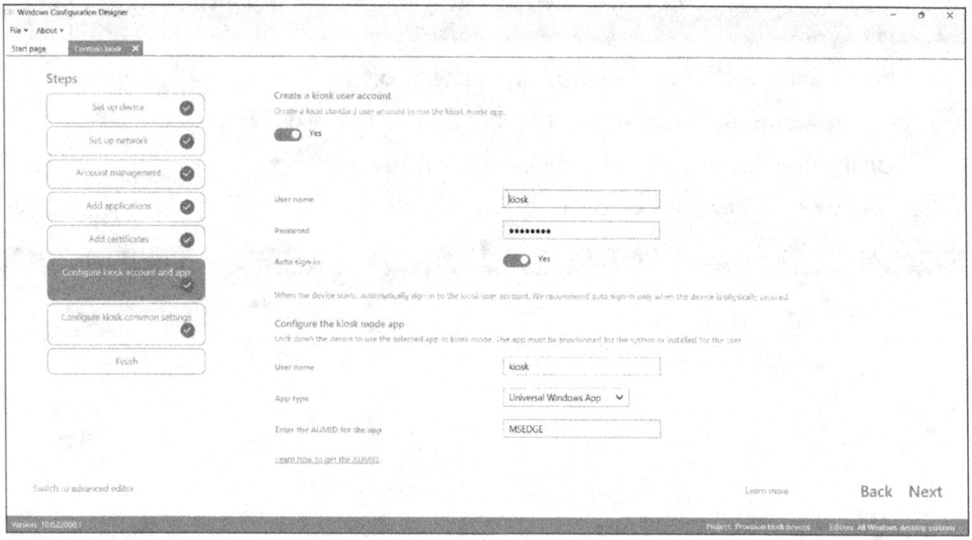

FIGURE 3-31 Creating a provisioning package for a kiosk

After creating the package, copy the generated .PPKG and .CAT files to appropriate media (such as a memory stick) and distribute them.

> ***NEED MORE REVIEW?*** **APPLY A PROVISIONING PACKAGE**
>
> **It's worth noting that a computer running OOBE detects the presence of PPKG files in attached storage devices, such as a memory stick. To review further details about automatically applying provisioning packages, refer to the Microsoft website at *https://learn.microsoft.com/windows/configuration/provisioning-packages/provisioning-apply-package*.**

Multiple computers using Intune

To configure computers as kiosks by using Intune, use the following procedure:

1. In the Microsoft Intune admin center, navigate to **Devices | Configuration profiles**.

2. Create a new profile for **Windows 10 and later**, using the **Kiosk** template.

3. In the Kiosk wizard, add a **Name** and **Description** on the **Basics** tab and click **Next**.

4. On the **Configuration settings** tab, in the **Select a kiosk mode** list, choose

    - **Single app, full-screen kiosk**
    - **Multi app kiosk**

5. Assuming **Single app, full-screen kiosk**, which is typical, then configure

    - **Use logon type**   Auto logon, Local user account, or Azure AD user or group
    - **Application type**   Microsoft Edge browser, Kiosk browser, or Store app

6. If you chose **Microsoft Edge browser**, specify the URL and related properties, as shown in Figure 3-32.

7. Click **Next**, and then define **Scope tags** as needed.

8. On the **Assignments** page, target the necessary group of devices.

9. On the **Applicability Rules** tab, define any necessary settings.

10. Finally, on the **Review + create** page, click **Create**.

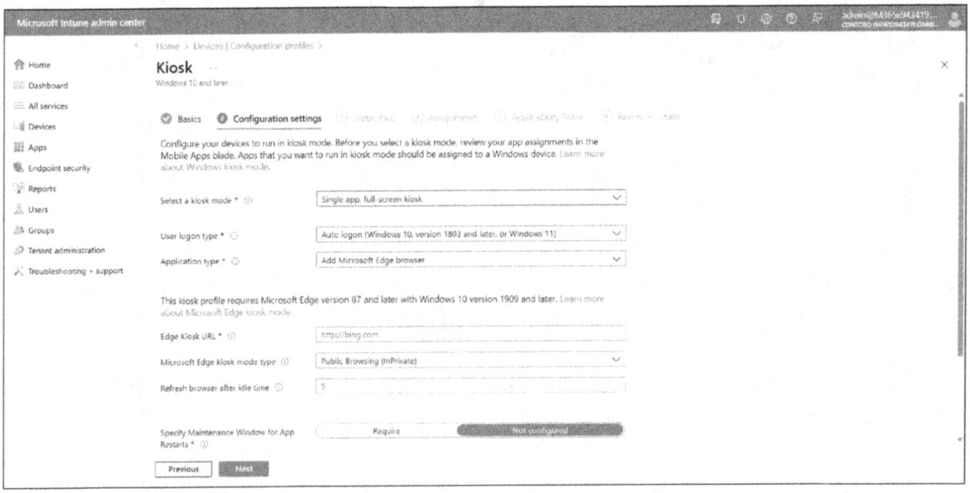

FIGURE 3-32 Provisioning a kiosk with Intune

Configure and implement profiles on Android devices

The process of creating configuration profiles for Android doesn't vary enormously from the process used for Windows, iOS, or macOS. However, since Intune supports several Android platforms, there is an additional step or two.

Intune supports the following Android platforms:

- Android device administrator
- Android Enterprise
- Android open source project devices (AOSP)

When you start creating, configuring, and assigning an Android configuration profile in Intune, you must select the appropriate platform. Depending on which platform you select will determine what type of profiles you can create. These are described in Table 3-12.

TABLE 3-12 Summary of Android profile types

Android device administrator	Android (AOSP)	Android enterprise
<ul><li>Custom</li><li>Device restrictions</li><li>Email</li><li>MX profile</li><li>Certificates</li><li>VPN</li><li>Wi-Fi</li></ul>	<ul><li>Device restrictions</li><li>Certificates</li><li>Wi-Fi</li></ul>	Fully-managed corporate:<ul><li>Derived credential</li><li>Device restrictions</li><li>Certificates</li><li>VPN</li><li>Wi-Fi</li></ul>Personally-owned work:<ul><li>Custom</li><li>Device restrictions</li><li>Email</li><li>Certificates</li><li>VPN</li><li>Wi-Fi</li></ul>

Plan and implement Microsoft Tunnel for Intune

Microsoft Tunnel is your organization's virtual private network (VPN) gateway for Android and iOS devices. It's designed to allow users of those devices to connect to your on-premises resources.

Microsoft Tunnel for Intune runs in a container on Linux in your on-premises environment and enables access to on-premises resources from iOS and Android devices. Tunnel has the following requirements:

- Microsoft Defender for Endpoint (as the Microsoft Tunnel client app)
- Intune VPN profiles

> **NOTE ADDITIONAL REQUIREMENTS**
> You might also need to provision a solution such as Azure ExpressRoute to extend your on-premises network to the cloud.

Prerequisites

Before you can set up the tunnel, you'll require the following:

- An Azure subscription
- An Intune subscription
- A Linux server running containers in your on-premises network
- A transport layer security (TLS) certificate for the Linux server
- Devices running iOS or Android
- Client apps:
    - **Android**   Microsoft Defender for Endpoint
    - **iOS**   Microsoft Defender for Endpoint or Microsoft Tunnel client app

Configuring the tunnel

To set up the tunnel, you'll need to perform the following high-level steps:

1. Create a server configuration on Intune.
2. Create a site in Intune.
3. Install a Microsoft Tunnel Gateway on a Linux server in your on-premises environment (by using an Intune script).
4. Deploy the Microsoft Tunnel client app to your iOS and Android devices.
5. Create and deploy VPN profiles to your iOS and Android devices.

Specifically, you'll use Intune to perform the following:

- Download the Microsoft Tunnel installation script which you must run on your Linux container
- Configure aspects of Microsoft Tunnel Gateway: IP addresses, DNS servers, and ports
- Deploy VPN profiles to devices
- Deploy the Microsoft Tunnel client apps

CREATE THE SERVER CONFIGURATIONS

Let's examine the process. We start by creating server configurations:

1. Open Microsoft Intune admin center.
2. In the navigation pane, select **Tenant administration**.
3. On the **Tenant admin | Tenant status** page, select **Microsoft Tunnel Gateway**.
4. Click the **Server configurations** tile on the **Tenant admin | Microsoft Tunnel Gateway** page, as shown in Figure 3-33.

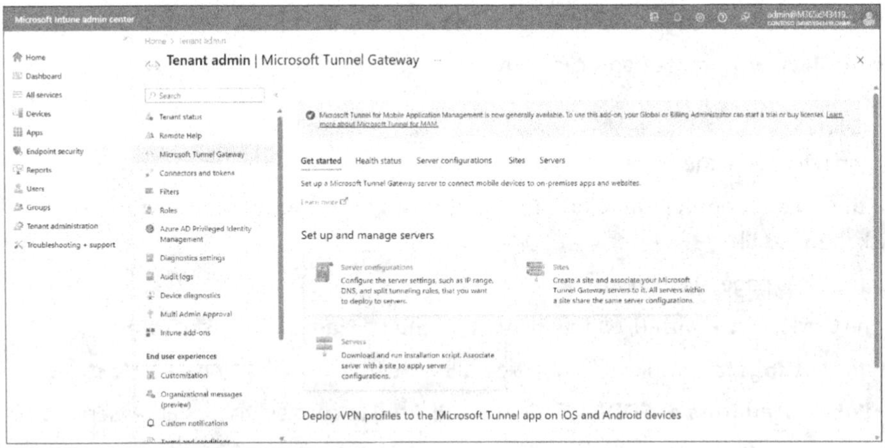

FIGURE 3-33 Provisioning the Microsoft Tunnel Gateway

5. Click **Create new**.

6. On the **Create server configuration** page, on the **Basics** tab, enter a **Name** and **Description** and click **Next**.

7. On the **Settings** page, displayed in Figure 3-34, enter the following information and click **Next**:

   - **IP address range** The addresses provided to Android and iOS devices when they connect through the tunnel.

   - **Server port** The listening TCP port used by your server. Typically, this will be 443.

   - **DNS servers** The IP addresses of DNS servers that are used by the remote client devices.

   - **DNS suffix search** The DNS suffix applied to the client devices for DNS searches.

   - **Split tunneling rules** Determine how IP routing is handled through the tunnel.

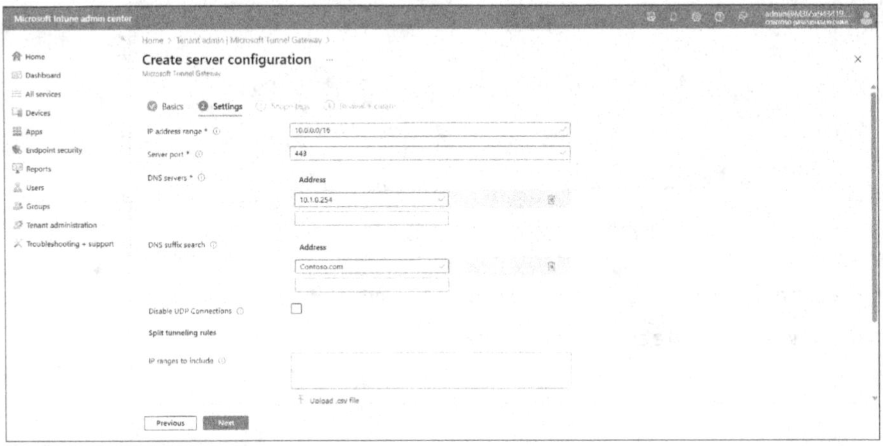

FIGURE 3-34 Creating the server configuration

8. On the **Scope tags** page, define any tags and click **Next**.

9. On the **Review + create** page, click **Create**.

CREATE THE SITES

The next step is to create the sites.

1. On the **Tenant admin | Microsoft Tunnel Gateway** page, as shown in Figure 3-33, click the **Sites** tile.

2. On the **Sites** page, click **Create**.

3. In the **Create a site** wizard, on the **Basics** tab, enter a **Name** and **Description**.

4. On the **Settings** tab, displayed in Figure 3-35, enter the following and click **Next**:

   ■ **Public IP address or FQDN**   The IP or URL used to connect to the target server.

   ■ **Server configuration**   The configuration you previously configured.

   ■ **URL for internal network access check**   Used to check network access every five minutes.

   ■ **Automatically upgrade servers as this site**   Enables you to keep your servers up to date automatically, which is recommended.

   ■ **Limit server upgrades to maintenance window**   Enables you to control when such upgrades might occur.

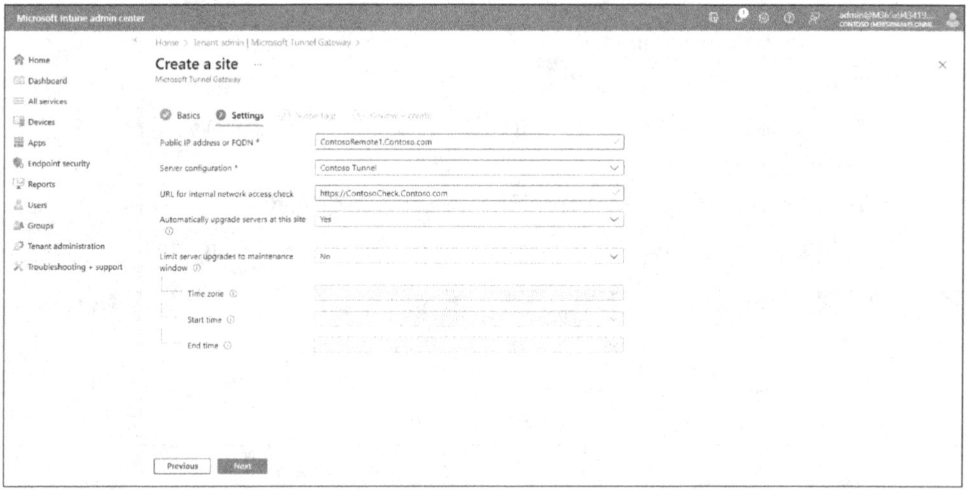

FIGURE 3-35 Creating a site configuration

5. On the **Scope tags** page, define any tags and click **Next**.

6. On the **Review + create** page, click **Create**.

CREATE THE SERVERS

The next step is to create your servers. You do this by generating and downloading a script. The script is already generated based on your previous settings. To download the script:

1. On the **Tenant admin | Microsoft Tunnel Gateway** page, click the **Servers** tile.

2. On the **Servers** page, click **Create**.

3. On the **Create a server** page, click **Download script.**

   Installing your Linux servers in your on-premises environment and running the script to enable the gateway is necessary.

CONFIGURE THE CLIENT DEVICES

Within Intune, your next steps are to deploy VPN profiles to your devices and to deploy the required app to your devices. You can perform these tasks from the **Tenant admin | Microsoft Tunnel Gateway** page.

Start by deploying the VPN profile:

1. Click the **Configuration profiles** tile on the **Tenant admin | Microsoft Tunnel Gateway** page. The **Configuration profiles** page in Intune displays.

2. Click **Create profile**, and then select the following:

   - **Platform**   Android Enterprise
   - **Profile type**   VPN

3. Click **Create**.

4. On the **Configuration settings** page, select **Microsoft Tunnel** in the **Connection type** list. Configure the settings, including selecting the appropriate Microsoft Tunnel site you configured earlier. For guidance, see the link in the Need More Review below.

5. Complete the wizard as usual, and assign the profile to the target Android devices.

6. Now, if necessary, create a VPN configuration profile for iOS. The process is very similar to that of Android.

   The final step is to deploy the required Microsoft Tunnel app to your devices.

1. Click the **Apps** tile on the **Tenant admin | Microsoft Tunnel Gateway** page. Intune's **All apps** page displays.

2. Click **Add**.

3. On the **Select app type** page, in the **App type** list, select **Android store app** and click **Select**.

4. Search for and copy the URL for the Microsoft Defender for Endpoint app in the Google Play Store.

5. Enter the required information on the **App information** page, including the Appstore URL you just copied.

6. Complete app deployment as usual. For guidance, see the Need More Review link below.

7. Now, if necessary, deploy the required app for iOS. The process is very similar to Android's (in many ways, easier).

This last step completes the process of enabling and configuring the tunnel. You can use the **Tenant admin | Microsoft Tunnel Gateway** page to monitor your configuration. Select the **Health status** tab.

> **NEED MORE REVIEW?** **CONFIGURE MICROSOFT TUNNEL FOR INTUNE**
>
> To review further details about configuring the Microsoft Tunnel for Intune, refer to the Microsoft website at *https://learn.microsoft.com/mem/intune/protect/microsoft-tunnel-configure*.

Skill 3.3: Monitor devices

You must understand what's happening on your users' devices within your organization. You must be able to identify situations in which a device has configuration problems or is experiencing device health issues. Intune provides a number of monitoring tools that can help you make these determinations.

> **This skill covers how to:**
> - Monitor devices by using Intune
> - Monitor devices by using Azure Monitor
> - Analyze and respond to issues identified in Endpoint analytics and Adoption Score

Monitor devices by using Intune

Knowing what devices are enrolled in your organization's MDM is important. Select the **Devices** node in the Microsoft Intune admin center to access device inventory reports. As shown in Figure 3-36, you can see a summary of enrolled devices.

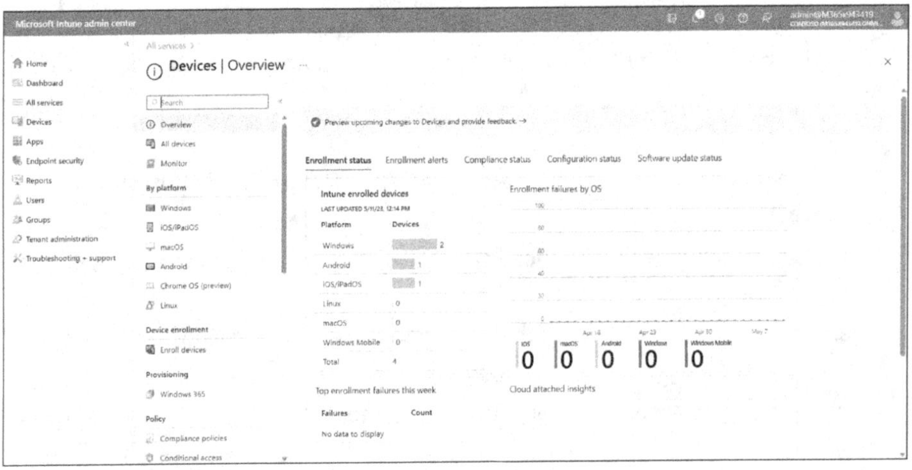

FIGURE 3-36 Overview report of Intune enrolled devices

To view additional information about enrolled devices, select **All Devices**. As shown in Figure 3-37, you can review a list of all devices.

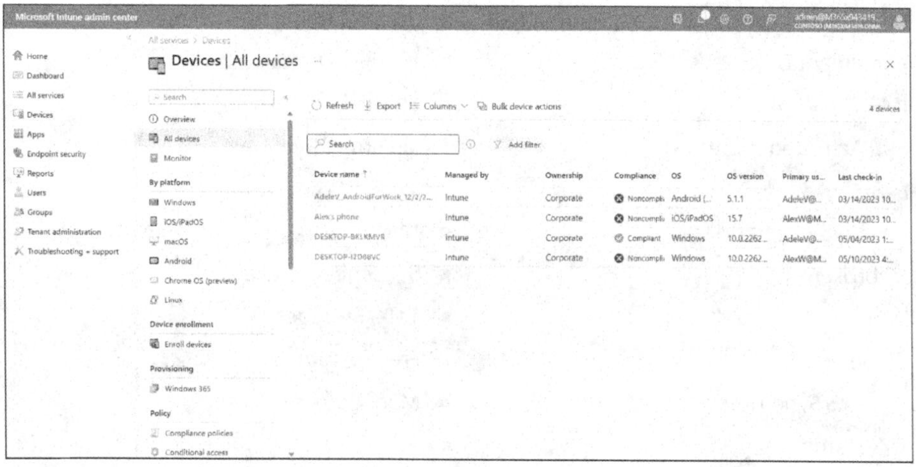

FIGURE 3-37 Reviewing all devices

SELECT COLUMNS

You can determine exactly what information is displayed using the **Columns** button shown in Figure 3-38. Select from the available columns to adjust the displayed information.

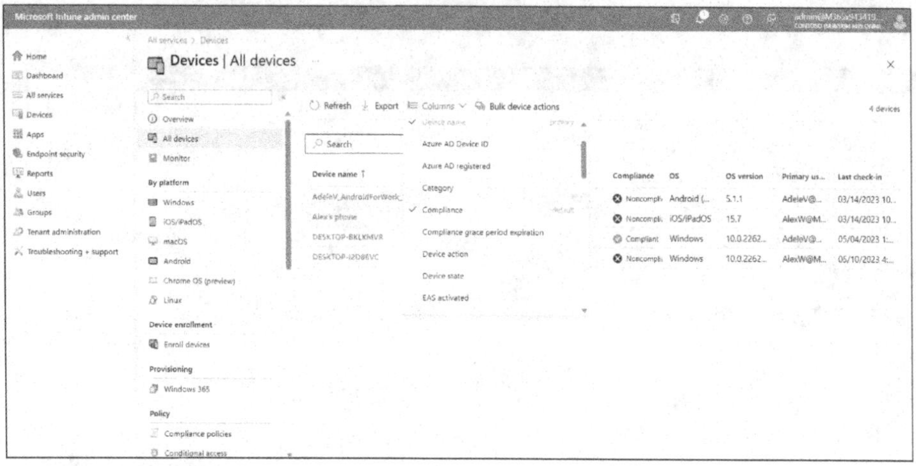

FIGURE 3-38 Selecting reporting columns for All Devices node

Available column options are as follows:

- Azure AD Device ID
- Azure AD registered
- Category
- Managed By

- Compliance Grace Period Expiration
- OS
- OS version
- Device Action

- Device State
- Enrolled By Email Address
- Last Check-In
- Enrollment Date
- IMEI
- EAS Activated
- EAS Activation ID
- Intune Registered
- Jailbroken
- Supervised
- Compliance
- Last EAS Sync Time
- EAS Status
- EAS Reason
- Encrypted
- Enrolled by user UPN

- Model
- Manufacturer
- Serial Number
- Phone Number
- Enrolled by user display name
- Security Patch Level
- Wi-Fi MAC
- MEID
- Subscriber Carrier
- Total Storage
- Free Storage
- Management Name
- Join Type
- Sku Family
- Ownership

FILTER RESULTS

You can also use filtering. Select **Add Filter**, as shown in Figure 3-39, and you can select criteria on which to filter.

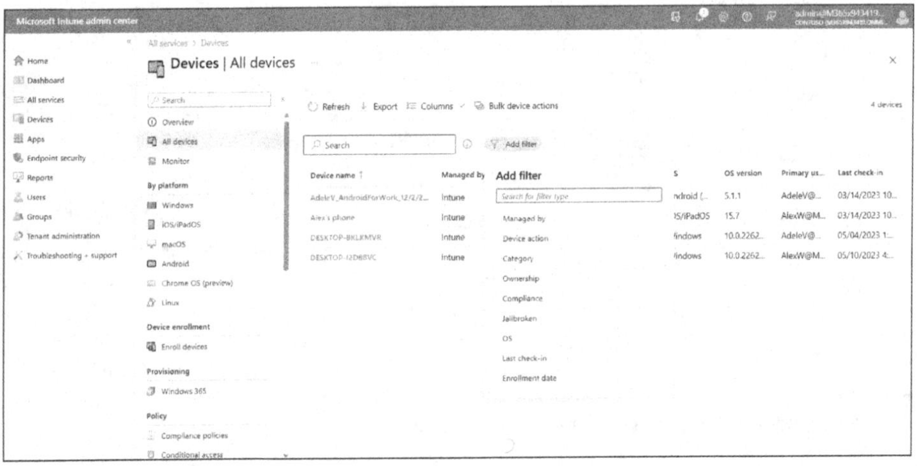

FIGURE 3-39 Selecting reporting filters for All Devices node

Filtering criteria are:

- Managed By
- Device Action
- Category

- Ownership
- Compliance
- Jailbroken
- OS
- Last Check-In, with Date And Time Ranges
- Enrollment Date, with Date And Time Ranges

EXPORT DEVICE INFORMATION

After you have filtered the devices in the list, select **Export**. You can then choose between two options:

- Only include selected columns in the exported file
- Include all inventory data in the exported file

Then select **Yes**, as shown in Figure 3-40, to export the data. A ZIP file is downloaded. You can access your report by selecting the **Open file** link in Microsoft Edge.

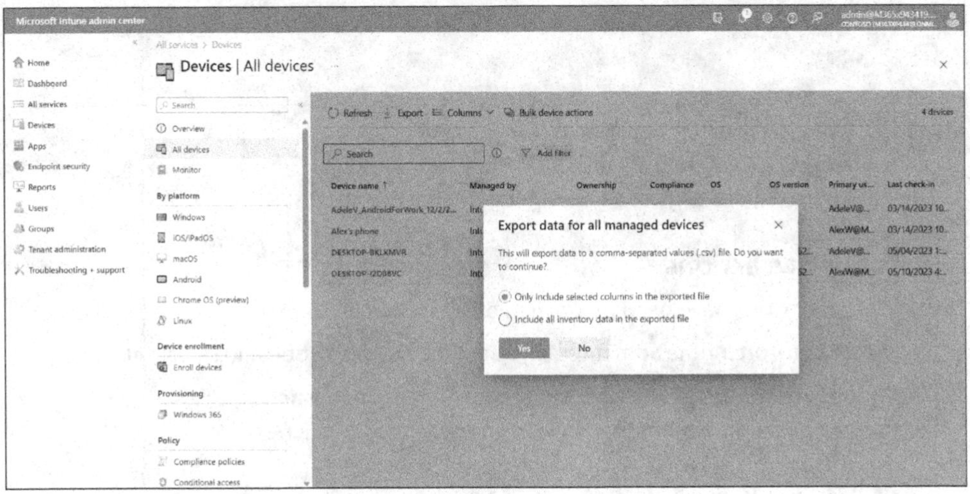

FIGURE 3-40 Exporting results for All Devices display

You can use Intune to monitor your enrolled devices. In Devices, select **Monitor**. You can then select and review the following information:

- **Configuration** Review reports on the assignment status and failures, devices with restricted apps, certificates, and a device encryption report.
- **Compliance** Review reports on noncompliant devices, devices without compliance policies, settings compliance, policy compliance, noncompliant policies, Windows health attestation reports, and threat agent status.
- **Enrollment** Review reports on Autopilot deployments, enrollment failures, and incomplete user enrollments.

- **Software updates**   Review reports on per update ring deployment state, installation failures for iOS, and feature update failures.

- **Other**   Review reports on device actions performed by administrators.

You can filter and export your required data for each reporting node, as shown in Figure 3-41.

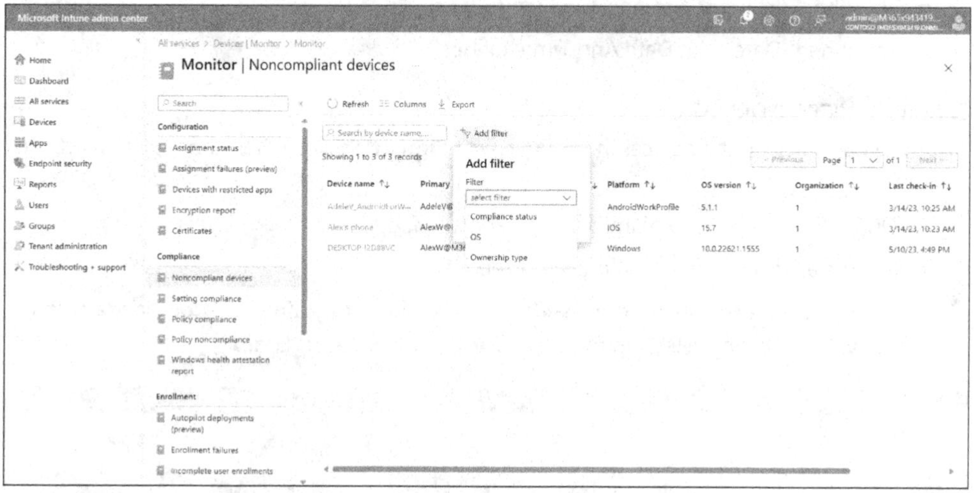

FIGURE 3-41 Filtering monitoring options

The following sections explore some of these reporting options.

Monitor device actions

To monitor actions that have been performed on your devices, use the following procedure:

1. In the Microsoft Intune admin center, select the **Devices** node and select **Monitor**.

2. On the **Monitor** page, in the **Other** section, select **Device actions**. Figure 3-42 displays the various device actions that have been performed or are pending.

3. If you want, you can filter and export the results.

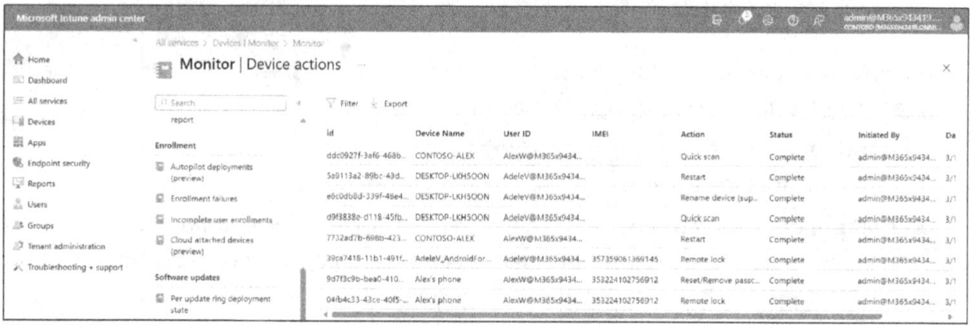

FIGURE 3-42 A list of recent and pending device actions

Review device audit logs

You can also use the device audit logs in Intune to view and analyze recent device actions, as shown in Figure 3-43. To access the logs, select the **Tenant Administration** node in the Microsoft Intune admin center in the navigation pane, and then select **Audit logs**.

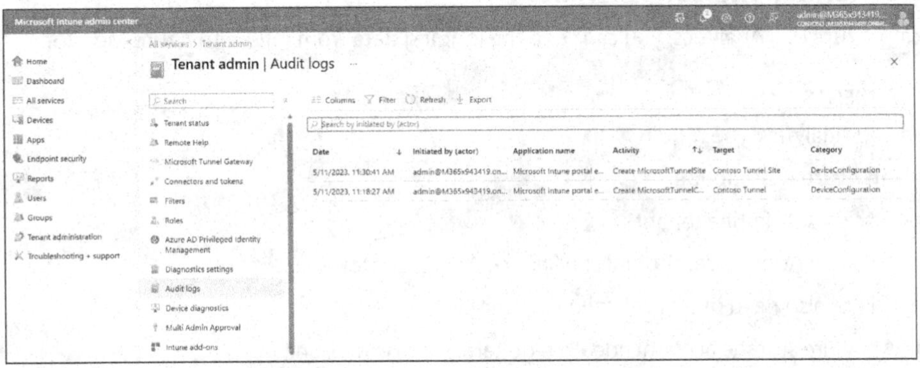

FIGURE 3-43 Viewing the Intune audit logs

You can filter and export the returned results if there are many actions or you are interested in specific devices. You can filter based on **Category**, **Activity**, and **Date Range**.

> **NEED MORE REVIEW?** **AUDIT LOGS FOR INTUNE ACTIVITIES**
>
> To review further details about using logs to analyze Intune activities, refer to the Microsoft website at *https://learn.microsoft.com/mem/intune/fundamentals/monitor-audit-logs*.

Windows Health Attestation Report

Using Windows Health Attestation in Intune enables you to view the health status of enrolled Windows devices using a number of factors, including:

- BitLocker
- Code integrity
- Early launch malware
- Boot debugging
- Secure boot
- Data execution prevention policy
- Virtual security mode
- Boot manager version

To access Windows Health Attestation data, select the devices in the Microsoft Intune admin center and then select **Monitor**. Select **Windows health attestation report**. As with many other Intune reporting features, you can filter the listed results and export the unfiltered or filtered results to a CSV file.

Monitor devices by using Azure Monitor

If your organization has an Azure subscription, you can enable additional analytics and reporting features by combining Intune and Azure Monitor.

Azure Monitor and Log Analytics

By using Azure Log Analytics, you can send the logging data from Intune to Azure Monitor.

REQUIREMENTS

To use Log Analytics, you require

- An Azure subscription
- A Microsoft Intune tenant
- A Global Administrator or Intune Service Administrator account

You might also need one of the following services:

- An Azure storage account, ideally a general storage account
- An Azure event hubs namespace to integrate with third-party solutions
- An Azure log analytics workspace to send logs to Log Analytics

To send the log data to Azure monitor, use the following high-level procedure:

1. Open the Microsoft Intune admin center.

2. In the navigation pane, select **Tenant administration**, and then select **Diagnostics settings**.

3. Select **Turn On Diagnostics** and enter the following properties:

   - Enter a name for the **Diagnostic Settings**.
   - Specify whether you want to archive to a storage account. This saves log data to an Azure storage account.
   - Select whether you want to stream to an Azure event hub.
   - Choose whether to send diagnostics to Log Analytics. If you choose this option, the data is sent to Azure Log Analytics. Choose this option if you want to use visualizations or monitoring and alerting for your logs.
   - Choose whether to send the Intune audit logs to your storage account, event hub, or Log Analytics.
   - Choose whether to send Operational logs (which show the success or failure of users and devices that enroll in Intune) to your storage account, event hub, or Log Analytics.

When you have completed the setup, you should have a dialog similar to Figure 3-44.

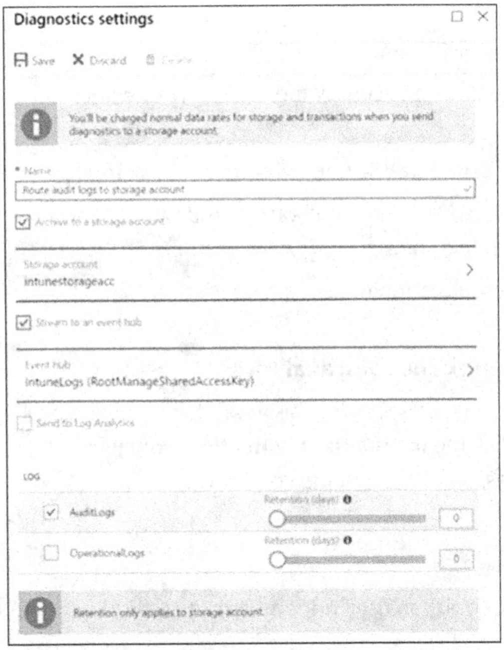

FIGURE 3-44 Verifying diagnostics settings in Intune

> **NEED MORE REVIEW?** **SEND LOGS TO AZURE MONITOR**
>
> To review further details about Azure monitor, refer to the Microsoft website at *https://learn.microsoft.com/en-us/mem/intune/fundamentals/review-logs-using-azure-monitor#send-logs-to-azure-monitor*.

Analyze and respond to issues identified in Endpoint analytics and Adoption Score

Built-in to Microsoft Endpoint Manager is Endpoint analytics. You can access this from the **Reports** node.

Implement Endpoint analytics

Before you can use Endpoint analytics, you must enable and configure it. Use the following procedure:

1. Open Microsoft Intune admin center.
2. Select **Devices** and then select **Configuration profiles**.
3. Click **Create profile**.
4. In the **Platform** list, choose **Windows 10 and later**.

5. In the **Profile type** list, choose **Templates**.

6. Select **Windows health monitoring** and click **Create**.

7. On the **Windows health monitoring** page, on the **Basics** tab, enter a **Name** and **Description**.

8. On the **Configuration settings** page, choose **Enable** in the **Health monitoring** list.

9. In the **Scope** list, select **Endpoint analytics**. You can also choose Windows updates, and although that's not directly related to Endpoint analytics, it is useful.

10. Click **Next**, and complete the wizard as usual, assigning to a group that contains all your Windows devices.

11. Then, in Intune, navigate to **Reports** and click **Endpoint analytics**.

12. Click **Settings**. Verify that the **Connected** status is shown. This might take a while to provision. When **Connected** is shown, click the **Intune data collection policy** link to verify the policy is applied to your devices, and data is being collected.

Using Endpoint analytics

After you've enabled your devices to gather data, you can use Endpoint analytics, displayed in Figure 3-45, to review the following:

- **Startup Performance** Determines and reviews startup performance for managed devices. Review the following:
  - Startup score compared to baseline
  - Model performance
  - Device performance
  - Startup processes
  - Restart frequency
- **Proactive remediations** Enables you to create and run script packages on devices that enable you to find and fix issues proactively.
- **Recommended software** Enables you to review the number of managed devices that have adopted organizational apps.
- **Application reliability** Determines and reviews application reliability in the following areas:
  - Overview
  - App performance
  - Model performance
  - Device performance
  - OS versions performance

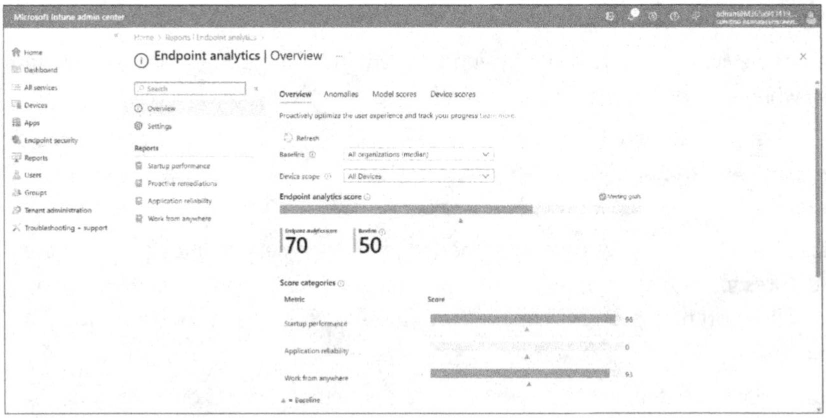

FIGURE 3-45 Reviewing Endpoint analytics overview details

Skill 3.4: Manage device updates for all supported device platforms by using Intune

Keeping computers safe and protected from external threats, such as malware and hackers, is challenging. In earlier versions of Windows, you could decide whether the operating system was automatically updated with the latest features, security updates, and fixes through the Windows Update feature. Some users choose to disable automatic updates, and these computers are vulnerable to attack. With over a billion Windows devices worldwide, even if this number is a small percentage, it might mean millions of devices were unprotected.

Windows 11 changes the game regarding updates and security because it continually and automatically benefits from new updates rolled out through Windows Update, just as with Windows 10. To enhance the security protection delivered in Windows 11, the consumer can no longer turn off security updates. Enterprise users will have some leeway on the timing of updates and upgrades, and they can still choose to test updates and deliver them internally, using other management tools to keep their devices updated. For organizations requiring a static installation of Windows 11 that will not have upgrades, Microsoft ships a special build of Windows 11, which is discussed later in this skill.

This skill covers how to:

- Plan for device updates
- Create and manage update rings by using Intune
- Configure Windows client delivery optimization by using Intune
- Create and manage update policies by using Intune
- Manage Android updates by using configuration profiles
- Monitor updates
- Troubleshoot updates in Intune

Plan for device updates

To keep your users' devices running efficiently and securely, installing updates from operating system vendors when they become available is important.

In the past, operating system updates were designed primarily to fix identified problems or security vulnerabilities for the Windows client platform. However, with Windows 10, Microsoft introduced a new update model: Windows as a service.

With Windows as a service, updates are designed to resolve perceived defects in software and add new features to the operating system. Instead of releasing new versions of Windows every few years, Microsoft now provides continual updates that provide new features to Windows 10 and newer.

As an IT professional supporting Windows client users, you must know how to manage updates within your organization. Much of this understanding is based on understanding the new Windows as a service model.

Windows as a service

Windows as a service is more about Windows deployment than it is updating; in other words, the update mechanism is used to deliver—or deploy—new builds of Windows instead of relying on more traditional deployment methods.

As an organization, this means that instead of planning and performing operating system upgrades, such as from Windows 7 to Windows 10, you use Windows Update to continually introduce new Windows client features as the operating system evolves. This means that the update process becomes a continual process, based on small incremental updates rather than significant upgrades every few years.

Two types of updates are delivered in this way:

- **Feature updates**   These add significant functionality to the Windows 11 operating system. With Windows 10, these updates were delivered twice annually. Now, both Windows 10 and Windows 11 receive Feature updates once per year, typically in the autumn. Each Feature update is referred to by its year of release and its release point in that year. Thus, 22H2 refers to the 2022 Feature updates released in the second half (H2) of 2022.

- **Quality updates**   These provide reliability and security updates and fixes. Microsoft deploys these updates monthly on the second Tuesday of the month. They are cumulative, meaning that even if you miss an update, you receive all previous updates by applying a subsequent update.

DEFERRALS

Business users of Windows 11 can determine when these updates apply. Broadly, you can configure deferral periods for both Feature and Quality updates. These deferrals define the number of days that you defer the application of released updates.

When an update is imminent, Microsoft makes it available to early adopters. When the update is finalized, the update is distributed to Windows devices worldwide.

As part of the update planning process, you should consider participating in the early release scheme for updates for some of your users' computers. This will enable you to test the effect of the updates on your organization's Windows 11 computers. You can also use deferrals to determine precisely when you will apply it to most of your computers after an update has been released.

You can continue to use a Windows 11 version typically for three years after it has been made widely available. You must then start the process over again. It's quite likely that many organizations will choose to perform continual, rolling updates. Consequently, some of your users' computers might be using one version of Windows 11 while other users are using earlier or later versions.

> **NEED MORE REVIEW?** **WINDOWS 11 RELEASE INFORMATION**
>
> If you want to know more about Windows update cadence and support windows, visit the Microsoft website at *https://learn.microsoft.com/windows/release-health/windows11-release-information*.

SELECT THE APPROPRIATE SERVICING CHANNEL

In order to implement updates within your organization, you must decide which computers will receive updates, and how quickly they will receive them after Microsoft releases them. Part of this decision is about selecting a servicing channel. Also, you must consider deferral periods for these updates.

Users of Windows 11 Home editions have no control over how their computers receive these updates. However, users in business and educational organizations who are using Windows 11 Pro, Windows 11 Enterprise, or Windows 11 Education editions can control their update experience using servicing channels. Microsoft provides several servicing channels. These channels determine when updates are applied to a computer. These channels are:

- **Windows Insider Program**   For early adopters/insiders. Three channels are available: Dev Channel, Beta Channel, and Release Preview:
  - **Dev Channel**   Receives early and frequent updates
  - **Beta Channel**   Receives less frequent updates
  - **Release Preview**   Receives what you might consider a pre-release beta of the finalized updates
- **General Availability Channel**   The default channel. Users receive updates fairly quickly after Microsoft releases them. This channel is referred to as the Retail Channel in the Microsoft Intune admin center.
- **Long-Term Servicing Channel**   A specialized version of Windows 11 Enterprise that doesn't receive feature updates. You don't configure this channel; instead, it's a licensed version of Windows 11 Enterprise (Windows 11 Enterprise LTSC).

USE DEPLOYMENT RINGS

You can create deployment rings by selecting an appropriate servicing channel and then configuring feature update and quality update deferral values. You might decide that you require a test group of computers that get updates early. You might also decide to create a group of computers that receive updates reasonably quickly after release. After testing, you might then want to enable the bulk of your remaining computers to receive the updates.

You could achieve this by using the deployment rings described in Table 3-13.

TABLE 3-13 Suggested deployment rings

Ring	Channel	Feature deferral	Quality deferral	Explanation
Test	Windows Insider – Release Preview	0 days	0 days	Enables you to evaluate and test prerelease updates before deploying them to your other devices. During this phase, you can begin to identify any potential issues with the updates.
Early	General Availability Channel (displayed as Retail Channel in Intune)	0 days	0 days	Enables you to evaluate released updates on a small subset of your devices. This enables you to identify any possible problems before you deploy updates to the rest of your computers.
Standard	General Availability Channel	90 days	15 days	For most of your users, the deferment values ensure you have had adequate time to test updates and identify possible problems.
Slow	General Availability Channel	180 days	30 days	This ring might be used to ensure that updates are applied as long as possible after their release. Devices configured into this ring might be running critical apps or services.

Create and manage update rings by using Intune

You can configure update deployment rings using the Microsoft Intune admin center, as shown in Figure 3-46.

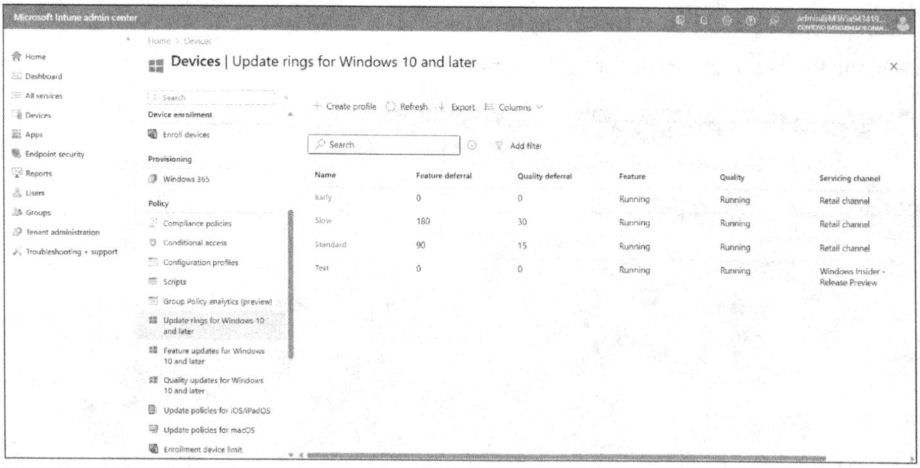

FIGURE 3-46 Implementing Microsoft Intune update rings

To create an update ring, use the following procedure:

1. Open **Microsoft Intune admin center** and navigate to **Devices**.

2. Select Windows and then select **Update rings for Windows 10 and later**.

3. Click **Create profile**.

4. On the **Create Update ring for Windows 10 and later** page, on the Basics tab, enter a **Name** and **Description**, and then click **Next**.

5. On the **Update ring settings** tab, shown in Figure 3-47, configure the following settings, and then select **Next**:

   - **Microsoft product updates**   Enables other Microsoft products, such as Office, to be updated by Windows Update.

   - **Windows drivers**   Enables driver updates to be delivered by Windows Update.

   - **Quality update deferral period (days)**   Defines the deferral period for the monthly quality updates; 30 days is the maximum value.

   - **Feature update deferral period (days)**   Defines the deferral period for the annual feature updates; 365 days is the maximum value.

   - **Upgrade Windows 10 devices to Latest Windows 11 release**   Enables you to quickly update your Windows 10 devices using the latest version of Windows 11.

   - **Set feature update uninstall period (2 – 60 days)**   Defines the uninstall period permitted on your updated devices.

   - **Enable pre-release builds**   When enabled, this setting allows you to select the pre-release channel. If set to **Not Configured**, the update ring uses the **Retail Channel**.

   - **User experience settings**   These include automatic update behavior, restart checks, and deadline settings.

6. Complete the **Scope tags** and **Assignments** tabs as required, and then click **Next**.

7. On the **Review + create** tab, click **Create**.

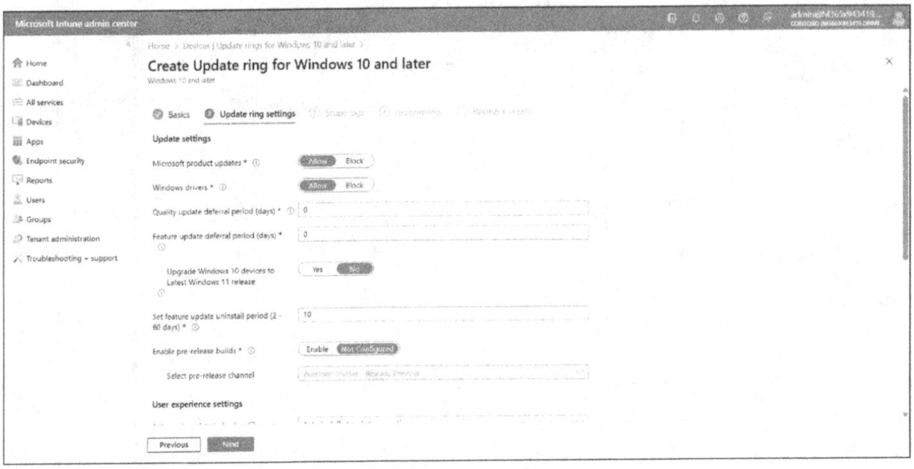

FIGURE 3-47 Creating an update ring for Windows 10 and later

> **NEED MORE REVIEW?** **MANAGE WINDOWS 10 AND WINDOWS 11 SOFTWARE UPDATES IN INTUNE**
>
> To learn more about managing updates using Intune, visit the Microsoft website at *https://learn.microsoft.com/intune/windows-update-for-business-configure*.

Configure Windows client delivery optimization by using Intune

In Windows 11, you have several options regarding how Windows updates and Microsoft Store apps are delivered to the computer. By default, Windows obtains updates from the Microsoft update servers, local network computers, and the Internet.

Windows Update Delivery Optimization enables the application of updates more quickly than previous versions of Windows. Once one PC on your local network has installed an update, other network devices can obtain the same updates without downloading directly from Microsoft.

This process is similar to popular peer-to-peer file-sharing apps. Only partial file fragments of the update files are downloaded from any source, which speeds up the delivery and increases the security of the process. If you allow delivery optimization to take place, you then can choose from the following options how your PC will obtain updates and apps from other PCs:

- **Devices on my local network**   Windows attempts to download from other PCs on your local network that have already downloaded the update or app.

- **Devices on the internet and my local network**   Windows attempts to download from the PCs on your local network, and Windows also looks for PCs on the Internet configured to share parts of updates and apps.

If Delivery Optimization is enabled, your computer can also send parts of apps or updates downloaded using Delivery Optimization to other PCs locally or on the Internet.

Typically, you'll want to configure delivery optimization settings for your Windows 11 devices by configuring device configuration profiles in Microsoft Intune. After creating a profile, assign or deploy that profile to your Windows 10/11 devices. Table 3-14 lists the available settings.

TABLE 3-14 Delivery Optimization settings

Setting	Description
Download Mode	Configure the use of Windows Update Delivery Optimization for downloads of Windows apps and updates as follows: ■ HTTP only, no peering ■ HTTP blended with peering behind the same NAT ■ HTTP blended with peering across a private group ■ HTTP blended with internet peering ■ Simple download mode with no peering ■ Bypass mode
Bandwidth optimization mode	Select the maximum bandwidth that Delivery Optimization uses across all concurrent download activities. Downloads from LAN peers are not throttled even when this policy is set. ■ Absolute ■ Percentage ■ Percentage with business hours
Delay background HTTP download (in seconds)	Delay the use of the HTTP source in a background download to prioritize the download from peers. After the max delay is reached, the download will resume from the HTTP source. The recommended value is 60 seconds.
Delay foreground HTTP download (in seconds)	Delays use of the HTTP source in a foreground download to prioritize the download from peers. After the max delay is reached, the download will resume from the HTTP source. The recommended value is 60 seconds (0-86,400).
Minimum RAM required for peer caching (in GB)	Minimum RAM required on devices to use peer caching. The recommended value is 4 GB (1-100,000).
Minimum disk size required for peer caching (in GB)	Minimum disk size required on devices to use peer caching. The recommended value is 32 GB. (1-100,000)
Minimum content file size for peer caching (in MB)	Minimum content file size required to use peer caching. The recommended value is 10 MB (1-100,000).
Minimum battery level required to upload (in %)	Minimum battery level required to upload data to peers while on battery power. Uploads will automatically pause when the battery level drops below the set minimum battery level. The recommended value is 40 percent (0-100)
Modify cache drive	The device drive that Delivery Optimization will use for its cache. The drive location can be specified using environment variables, drive letter, or full path.
Maximum cache age (in days)	The maximum retention period for each content item in the cache. The recommended value is 7 days (0-3650).
Maximum cache size type	Delivery Optimization can utilize the maximum cache size as a percentage of disk size or an absolute value (in GB).

Setting	Description
VPN peer caching	Enables the device to participate in peer caching while connected via VPN to the domain network.
Cache server host names	This policy allows you to set one or more Delivery Optimization in Network Cache servers that will be used by your client(s). One or more values can be added as either fully qualified domain names (FQDN) or IP addresses.
Delay foreground download Cache Server fallback (in seconds)	Set this policy to delay the fallback from Cache Server to the HTTP source for a foreground content download by X seconds. Note: if you set the policy to delay foreground download from HTTP, it will apply first to allow downloads from peers first (0-2,592,000).
Delay background down-load Cache Server fallback (in seconds)	Set this policy to delay the fallback from Cache Server to the HTTP source for a background content download by X seconds. Note: If you set the policy to delay background download from HTTP, it will apply first (to allow downloads from peers first) (0-2,592,000).

To create a device configuration profile that configures your required delivery optimization settings, use the following procedure:

1. Open the Microsoft Intune admin center.

2. Navigate to the **Devices**, select **Windows**, and then select **Configuration profiles**.

3. Select **Create profile**, and on the **Create a profile** page, in the **Platform** list, choose **Windows 10 and later**, and then in the **Profile Type** list, select **Templates**.

4. Select **Delivery optimization** and click **Create**.

5. On the **Delivery Optimization** page, on the **Basics** tab, enter a **Name** and **Description**, and then click **Next**.

6. On the **Configuration settings** tab, shown in Figure 3-48, enter the settings you want to configure and select **Next**.

7. Assign the profile, select **Next**, and then, optionally, configure applicability rules.

8. Select **Next**, and on the **Review + Create** tab, select **Create**.

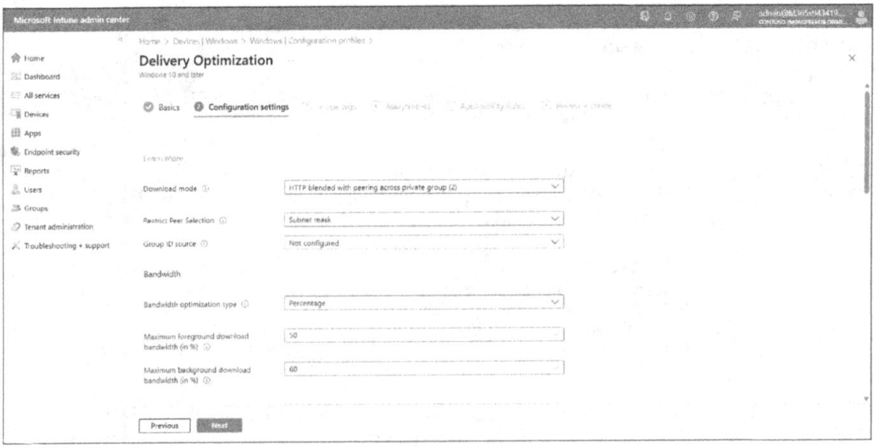

FIGURE 3-48 Device configuration profile

After the delivery optimization settings are configured in Intune or Group Policy and assigned to your devices, they replace the Delivery Optimization settings in the Settings app. Users will see the **Some settings are managed by your organization** notification.

Create and manage update policies by using Intune

It's important to be able to manage updates for all your users' devices, even if those devices are running operating systems other than Windows. Intune supports the capability to manage updates for iOS and macOS devices. For both these platforms, you create update policies.

Managing updates for iOS

Use the following procedure to create an update policy for iOS:

1. Open Microsoft Intune admin center and navigate to **Devices**.
2. Select **iOS/iPadOS**.
3. On the **iOS/iPadOS | iOS/iPadOS devices** page, click **Update policies for iOS/ iPadOS**.
4. On the **Update policies for iOS/iPadOS** page, click **Create profile**.
5. In the **Create profile** wizard, on the **Basics** tab, enter a **Name** and **Description** and click **Next**.
6. On the **Update policy settings** tab, shown in Figure 3-49, select the following, and click **Next**:
   - **Select version to install** Defaults to **Latest update**
   - **Schedule type** Defaults to **Update at next check-in**
7. Complete the wizard by configuring **Scope tags** and **Assignments**, and then create the profile.

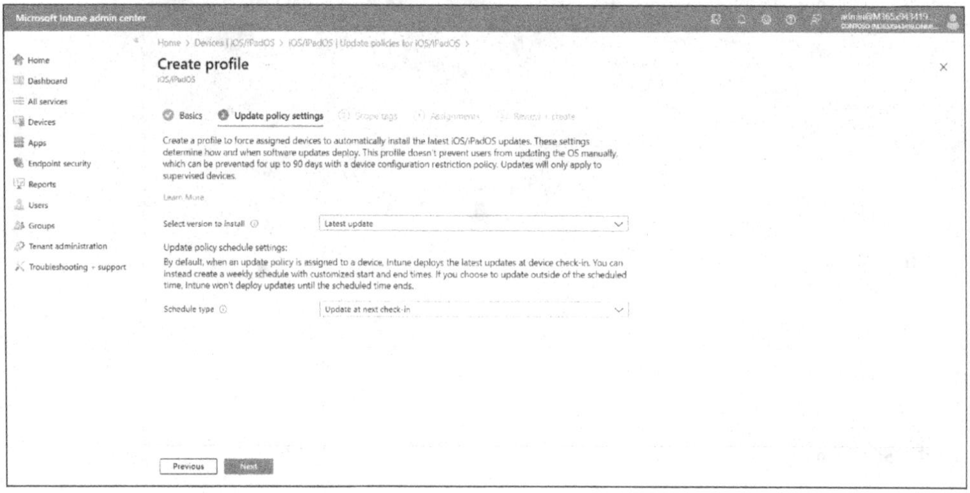

FIGURE 3-49 Creating an iOS update ring

Managing updates for macOS

To create an update policy for macOS, use the following procedure:

1. Open Microsoft Intune admin center and navigate to **Devices**.

2. Select **macOS**.

3. On the **macOS | macOS devices** page, click **Update policies for macOS**.

4. On the **Update policies for macOS** page, click **Create profile**.

5. In the **Create profile** wizard, on the **Basics** tab, enter a **Name** and **Description** and click **Next**.

6. On the **Update policy settings** tab, shown in Figure 3-50, select the following, and click **Next**:

   - **Critical updates**   Choose between **Download and install**, **Download only**, **Install immediately**, **Notify only**, and **Install later**

   - **Firmware updates**   Choose between **Download and install**, **Download only**, **Install immediately**, Notify only, and **Install later**

   - **Configuration file updates**   Choose between **Download and install**, **Download only**, **Install immediately**, **Notify only**, and **Install later**

   - **All other updates (OS, Built-in apps)**   Choose between: **Download and install**, **Download only**, **Install immediately**, **Notify only**, and **Install later**

   - **Schedule type**   Choose between **Update at next check-in**, **Update during scheduled time**, and **Update outside of scheduled time**

7. Complete the wizard by configuring **Scope tags** and **Assignments**, and then create the profile.

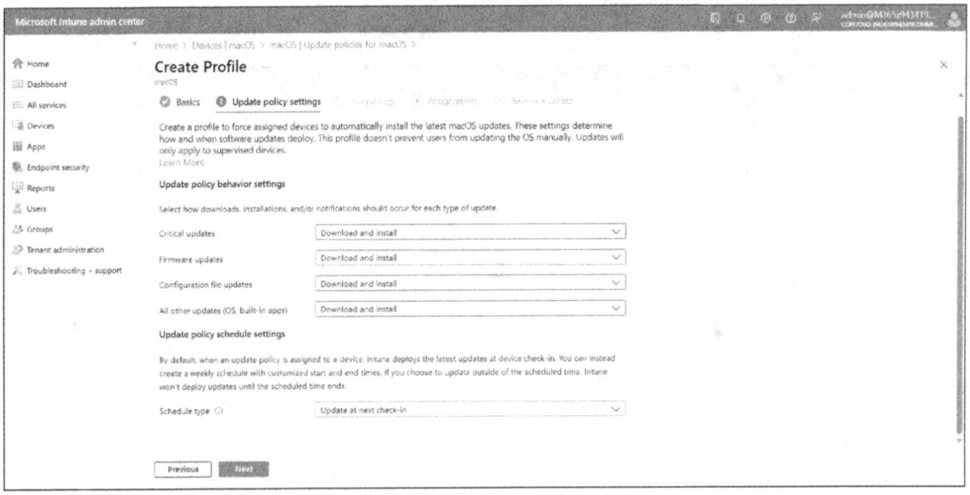

FIGURE 3-50 Creating an macOS update ring

Manage Android updates by using configuration profiles

You can also use Intune to exert a degree of control over Android Enterprise updates. This only applies to devices with Android using the fully managed, dedicated, and corporate-owned work profile. Rather than using specific update rings like you would do with Windows, iOS, and macOS, Android updates are managed though a device configuration profile.

To create a profile that includes the update settings, use the following procedure:

1. Open Microsoft Intune admin center.

2. Select **Devices** and then select **Android**.

3. On the **Android | Overview** page, click **Configuration profiles**.

4. Click **Create profile**.

5. On the **Create a profile** page, select the **Android Enterprise** and then select **Device restrictions** under the **Fully managed, Dedicated, and Corporate-Owned Work Profile** heading.

6. Click **Create**.

7. On the **Basics** tab, enter a **Name** and **Description** and click **Next**.

8. On the **Configuration settings** page, shown in Figure 3-51, expand **General** and then click **System update**. This setting ensures that when over-the-air updates are available for targeted devices, those updates are installed based on this policy. Choose between **Device Default**, **Automatic**, **Postponed**, and **Maintenance window**.

9. Depending on the option selected determines what other settings must be configured. For example, selecting **Automatic** requires no other settings.

10. Complete the wizard by configuring **Scope tags** and **Assignments**, and then create the profile.

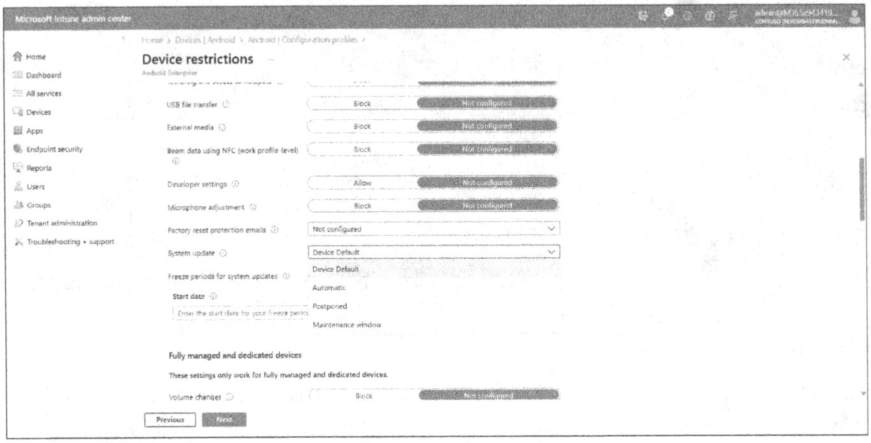

FIGURE 3-51 Using a device restrictions profile to configure Android updates

It's important to realize that the application of updates depends on the hardware vendor of your users' Android devices releasing those updates.

Monitor updates

Using the Intune admin center, you can review the current status of updates and monitor the application of those updates using the configured update rings. For Windows, use the following procedure:

1. Open Microsoft Intune admin center.

2. Navigate to **Devices | Windows** and then choose **Update rings for Windows 10 and later**.

3. Select the appropriate update ring. You can now review the application of update on the Overview tab. Select the **Device status** tab for details about specific device updates.

You can also use the Intune reporting node:

1. In the Microsoft Intune admin center, select **Reports** and then select **Windows updates**.

2. Click **Refresh** to generate reports.

From this page, you can review the following:

- **Windows Feature updates:**
  - In progress
  - Success
  - Error
  - Rollback initiated
  - Canceled
  - On hold
  - Total
- **Windows Expedited Quality updates:**
  - In progress
  - Success
  - Error
  - Canceled
  - Total

Troubleshoot updates in Intune

Updates are necessary to maintain the security and reliability of Windows 11. You should ensure that devices are receiving updates, know how to review installed updates, and find more information regarding an update.

After you have created your Windows 11 Update Rings, you can manage them with Intune. Select the appropriate update ring, and on the **Overview** page, you can view the assignment status, showing that the ring has been successfully assigned to one group, and take the following actions to manage the ring:

- **Delete** Stops enforcing the settings of the Update Ring and removes its configuration from Intune. The settings on devices that were assigned to the Update Ring remain in place.

- **Pause**   Prevents assigned devices from receiving either Feature Updates or Quality Updates for up to 35 days from the time you pause the ring. Pause functionality automatically expires after 35 days.
- **Resume**   Used to restore an Update Ring that was paused.
- **Extend**   When an Update Ring is paused, you can select **Extend** to reset the pause period.
- **Uninstall**   Use Uninstall to uninstall (roll back) the latest Feature Update or Quality Update on a device running Windows 11.

You can also modify the settings contained within an Update Ring by selecting **Properties** under the **Manage** heading and then amending the settings.

View update history

You can also review and remove any specific updates on an individual computer. Follow these steps to view your update history and see which Windows updates failed or were successfully installed on your Windows 11 device:

1. Open the **Settings** app and click **Windows Update**.
2. In **Windows Update**, click **Update History**.
3. On the **Update History** page, as shown in Figure 3-52, you can see a list of your installed Windows updates.

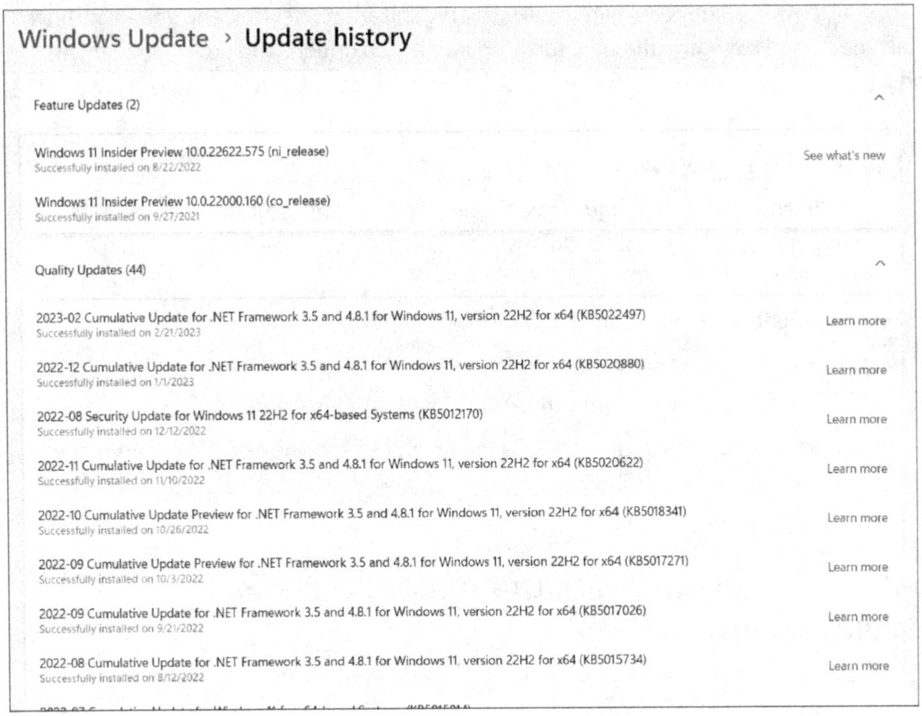

FIGURE 3-52 View Update History

4. Click one of the successfully installed updates to see more details about it.

5. In the bottom part of the screen, you can view **Definition Updates**, which relate to Microsoft Defender Antivirus and threat protection, and **Other Updates**.

Each update contains a summary of the payload. If you click the **Update** link, you are directed to the detailed Knowledge Base description on the Microsoft support pages relating to the update, which allows you to review the details about the update. You can also remove any updates you want. Click **Uninstall updates**, and then review the returned list. Choose **Uninstall** for any updates you want to remove.

NEED MORE REVIEW? **WINDOWS 11 UPDATE HISTORY**

Microsoft publishes the contents of each Windows 11 update for you to review and understand what is contained in each periodic software update. View this list at *https://support.microsoft.com/ en-us/topic/windows-11-version-22h2-update-history-ec4229c3-9c5f-4e75-9d6d-9025ab70fcce.*

Skill 3.5: Implement endpoint protection for all supported device platforms

Windows 11 contains a number of built-in features that are part of the Microsoft Defender suite of security apps. It's important that you are familiar with each of these, you can determine what they do, you know how they can help secure your organization's devices, and you know how you can enable and configure these features. You must also understand how to implement, configure, and manage these security features by using Microsoft Intune.

This skill covers how to:

- Create and manage configuration policies for Endpoint security, including antivirus, encryption, firewall, endpoint detection and response (EDR), and attack surface reduction (ASR)
- Implement and manage security baselines in Intune
- Onboard devices to Defender for Endpoint
- Implement automated response capabilities in Defender for Endpoint
- Review and respond to device issues identified in the Microsoft Defender Vulnerability Management dashboard

---

Create and manage configuration policies for Endpoint security

In this section, you'll learn how to secure your Windows 11 devices. You'll also learn about the various security features in Windows 11.

Implement enterprise-level disk encryption

It's important to be able to protect your computers against data loss and data leakage. One way in which you can do this is to enable disk encryption. Windows 11 supports BitLocker.

BitLocker enables you to encrypt an entire hard disk, including the operating system drive. BitLocker is available in Windows 11 Pro, Enterprise, and Education editions.

With BitLocker enabled, the drive is no longer susceptible to data theft. On a system that is not encrypted simply removing the drive from the PC and attaching it as a slave to another PC allows the data to be read, bypassing all NTFS security.

TRUSTED PLATFORM MODULES

Most modern computers contain a security component known as a Trusted Platform Module (TPM). This component securely stores cryptographic information, such as BitLocker's encryption keys.

BitLocker supports versions 1.2 and 2.0 of the TPM specification, and information contained on the TPM is more secure from external software attacks and physical theft.

If a device has been tampered with, such as removing the hard drive from the original computer, BitLocker prevents the drive from being unlocked. BitLocker will seek remediation from the user by entering BitLocker recovery mode and requiring the user to enter a 48-digit recovery key.

While a TPM is the most secure option, BitLocker can also be used on devices without a TPM. To enable this capability, you must configure the appropriate settings in Intune, and we'll discuss those shortly.

UNDERSTAND BITLOCKER AUTHENTICATION OPTIONS

It's important to consider the available authentication options. You can use the following methods:

- **TPM + startup PIN + startup key**   This is the most secure combination. The encryption key is stored on the TPM chip. The user might find this option cumbersome because this requires multiple authentication tasks.
- **TPM + startup key**   The encryption key is stored on the TPM chip. The user must insert a USB flash drive containing a startup key.
- **TPM + startup PIN**   The encryption key is stored on the TPM chip. The user needs to enter a PIN to unlock the device.
- **Startup key only**   The user needs to insert a USB flash drive with the startup key on it. The device doesn't need to have a TPM chip. The BIOS must support access to the USB flash drive before the operating system loads.
- **TPM only**   The encryption key is stored on the TPM chip, and no user action is required.

With all the BitLocker authentication methods, the drive is encrypted until unlocked. When the BitLocker encrypted drive is in recovery mode, you can also unlock the drive by using either the recovery password or recovery key:

- **Recovery password** This is a 48-digit number typed on a regular keyboard or by using the function keys (F1-F10) to input the numbers.

- **Recovery key** This is an encryption key created when the BitLocker is first employed and is for recovering data encrypted on a BitLocker volume. Often the encryption key is stored on removable media.

Because the TPM chip and BitLocker protect the hard drive, administrators can also configure BitLocker to operate without additional unlock steps, so long as the device (and TPM) recognize the drive, it will be unlocked.

CONFIGURE BITLOCKER WITH INTUNE

If you have many devices on which you want to enable and manage BitLocker, you can use Microsoft Intune. To configure BitLocker, use the following procedure:

1. Open Microsoft Intune admin center.

2. Navigate to **Endpoint security** and select **Disk encryption**.

3. In the details pane, select **Create Policy**.

4. On the **Create a profile** page, displayed in Figure 3-53, in **Platform**, select **Windows 10 and later**.

5. In the **Profile**, select **BitLocker**, and then select **Create**.

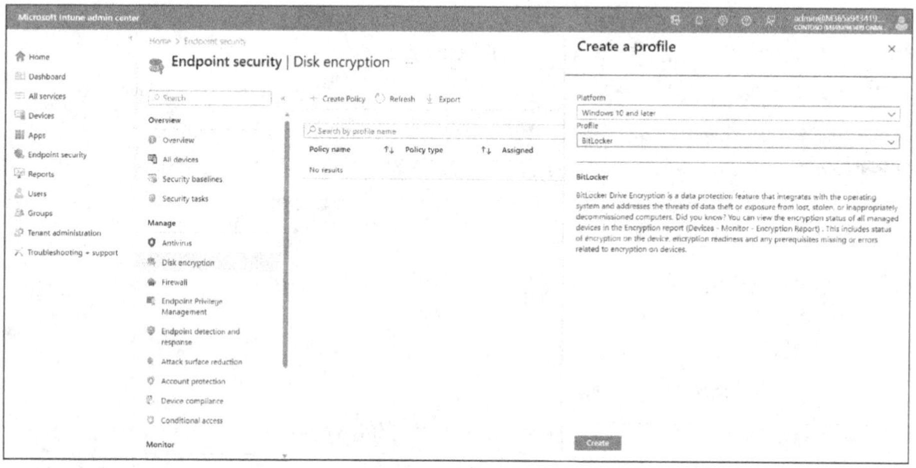

FIGURE 3-53 Creating a BitLocker profile in Intune

6. On the **Create profile** page, on the **Basics** tab, enter a **Name** and **Description**, and then select **Next**.

7. On the **Configuration settings** tab, shown in Figure 3-54, configure the following settings, and then select **Next**:

- **BitLocker – Base Settings** Including whether to enable full disk encryption for OS and fixed data drives.
- **BitLocker – Fixed Drive Settings** Including drive recovery settings and encryption methods for fixed data drives.
- **BitLocker – OS Drive Settings** Including whether Startup authentication is required, such as TPM startup options as discussed earlier. You can also define the system drive recovery options.
- **BitLocker – OS Drive Settings** Including blocking write access to removable data drives not protected by BitLocker.

8. Optionally, configure scope tags, and then, in the **Assignments** tab, assign the profile to the required groups.

9. Finally, on the **Review + create** tab, select **Create**.

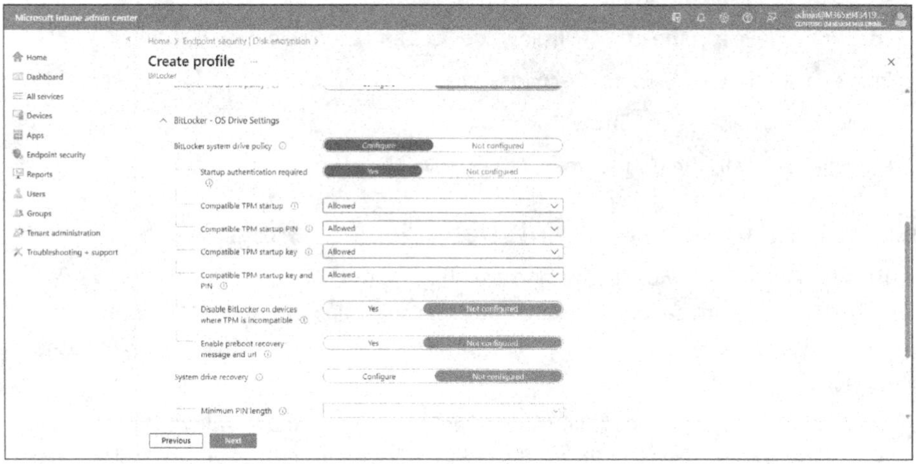

FIGURE 3-54 Configuring BitLocker – OS Drive Settings in an Intune profile

You can also configure BitLocker settings in Intune by using Configuration Profiles in the Devices node. Use the following procedure:

1. Select **Devices**, select **Windows**, and then select **Configuration profiles**.

2. Select **Create profile**, and in the **Platform** list, select **Windows 10 and later**.

3. In the **Profile type** list, select **Templates**. You can now choose either:

- **Administrative templates** Choose this option to use an interface that's broadly similar to that used when configuring GPO settings. Create the profile as usual, and on the **Configuration Settings** tab, expand **Computer Configuration > Windows Components > BitLocker Drive Encryption > Operating System Drives** and configure the required values. Then complete the process of configuring and assigning the profile. The advantage of configuring BitLocker this way is that you can combine settings with others which are also configurable in the Administrative Template profile.

- **Endpoint protection**   You can use Endpoint Protection profiles to configure a range of security settings, including those for BitLocker. Create the profile in the usual way, and on the **Configuration settings** tab, in addition to any other settings, make sure to expand **Windows Encryption**. You can then require BitLocker encryption and go on to configure BitLocker base settings, OS drive settings, and fixed data-drive settings. Complete the process of configuring and assigning the profile.

BITLOCKER RECOVERY

If your users' computers experience a situation where BitLocker will not unlock their operating system drive, they must enter a recovery key, as mentioned earlier. You can store and access the keys using Intune.

To access the BitLocker key for a user, use the following procedure:

1. In the Microsoft Intune admin center, navigate to **Devices** and select **Windows devices**.
2. Locate the device in the list of Windows devices and then select it.
3. In the navigation pane, select **Recovery keys**.
4. In the details pane, select **Show Recovery Key**.
5. Provide the key to the user to unlock their drive.

Implement and manage Microsoft Defender Credential Guard

When users sign in, they provide their user credentials via the Local Security Authority subsystem (LSA) to an authentication service. These user credentials are stored temporarily in memory in the LSA as hashes. Certain malicious software can access the LSA and exploit the stored hashes.

To help protect against this possibility, Windows 11 Enterprise and Windows 11 Education editions have a feature called Microsoft Defender Credential Guard, which implements virtualization-assisted security technology, enabling Microsoft Defender Credential Guard to block access to credentials stored in the Local Security Authority.

REQUIREMENTS

In addition to requiring the appropriate edition of Windows 11, the following are the requirements for implementing Microsoft Defender Credential Guard:

- Support for Virtualization-based security.
- UEFI 2.3.1 or greater.
- Secure Boot.
- TPM 1.2 or 2.0, either discrete or firmware.
- UEFI (firmware) lock preferred.
- Virtualization features: Intel VT-x or AMD-V; SLAT must be enabled.
- Windows hypervisor, although Hyper-V doesn't need to be installed.

Implement Microsoft Defender Credential Guard

After verifying that your computer meets the requirements, you can enable Microsoft Defender Credential Guard by using Group Policy or Microsoft Intune. To use Intune, perform the following steps:

1. Open Microsoft Intune admin center.

2. Navigate to **Endpoint security** and select **Account protection**.

3. In the details pane, select **Create Policy**.

4. On the **Create a profile** page, displayed in Figure 3-55, in **Platform**, select **Windows 10 and later**, and in the **Profile** list, choose **Account protection**.

5. Click **Create**.

6. In the **Create profile** wizard, on the **Basics** tab, enter a **Name** and **Description** and click **Next**.

7. On the **Configuration settings** page, select **Enable with UEFI lock** in the **Turn on Credential Guard** list and click **Next**.

8. Complete the wizard by defining scope tags and assignments and click **Create** on the **Review + create** page.

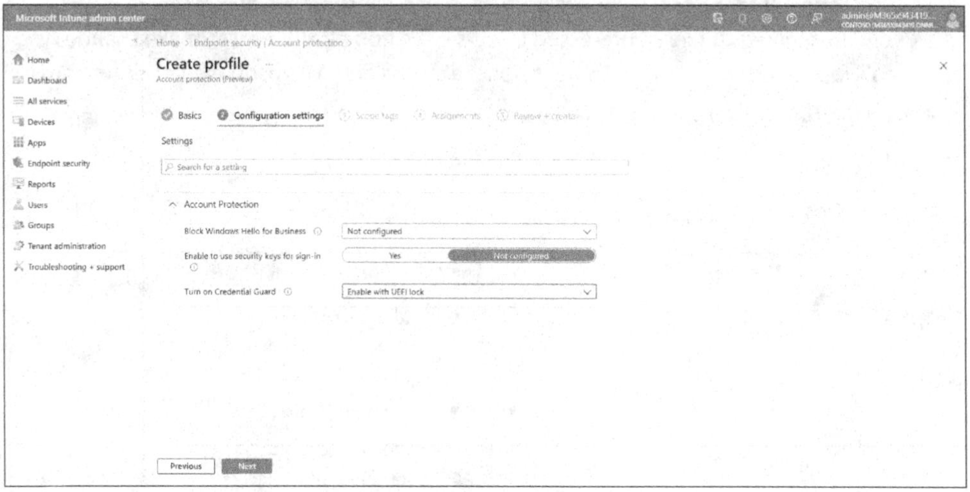

FIGURE 3-55 Enabling Microsoft Defender Credential Guard

You can also use a configuration profile of type Endpoint protection:

1. Select **Devices**, select **Windows**, and then select **Configuration profiles**.

2. Select **Create profile**, and in the **Platform** list, select **Windows 10 and later**.

3. In the **Profile type** list, select **Templates**.

4. In the list of templates, select **Endpoint protection**, and click **Create**.

5. On the **Configuration settings** page, expand **Microsoft Defender Credential Guard** and configure the desired settings.

NEED MORE REVIEW? **MANAGE MICROSOFT DEFENDER CREDENTIAL GUARD**

To review further details about how Microsoft Defender Credential Guard works, refer to the Microsoft website at *https://learn.microsoft.com/windows/security/identity-protection/credential-guard/credential-guard-manage*.

Implement Microsoft Defender Exploit Guard

You can use Microsoft Defender Exploit Guard to help to reduce the attack surface of your users' apps. Microsoft Defender Exploit Guard consists of four components:

- **Exploit protection** Uses Microsoft Defender Antivirus or, if installed, third-party antivirus software to help mitigate exploit techniques used against your organization's apps.
- **Attack surface reduction rules** Uses rules to help prevent attack vectors implemented by scripts, email, and Office-based malware. Based on Microsoft Defender Antivirus.
- **Network protection** Extends Microsoft Defender SmartScreen protection in Microsoft Edge to other applications to prevent access to Internet domains that might host phishing scams, exploits, and other malicious content. Requires Microsoft Defender Antivirus and cloud-delivered protection enabled.
- **Controlled folder access** Helps protect against ransomware and malware by preventing changes to files in protected folders if the app attempting to make changes is malicious or exhibits suspicious behavior. It also requires Microsoft Defender Antivirus.

Note that different features are available in different Windows 11 edition, as shown in Table 3-15.

TABLE 3-15 Windows Defender Exploit Guard features

Edition of Windows 11	Features supported
Windows 11 Home	■ Exploit protection ■ Controlled folder access
Windows 11 Pro	■ Exploit protection ■ Controlled folder access
Windows 11 Enterprise E3 Windows 11 Education E3	■ Exploit protection ■ Controlled folder access ■ Network protection
Windows 11 Enterprise E5 Windows 11 Education E5	■ Exploit protection ■ Controlled folder access ■ Network protection ■ Attack surface reduction rules

EXPLOIT PROTECTION

Exploit Protection helps to protect your users' devices against malware that uses exploits to spread through your organization. Exploit Protection consists of a number of specific mitigations that you must enable and configure separately.

By default, Exploit Protection already enables several mitigations that apply to the operating system and specific apps. However, if you want to configure these and other mitigations, use the following procedure:

1. Open the **Windows Security** app.

2. Select the **App & browser control** tab.

3. Scroll down and select the **Exploit protection settings** link.

4. Configure the required settings on the **Exploit protection** page, shown in Figure 3-56. You can configure **System** settings and also specific **Program** settings. Review Table 3-16 for an overview of available settings.

5. Select the **Export settings** link to export the settings to an XML file.

6. Distribute the XML file to other devices by using Microsoft Intune.

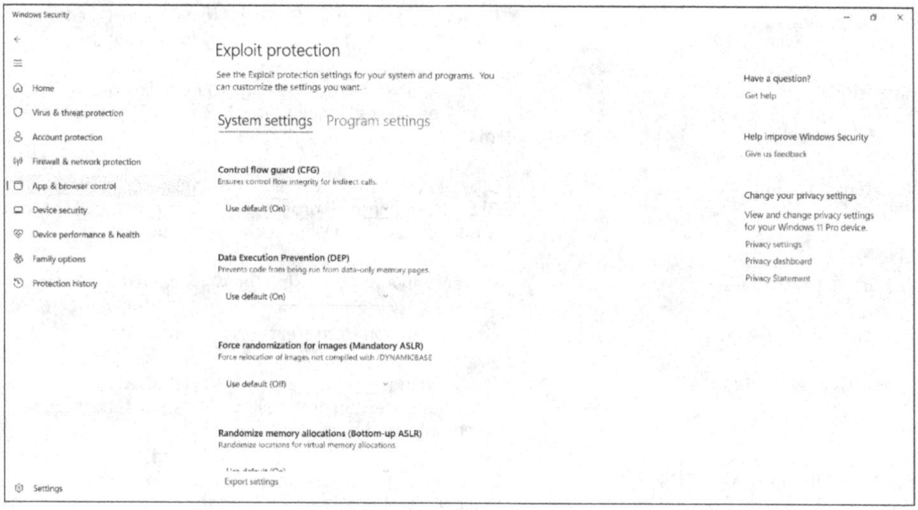

FIGURE 3-56 Configuring exploit protection settings

TABLE 3-16 Exploit protection mitigations

Mitigation	Explanation
Control Flow Guard (CFG)	Control Flow Guard combats memory corruption vulnerabilities.
Data Execution Prevention (DEP)	Helps to prevent executable code from being run from pages that contain data.
Force Randomization For Images (Mandatory ASLR)	Helps prevent attacks by putting processes into memory at random locations.
Randomize Memory Allocations (Bottom-Up ASLR)	Helps prevent attacks by putting processes into memory at random locations.
High-Entropy ASLR	Helps prevent attacks by increasing variability when using Randomize memory allocations.

Mitigation	Explanation
Validate Exception Chains (SEHOP)	Helps prevent the use of a structured exception-handler attack.
Validate Heap Integrity	Helps to prevent attacks that seek to use memory corruption.
Arbitrary code guard (ACG)	Prevents the introduction of non-image-backed executable code and prevents code pages from being modified. Optionally, it can allow thread opt-out and remote downgrade (configurable only with PowerShell).
Block low integrity images	Prevents the loading of images marked with Low Integrity.
Block remote images	Prevents loading of images from remote devices.
Block untrusted fonts	Prevents loading any GDI-based fonts not installed in the system fonts directory, notably fonts from the web.
Code integrity guard	Restricts loading of images signed by Microsoft, WHQL, or higher. Can optionally allow Microsoft Store signed images.
Disable extension points	Disables various extensibility mechanisms that allow DLL injection into all processes, such as AppInit DLLs, window hooks, and Winsock service providers.
Disable Win32k system calls	Prevents an app from using the Win32k system call table.
Do not allow child processes	Prevents an app from creating child processes.
Export address filtering (EAF)	Detects dangerous operations being resolved by malicious code. Can optionally validate access by modules commonly used by exploits.
Import address filtering (IAF)	Detects dangerous operations being resolved by malicious code.
Simulate execution (SimExec)	Ensures that calls to sensitive APIs return to legitimate callers. Only configurable for 32-bit (x86) applications. Not compatible with ACG
Validate API invocation (CallerCheck)	Ensures that legitimate callers invoke sensitive APIs. Only configurable for 32-bit (x86) applications. Not compatible with ACG
Validate handle usage	Causes an exception to be raised on any invalid handle references.
Validate image dependency integrity	Enforces code signing for Windows image dependency loading.
Validate stack integrity (StackPivot)	Ensures that the stack has not been redirected for sensitive APIs. Not compatible with ACG

ATTACK SURFACE REDUCTION RULES

Attack Surface Reduction rules can help prevent actions and apps often used by exploit-seeking malware from infecting your organization's devices. Each rule is identified by a unique identity known as a GUID. Table 3-17 lists and describes the available Attack Surface Reduction rules and their respective GUIDs.

TABLE 3-17 Attack Surface Reduction rules

Rule and description	GUID
Block executable content from email client and webmail.	be9ba2d9-53ea-4cdc-84e5-9B1eeee46550
Block all Office applications from creating child processes.	d4f940ab-401b-4efc-aadc-ad5f3c50688a
Block Office applications from creating executable content.	3b576869-a4eC-4529-8536-b80a7769e899
Block Office applications from injecting code into other processes.	75668c1f-73b5-4Cf0-bb93-3ecf5cb7cc84
Block JavaScript or VBScript from launching down-loaded executable content.	d3e037e1-3eb8-44c8-a917-57927947596d
Block execution of potentially obfuscated scripts.	5beb7efe-fd9A-4556-801d-275e5ffc04cc
Block Win32 API calls from Office macro.	92e97fa1-2edf-4476-bdd6-9dd0B4dddc7b
Block executable files from running unless they meet a prevalence, age, or trusted list criteria.	01443614-cd74-433a-b99e-2ecdc07bfc25
Use advanced protection against ransomware.	c1db55ab-c21a-4637-bb3f-a12568109d35
Block credential stealing from the Windows local security authority subsystem (lsass.exe).	9e6c4e1f-7d60-472f-ba1a-a39ef669e4b2
Block process creations originating from PSExec and WMI commands.	d1e49aac-8f56-4280-b9ba-993a6d77406c

Rule and description	GUID
Block untrusted and unsigned processes that run from USB.	b2b3f03d-6a65-4f7b-a9c7-1c7ef74a9ba4
Block Office communication applications from creating child processes.	26190899-1602-49e8-8b27-eb1d0a1ce869
Block Adobe Reader from creating child processes.	7674ba52-37eb-4a4f-a9a1-f0f9a1619a2c

> **NEED MORE REVIEW?** **ENABLE ATTACK SURFACE REDUCTION RULES**
>
> To review further details about configuring Attack Surface Reduction rules, refer to the Microsoft website at *https://learn.microsoft.com/en-us/microsoft-365/security/defender-endpoint/ enable-attack-surface-reduction?view=o365-worldwide*.

NETWORK PROTECTION

Network Protection helps prevent your users from using apps to access Internet-based domains that might present a risk of malware, scams, or other malicious content. You can use GPOs, Microsoft Intune, or Windows PowerShell to enable network protection.

> **NEED MORE REVIEW?** **ENABLE NETWORK PROTECTION**
>
> To review further details about enabling and configuring Network Protection, refer to the Microsoft website at *https://docs.microsoft.com/en-us/windows/security/threat-protection/ microsoft-defender-atp/network-protection*.

CONTROLLED FOLDER ACCESS

You can use Controlled Folder Access to help prevent the spread of malicious software. Specifically, controlled folder access helps protect valuable data stored in specific folders. You can use Windows PowerShell, GPOs, or MDM to configure controlled folder access.

> **NEED MORE REVIEW?** **ENABLE CONTROLLED FOLDER ACCESS**
>
> To review further details about configuring folder access, refer to the Microsoft website at *https://docs.microsoft.com/en-us/windows/security/threat-protection/microsoft-defender-atp/ controlled-folders*.

IMPLEMENTING MICROSOFT DEFENDER EXPLOIT GUARD

Having learned about each of the elements of Exploit Guard, it's important that you know how to enable and configure these settings in Intune. Use the following procedure:

1. Open Microsoft Intune admin center.
2. Navigate to **Devices** and then select **Windows**.

3. Click **Configuration profiles**.

4. Click **Create profile**.

5. On the **Create a profile** page, select **Windows 10 and later** and then select **Templates**.

6. In the list of templates, select **Endpoint protection** and click **Create**.

7. Enter a **Name** and **Description** on the **Basics** tab, and then, on the **Configuration settings** page, expand **Microsoft Defender Exploit Guard**.

8. As shown in Figure 3-57, configure the required settings in the following folders:

   ▪ **Attack Surface Reduction**   Select the desired protections.

   ▪ **Controlled folder access**   Enable the setting and define apps and folders.

   ▪ **Network filtering**   Enable the setting or enable in Audit mode.

   ▪ **Exploit protection**   Browse and locate a previously created XML file that contains exploit settings you exported from the Windows Security app on a properly configured device.

9. Click **Next**, configure scope tags and assignments as necessary, and then **Create** the profile.

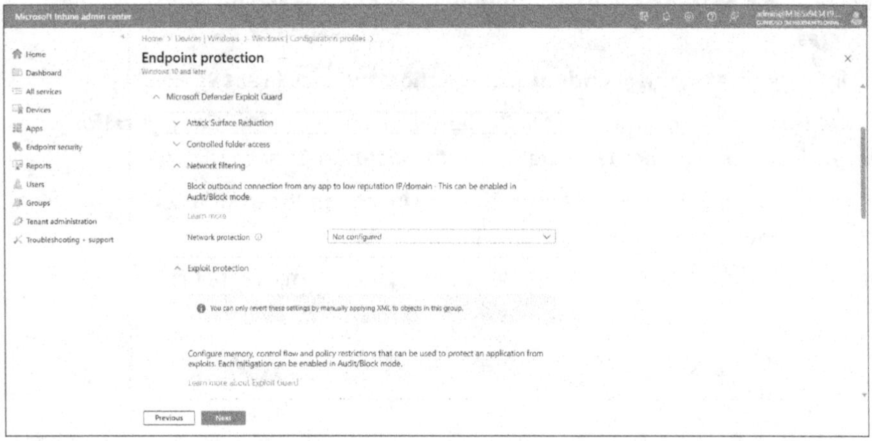

FIGURE 3-57 Configuring Exploit Guard settings

Implement Microsoft Defender Application Guard

Microsoft Defender Application Guard isolates browser sessions from the local device by running those sessions in a virtual machine environment; this helps prevent malicious apps or content from accessing the local device.

REQUIREMENTS
The requirements for Microsoft Defender Application Guard are as follows:

   ▪ 64-bit version of Windows 11 Enterprise, Education, or Professional.

   ▪ 8 GB of physical memory is recommended.

- Support for Virtualization-based security.
- Secure Boot.
- Virtualization features: Intel VT-x, AMD-V, and SLAT must be enabled.
- An Intel VT-d or AMD-Vi input-output memory management unit.

CONFIGURE MICROSOFT DEFENDER APPLICATION GUARD

You can configure Microsoft Defender Application Guard in one of two modes:

- **Standalone Mode**   In standalone mode, users can manage their own device settings.
- **Enterprise-Managed Mode**   With Enterprise mode, an administrator configures appropriate device settings using GPOs, MDM, or Windows PowerShell.

You can enable and configure Microsoft Defender Application Guard from Windows Security. However, to configure the relevant settings in Intune, use the following procedure:

1. Open Microsoft Intune admin center.
2. Navigate to **Devices** and then select **Windows**.
3. Click **Configuration profiles**.
4. Click **Create profile**.
5. On the **Create a profile** page, select **Windows 10 and later** and then select **Templates**.
6. In the list of templates, select **Endpoint protection** and click **Create**.
7. Enter a **Name** and **Description** on the **Basics** tab, and then, on the **Configuration settings** page, expand **Microsoft Defender Application Guard**.
8. As shown in Figure 3-58, select **Enabled for Edge** in the **Application Guard** list, and then configure supplemental settings, such as clipboard behavior and printing. Click **Next**.
9. Configure scope tags and assignments as necessary, and then choose **Create** to create the profile.

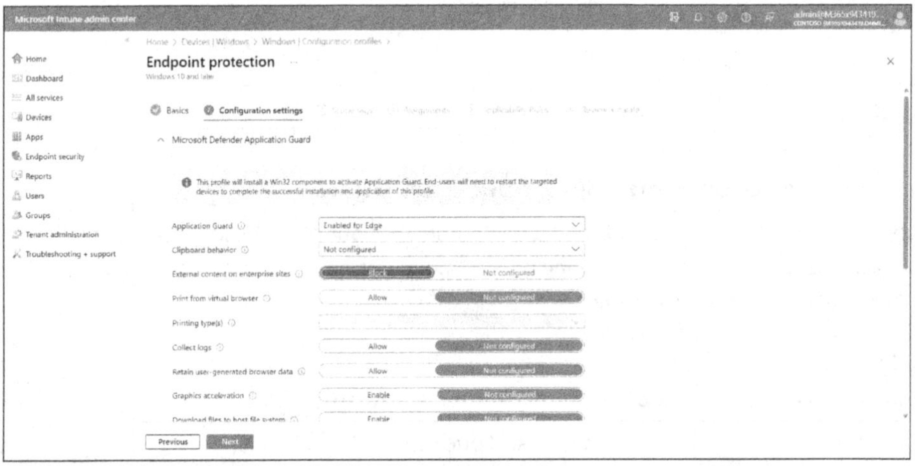

FIGURE 3-58 Enabling and configuring Application Guard

To use Microsoft Defender Application Guard in standalone mode, select the ellipsis button in Microsoft Edge and then select **New Application Guard window**, as shown in Figure 3-59. The Microsoft Defender Application Guard service starts, and then a new instance of Microsoft Edge opens.

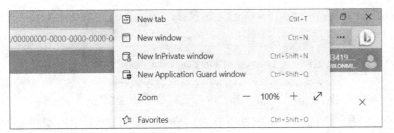

FIGURE 3-59 Opening a new Application Guard window

NEED MORE REVIEW?   **CONFIGURE MICROSOFT DEFENDER APPLICATION GUARD POLICY SETTINGS**

To learn how to configure Microsoft Defender Application Guard policies, refer to the Microsoft website at *https://learn.microsoft.com/windows/security/threat-protection/microsoft-defender-application-guard/md-app-guard-overview.*

Implement Microsoft Defender Application Control

Microsoft Defender Application Control enables you to determine precisely which apps your users are allowed to run by blocking any unsigned apps and scripts. You configure Microsoft Defender Application Control with policies that specify whether a code that runs in kernel mode, such as device drivers or apps, can run.

A policy typically includes rules that

- Control options such as whether audit mode is enabled
- Determine whether user mode code integrity (UMCI) is enabled
- Specify the level at which apps are to be identified and/or trusted

Each Windows 11 device has a single Microsoft Defender Application Control policy defined for it. Typically, you configure this using GPOs in an AD DS environment or Intune for enrolled devices. Either way, the policy is stored as a local file called SIPolicy.p7b that resides in the C:\Windows\System32\CodeIntegrity folder; for UEFI-based computers, the file is <EFI System Partition>\Microsoft\Boot.

SIGN APPS

To enable Microsoft Defender Application Control in your organization, you must digitally sign all the trusted apps that you want to allow to run on your devices. You can do this in a number of ways, as listed below:

- **Publish your apps by using the Microsoft Store**   All apps in the Microsoft Store are automatically signed with signatures from a trusted certificate authority (CA).

- **Use your own digital certificate or public key infrastructure (PKI)**   You can sign the apps by using a certificate issued by a CA in your own PKI.
- **Use a non-Microsoft CA**   You can use a trusted non-Microsoft CA to sign your own desktop Windows apps.
- **Use the Microsoft Defender Application Control signing portal**   In Microsoft Store for Business, you can use a Microsoft web service to sign your desktop Windows apps.

CREATE A DEFAULT MICROSOFT DEFENDER APPLICATION CONTROL POLICY

To create a default policy, create a virus- and malware-free reference computer that contains the set of apps your users require to run. You might need to create several reference computers, each representing a typical device configuration within your organization. For example, you create a standard device for the research department, and perhaps you create a kiosk-type device for use in the library.

Having created the reference computer, sign in and then complete the following procedure:

1. Open an elevated Windows PowerShell command prompt.

2. Create the required variables for the process by running the following three commands:

```
$CIPolicyPath=$env:userprofile+"\Desktop\"
$InitialCIPolicy=$CIPolicyPath+"InitialScan.xml"
$CIPolicyBin=$CIPolicyPath+"DeviceGuardPolicy.bin"
```

3. Scan the system for installed apps using the New-CIPolicy cmdlet:

```
New-CIPolicy -Level PcaCertificate -FilePath $InitialCIPolicy -UserPEs
3> CIPolicyLog.txt
```

4. Convert the WDAC policy to a binary format (for import) using the ConvertFrom-CIPolicy cmdlet:

```
ConvertFrom-CIPolicy $InitialCIPolicy $CIPolicyBin
```

ENABLE MICROSOFT DEFENDER APPLICATION CONTROL

After creating the default WDAC policy, you can configure the settings with GPOs or Microsoft Intune. To use Intune, use the following procedure:

1. Open Microsoft Intune admin center.

2. Navigate to **Devices** and then select **Windows**.

3. Click **Configuration profiles**.

4. Click **Create profile**.

5. On the **Create a profile** page, select **Windows 10 and later** and then select **Templates**.

6. In the list of templates, select **Endpoint protection** and click **Create**.

7. Enter a **Name** and **Description** on the **Basics** tab, and then, on the **Configuration settings** page, expand **Microsoft Defender Application Control**.

8. In the **Application control code integrity policies** list, select **Enforce** or **Audit** only as appropriate.

9. Then in the **Trust apps with good reputation** list, select **Enable**. Click **Next**.

10. Configure scope tags and assignments as necessary, and then **Create** the profile.

> ***NEED MORE REVIEW?*** **PLANNING AND GETTING STARTED ON THE MICROSOFT DEFENDER APPLICATION CONTROL DEPLOYMENT PROCESS**
>
> To review further details about deploying Microsoft Defender Application Control, refer to the Microsoft website at *https://learn.microsoft.com/windows/security/threat-protection/ windows-defender-application-control/windows-defender-application-control*.

Implement Microsoft Defender Antivirus

Malicious software can do many things to your computer, such as allowing unauthorized parties remote access to your computer or collecting and transmitting information that is sensitive or confidential to unauthorized third parties.

Some types of malware include:

- **Computer viruses** Replicating malware, normally with email attachments or files.
- **Computer worms** Replicate, without direct intervention, across networks.
- **Trojan horses** Trick the user into providing an attacker with remote access to the infected computer.
- **Ransomware** Harms the user by encrypting user data. A ransom (fee) needs to be paid to the malware authors to recover the data.
- **Spyware** Tracking software that reports to the third party how a computer is used.

The most common attack vector for malware is still by email, although attacks from websites, pirated software, video, and music files are becoming increasingly common.

You can help protect against malware infection by following these guidelines:

- All software should be from a reputable source.
- All software and operating system updates are applied.
- Antimalware software is installed and enabled on your devices.
- Antimalware definitions are up to date.
- Avoid using or accessing pirated software or media-sharing sites.
- Be suspicious of out-of-the-ordinary email attachments, and don't open links in spam or phishing emails.

Although no antimalware solution can provide 100 percent safety, modern solutions can reduce the probability that malware compromises your device.

Microsoft Defender Antivirus can help protect your device by actively detecting spyware, malware, and viruses in the operating system and on Windows 11 installed on Hyper-V virtual machines. Windows Defender runs in the background and automatically installs new definitions as they are released, often daily.

You can use Microsoft Defender Antivirus manually to check for malware with various scan options listed in Table 3-18.

TABLE 3-18 Microsoft Defender Antivirus scan options

Scan options	Description
Quick	Checks the most likely areas that malware, including viruses, spyware, and software, commonly infect.
Full	Scans all files on your hard disk and all running programs.
Custom	Enables users to scan specific drives and folders to target specific areas of their computers, such as removable drives.
Microsoft Defender Offline Scan	Allows users to find and remove difficult-to-remove malicious software. The system must reboot, and the scan can take about 15 minutes.

You should routinely check your system for malware. If it becomes infected or you suspect malware is on your system, you can run a full scan.

Implement Windows Defender Firewall

You can implement Windows Defender Firewall rules and settings in Intune as follows:

1. Open Microsoft Intune admin center.
2. Navigate to **Endpoint security** and select **Firewall**.
3. In the details pane, select **Create Policy**.
4. On the **Create a profile** page, in **Platform**, select **Windows 10, Windows 11, and Windows Server**.
5. In the **Profile**, select **Microsoft Defender Firewall**, and then select **Create**.
6. In the **Create a profile** wizard, on the **Basics** tab, enter a **Name** and **Description** and click **Next**.
7. On the **Configuration settings** tab, configure the following settings, and click **Next**:
    -   **Firewall**, which determines the fundamental state of the firewall for domain, private, and public network location profiles.
    -   **Auditing** settings.
    -   **Network List Manager**, which defines TLS endpoint settings.
8. Configure scope tags and assignments as needed, and then choose **Create** to create the profile.

You will also need to define firewall rules, as shown in Figure 3-60. Use the following procedure:

1. Open Microsoft Intune admin center.
2. Navigate to **Endpoint security** and select **Firewall**.
3. In the details pane, select **Create Policy**.

4. On the **Create a profile** page, in **Platform**, select **Windows 10, Windows 11, and Windows Server**.

5. In the **Profile**, select **Microsoft Defender Firewall rules**, and then select **Create**.

6. In the **Create a profile** wizard, on the **Basics** tab, enter a **Name** and **Description** and click **Next**.

7. On the **Configuration settings** tab, click **Add** to create and configure specific firewall rules. When you are done, click **Next**. When adding a rule, you must set numerous settings, including

    - **State** (enabled or disabled)
    - **Name**
    - **Interface Types**
    - **Remote Port Ranges**
    - **Action (Allow** or **Block)**
    - **Protocol**

8. Configure scope tags and assignments as needed, and then **Create** the profile.

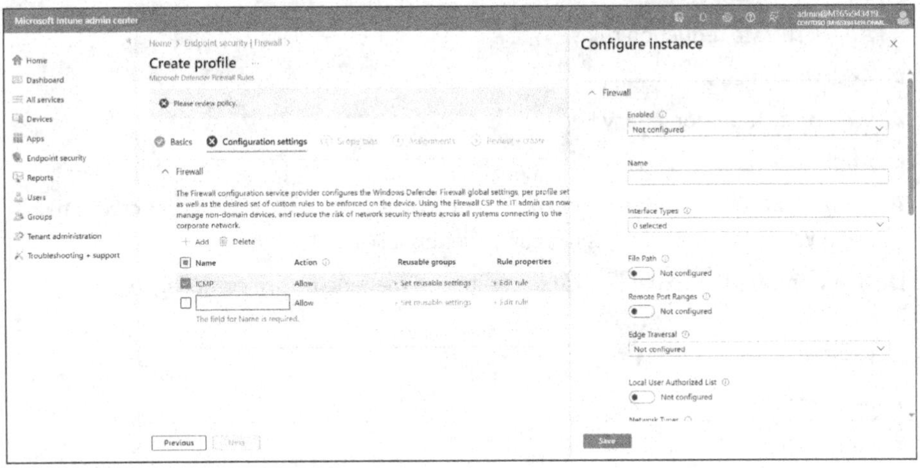

FIGURE 3-60 Defining firewall rules

You can also create an endpoint protection configuration profile in Devices and configure the required firewall settings in the Microsoft Defender Firewall section.

How to apply the required security settings to your endpoints

During this skill, you've learned about the various security features in Windows 11. You've also learned how to use either Endpoint security policies or a device configuration profile (using the Endpoint protection template) to enforce the required configurations.

In fact, you can generally use either of these methods. An advantage of using the Endpoint security policies is that you can also implement security baselines to help keep those policies aligned with security improvements. By using Endpoint security policies, you can configure the following:

- **Antivirus**   Enables you to review Windows 11 unhealthy endpoints and devices with active malware. You also can use this option to create and assign antivirus profiles:
  - Microsoft Defender Antivirus exclusions
  - Microsoft Defender Antivirus
  - Windows Security Experience
- **Disk Encryption**   Enables you to create and configure BitLocker profiles for Windows 11 devices and macOS encryption settings.
- **Firewall**   Enables you to create and configure firewall profiles and firewall rules.
- **Endpoint Detection and Response**   Enables you to create profiles that provide advanced attack detections that are near real-time and actionable.
- **Attack Surface Reduction**   Enables you to create and configure the following profiles to help reduce the attack surface on your managed devices:
  - App and browser isolation
  - Device control
  - Attack surface reduction rules
  - Exploit protection
  - Web protection (for legacy Edge)
  - Application control
- **Account Protection**   Enables you to create profiles that help protect user credentials by using Windows Hello for Business and Credential Guard technology.
- **Device Compliance**   Enables you to create and manage device compliance settings. These include
  - Policies
  - Notifications
  - Retire Noncompliant devices
  - Locations
  - Compliance policy settings
- **Conditional access**   Enables you to create and configure conditional access policies. These policies enable you to enforce access requirements when specific conditions occur. For example, deny access to cloud apps for non-compliant devices.

In fact, some elements can only be configured in these settings, such as Local user group membership and Local admin password solution (Windows LAPS).

An advantage of using an Endpoint protection configuration profile is combining and configuring all your Microsoft Defender security settings in a single profile. These settings are

- Microsoft Defender Application Guard
- Windows Defender Firewall
- Microsoft Defender SmartScreen
- Windows Encryption
- Microsoft Defender Exploit Guard
- Microsoft Defender Application Control
- Microsoft Defender Credential Guard
- Microsoft Defender Security Center
- Xbox services
- User Rights

EXAM TIP

Familiarize yourself with the available options in each of these methods for securing your endpoints.

Implement and manage security baselines in Microsoft Intune

Implementing security and related settings is one of the more important tasks you'll need to perform. As discussed, Microsoft has begun consolidating the security-related settings into a single Intune: Endpoint security folder.

Here, you'll find options to manage the various security settings we've been discussing. But you'll also find a link to review security baselines.

You can use the security baselines to manage and monitor the security status of enrolled devices within your organization. By default, there are three security baselines, as shown in Figure 3-61:

- Security Baseline for Windows 10 and later
- Microsoft Defender for Endpoint Baseline
- Microsoft Edge Baseline
- Windows 365 Security Baseline

The security baselines provide preconfigured groups of settings that enable you to configure security on your devices more easily. When you create and apply a security baseline profile, you create multiple device configuration profiles.

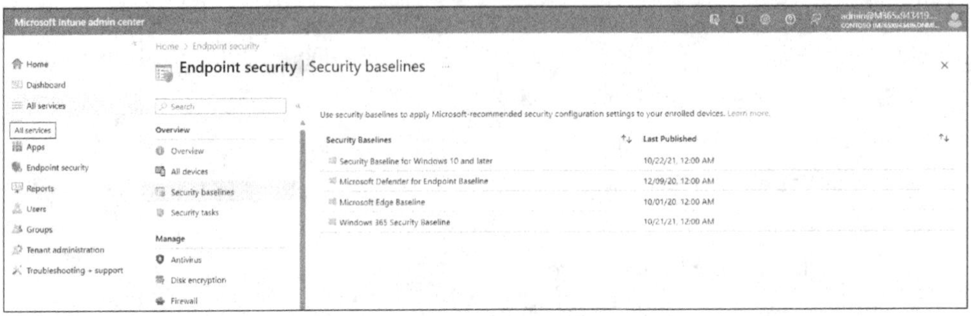

FIGURE 3-61 Configuring Security Baselines in Intune

Periodically, Microsoft releases new baselines. When viewing profile details, the baseline used is identified in the **Current Baseline** column, displayed in Figure 3-62.

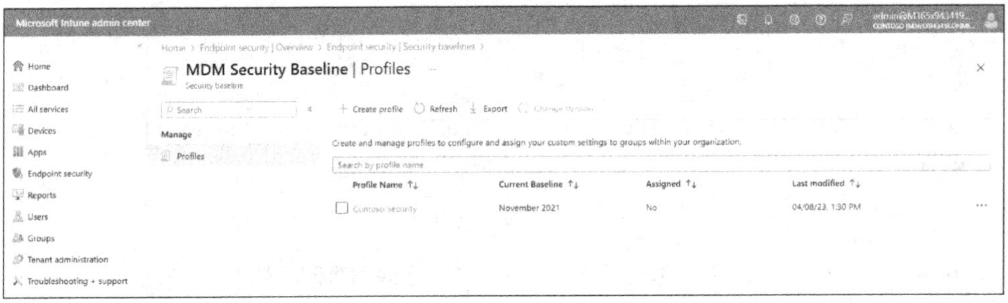

FIGURE 3-62 Reviewing versions for a security baseline

Create a profile

To create a profile based on a security baseline, use the following procedure:

1. In the Microsoft Intune admin center, select **Endpoint security** in the navigation pane.

2. Select **Security baselines**, and then select the appropriate baseline.

3. Select the **Profiles** tab, and then select **Create profile**.

4. On the **Create profile** page, on the **Basics** tab, enter the **Name** and **Description** and select **Next**.

5. On the **Configuration settings** tab, configure the appropriate settings. These will vary based on the baseline you select. When you've completed the configuration, select **Next**.

6. Optionally, use the **Scope tags** tab to scope the profile, select **Next**, and then assign the profile in the usual way.

7. Select **Next**, and then on the **Review + create** tab, select **Create**.

Your profile displays in the list of profiles. Notice that the **Current Baseline** column indicates the baseline used to create the profile.

Update a profile

If you create a profile on an earlier baseline and Microsoft releases a newer version of that baseline, you might decide to update the profiles. However, existing profiles do not update automatically.

In fact, profiles using an older version of a baseline become read-only. They can still be used to secure your devices, and you can edit their name, description, and assignments. But you should consider updating them to the new baseline.

If Microsoft releases a baseline update, you can choose to update the baseline version used for a profile. You do this by using the following procedure:

1. In the Microsoft Intune admin center, navigate to **Endpoint security**.
2. Select **Security baselines**.
3. Select the appropriate baseline.
4. Select the check box next to the target profile.
5. Click **Change Version** on the toolbar (see Figure 3-63).
6. If a new baseline is available (none are in the screenshot), then choose either
   - **Accept baseline changes but keep my existing setting customizations**
   - **Accept baseline changes and discard existing setting customizations**
7. Click **Submit**.

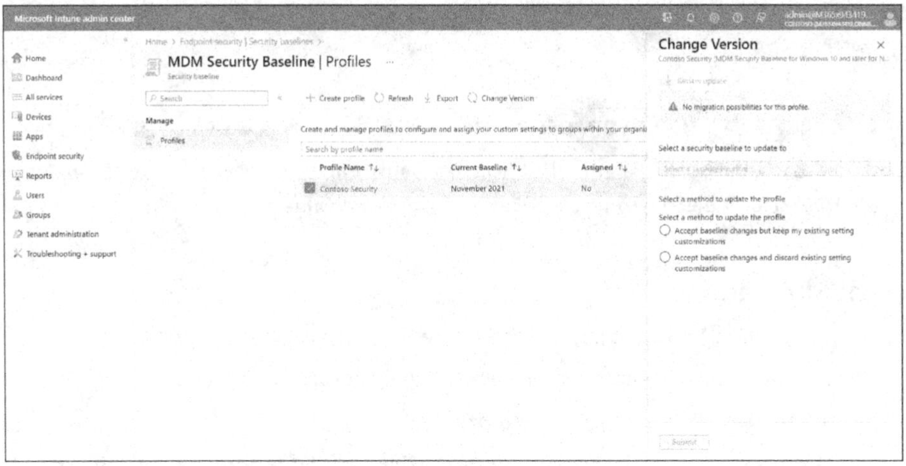

FIGURE 3-63 Changing the version for a security profile based on a baseline

> **NEED MORE REVIEW?** **USE SECURITY BASELINES TO CONFIGURE WINDOWS DEVICES IN INTUNE**
>
> To review further details about managing security baselines, refer to the Microsoft website at *https://learn.microsoft.com/mem/intune/protect/security-baselines*.

Onboard devices to Defender for Endpoint

Microsoft Defender for Endpoint (formerly Windows Defender Advanced Threat Protection) is a security platform built into Windows 11 and integrated with Microsoft cloud-based security services. Microsoft Defender for Endpoint integrates many of the security features we have already discussed to help you secure your devices.

Requirements

To use Microsoft Defender for Endpoint, you require one of the following Microsoft Volume licensing options:

- Windows 10/11 Enterprise E5
- Windows 10/11 Education A5
- Microsoft 365 E5 (M365 E5), which includes Windows 11 Enterprise E5
- Microsoft 365 A5 (M365 A5)
- Microsoft 365 E5 Security
- Microsoft 365 A5 Security
- Microsoft Defender for Endpoint

The Portal

You use the Microsoft 365 Defender portal to manage Microsoft Defender for Endpoint settings and to view reports and alerts. You can access the portal at *https://securitycenter.windows.com*.

> **NEED MORE REVIEW?** **MICROSOFT DEFENDER FOR ENDPOINT PORTAL OVERVIEW**
>
> To learn how to use the portal, refer to the Microsoft website at *https://learn.microsoft.com/microsoft-365/security/defender/microsoft-365-security-center-mde*.

Setup and onboarding

To onboard your devices, use the following procedure:

1. In the Microsoft Intune admin center, navigate to **Endpoint security**.
2. Select **Microsoft Defender for Endpoint**.
3. In the **Details** pane, click the link for **Connect Microsoft Defender for Endpoint to Microsoft Intune in the Microsoft Defender Security Center**.
4. In **Microsoft 365 Defender**, select **Settings** > **Endpoints** >**Advanced features**.
5. Turn on the **Microsoft Intune connection**.
6. Click **Save preferences**.

After you've enabled the connection, Microsoft 365 Defender sends an onboarding configuration package to Intune. Deploy this package to your Windows devices. Alternatively, you can create and assign an Endpoint detection and response profile from Endpoint security in Intune. Use the following procedure:

1. In the Microsoft Intune admin center, navigate to **Endpoint security**.
2. Select **Endpoint detection and response**.
3. In the details pane, click **Create Policy**.
4. On the **Create a profile** page, in **Platform**, select **Windows 10 and later**.
5. In the **Profile**, select **Endpoint detection and response**, and then select **Create**.
6. On the **Basics** tab, enter a **Name** and **Description** and click **Next**.
7. On the **Configuration settings** page, in the Microsoft Defender for Endpoint client configuration package type list, choose the appropriate file type, and then browse and select the onboarding file. Click **Next**.
8. Configure scope tags and assignments, and then **Create** the profile.

NEED MORE REVIEW? **CONFIGURE MICROSOFT DEFENDER FOR ENDPOINT IN INTUNE**

To learn more about setup and onboarding, refer to the Microsoft website at
https://learn.microsoft.com/mem/intune/protect/advanced-threat-protection-configure.

Implement automated response capabilities in Defender for Endpoint

Microsoft Defender for Endpoint provides numerous capabilities that can help you secure your endpoint devices. Table 3-19 describes some of these capabilities.

TABLE 3-19 Capabilities of Microsoft Defender for Endpoint

Capability	Description
Attack surface reduction	Implementing several Windows Defender ATP features helps reduce the attack surface of a computer, its applications, and the data it consumes.
Endpoint detection and response	Continuously monitors your organization's endpoints for possible attacks against devices or networks in your organization and provides the features you can use to mitigate and remediate threats.
Automated investigation and remediation	Offers automatic investigation and remediation capabilities that help reduce the volume of alerts and actions an administrator needs to perform to fix breaches.
Secure score	Enables you to assess the security posture of your organization and identify devices that might need attention, as well as recommendations for actions to improve your score
Management and APIs	Provides a means for you to interact with the platform by providing APIs.

Review and respond to device issues identified in the Microsoft Defender Vulnerability Management dashboard

The Microsoft Defender Vulnerability Management Dashboard in Microsoft 365 Defender
provides a wide variety of useful information that can help you identify issues and respond to
those issues. Figure 3-64 displays a typical dashboard for an enterprise organization.

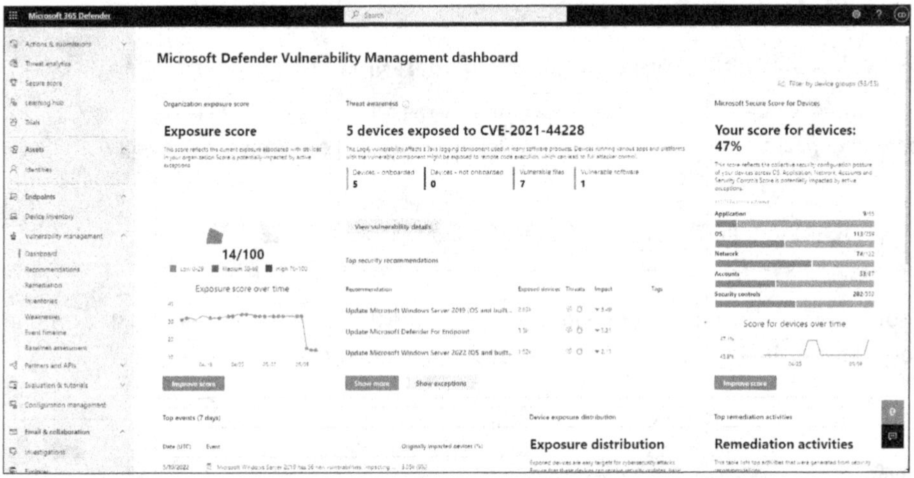

FIGURE 3-64 Reviewing the Microsoft Defender Vulnerability Management Dashboard

Use the information summary in Table 3-20 to determine how to use the Microsoft
Defender Vulnerability Management Dashboard.

TABLE 3-20 The features and elements in the Microsoft Defender Vulnerability Management Dashboard

Area	Description
Selected device groups (#/#)	Enables you to filter the data you want to review.
Organization exposure score	Displays a headline figure that indicates your organization's device exposure to threats and vulnerabilities. Click **Improve score** to review insights that can help you improve the score and your security posture.
Microsoft Secure Score for Devices	Enables you to review the security relating to your organization's operating system, applications, network, accounts, and security controls. Again, you can use the **Improve score** link to review insights and suggestions for improvements in this area.

Area	Description
Device exposure distribution	Displays the number of devices that are exposed to threats based on their configuration. Presented graphically as a doughnut chart. By selecting sections of the chart, you can review ■ Device names ■ Exposure level and risk levels ■ Details such as operating system, health state, and tags
Expiring certificates	Displays a list of expired certificates or those imminently expiring in the next 30, 60, or 90 days.
Top security recommendations	Review top recommendations for improving the security posture of your organization's devices.
Top vulnerable software	Review your software inventory. Identify those apps with security vulnerabilities.
Top remediation activities	Review the security remediations that are recommended in one convenient location. This enables you to track changes as you make them more easily.
Top exposed devices	Review devices and their details that have a high security exposure score. From **Device details**, you can ■ Manage tags ■ Initiate automated investigations ■ Initiate a live response session ■ Collect an investigation package ■ Run antivirus scan ■ Restrict app execution ■ Isolate devices

> **NEED MORE REVIEW?** **DASHBOARD INSIGHTS**
>
> To learn more about the dashboard in Microsoft Defender, refer to the Microsoft website at *https://learn.microsoft.com/microsoft-365/security/defender-vulnerability-management/ tvm-dashboard-insights.*

Chapter summary

- Intune device configuration policies are used to configure device settings using MDM.
- Intune can deploy PowerShell scripts to Windows devices using an MDM extension. This allows administrators to deploy Win32 apps if required.
- Scope tags are used to assign and filter Intune policies to specific Azure AD groups.
- You can configure custom policies with Intune by configuring an Open Mobile Alliance Uniform Resource Identifier (OMA-URI) policy.
- Microsoft Defender Credential Guard requires a TPM and virtualization features to be enabled in a 64-bit edition of either Windows 11 Enterprise or Windows 11 Education.

- Microsoft Defender Exploit Guard consists of four components: Exploit Protection, Attack Surface Reduction Rules, Network Protection, and Controlled Folder Access.
- Microsoft Defender Application Guard has similar requirements to Credential Guard, enabling you to open new browser windows in a virtualized environment.
- Microsoft Defender Application Control lets you determine which apps are safe to run in your organization.
- Most of these Windows Defender features are managed through Windows PowerShell, Group Policy, and Microsoft Intune.
- Automatic enrollment lets you enroll Windows devices when they register with or join Azure AD.
- Device Enrollment Manager Accounts enable a specified account to enroll up to 1,000 devices.
- There are a number of ways to enroll Windows devices:
  - Add a Work Or School account
  - Enroll In MDM Only (user-driven)
  - Azure AD Join during OOBE
  - Azure AD Join using Windows Autopilot
  - Enroll In MDM only (using a Device Enrollment Manager)
  - Azure AD Join using bulk enrollment
- To enroll Android and iOS devices, you can download the Company Portal app from the relevant device store and sign in to the app using an organizational or school account.
- Log Analytics requires an Azure subscription.
- Windows Update Delivery Optimization is a method of peer-to-peer sharing of Windows update files.
- Administrators can use Intune to centrally configure and manage Windows Update behavior and Windows Update Delivery Optimization settings.
- Scope tags enable you to more specifically target the application of configuration profiles.
- You can configure Kiosk mode by using the Settings app and by using Intune.
- The Microsoft Tunnel for Intune enables iOS and Android devices to access your on-premises resources and apps.
- You can use Endpoint analytics to gain insights into Startup Performance, Proactive remediations, Recommended software, and Application reliability.
- You configure the application of updates for iOS, macOS, and Windows by using update rings in Intune.
- You configure the application of updates for Android by using a Device Restrictions configuration profile.
- Microsoft Defender Exploit Guard provides four functions: Exploit protection, Attack surface reduction rules, Network protection, and Controlled folder access.

Thought experiment

In this thought experiment, demonstrate your skills and knowledge of the topics covered in this chapter. You can find the answers in the section that follows.

Scenario 1

Your organization has 500 employees and has implemented a bring-your-own-device (BYOD) strategy that enables users to use their personal mobile phones and tablets for corporate purposes as long as they comply with company policy regarding security and management features. After consulting an employee survey, you find that the users in your organization have iOS, Android, or Windows 11 devices.

1. What technology should you use to manage the devices?
2. You want to simplify enrollment for your Windows device users. What should you do?
3. To support your iOS devices, what additional step is required to enable MDM?

Scenario 2

Like many large organizations, security is a big concern at Contoso. You decide to implement MDM with Intune to help to manage and secure your users' devices.

1. What feature of Intune could you use to verify the current status of Microsoft Defender on your users' Windows 11 devices?
2. You want to be able to configure Microsoft Defender Application Guard settings for enrolled Windows 11 devices. How can you achieve this in Intune?
3. You don't want users with Android devices to be able to enroll them. How could you enforce this restriction?

Scenario 3

Adatum Corporation uses Microsoft 365 and has implemented Windows 11 Enterprise for all devices. You configure Windows Update and deploy update rings using Microsoft Intune.

Answer the following questions for your manager:

1. Two remote offices are in an area with poor Internet bandwidth, and the IT team is concerned that operational requirements might be difficult to maintain. What measure could you implement for the devices located at the remote locations to reduce bandwidth consumption from Windows updates?
2. Windows updates received by the head office devices are consuming too much of the available bandwidth. Users are reporting that access to the Internet is slow. What settings can you configure within Microsoft Intune to help relieve congestion at the head office?
3. Your Compliance Manager has received confirmation that your regulatory body has approved Windows 11 Enterprise, version 22H2 as being compliant. You need to ensure

that all devices use only this version of Windows until the Compliance Manager confirms that a new version is compliant. How will you proceed?

4. You need to work with the Compliance Manager to ensure that future versions of Windows 11 Enterprise obtain regulatory compliance before the deployed version of Windows 11 becomes unsupported. What will you do to ensure that you can proactively evaluate the compatibility of new versions of Windows 11?

Scenario 4

Your users use both Android and iOS devices. Lately, it's been necessary for these users to access a database application that runs on an on-premises server. Intune manages your users' devices.

Answer the following questions:

1. How could you facilitate access for your users?
2. What high-level steps are necessary to facilitate your solution?

Thought experiment answers

This section contains the solution to the thought experiment. Each answer explains why the answer choice is correct.

Scenario 1

1. Microsoft Intune with Mobile Device Management enabled.
2. Enable and configure Windows Autoenrollment.
3. You require an Apple MDM Push Certificate for your organization.

Scenario 2

1. You can monitor Threat Agent Status to determine the current status of Microsoft Defender on your users' enrolled Windows devices.
2. You can use the Microsoft Intune admin center to create an Endpoint Protection Profile that contains the necessary Microsoft Defender Application Guard settings and assign the profile to the appropriate group(s) of devices.
3. In the Microsoft Intune admin center, create a Device Enrollment Restriction and define a Platform Restriction that prevents the enrollment of Android devices.

Scenario 3

1. You should configure Delivery Optimization and select that updates are downloaded from Devices on my local network on all devices except one device which needs to receive the updates from the Microsoft update service.

2. You can implement Delivery Optimization for the head office devices so that updates are received from other devices on the network. You can also configure bandwidth optimization measures that restrict the bandwidth consumed by updates during defined business hours.

3. You should install Windows 11 Enterprise, version 22H2 (General Availability Channel), and then implement policy using Windows Update to defer Windows Feature Updates for the maximum allowed duration of 365 days.

4. Enroll into the Windows Insider Program and install Windows 11 preview builds. Test these builds for compatibility issues. This should allow you to be ready to test the next General Availability Channel release and obtain compliance sign-off.

Scenario 4

1. You could implement Microsoft Tunnel for Intune. Microsoft Tunnel provides a VPN gateway for Android and iOS devices in your organization for access to on-premises resources.

2. You must perform the following high-level steps:

    - Create a server configuration on Intune.

    - Create a site in Intune.

    - Install a Microsoft Tunnel Gateway on a Linux server in your on-premises environment (by using an Intune script).

    - Deploy the Microsoft Tunnel client app to your iOS and Android devices.

    - Create and deploy VPN profiles to your iOS and Android devices.

CHAPTER 4

Manage applications

Using Microsoft Intune or the Microsoft Store for Business, you can deploy and configure apps for your organization's enrolled devices. You can use Intune's Mobile Application Management (MAM) features to manage apps on your users' devices. This chapter explores these app and data management capabilities.

Skills covered in this chapter:
- Skill 4.1: Deploy and update apps for all supported device platforms
- Skill 4.2: Plan and implement app protection and app configuration policies

Skill 4.1: Deploy and update apps for all supported device platforms

Within an organization, you can use on-premises tools, such as Microsoft Endpoint Configuration Manager (CM) and the Microsoft Deployment Toolkit (MDT), to manage Windows desktop images. Using these tools, you can integrate your organization's applications into standard desktop builds and deploy and manage additional applications and updates.

You might consider using Microsoft Intune to deploy and manage apps for devices not part of your on-premises Active Directory Domain Services (AD DS) environment or cloud-managed. If enrolled in Intune, you can deploy apps to Windows, iOS, Android, and macOS devices. The Microsoft Store for Business provides another method for distributing apps for your organizational users.

Windows Configuration Designer, part of the Windows Assessment and Deployment Toolkit (Windows ADK) mentioned in chapter 1, enables you to create provisioning packages for your Windows devices. You can use these packages to add, remove, and configure applications on your users' Windows devices.

This skill covers how to:

■ Deploy apps by using Intune

■ Configure Microsoft 365 Apps deployment by using the Microsoft Office Deployment Tool or Office Customization Tool (OCT)

■ Manage Microsoft 365 Apps by using the Microsoft 365 Apps admin center

■ Deploy Microsoft 365 Apps by using Intune

■ Configure policies for Office apps by using Group Policy or Intune

■ Deploy apps to platform-specific app stores by using Intune

Deploy apps by using Intune

Using Intune, you can deploy and maintain apps from the cloud onto your users' devices. A copy of the software can be made available across multiple devices such as their iPhone, Windows laptop, or tablet. You deploy, configure, and manage apps in Intune using the Apps node in the Microsoft Intune admin center, displayed in Figure 4-1.

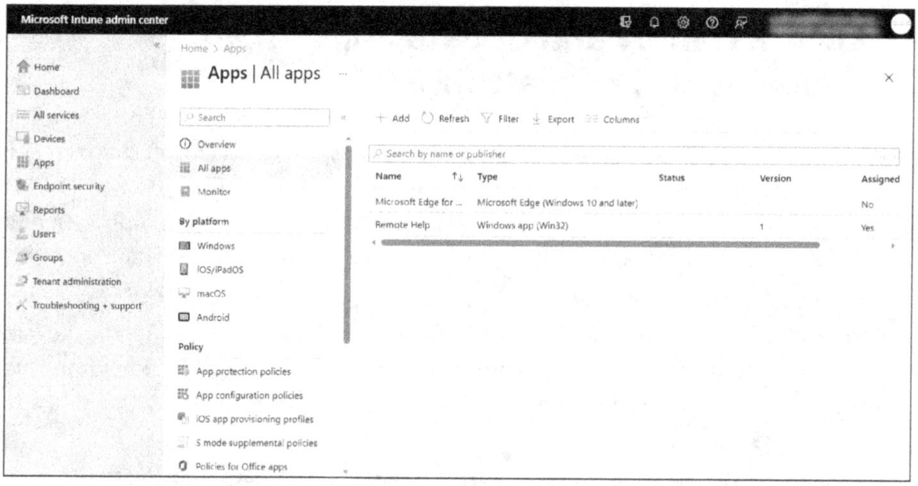

FIGURE 4-1 Managing apps in Microsoft Intune

From the **Apps** node, the following options are available:

■ **All apps**   Use this node to add, configure, and assign apps to your enrolled devices, irrespective of operating system (platform).

■ **Monitor**   Select this node to review:

   ■ **App licenses**   Enables you to identify volume-purchased apps from the app stores.

   ■ **Discovered apps**   Displays information about apps assigned by Intune or installed on devices.

- **App installation status**   Reports on the status of assigned apps.
  - **App protection status**   Displays information about app protection policy status.
- **Windows, iOS/iPadOS, macOS, and Android**   Under **By Platform**, select one of the listed operating systems to review and manage apps for a specific operating system.
- **App protection policies**   Use this node to configure policies that help to protect against data leakage from deployed apps. You can create policies for iOS/iPadOS, Android, and Windows.
- **App configuration policies**   You can create app configuration policies to configure apps on both iOS and Android devices, enabling you to customize the targeted app. You can create a policy that targets either the platform, or a specific app.
- **iOS app provisioning profiles**   When you deploy apps to iOS devices by using Intune, you must use an enterprise signing certificate. This certificate helps ensure the integrity of apps you deploy and typically has a lifetime of three years. However, the provisioning profile used to deploy the app lasts for a year. You can only assign and use a new app provisioning profile while the certificate is still valid.
- **S Mode supplemental policies**   Windows S Mode helps protect Windows computers by limiting configured devices to only installing and running apps distributed from the Microsoft Store. By using these policies, you can authorize additional apps so that S Mode–protected devices can run those additional apps. You must sign these policies using the Device Guard Signing Portal.
- **Policies for Office apps**   Create policies that enable you to manage Office app features and capabilities on mobile devices. There are currently more than 2,000 settings that you can assign.
- **Policy sets**   Using Policy sets enables you to group application management, device management, and device enrollment policies into a single grouping for assignment to specified groups of users or devices. This can help streamline the application process.
- **App selective wipe**   Enables you to create a wipe request that will remove company app data from a selected user and device.
- **App categories**   Enables you to define app category names to help your users locate suitable apps.
- **E-books**   Enables you to access your organization's e-books and related settings.
- **Filters**   Enables you to filter apps by platform and other criteria to assign a policy based on rules you create.

In an earlier version of Intune, the following settings were also accessible through the Apps node. However, they now reside in the Tenant Administration node. Select **Tenant Administration**, and then select **Connectors And Tokens**. In this node, the following app-related options are available:

- **Windows enterprise certificate**   Enables you to view and apply your code-signing certificate. This certificate is used to distribute your line-of-business (LOB) apps to managed Windows devices.

- **Windows 365 Citrix connector**   Enables you to integrate Citrix Cloud with Windows 365. to access Citrix HDX technologies for enhanced Cloud PC security and manageability.

- **Apple VPP Tokens**   Enables you to view and apply your iOS Volume Purchase Program (VPP) licenses.

- **Managed Google Play**   Enables you to approve Google Android apps for your organization.

Other options are accessible in **Connectors and Tokens**, but they do not relate to app management.

NEED MORE REVIEW?   WHAT IS MICROSOFT INTUNE APP MANAGEMENT?

To review further details about using Intune for app management, refer to the Microsoft website at *https://learn.microsoft.com/mem/intune/apps/app-management*.

When you deploy apps to your devices, there are several different app types that you can select, as shown in Figure 4-2.

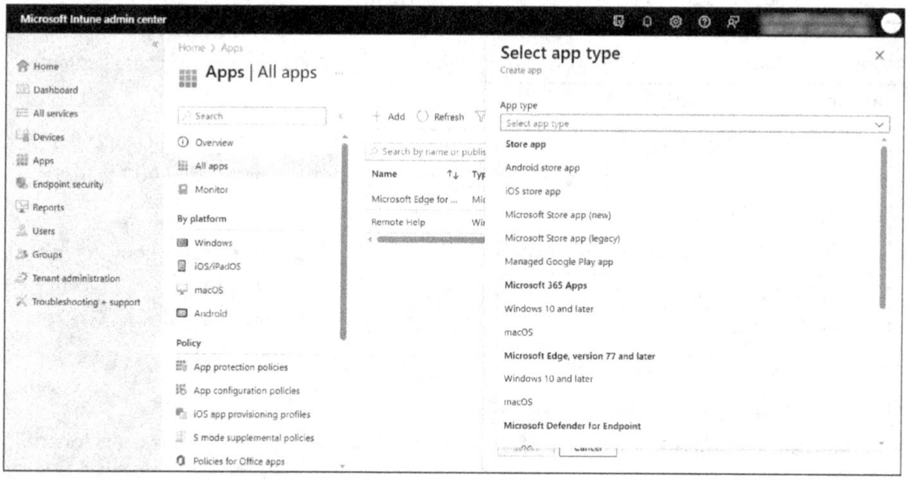

FIGURE 4-2 Adding a new client app

These app types are as follows:

- **Store App**   Use this option to deploy apps to your users' devices to avoid requiring users to directly deploy the apps from the specified store. The available options are as follows:

  - **Android store app**   Enter the app's Google Play Appstore URL and then define its minimum operating system level.

  - **iOS store app**   Enter a search string, and search the Apple Store directly for the appropriate app. Then configure the requirements for the app, including the operating system version.

- **Microsoft Store app (new)**   Enter the app's URL.
- **Microsoft Store app (legacy)**   Enter the app's URL.
- **Managed Google Play app**   Approve apps in Managed Google Play and then assign the apps.
- **Microsoft 365 Apps**   Use this option to assign Microsoft 365 apps to your users' devices. Available options are:
  - **Windows 10 and later**   Specify which apps within Microsoft 365 you want to deploy. Then define a suite name, description, and options, such as whether the app suite will be displayed in the Company Portal. You also must choose the architecture (32-bit or 64-bit), Update channel [Current Channel (Preview), Current Channel, Monthly Enterprise Channel, Semi-Annual Enterprise Channel (Preview), and Semi-Annual Enterprise Channel], and other options (Software License Terms Acceptance and Languages).
  - **macOS**   You cannot control which apps are deployed from the suite. However, you must define a name, description, and whether the app displays in the Company Portal.
- **Microsoft Edge, version 77 and later**
  - **Windows 10 and later**   Add Microsoft Edge for Windows to install the Microsoft Edge browser on managed devices running Windows 10 or later.
  - **macOS**   Add Microsoft Edge for macOS to install the Microsoft Edge browser on managed macOS devices.
- **Microsoft Defender for Endpoint**
  - **macOS**   Add Microsoft Defender for Endpoint to managed macOS devices.
- **Web Application**
  - **iO/iPadOS web clip**   Add a website URL into App information to place a shortcut to the web clip to the Home screen.
  - **Windows web link**   Add a website URL into App information. A shortcut to the website is added to the Start menu.
- **Other**   Use for any other type of app. The options are as follows:
  - **Web link**   Use to assign a web app for which you have a valid URL. These are client-server apps, and the URL identifies the server that contains the web app.
  - **Built-In app**   Use to assign curated apps to iOS or Android devices. After you assign the app(s), it appears as either a built-in iOS app or a built-in Android app.
  - **Line-of-business app**   Use to assign a Line-Of-Business (LOB) app. You can use this approach to sideload apps for which you have the application package file. Windows devices use .appx packages. Browse and select the package file, then configure supplemental options such as category and description.
  - **Windows app (Win32)**   Use to assign apps to Windows devices. Like an LOB app, you browse and select the package file (in this case, a file with an `.intunewin`

file extension), then complete the configuration as above. Note that to create a file with the appropriate extension, you must convert your Win32 app to the Intune format using the Microsoft Win32 Content Prep Tool. This tool packages the app correctly for upload to Intune and is available at *https://github.com/Microsoft/Microsoft-Win32-Content-Prep-Tool*.

- **macOS app (DMG)**   To add a macOS application, upload the app's installation file. Intune supports .dmg files containing .app files.

- **Android Enterprise system app**   Use to assign an Android Enterprise system app to your users' devices.

Add a Microsoft Store app

To add a Microsoft Store app, use the following procedure:

1. Open the Microsoft Intune admin center and select **Apps** in the navigation pane.

2. Select **All apps**, and then select **Add**.

3. On the **Select add type** blade displayed in Figure 4-2, in the **App Type** list, under the **Store app** heading, select **Microsoft Store app (new)** and click **Select**.

4. On the **Add App** blade, select **Search the Microsoft Store app (new)**.

On the **Search the Microsoft Store app (new)** blade, search for an app and then choose **Select.** as displayed in Figure 4-3.

EXAM TIP

To obtain the URL, visit the Appstore using a web browser, locate the app you want, and then copy the URL for the app's page.

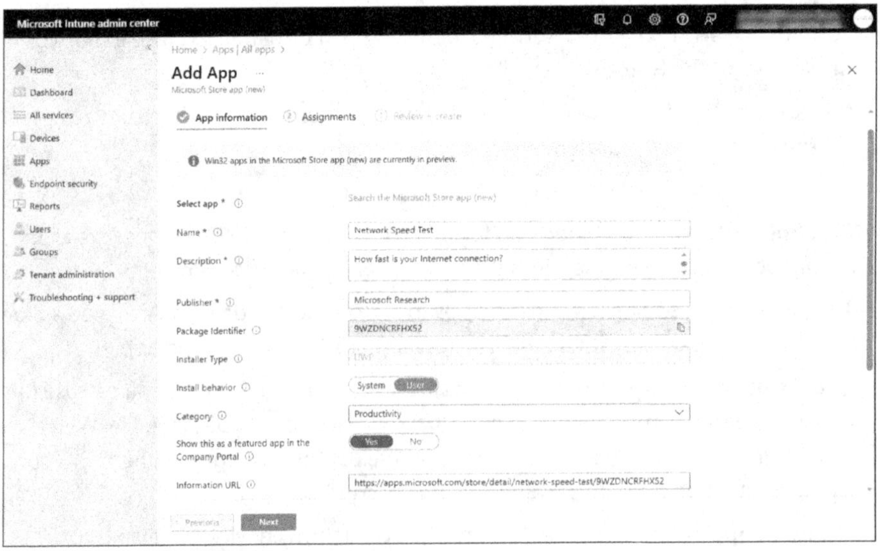

FIGURE 4-3 Adding a Microsoft Store app

5.   Select **Next**, and on the **Assignments** tab select the appropriate groups for assignment, or select **Add all users** as displayed in Figure 4-4. Then select **Next**.

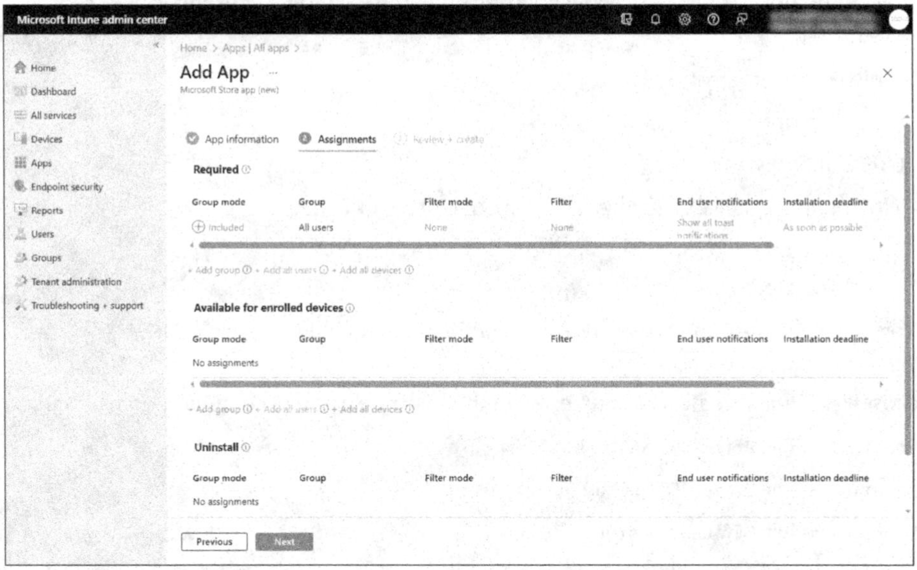

FIGURE 4-4 Assigning a Microsoft Store app

6.   On the **Review + create** tab, select **Create**.

After you create the app, you can use the **Device install status** and **User install status** options in the **Monitor** section to monitor the installation of the selected app.

NOTE INSTALLING IOS AND ANDROID STORE APPS

Installing store apps for iOS and Android is fairly similar to this process.

NOTE ARM64 APPS

Microsoft Store apps do not support any app with an ARM64 installer.

Configure Microsoft 365 Apps deployment by using the Microsoft Office Deployment Tool or Office Customization Tool (OCT)

You can configure Microsoft 365 Apps by using specialist tools that allow you to customize and configure the Office installation for your company's needs. Two tools are available:

- Office Deployment Toolkit (ODT)
- Office Customization Tool

Using the Microsoft Office Deployment Tool

The ODT is a command-line utility that can deploy Microsoft 365 Apps to client devices. The ODT provides granular control over how to install Office installation. For example, you can configure the following:

- Which products are installed
- Language options
- Office updates
- Whether the install experience is displayed to users

> **NOTE   ODT DOWNLOAD**
>
> You can download the ODT at *www.microsoft.com/download/details.aspx?id=49117*.

The installer file will create the setup.exe and the following sample configuration files:

- configuration-Office365-x64.xml
- configuration-Office365-x86.xml
- configuration-Office2019Enterprise.xml
- configuration-Office2021Enterprise.xml

The configuration-Office365-x64.xml sample configuration file looks like this:

```
<!-- Office 365 client configuration file sample. To be used for Office 365 ProPlus apps,
    Office 365 Business apps, Project Pro for Office 365, and Visio Pro for Office 365.
    For detailed information regarding configuration options visit: http://aka.ms/ODT.
    To use the configuration file be sure to remove the comments
    The following sample allows you to download and install the 64-bit version of the
Office 365 ProPlus apps
    and Visio Pro for Office 365 directly from the Office CDN using the Current Channel
    settings -->
<Configuration>
 <Add OfficeClientEdition="64" Channel="Current">
  <Product ID="O365ProPlusRetail">
   <Language ID="en-us" />
  </Product>
  <Product ID="VisioProRetail">
   <Language ID="en-us" />
  </Product>
 </Add>
 <!-- <Updates Enabled="TRUE" Channel="Current" /> -->
 <!-- <Display Level="None" AcceptEULA="TRUE" /> -->
 <!-- <Property Name="AUTOACTIVATE" Value="1" /> -->
</Configuration>
```

You edit the configuration file that matches the version of Office that you want to customize and then run setup.exe from the command line using either the download mode or the configure mode. The following syntax can be used.

```
setup.exe /download <yourconfigurationfile.xml>
setup.exe /configure <yourconfigurationfile.xml>
```

The download mode is useful when you need to add additional Microsoft 365 Apps products and languages as these are downloaded to the download folder ready for deployment.

The configure mode installs the downloaded Microsoft 365 Apps products and languages onto a client computer. You also use the configure mode to remove and update Office products and languages.

> **NEED MORE REVIEW?** **CONFIGURATION OPTIONS FOR THE OFFICE DEPLOYMENT TOOL**
>
> To review further details about using the Office Deployment Tool, refer to the Microsoft website at *https://learn.microsoft.com/mem/intune/apps/app-management*.

Using the Office Customization Tool

The Office Customization Tool offers a web-based interface that creates configuration files that you can use to deploy Office at scale. Like the ODT, you can define which applications and languages are installed and how the Office applications will be updated.

To use the Office Customization Tool, as shown in Figure 4-5, go to *https://config.office.com/deploymentsettings* and optionally sign in using a Global Administrator account.

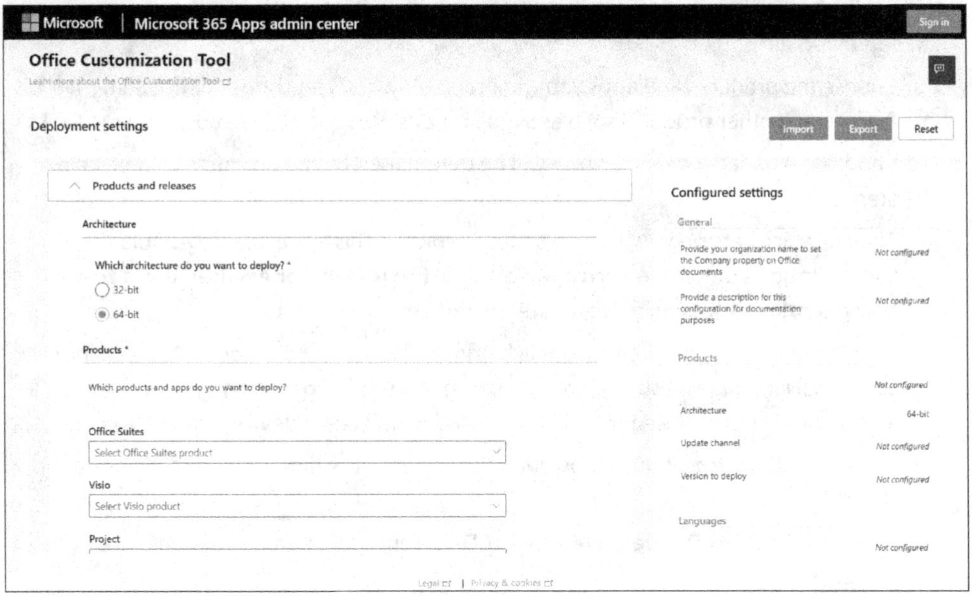

FIGURE 4-5 Configuring Office using the Office Customization Tool

Within the Office Customization Tool, you will choose the products, languages, and application preferences to configure. For example, you can configure the following settings.

- 64-bit German version of Microsoft 365 Apps
- All Microsoft 365 Apps except Access
- Automatically accept the EULA

EXAM TIP

Microsoft recommends that you uninstall any previous versions of Office before installing volume-licensed versions of Office 2019 or 2021 products. When using the Office Deployment Tool, you can use the RemoveMSI element in your configuration.xml file to uninstall versions of Office that use the Windows Installer installation technology.

Follow these steps to create a configuration file using the Office Customization Tool that can be used to install a customized version of Office.

1. Launch the Office Customization Tool at *https://config.office.com/deploymentsettings* and sign in as a Global Administrator.

2. In the **Product and releases** section, choose the architecture you want to deploy—either the 32-bit or 64-bit version of Office. You can deploy one architecture per configuration file.

3. Choose the products and apps you want to deploy. You can choose Office Suites, Visio, Project, and other products such as Skype for Business Basic 2019 and Language Packs.

4. Choose the update channel, which will be determined by the products you select in Step 3.

5. Choose which version you want to deploy. Typically, this is the latest available version. Use the toggles under the **Turn apps on or off to include or exclude them from being deployed** section to select the desired apps and select **Next**.

6. In the **Language** section, choose which primary language you require. You can include additional languages. You can use the option to **Match Operating System**, which will automatically install the same languages used on the client device. Select **Next**.

7. In the **Installation** section, choose whether to install the Office files directly or from the cloud:

    - **Office Content Delivery Network (CDN)** from a location on your network
    - **Local source**
    - **Microsoft Endpoint Configuration Manager**

8. Choose whether the installation is displayed to the users and whether the process can shut down any running applications. Select **Next**.

9. In the **Update and upgrade** section, choose whether to install the Office files directly or from the cloud:

    ■ **Office Content Delivery Network (CDN)** from a location on your network.

    ■ **Local source**

    ■ **Microsoft Endpoint Configuration Manager**

10. Choose whether the installation process will automatically check for updates.

11. In the **Upgrade** section, choose whether to uninstall all MSI-versions of Office, including Visio and Project, and whether to automatically install the same language versions as the removed MSI-version of Office. Select **Next**.

12. In the **Licensing and activation** section, choose between **User based**, **Shared Computer**, and **Device based** licensing. Select **Next**.

13. In the **General** section, you can provide your organization name and a description that will populate the **Company** property on Office documents. Select **Next**.

14. In the **Application preferences** section, choose what preferences to apply for when deploying Office. There are more than 30 options to fine-tune the behavior of Office. Most settings can be configured or set to **True**, **False**, or **Not configured**.

15. Select **Finish**. You can review the configured settings in the right-hand pane throughout the configuration process.

16. Once complete, you can select **Export**. Before creating the file, you must specify the default file format that Office uses or choose **Keep Current Settings** to keep the current settings. File formats can be either **Office Open XML formats** or **OpenDocument formats**. Select **OK**.

17. Accept the terms in the license agreement, then provide a name for the configuration file, and then select **Export**.

After creating the configuration files, you can now use the file in your deployment workflow with the Office Deployment Tool or another software distribution solution.

Manage Microsoft 365 Apps by using the Microsoft 365 Apps admin center

Microsoft 365 includes Microsoft 365 Apps. Microsoft 365 Apps includes the following apps: Access, Excel, OneNote, Outlook, PowerPoint, Publisher, Skype for Business, and Word. Microsoft 365 Apps installs as a single package, although you have some control over the details.

Users who have an Office 365 license associated with their accounts can download and install Microsoft 365 Apps, depending on the subscription. To do this, they must sign in to *www.office.com* using their Microsoft 365 accounts. Then on the Microsoft 365 homepage, they can select the **Install apps** link, as shown in Figure 4-6).

FIGURE 4-6 Installing Microsoft 365 Apps manually from the Microsoft 365 portal

Users can select from these two options:

- **Microsoft 365 apps**   Installs the default apps. The defaults are configurable by the Microsoft 365 administrator.
- **Other install options**   Enables users to choose additional options, as shown in Figure 4-7.

Users can choose to install Office in either 32-bit or 64-bit versions. Skype For Business can install the Basic (for Office 365) or 2015 versions. Optionally, users can also install Office on their iOS, Android, or Windows mobile devices and tablets. (As of June 11, 2019, Windows 10 Mobile is no longer supported.) Users can install Office on up to five PCs or Macs, five tablets, and five smartphones.

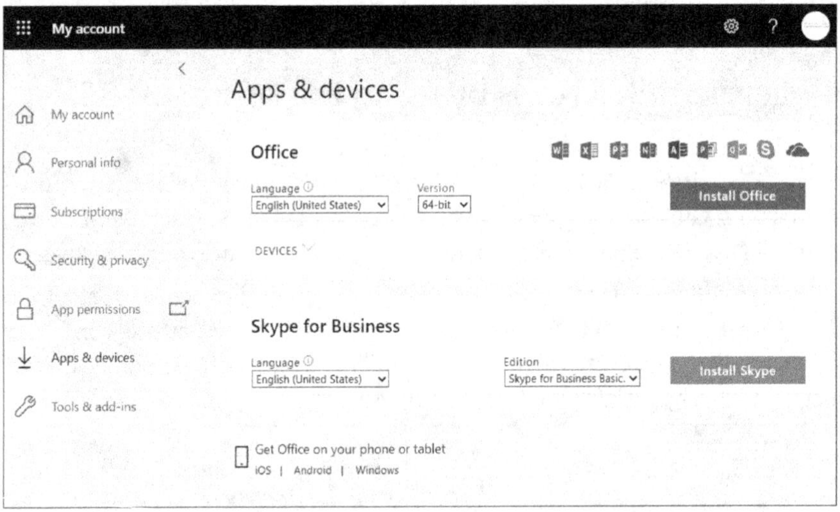

FIGURE 4-7 Choosing the Office 365 components for installation

Administrative control over deployment options

As an administrator, you can control what users can install. Open the Microsoft 365 admin center by navigating to *https://admin.microsoft.com* and signing in using your Global Administrator account. On the **Home** page, search for and select **Microsoft 365 installation options**.

On the **Microsoft 365 app installation options** blade shown in Figure 4-8, select the update interval for Microsoft 365 app updates. When you have finished configuring the options, select **Save**.

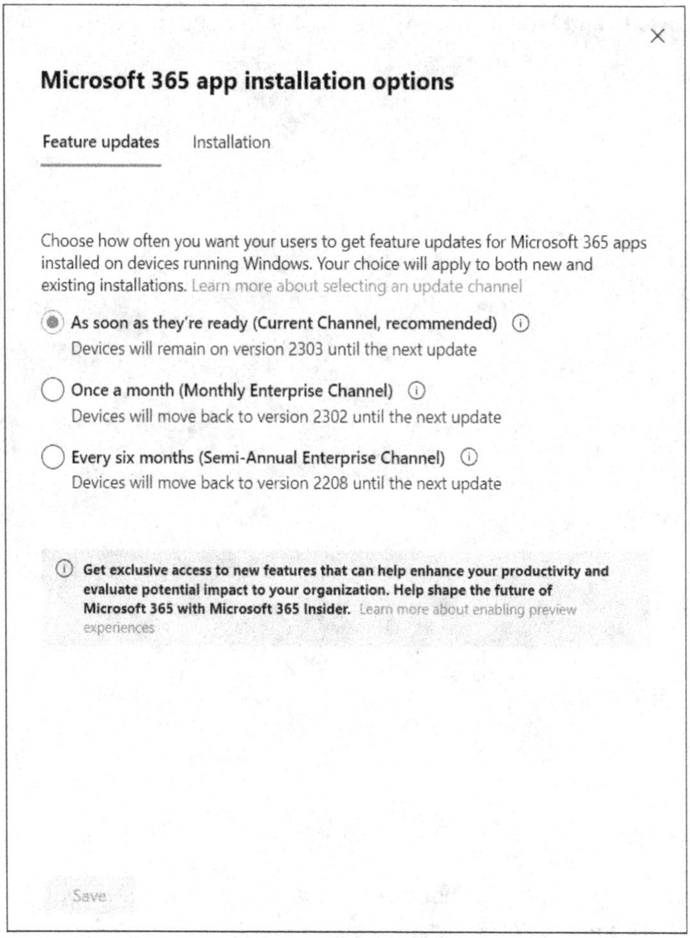

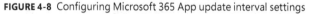

×

Microsoft 365 app installation options

Feature updates   Installation

Choose how often you want your users to get feature updates for Microsoft 365 apps installed on devices running Windows. Your choice will apply to both new and existing installations. Learn more about selecting an update channel

◉ **As soon as they're ready (Current Channel, recommended)** ⓘ
    Devices will remain on version 2303 until the next update

◯ **Once a month (Monthly Enterprise Channel)** ⓘ
    Devices will move back to version 2302 until the next update

◯ **Every six months (Semi-Annual Enterprise Channel)** ⓘ
    Devices will move back to version 2208 until the next update

ⓘ **Get exclusive access to new features that can help enhance your productivity and evaluate potential impact to your organization. Help shape the future of Microsoft 365 with Microsoft 365 Insider.** Learn more about enabling preview experiences

Save

FIGURE 4-8 Configuring Microsoft 365 App update interval settings

> ***NOTE***   **AFTER INSTALLING OFFICE**
>
> After installation, if users open Control Panel and review the Programs and Features installed on their computer, Office is listed as Microsoft 365 Apps for Enterprise.

Deploy Microsoft 365 Apps by using Intune

You can also use Intune to deploy Microsoft 365 Apps to your enrolled devices. To add a Microsoft 365 suite app to Windows 10 devices, use the following procedure:

1. In the Microsoft Intune admin center, select **Apps**, and then under **By Platform**, select **Windows**.

2. On the **Windows apps** blade, select **Add**.

3. On the **Select add type** blade, in the **App type** list, under the **Microsoft 365 Apps** heading, select **Windows 10 and later**, as shown in Figure 4-9, and choose **Select**.

FIGURE 4-9 Adding Microsoft 365 apps to Windows 10 devices

4. On the **App suite information** tab, most properties are preconfigured. However, you can feature the app in the Company Portal and add notes. Select **Next**.

5. On the **Configure app suite** tab, in the **Select Office apps** list, select the components of Office you want to deploy: Access, Excel, OneNote, Outlook, PowerPoint, Publisher, Skype for Business, Teams, and Word. All are selected except Skype for Business.

6. In the **Select other Office apps (license required)** list, select any additional Office products you want to deploy. For example, **Project Online Desktop Client**.

7. Next, choose the architecture (32-bit or 64-bit), the **Default file format** Office will use, and the **Update channel**, as shown in Figure 4-10. You can also remove other software

versions on targeted devices and select a specific version of Microsoft 365 apps. The default is the latest version available.

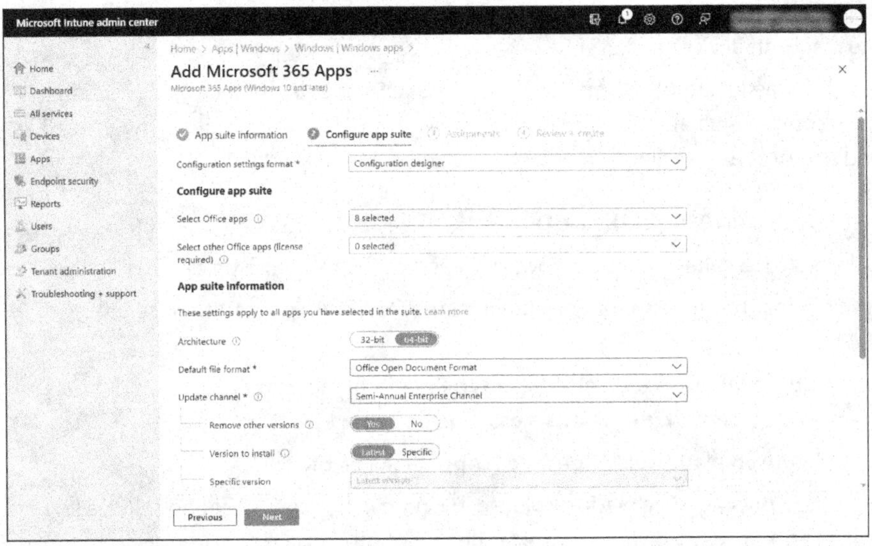

FIGURE 4-10 Configuring Microsoft 365 app suite properties

8. There are several additional properties that you can configure, including supported languages. When you're ready, select **Next**.

9. On the **Assignments** tab displayed in Figure 4-11, you can assign the suite to a group, all users, or all devices. You can require the app suite or make it available for enrolled devices. If you make an app available, you can only assign it to user groups. The available app is displayed in the Company Portal app for assigned users to install.

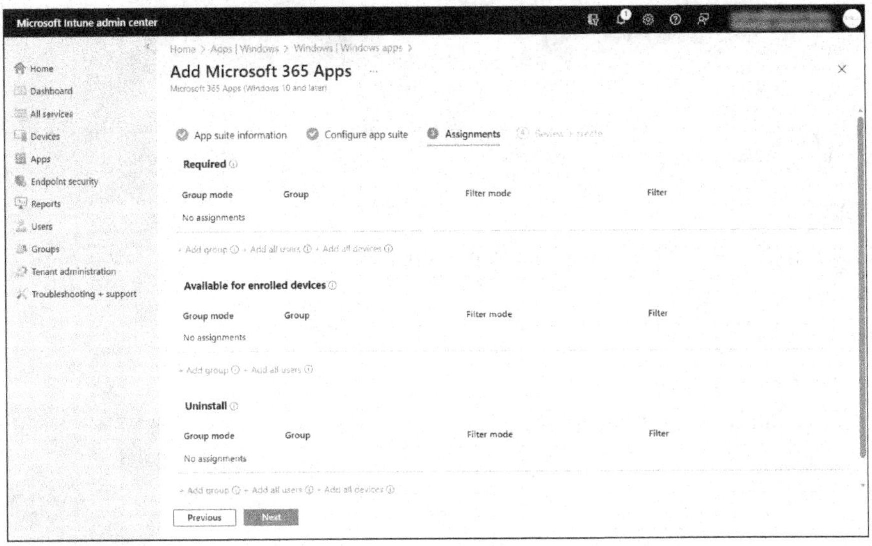

FIGURE 4-11 Configuring Microsoft 365 app suite assignments

10. Select **Next**, and review your choices on the **Review + create** tab. When you're ready, select **Create**.

11. After creating the app, you can use the monitoring options to view the installation status for both devices and users.

The process for assigning Microsoft 365 apps to macOS varies in as much as you cannot control which components of Office you deploy, nor can you define app suite settings, such as **Update** and **Architecture** settings.

Add a line-of-business (LOB) app

To add a Microsoft 365 suite app to Windows devices, use the following procedure:

1. In the Microsoft Intune Manager admin center, select **Apps**, and then select **All Apps**.

2. Select **Add**, and then on the **Select app type** blade, in the **App type** list, under the **Other** heading, select **Line-of-business app**, and click **Select**.

3. On the **Add App** blade, select the **Select app package file** link.

4. On the **Add package file** blade displayed in Figure 4-12, browse for and select a line of business app. This can include Android (.apk), iOS (.ipa), macOS (.intunemac), and Windows (.msi, .appx, .appxbundle, .msix, and .msixbundle) app files.

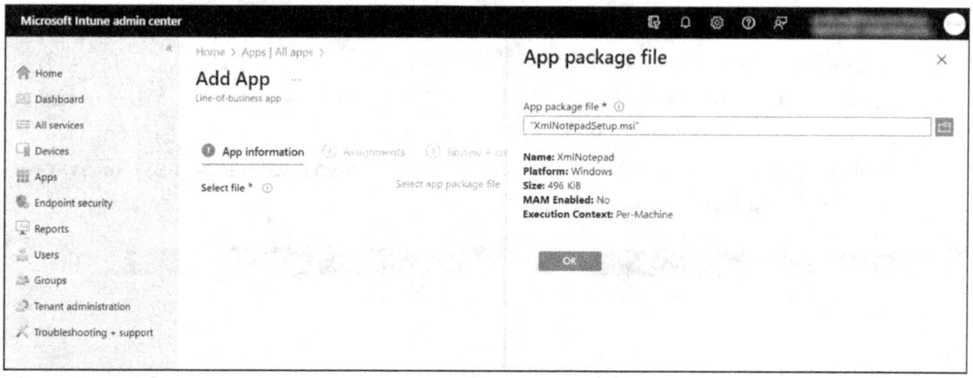

FIGURE 4-12 Adding a Windows 10 Line-of-business app

5. Select **OK**.

6. On the **App** tab, enter the following information:
   - **Name** (required)
   - **Description** (required)
   - **Publisher** (required)
   - **App install context** (**User** or **Device**)
   - **Ignore app version**

- **Command-line arguments** (for installation purposes)
- **Category** (**Business**, **Productivity**, **Photos & Media**, and so on)
- **Show this as a featured app in the Company Portal** (set the toggle to **Yes** or **No**)
- **Information URL**, **Privacy URL**, **Developer**, **Owner**, **Notes**, and a **Logo** image

7. Select **Next**, and assign the app using the previously described procedure on the **Assignments** tab.

8. Select **Next**, and then select **Create**.

NEED MORE REVIEW? **ADD APPS TO MICROSOFT INTUNE**

To review further details about using Intune to assign apps, refer to the Microsoft website at *https://learn.microsoft.com/mem/intune/apps/apps-add*.

Gather Microsoft 365 Apps readiness data

Before deploying Microsoft 365 Apps to your users' devices, you must ensure the devices are ready for those apps. Before deploying Office apps, you should verify that your users' devices support the current version. Also, there might be compatibility issues with older versions of Office documents and newer versions of the apps.

Many organizations use Office add-ins such as Microsoft Visual Basic for Applications (VBA) macros to help automate Office-based tasks. These add-ins might not be compatible with Microsoft 365 Apps. To help you identify potential add-in compatibility issues within your organization, you can use the Readiness Toolkit to assess your organization's readiness for Microsoft 365 Apps.

NOTE **READINESS TOOLKIT FOR OFFICE ADD-INS AND VBA**

To download the Readiness Toolkit for Office add-ins and VBA, visit the following website at *https://www.microsoft.com/en-us/download/details.aspx?id=55983*.

To use the Readiness Toolkit, your computers must meet the following requirements:

- Windows 8.1 or newer operating system
- Microsoft .NET Framework 4.7.2 or newer
- Excel 2010 or newer to view the reports

After installing the Readiness Toolkit, you can decide what type of report you want to run. Available options are detailed in Table 4-1.

TABLE 4-1 Readiness Toolkit reporting options

Reporting options	Description
Most recently used Office documents and installed add-ins on this computer	■ Scans Office documents in the user's list of most recently used files. ■ Also looks for any Add-Ins for Office that are installed. ■ Report type: VBA and Add-In.
Office documents in a local folder or network share	■ Scans the Office documents in the folder or network share that you specify. ■ Report type: VBA only. Does not scan for Add-Ins.
Previous readiness results saved in a local folder or network share	■ Enables you to create a consolidated report comprised of individual readiness results from multiple computers. Useful for departmental analysis. ■ Report type: Configurable depending on what you previously scanned for.
Add-in data from the Office Telemetry dashboard	■ Scans data from the Office Telemetry dashboard. ■ Report type: Add-In only.

> **NEED MORE REVIEW?** **TELEMETRY DASHBOARD TOPOLOGY, SIZING, AND BANDWIDTH PLANNING**
>
> To learn about the Office Telemetry Dashboard, visit the Microsoft website at *https://learn.microsoft.com/deployoffice/compat/plan-telemetry-dashboard-deployment*.

You can then choose either a basic or an advanced report. Advanced reports are recommended because they provide more complete information on which to base your decisions. The Readiness Report Creator tool generates an Excel spreadsheet comprised of several worksheets. Each worksheet contains information about different aspects of your existing devices' compatibility.

Depending on the report type, the following worksheets are available:

- VBA Overview
- VBA Summary
- VBA Results
- VBA Remediation
- VBA References
- Add-In Summary
- Add-In Details
- By Computer Name

> **NEED MORE REVIEW?** **USE THE READINESS TOOLKIT TO ASSESS APPLICATION COMPATIBILITY FOR MICROSOFT 365 APPS**
>
> To learn how to use the Readiness Toolkit, visit the Microsoft website at *https://learn.microsoft.com/deployoffice/readiness-toolkit-application-compatibility-microsoft-365-apps*.

Configure policies for Office apps by using Group Policy or Intune

Once you have deployed Microsoft 365 apps to your users, you might need to fine-tune the configuration or deploy policies. You can apply specific Microsoft Office app policies using Intune or Group Policy.

You will see how both solutions are implemented with specific management examples.

Configure policies for Office apps by using Group Policy

With Group Policy, you choose from hundreds of available policies that can be set locally on a Windows device or applied on Windows devices across your whole enterprise using Group Policy with the Microsoft Office administrative templates.

To manage Microsoft Office with Group Policy, you need to install the Administrative Template files for Microsoft Office, which contain the specific GPOs that allow you to configure settings for all supported versions of Microsoft Office, including Microsoft 365 apps.

The Administrative Templates (ADMX/ADML) for Microsoft Office and Microsoft 365 are not installed by default, so you first need to download the latest Administrative Template files from *https://www.microsoft.com/en-us/download/details.aspx?id=49030*. The Administrative Templates files define the available Group Policy settings.

The Group Policy Administrative Template is supported by Windows 8.1 and later and works with the following Office programs:

- Microsoft 365 Apps for enterprise.
- Desktop versions of Project and Visio (subscription plans only).
- Volume licensed versions of Office LTSC 2021, Project 2021, and Visio LTSC 2021 (such as Office LTSC Professional Plus 2021, Project Standard 2021, and Visio LTSC Professional 2021).
- Volume licensed versions of Office 2019, Project 2019, and Visio 2019 (such as Office Standard 2019 and Visio Professional 2019.).
- Volume-licensed versions of Office 2016, Project 2016, and Visio 2016 (such as Office Professional Plus 2016 and Project Standard 2016).

Once you have downloaded the Administrative Templates, you need to extract the files by executing the file as an administrator. The files must be copied to your Central Store for Group Policy Administrative Templates on your domain controller. The Administrative Templates must be placed in the local domain controller store if you only have one domain controller.

It is recommended to copy all the ADMX files so that you have access to all the policies. Add the downloaded ADMX files to your domain controller using the following procedure.

1. Copy all the downloaded ADMX files, as shown in Figure 4-13.

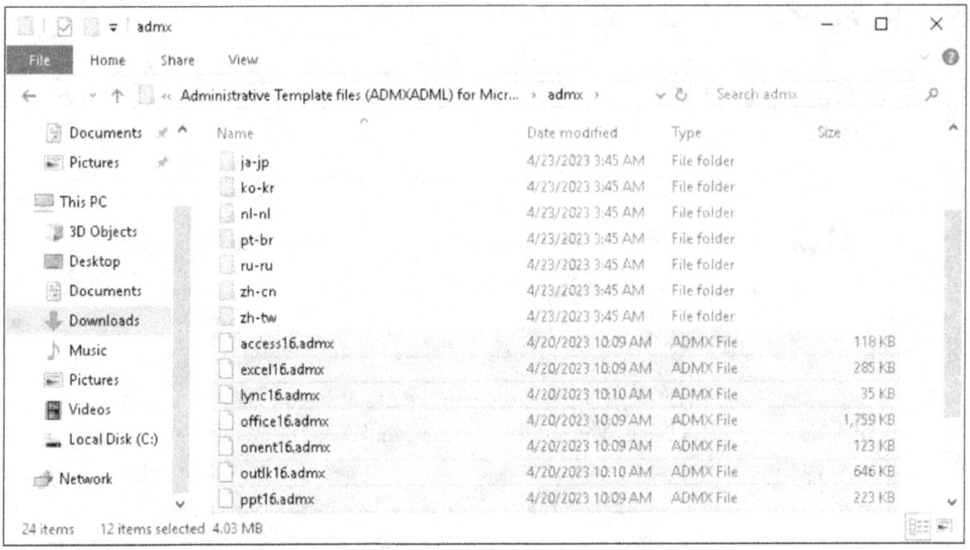

FIGURE 4-13 Adding ADMX files

2. Copy and paste the ADMX files to your domain controller at `C:\Windows\PolicyDefinitions`.

3. Allow File Manager to overwrite the files. If prompted, select **Yes to All**. Overwriting the ADMX files makes the latest Microsoft Office and Microsoft 365 Policy settings available.

4. Repeat this task for the ADML language files. You can copy all the files or just the language folders you want. For example, you could select only the **en-Us language (English – United States)** folder, select all the files in the folder, and choose **Copy**.

5. Paste the ADML files to your domain controller at `C:\Windows\PolicyDefinitions`.

Verify that the Administrative Templates installation is successful by viewing the new templates within Group Policy Management using the following steps.

1. On your domain controller, select **Start > Windows Administrative Tools > Group Policy Management.**

2. Right-click the **Default Domain Policy** and click **Edit**.

3. Expand the **Computer Configuration\Policies\Administrative Templates Policy definiations** folder.

4. You should see Office policies appear in the Group Policy Management console, as shown in Figure 4-14.

5. You can verify that Office policies also appear in the User `Configuration\Policies\ Administrative Templates` folder.

6. The policies can now be configured using Group Policy.

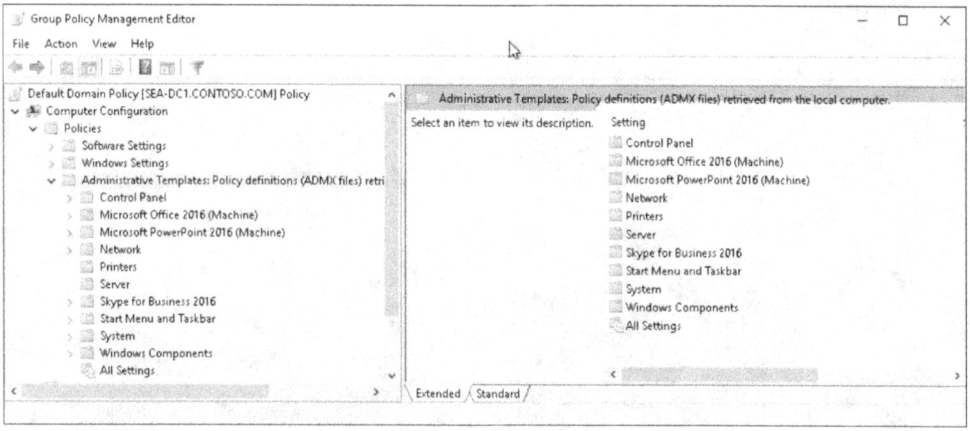

FIGURE 4-14 Verify Office Administrative Templates

Once you have installed the Administrative Template files for Microsoft Office, you can manage Microsoft Office settings with Group Policy. Group Policy allows you to control thousands of settings by configuring Group Policy Objects (GPO) in the Group Policy Management Console and then applying the GPOs to users and devices in your domain.

In the following example, we will create a new policy to enable week numbers in the Outlook calendar using the following procedure.

1. On your domain controller, select **Start, Windows Administrative Tools, Group Policy Management.**

2. Expand the **Group Policy Management** tree, right-click **Group Policy Objects**, and click **New**.

3. Name the new GPO **User_Outlook** and select **OK**.

4. Expand **Group Policy Objects**. Right-click **User_Outlook** GPO and select **GPO Status.** Ensure that **Computer Configuration Settings** is set to **Disabled**.

5. Right-click **User_Outlook** and click **Edit**.

6. In the **Group Policy Management Editor**, navigate to User Configuration\Policies\ Administrative Templates to view the Microsoft Office ADMX templates you imported earlier.

7. Navigate to User Configuration\Administrate Templates\Microsoft Outlook 2016\Outlook Options\Preferences\Calendar Options and double-click **Calendar week numbers**.

8. Select **Enabled** and select **OK**, as shown in Figure 4-15.

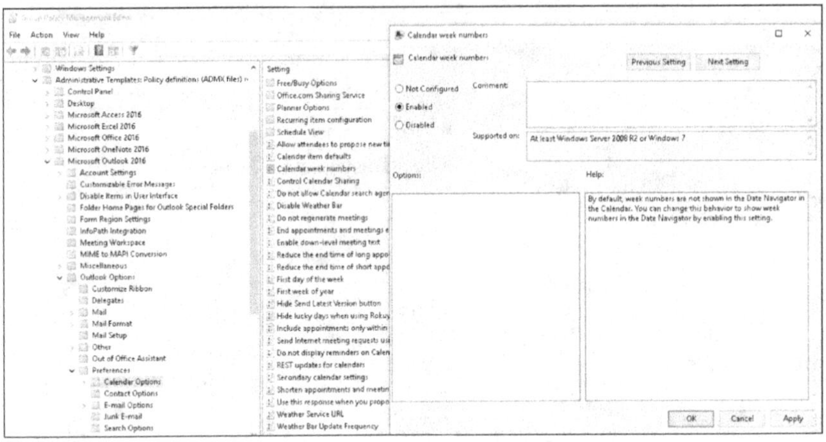

FIGURE 4-15 Enable the Outlook week numbers Group Policy setting

9. Close the **Group Policy Management Editor.**

10. In **Group Policy Management**, right-click the Organizational Unit (OU) containing the users to which you want the GPO to apply and select **Link an Existing GPO**.

11. On the **Select GPO** dialog box, select the **User_Outlook** GPO and select **OK**.

The group policy is now configured and will be applied to users within the OU when they next log in to their Windows computers. By default, Group Policy refreshes in the background every 90 minutes. You can force an individual computer to update the polices by using the `gpupdate /force` command from an elevated command prompt. You can then start Outlook and verify that the calendar week numbers are visible, as shown in Figure 4-16.

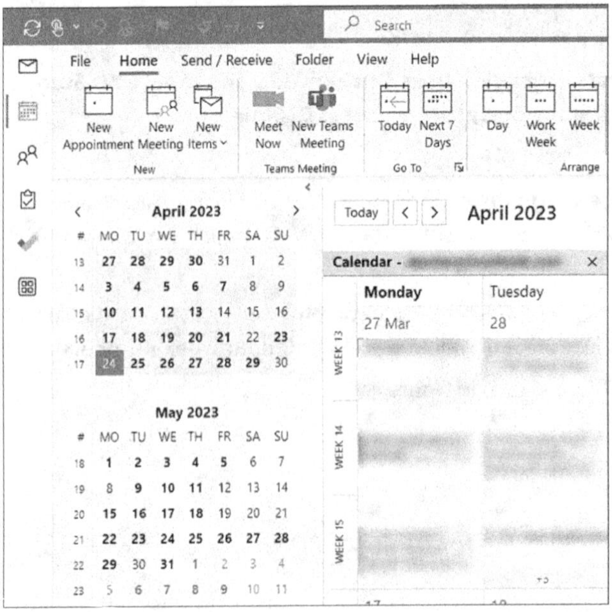

FIGURE 4-16 Display week numbers in Outlook

Configure policies for Office apps by using Intune

Intune is the mobile application management solution to configure and manage policies
related to the software deployed within your organization. These policies are assigned to your
users and devices and control how applications behave.

Just as you saw with Group Policy, Intune also provides policies specifically for controlling how Microsoft Office apps behave. Mobile app management policies within Intune allow
cloud-based management of your Office apps that can be applied to groups of end users. In
addition to configuring app features available to users, you can control how apps access Microsoft 365 services, control data sharing, and enforce security requirements.

Some examples of Office app policies are shown in Table 4-2.

TABLE 4-2 Examples Office app policies

Office app	App policy
Microsoft PowerPoint	Turn off Protected View for attachments opened from Outlook
Microsoft Visio	Block macros from running in Office files from the Internet
Microsoft Word	Turn off Protected View for attachments opened from Outlook
Microsoft Publisher	Publisher Automation Security Level
Microsoft Project	Allow Trusted Locations on the network

Organizations can use the Microsoft 365 Apps admin center to configure the Cloud Policy
service for Microsoft 365 (known as *Cloud Policy*). If you have an Intune subscription, you can
use Cloud Policy directly in the Microsoft Intune admin center under Apps\Policy\Policies for
Office apps. Both services include many of the same user-based policy settings available in
Group Policy. Once defined, Cloud Policies are automatically enforced as users sign in and use
Office.

Before you can use the Cloud Policy with Microsoft 365 Apps for enterprise, you need to
meet the following requirements:

- A supported version of Microsoft 365 Apps for enterprise.
- User accounts created in or synchronized to Azure Active Directory (Azure AD). Users
  must be signed into Microsoft 365 Apps for enterprise with an Azure AD-based account.
- Cloud Policy supports Microsoft 365 Groups and Azure AD Security Groups created in
  or synchronized to Azure AD. The group membership type can be either **Dynamic** or
  Assigned.

- The required URLs and IP address ranges listed here must be properly configured on your network: *https://learn.microsoft.com/en-us/microsoft-365/enterprise/urls-and-ip-address-ranges?view=o365-worldwide#microsoft-365-common-and-office-online*.

- Do not use authenticated proxies.

- Only users who are members of one of the following roles in Azure AD can create a policy configuration:

  - Global Administrator

  - Security Administrator

  - Office Apps Admin

> **NOTE CLICK-TO-RUN VOLUME LICENSED VERSIONS OF OFFICE**
>
> You cannot apply policy configuration to volume-licensed versions of Office that use Click-to-Run, such as Office LTSC Professional Plus 2021 or Office Standard 2019.

Create Office App Policy in Intune

Use this procedure in Intune to create Cloud Policy for Office applications that access Microsoft 365 services:

1. Sign in to the Microsoft Intune admin center as a Global Administrator.

2. Select **Apps** > **Policies for Office apps** > **Create**.

3. If this is your first time creating a cloud policy configuration, you will see the **Create** button in the center of the pane. Otherwise, the **Create** button is on the menu bar.

4. On the **Start with the basics** page, provide a name and description for the policy configuration, then select **Next**.

5. On the **Choose the scope** page, choose the scope for the policy. This can apply to a specific group of users or users who access documents anonymously using **Office on the web**. If you choose the first option, you need to select the group and then select **Next**.

6. On the **Configure Settings** page, select the policy or policies you want to include in the policy configuration, as shown in Figure 4-17, and select **Apply**.

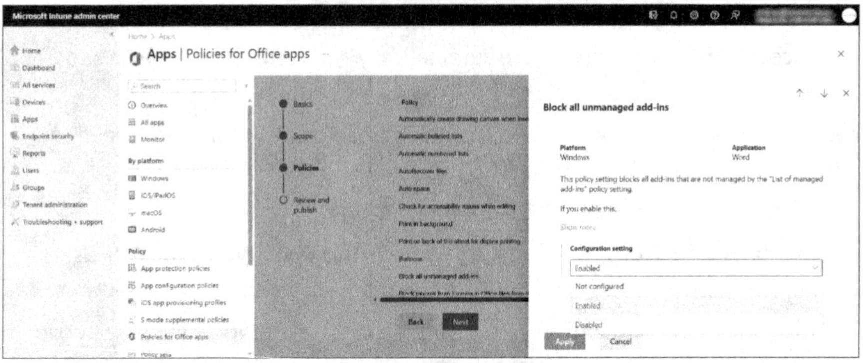

FIGURE 4-17 Configure Cloud Policy using Intune

7. You can configure additional policies by selecting additional policies on the **Configure Settings** page. Once complete, select **Next**.

8. On the **Review configuration and create** page, review your selections and then select **Create** to create the policy configuration.

> **NOTE   USE POLICY FILTERS**
>
> When this book was written, the Cloud Policy service offered 2,206 policies relating to Office apps and multiple platforms. You can use the filter to show only the apps and platforms you want to view.

9. On the **Policy configuration created** page, you will see the successful message indicating the policy configuration has been created; select **Done**.

10. On the **Policy configurations** page, you will see the policy configuration listed.

When a user launches a Microsoft 365 app, the Click-to-Run service used by Microsoft 365 Apps for enterprise will sync with the Cloud Policy to see if a policy configuration should be applied to the user.

> **NOTE   CLOUD POLICY COMPLEMENTS GROUP POLICY-BASED MANAGEMENT**
>
> Cloud Policy service does not replace Group Policy management. Cloud Policy manages user-based policies for Office apps used on any device (iOS, Android, Windows) where the user signs in using Azure Active Directory. Conversely, Group Policy can manage both user-based and machine-based policies on Windows PCs devices joined to an Active Directory domain.

Deploy apps to platform-specific app stores by using Intune

When you deploy apps to your devices, Intune supports several app stores. Before you can deploy the apps, you must add them to Intune.

In a modern workplace, users have multiple devices and platforms your company needs to support. Therefore, you might have several app requirements to consider. In this skill, you will first learn about the various app types supported by Intune and then review how to deploy apps using Intune to various platform-specific app stores. You learned how to deploy a Microsoft Store app earlier in this skill, so now you will now focus on other app stores.

To offer cloud-based app deployment, you can upload your apps to Intune or provide a link to the platform-specific ap store. A full Intune storage subscription offers unlimited storage space for apps. If you use a trial Intune subscription, you have 2 GB of cloud storage.

Intune supports the following general app types.

- Apps from the store (store apps)
- Apps written in-house or as a custom app (line-of-business)
- Apps that are built-in (built-in apps)
- Apps on the web (web link)
- Apps from other Microsoft services

You can add an app in Intune by selecting **Apps** > **All apps** > **Add**. The **Select app** type pane is displayed and allows you to select the app type. Intune supports specific app types, as shown in Table 4-3.

TABLE 4-3 App types supported by Intune

App-specific type	General type	App-specific procedures
Android store apps	Store app	Enter the Google Play store URL for the app.
iOS/iPadOS store apps	Store app	Search for the app and select the app in Intune.
Microsoft store apps	Store app	Enter the app's Microsoft Store URL.
Managed Google Play apps	Store app	Search for the app and select the app in Intune.
Android Enterprise apps	Store app	Search for the app and select the app in Intune.
Microsoft 365 apps for Windows 10 and later	Store app (Microsoft 365)	Select the Microsoft 365 app you want to install.
Microsoft 365 apps for macOS	Store app (Microsoft 365)	Select the Microsoft 365 app suite.
Microsoft Edge, version 77 and later for Windows 10 and later	Store app	Select **Windows 10 and later** under **Microsoft Edge**, and choose **version 77 and later**.
Microsoft Edge, version 77 and later for macOS	Store app	Select **macOS** under **Microsoft Edge**, and choose **version 77 and later**.
Android line-of-business (LOB) apps	LOB app	Enter an Android installation file with the .apk extension.
iOS/iPadOS LOB apps	LOB app	Enter an iOS/iPadOS installation file with the .ipa extension.

App-specific type	General type	App-specific procedures
Windows LOB apps	LOB app	Enter a Windows installation file with one of the .msi, .appx, .appxbundle, .msix, and .msixbundle extensions.
Built-in iOS/iPadOS apps	Built-in app	Select the built-in app in the list of provided apps.
Built-in Android apps	Built-in app	Select the built-in app in the list of provided apps.
Web apps	Web app	Enter a valid URL pointing to the web app.
iOS/iPadOS web clip	Web app	Enter a valid URL pointing to the web app.
Windows web link	Web app	Enter a valid URL pointing to the web app.
Cross-platform web apps	Web app	Enter a valid URL pointing to the web app.
Android Enterprise system apps	Store app	Enter the app name, publisher, and package file.
macOS LOB apps	LOB app	Select an installation file with the extension .pkg.
macOS apps (.dmg)	LOB app (non-store app)	Select an installation file with the .dmg extension.
Microsoft Defender for Endpoint (macOS)	Store app (Microsoft Defender ATP)	Under Microsoft Defender for Endpoint, select macOS as the app type, and then continue by setting up the app in Intune.

App Categories within Intune

An organization with many apps can become overwhelming for users. To help users find an app in the company portal, you can assign apps to one or more categories, such as **Accounting apps** or **Marketing apps**.

When adding apps, you can assign a category in Intune using the following procedure:

1. Sign in to the Microsoft Intune admin center as a Global Administrator.
2. Select **Apps** , then select **App categories**.
3. The **App categories** pane displays a list of current categories.
4. To add a category, select **Add** in the **Create category** pane, and then provide a name for the category.
5. To edit a category, select the ellipsis (...) next to the category, and then select **Pin to dashboard** or **Delete**.
6. Select **Create**.

Add Android store apps to Microsoft Intune

Use the following procedure to add an Android store app to Intune:

1. Sign in to the Microsoft Intune admin center as a Global Administrator.
2. Select **Apps** > **All apps** > **Add**.
3. In the **Select app type** pane, under **Store app**, select **Android store app**.

4. Click **Select**.

5. To configure the app information for the Android app, you must provide the Google Play store's app details. (The Google Play store is located at *https://play.google.com*.)

6. In the **App information** page, add the app details, as shown in Figure 4-18:

   - Name
   - Description
   - Publisher
   - Appstore URL
   - Minimum operating system
   - Category (Optional)
   - Show this as a featured app in the Company Portal
   - Information URL (Optional)
   - Privacy URL (Optional)
   - Developer (Optional)
   - Owner (Optional)
   - Notes (Optional)
   - Logo (Optional)

7. Select **Next.**

8. On the **Assignments** page, select the group assignments for the append and select **Next**.

9. On the **Review + create** page, review the values and settings you entered for the app and select **Create** to add the app to Intune.

10. The app's **Overview** blade is displayed.

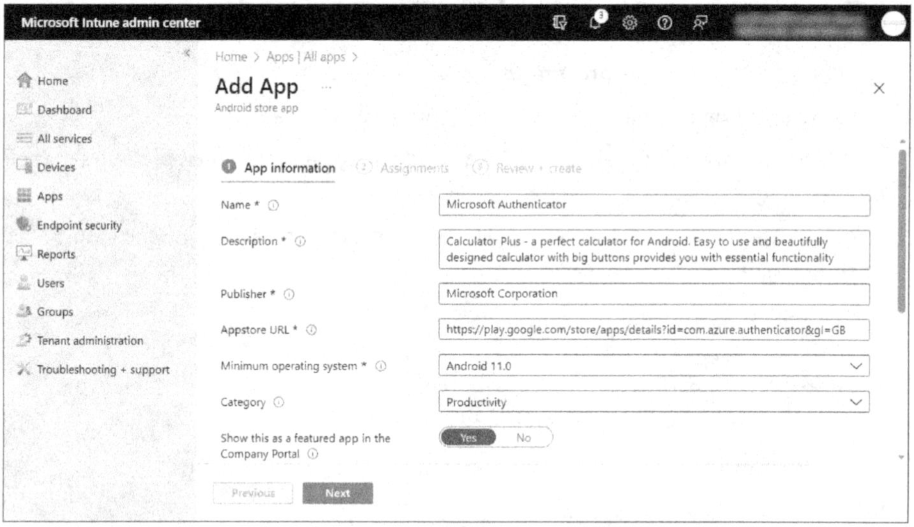

FIGURE 4-18 Adding a Windows 10 Line-of-business app

Add iOS store apps to Microsoft Intune

When you add an iOS store app to Intune, it will be available to be installed on your users' devices. iOS store apps are automatically updated once they are installed.

Only new iOS store apps can be deployed by using Intune. Built-in apps removed by a user, such as the Maps app, cannot be redeployed by Intune. A user must manually reinstall apps that they have removed.

> **NOTE** **FREE IOS APPS ONLY**
>
> Only free iOS apps can be deployed using the following method. If you want to deploy purchased apps using Intune, you should consider the Apple Business Manager program's licensing options. More information about the iOS/iPadOS volume-purchase program can be found at *https://learn.microsoft.com/mem/intune/apps/vpp-apps-ios*.

To add a free iOS store app to Microsoft Intune, use the following procedure:

1. Sign in to the Microsoft Intune admin center as a Global Administrator.
2. Select **Apps** > **All apps** > **Add**.
3. In the **Select app type** pane, under **Store app**, select **iOS store app**.
4. Click **Select**.
5. On the **App information** page, select **Search the App Store**.
6. On the **Search the App Store** pane, select the appropriate country/region locale and enter the app's name (or part of the name). Intune searches the store and returns a list of relevant results.
7. In the results list, find and select the app you want and choose **Select**.
8. On the **App information** page, the app details are partially pre-populated and include:
   - **Name**
   - **Description**
   - **Publisher**
   - **Appstore URL**
   - **Minimum operating system**
   - **Applicable device type**
   - **Category (Optional)**
   - **Show this as a featured app in the Company Portal**
   - **Information URL (Optional)**
   - **Privacy URL (Optional)**
   - **Developer (Optional)**

- **Owner (Optional)**
- **Notes (Optional)**
- **Logo (Optional)**

9. Select **Next.**

10. On the **Assignments** page, select the group assignments for the append and select **Next**.

11. On the **Review + create** page, review the values and settings you entered for the app and select **Create** to add the app to Intune.

12. The app's **Overview** blade is displayed.

Microsoft Store for Business apps

The Microsoft Store for Business provides your organization with a cloud-based storefront for users to find and purchase apps you have made available. You can connect the Microsoft Store for Business to Microsoft Intune and manage the apps from the portal.

Microsoft Store for Business provides the following functionality:

- Synchronize the list of (free or purchased) apps from the store with Intune.
- Synchronized apps can be assigned to groups, users, and devices. Both Online and Offline apps are synchronized to Intune.
- App names are appended with "Online" or "Offline" in the portal.
- Track how many licenses have been used and how many are available in the admin center.
- Intune takes care of the accounting of apps. Assigning and installing apps is blocked if insufficient licenses are available.
- Intune revokes app licenses for apps when the user is deleted from Azure AD.

Use the following procedure to sign up for Microsoft Store for Business:

1. Open a web browser and navigate to *https://www.microsoft.com/business-store.*

2. On the **Sign In** page, enter your company's Global Administrator account credentials.

3. On the **Microsoft Store for Business** webpage, select **Manage**.

4. On the **Overview** page, select **Products & Services** in the navigation pane.

5. If promoted, select a valid certificate for authentication and select **OK**.

Provisioning the Business Store can take up to 36 hours.

> *NOTE* **MICROSOFT STORE FOR BUSINESS RETIREMENT**
> Microsoft Store for Business retirement is due in 2023, though when this book was written, the Microsoft Store for Business retirement was delayed. Organizations can still use the Microsoft Store for Business to deploy apps to managed Windows 11 devices until the store is retired.

Manage Microsoft Store for Business administrative roles

Both the Global Administrator and Billing Administrator have equal full permissions to access and manage the Microsoft Store for Business. They can do everything allowed in the Microsoft Store Admin role. In detail, they can

- Sign up for Microsoft Store for Business and Education
- Modify company profile settings
- Purchase apps
- Distribute apps
- Purchase subscription-based software

Although you can administer everything in Microsoft Store for Business using your Azure AD Global Administrator account, you can also assign administrative roles to your organization's users. The relevant available roles are:

- **Admin**   Can perform all tasks and assign roles to others
- **Purchaser**   Can acquire and distribute products for your organization
- **Basic Purchaser**   Can acquire and distribute products they own
- **Device Guard Signer**   Can manage Device Guard settings

Table 4-4 lists each role's administrative abilities.

TABLE 4-4 Microsoft Store for Business administrative and purchasing roles

Ability	Admin	Purchaser	Device guard signer
Assign roles	X		
Manage Microsoft Store for Business and Education settings	X		
Acquire apps from Microsoft Store and add them to the inventory.	X	X	
Distribute apps that are in your inventory	X	X	
Sign policies and catalogs	X		X

Use the following procedure to assign a Microsoft Store for Business role to a user:

1. Sign in to Microsoft Store for Business as a Global Administrator, Billing Admin, or a user with the Microsoft Store Admin role.
2. On the Microsoft Store for Business portal, select **Manage**.
3. Select the **Permissions** tab in the navigation pane.
4. In Permissions, select the **Roles** tab and select **Assign roles**.
5. In the **Enter a name or email address** box, enter the name or email address of the user to which you want to assign a specific role and select **Save**.
6. Select the appropriate role or roles and then select **Save**, as shown in Figure 4-19.

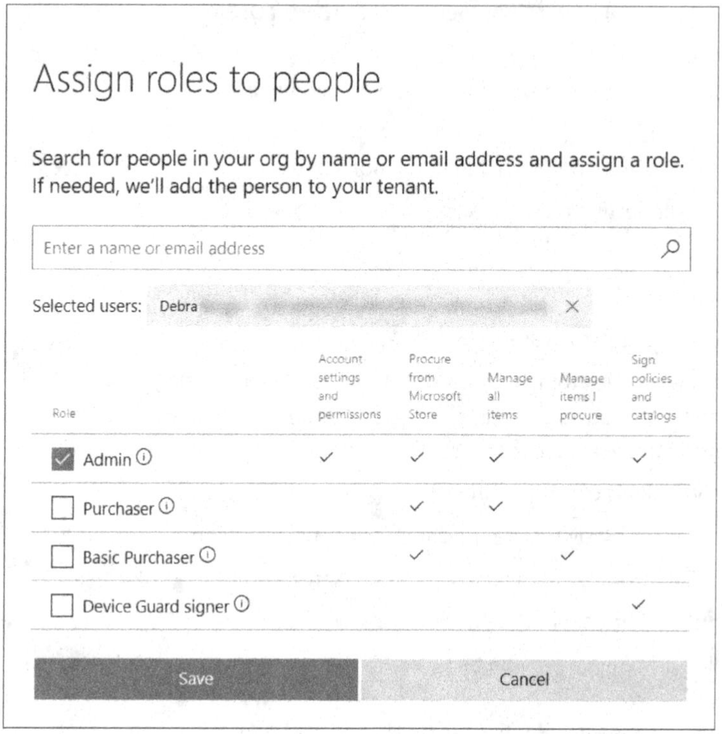

FIGURE 4-19 Assigning Microsoft Store for Business admin roles

You can review the assigned roles by selecting the **Roles** tab, as shown in Figure 4-20.

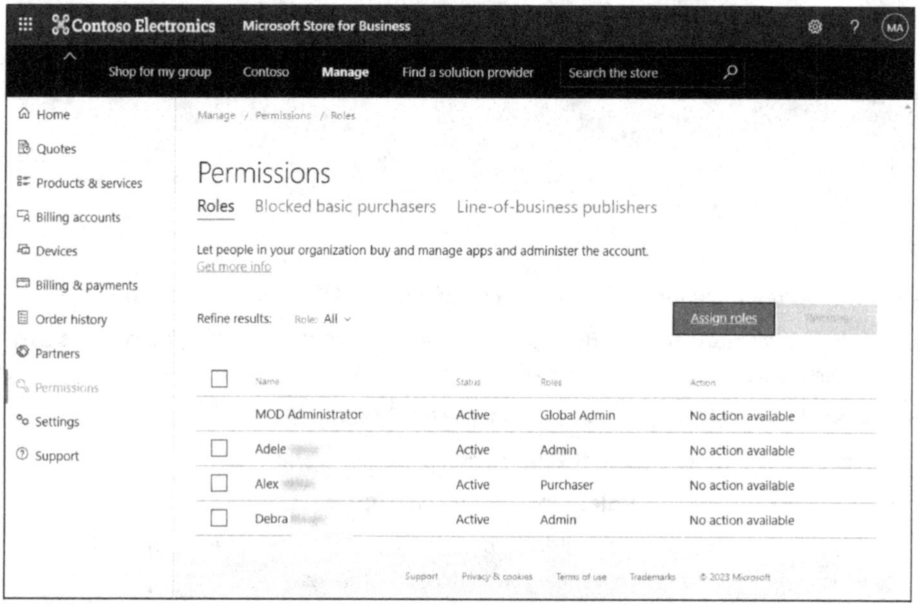

FIGURE 4-20 Reviewing assigned roles

You can also configure permissions for standard users within your organization. To do this, in the navigation pane, select **Settings**. You can review and edit these permissions on the **Shop** tab shown in Figure 4-21.

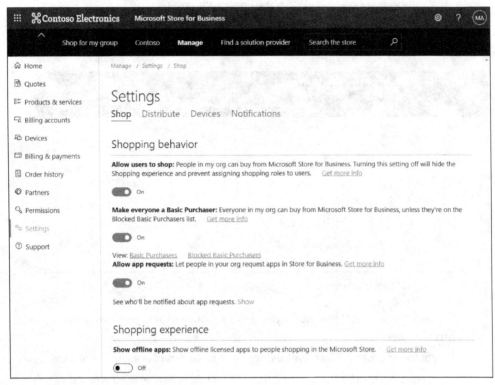

FIGURE 4-21 Reviewing the Microsoft Store for Business shopping behavior

You can edit the following permissions:

- **Allow users to shop** By default, anyone can buy apps from the Microsoft Store for Business. If you disable this setting, the store's shopping experience is hidden, and users cannot purchase apps.

- **Make everyone a basic purchaser** By default, everyone in your organization can buy from Microsoft Store for Business unless you added them to the Blocked Basic Purchasers role on the **Permissions** page. They can also manage the items they purchase.

- **Allow app requests** Enables users to request specific apps be available. Select the **Show** link to determine who receives these requests.

Enable the Private Store

You can create a Private Store for your users with the Microsoft Store for Business. When your users open the Store app in Windows 11, they can see a **Private Store** tab. You can configure this tab with your organization name if you wish.

To configure and enable the **private store**, use the following procedure:

1. In Microsoft Store for Business, select **Settings**, from the navigation bar and select the **Distribute** tab.

2. Under the **private store** heading, select the **Change** link.

3. In the **private store** window, enter the name of the private store and select **Save**.

4. Figure 4-22 shows that the store name is changed in the menu.

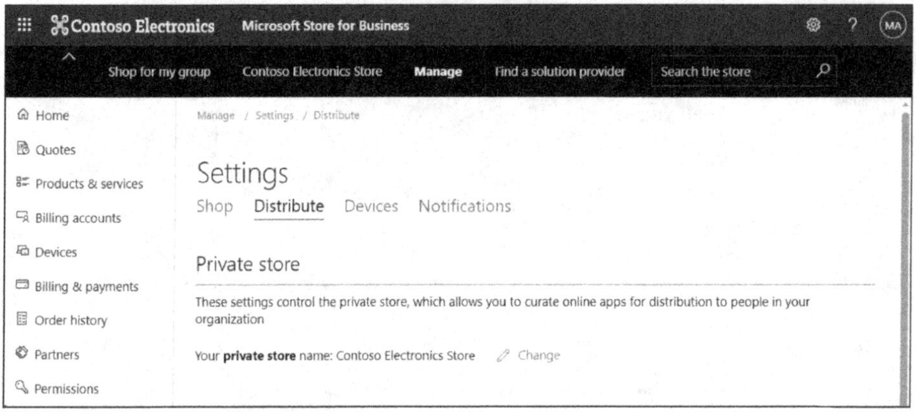

FIGURE 4-22 Editing the private store details

5. In the menu bar, select the link for your private store and then select **Activate private store**.

6. Accept the **Microsoft Store for Business and Education Services agreement.**

The private store is provisioned and enabled and should be visible to your users.

Licensing Store apps

For a user to install and use an app, the app must be licensed. The Microsoft Store for Business supports two methods for licensing apps:

- **Online**   All apps in the Store support online licensing; this is the default licensing mode. Users require an Azure AD account and must authenticate with the Store before acquiring online licensed apps. You can distribute online licensed apps using the Store, Microsoft Intune, or Microsoft Endpoint Configuration Manager.

- **Offline**   Only certain apps support this licensing mode. Using offline licensing enables an organization to obtain the app and install it on the organizational network for distribution to users' devices. These apps can be deployed using Intune or Microsoft Endpoint Configuration Manager and can even be embedded into a standard Windows 11 desktop image. Using the offline mode requires purchasing the required licenses from the software vendor. Note that this mode enables you to make apps available to users that do not have an Azure AD account and/or cannot connect to the Store.

Offline apps can be made visible in the Store by using the following procedure:

1. In the **Microsoft Store for Business** portal, select **Shop** from the **Settings** node in the navigation bar.

2. Under **Shopping experience**, beneath the **Show offline apps** option, select **On**.

Add apps to the Microsoft Store

You can deploy and manage apps after provisioning and configuring the Microsoft Store for Business. To do this, you must add apps to your private store. Next, you must determine how the apps will be made available to your users. There are three approaches you can take when adding apps to the store:

- **Use the Store**   Instruct your users to sign in to the store, select the Private Store tab, and then browse and select the appropriate app.

- **Assign apps from the Store**   Assign apps using the Store. Users will receive an email that provides a link to the app. Users who follow the link must authenticate with the Store, and then the app deploys without further user intervention.

- **Use a management tool**   You can use Intune (or Endpoint Configuration Manager) to deploy the app. You can sync the list of apps you want to make available for deployment to Intune. The Intune administrator can then deploy the app like any other app.

ACQUIRE AN APP AND DISTRIBUTE FROM THE PRIVATE STORE

To acquire an app and make it available in the private store, use the following procedure:

1. Sign in to **Microsoft Store for Business**, and on the menu, select **Shop for my group**.

2. Search for the required app.

3. Select the app, as shown in Figure 4-23, choose the **License type**, and then select **Get the app.**

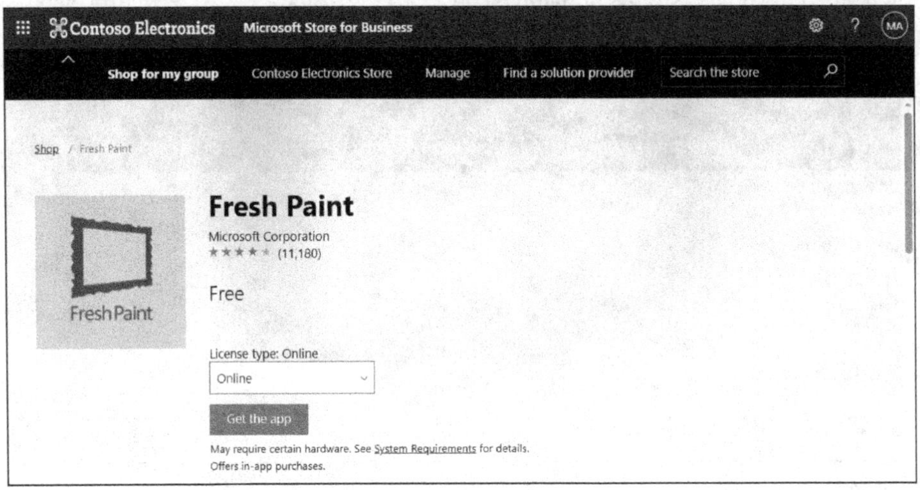

FIGURE 4-23 Selecting an app for inclusion in the Private Store

4. In the **Thanks for your order** window, select **Close**.

5. Select the ellipsis (**...**), and then select **Manage**.

6. Select the **Private store availability** tab.

7. In the **Choose groups of people who can see this app** list, select **No one** or **Everyone**, as shown in Figure 4-24, or select **Specific groups**. In Figure 4-24, **Everyone** is selected; if you choose **Specific groups**, select the appropriate groups.

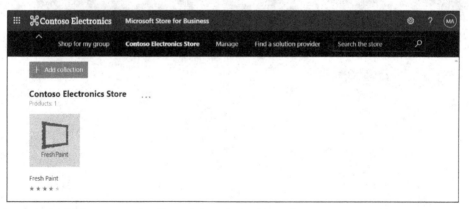

FIGURE 4-24 Enabling all users to see the Fresh Paint app

8. Verify that the private store is updated by selecting the **Private store** link on the menu bar. The newly acquired app is displayed, as shown in Figure 4-25.

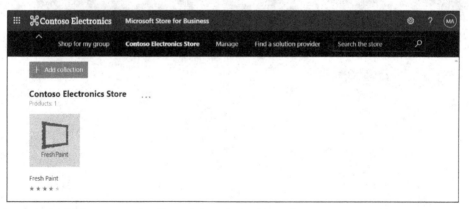

FIGURE 4-25 Adding apps to the Microsoft Store for Business private store

ASSIGNING APPS FROM THE PRIVATE STORE

To assign apps from the Private Store, use the following procedure:

1. Sign in to **Microsoft Store for Business** and select **Manage** from the menu bar.
2. In the navigation pane, select **Products & services**.
3. Locate and select the app that you want to assign.
4. On the **Users** tab, click **Assign to users**, as shown in Figure 4-26.

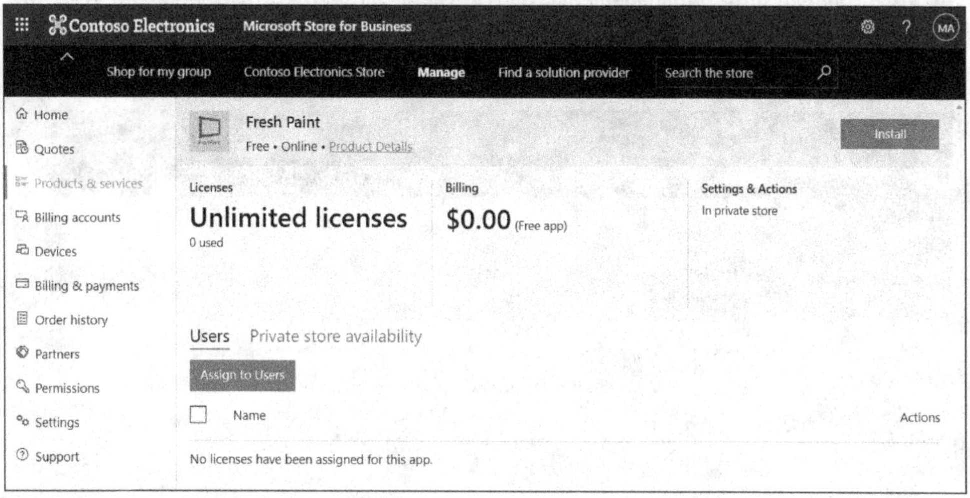

FIGURE 4-26 Assigning Microsoft Store apps to users

5. Select one or more users, and then click **Assign**.
6. You can select Download Results to view a CSV file detailing the assignments when the process is complete or select **Close**.
7. On the **Users** page, you should now see that the license count has increased by the number of assignments made.

Configure Intune MDM Authority and sync with the Microsoft Store for Business

Before you can use Microsoft Store for Business to deploy and manage apps within Intune, you must configure Intune as your organization's mobile device management authority and sign up for an account on the Microsoft Store for Business portal.

To configure the connection between Intune and the Microsoft Store for Business follow this procedure.

1. Sign in to the Microsoft Store for Business as a Global Administrator.
2. Select **Manage**, and then select **Settings** in the navigation bar.
3. On the Setting page, select **Distribute**.

4.   Under **Management tools**, as shown in Figure 4-27, you need to ensure that the MDM tool that your organization is using is active. Your management tool might be **Microsoft Intune Enrollment**, **Microsoft Intune**, or another management tool. If the tool is set to inactive, select **Activate**.

> **NOTE AUTOMATIC MDM ENROLLMENT IS AVAILABLE ONLY FOR AZURE AD PREMIUM SUBSCRIBERS.**
>
> Auto-enrollment with co-management requires licenses for both Azure AD Premium (AADP1) and Microsoft Intune Plan 1.

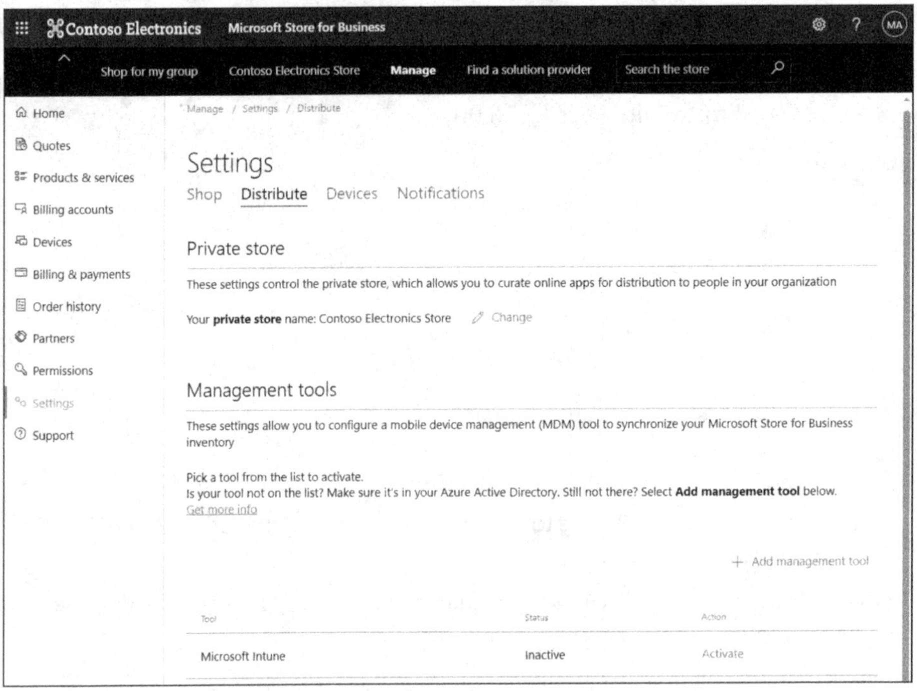

FIGURE 4-27 Microsoft Store for Business management tools setting

USE INTUNE TO DISTRIBUTE THE APP

To distribute an app with Intune, use the following procedure:

1.   Sign in to **Microsoft Store for Business** and add the desired app to the store.

2.   Sign in to the **Microsoft Intune Admin Center** with a Global Administrator account.

3.   If you recently added new apps, you may need to force the sync using the abovementioned procedure.

4.   Select the **Apps** node and then select **Windows Apps**.

5.   Your Microsoft Store for Business apps should be listed with the other app types, as shown in Figure 4-28.

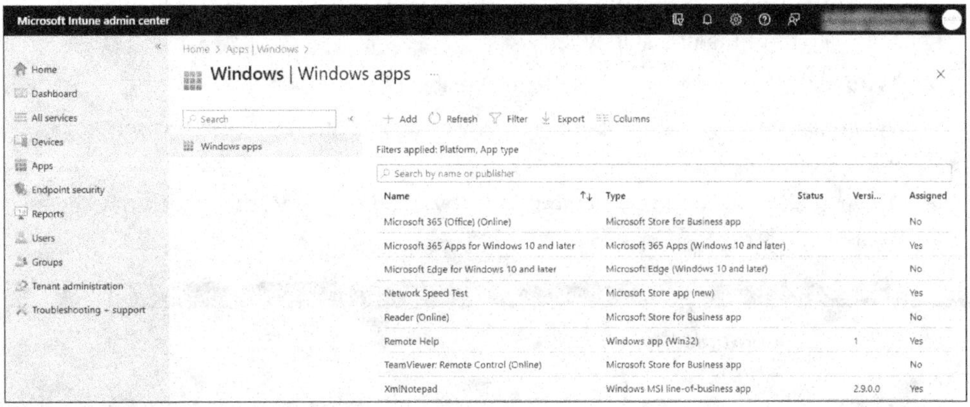

FIGURE 4-28 Viewing Microsoft Store for Business apps in Intune

6. You must now assign the app(s) within Intune as usual. Select the app, select **Properties**, and then edit **Assignments**.

7. You can then define to which users/devices the app will be deployed. This process was described in "Adding a Microsoft Store app" earlier in this chapter.

> **NEED MORE REVIEW?** **DISTRIBUTE APPS TO YOUR EMPLOYEES FROM MICROSOFT STORE FOR BUSINESS**
>
> To review further details about deploying apps with the Microsoft Store for Business, refer to the Microsoft website at *https://learn.microsoft.com /microsoft-store/ distribute-apps-to-your-employees-microsoft-store-for-business*.

Create and manage groups for app assignment

We have already looked at assigning apps to groups, making the app available to users. However, it's important that you also know how to create groups in the Intune portal. You can then assign apps to those groups.

In Intune, there are several different group types. These groups are stored in Azure AD. These groups are

- **Security** These groups give group members access to applications and resources and assign licenses. Group members can be users, devices, and other groups.
- **Microsoft 365** These groups are used for collaboration between other users. Members can access a shared mailbox, calendar, files, SharePoint sites, and so on. Group members can only be users.

The only significant difference from the app distribution perspective is that Security groups can contain other groups and devices as members, while Microsoft 365 groups can only contain users. However, that might not make any difference because, in many organizations, devices are associated with a specific user.

After you have selected the type of the group, you must select the membership type. There are the following three membership types:

- **Assigned**   You specify the group's membership by selecting users.
- **Dynamic user**   You define membership by creating a query that selects users automatically.
- **Dynamic device**   You define membership by creating a query that selects devices, as Figure 4-29 shows.

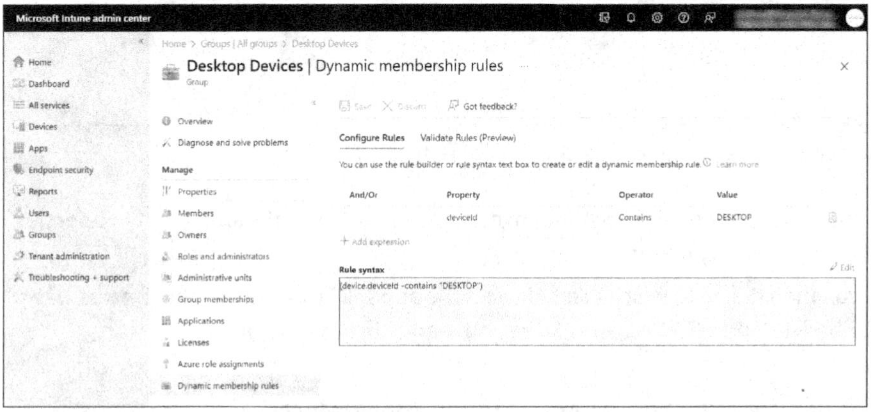

FIGURE 4-29 Reviewing the properties of a dynamic membership device group

---

EXAM TIP

Using dynamic groups is restricted to Azure AD premium subscriptions.

Remember, only security groups can contain devices. To create groups in the Microsoft Intune admin center, use the following procedure:

1. Select the **Groups** node in the navigation pane, and then select **New Group**.
2. Select the **Group type** from the list.
3. Enter a **Group name**.
4. Enter a **Group description** (optional).
5. Select the **Membership type**, and complete one of the following steps:
    - If you choose **Assigned**, select the **No members selected** link, add the members to the group, and select **Create**.
    - If you choose **Dynamic User**, select **Add dynamic query** > **Edit** to enter a query manually. Otherwise, use the **Add expression** link to build a query. When you're finished, select **Save**.
    - If you choose **Dynamic device**, select **Add dynamic query** > **Edit** to enter a query manually. Otherwise, use the **Add expression** link to build a query. When you're finished, select **Save**.
6. Review your choices, and then select **Create**.

After you create the group, you can assign apps to the group, as described in the "Add a Microsoft Store app" section earlier in this chapter.

NEED MORE REVIEW? **COMPARE GROUPS**

To review further details about groups in Intune, refer to the Microsoft website at *https://learn.microsoft.com/microsoft-365/admin/create-groups/compare-groups?view=o365-worldwide.*

Microsoft will send an email to users who have been assigned the app. The email will include a link to the app, as shown in Figure 4-30.

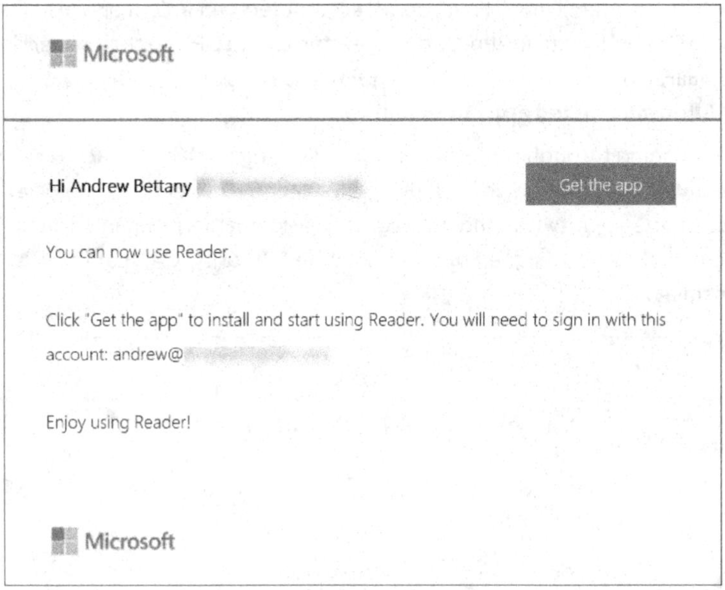

FIGURE 4-30 Email confirming app availability

Enable sideloading of apps

If you want to deploy an app that your development team has created, you cannot use traditional deployment methods since the app has not been securely signed by a trusted authority such as Microsoft. In these situations, your company can sign the app and allow it to be deployed.

Sideloading is the process of installing an LOB app in Windows 11 without needing to use a Store to deploy the app to users' devices. The app might only be internal to your company or originate in the Microsoft Store. To be able to sign an app, it must support offline licensing, and you have acquired adequate licenses for your needs. You can then choose to sideload the app.

Some organizations create their own apps. These apps have the same characteristics as the Universal Windows Platform (UWP) apps found in the Microsoft Store. Enterprise administrators can make these apps available publicly if they want to go through the Microsoft Store certification process or make them available to their enterprise users through a process known as sideloading. Universal apps can be deployed by using provisioning packages created with the Windows Configuration Designer or deployed to Windows devices using Intune.

> **NOTE** **WINDOWS 8.1 INTUNE SUPPPORT**
>
> Microsoft Intune ended support on October 21, 2022, for devices running Windows 8.1 and no longer supports Windows 8.1 sideloading.

Enable sideloading in Windows 11

By default, the sideloading option in Windows 11 is disabled. To enable sideloading, you can use a Group Policy setting. To configure Group Policy so that computers can accept and install sideloaded apps you created for your organization, open the appropriate GPO for editing, and navigate to `Computer Configuration\Administrative Templates\Windows Components\App Package Deployment`. Double-click **Allow all trusted apps to install**.

You can also enable sideloading through the Settings app. In **Settings**, select **Privacy & security**, and on the **For developers** tab shown in Figure 4-31, select **On** under the **Developer mode** heading. Select **Yes** on the security warning message. After sideloading is enabled, any line of business (LOB) Microsoft Store app signed by a Certification Authority (CA) that the computer trusts can be installed.

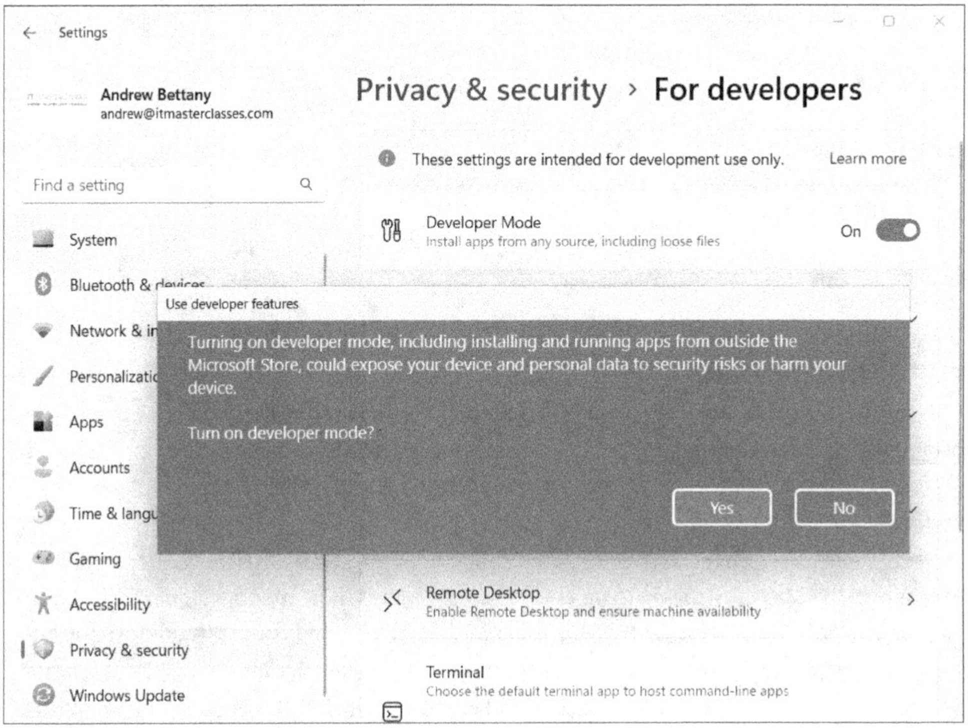

FIGURE 4-31 Enabling sideloading

Sideload an app

After enabling sideloading, you can sideload the app using the AppX Windows PowerShell module and the associated cmdlets. To manually sideload an app for the currently logged-in user, perform the following steps from a Windows PowerShell prompt:

Type **Add-appxpackage "path and name of the app"** to add the app and press Enter. Table 4-5 shows the available AppX cmdlets. If you need to add app dependencies, use this command: Add-appxpackage C:\MyApp.appx DependencyPath C:\appplus.appx.

The app installs and then is available to the user. If multiple users share a single computer, follow the process for each user. The AppX module for Windows PowerShell includes several cmdlets to install and manage LOB Microsoft Store apps, some of which are described in Table 4-5.

TABLE 4-5 Cmdlets in the AppX module for Windows PowerShell

Cmdlet	Description
Add-AppxPackage	Add a signed app package to a single user account
Get-AppxLastError	Review the last error reported in the app package installation logs
Get-AppxLog	Review the app package installation log
Get-AppxPackage	View a list of the app packages installed for a user profile
Get-AppxPackageManifest	Read the manifest of an app package
Remove-AppxPackage	Remove an app package from one or more user accounts

Use DISM to sideload apps into Windows images

If you want to sideload the apps to multiple computers, use Deployment Image Servicing and Management (DISM) commands. You can use DISM commands to manage app packages in a Windows image. When you use DISM to provision app packages, those packages are added to a Windows image and installed for the desired users when they log on to their computers.

You should be familiar with the DISM syntax when servicing a Windows image, whether a computer is offline or online. Table 4-6 describes a few cmdlets to keep in mind.

TABLE 4-6 Commands for use with DISM

Command	Description
DISM.exe {/Image:<path_to_image_directory>	/ Online} [dism_global_options] {servicing_option} [<servicing_argument>]	To service a Windows image with DISM
DISM.exe /Image:<path_to_image_directory> [/Get-ProvisionedAppxPackages | /Add-Provisioned AppxPackage | /Remove-ProvisionedAppxPackage | /Set-ProvisionedAppxDataFile]	To service an app package (.appx or .appxbundle) for an offline image
DISM.exe /Online [/Get-ProvisionedAppxPackages | /Add-ProvisionedAppxPackage | /Remove-ProvisionedAppxPackage | /Set-ProvisionedAppxDataFile	To service an app package (.appx or .appxbundle) for a running operating system

Other command-line service options include /Get-ProvisionedAppxPackages, /FolderPath, /PackagePath, /LicensePath, and /Add-ProvisionedAppxPackage. Becoming familiar with these is very important because you'll likely be tested on them. You can learn about all available commands and options at *https://learn.microsoft.com/windows-hardware/manufacture/desktop/dism-app-package--appx-or-appxbundle--servicing-command-line-options?view=windows-11.* Review this article and make sure you can make sense of commands you might come across, such as

```
Dism /Online /Add-ProvisionedAppxPackage /FolderPath:C:\Test\Apps\MyUnpackedApp /
SkipLicense
```

Another example is:

```
Dism /Image:C:\test\offline /Add-ProvisionedAppxPackage /FolderPath:c:\Test\Apps\
MyUnpackedApp /CustomDataPath:c:\Test\Apps\CustomData.xml
```

Skill 4.2: Plan and implement app protection and app configuration policies

Using Microsoft Intune, you can implement Mobile Application Management (MAM) to assign, configure, update, secure, and monitor your users' apps. You use MAM to manage app usage and protect app data on your users' Windows, iOS, and Android devices.

> **This skill covers how to:**
> - Plan and implement app protection policies for iOS and Android
> - Manage app protection policies
> - Implement Conditional Access policies for app protection policies
> - Plan and implement app configuration policies for managed apps and managed devices
> - Manage app configuration policies

Plan and Implement App Protection policies for iOS and Android

When you start working with Intune, you need to establish your organization's objectives and what devices, apps, and data your users use. This will help define your goals and objectives for controlling and securing your organizational data.

Intune introduces the feature of managed apps, which allows you to granularly manage the use of apps that run on users' devices. Typically, the device used within an organization will be enrolled and managed by Intune, though MDM and MAM are separate, and this allows applications to be managed using MAM even on devices not managed by MDM, such as a users' personal devices.

Once you understand what and how your users use data, you can consider how you control and secure it using Intune MAM. You can use managed apps to enforce the following behaviors in your users' apps:

- Restrict copying and pasting
- Restrict Save As
- Specify a managed browser for opening web links
- Define app-level Conditional Access
- Enable multi-identity use
- Provide app protection both with and without device enrollment

The precise details of management options vary based on the type of device being managed. Table 4-7 identifies the key app management capabilities.

TABLE 4-7 Management options in Intune MAM

App management function	Android /Android enterprise	iOS/ iPadOS	macOS	Windows 10/11
Add and assign apps to devices and users	Yes	Yes	Yes	Yes
Assign apps to devices not enrolled with Intune	Yes	Yes	No	No
Use app configuration policies to control the startup behavior of apps	No	Yes	No	No
Use mobile app provisioning policies to renew expired apps	No	Yes	No	No
Protect company data in apps with app protection policies	Yes	Yes	No	No
Remove only corporate data from an installed app (app selective wipe)	Yes	Yes	No	Yes
Monitor app assignments	Yes	Yes	Yes	Yes
Assign and track volume-purchased apps from an app store	No	Yes	No	Yes
Mandatory install of apps on devices (required)	Yes	Yes	Yes	Yes
Optional installation on devices from the Company Portal (available installation)	Yes	Yes	Yes	Yes
Install shortcut to an app on the web (web link)	Yes	Yes	Yes	Yes
In-house (line-of-business) apps	Yes	Yes	Yes	Yes
Apps from a store	Yes	Yes	No	Yes
Update apps	Yes	Yes	No	Yes

To implement app protection policies, open the Microsoft Intune admin center, and sign in as a Global Administrator. Navigate to the **Apps** node, as shown in Figure 4-32. Under **Policy**, select the **App Protection Policies** node.

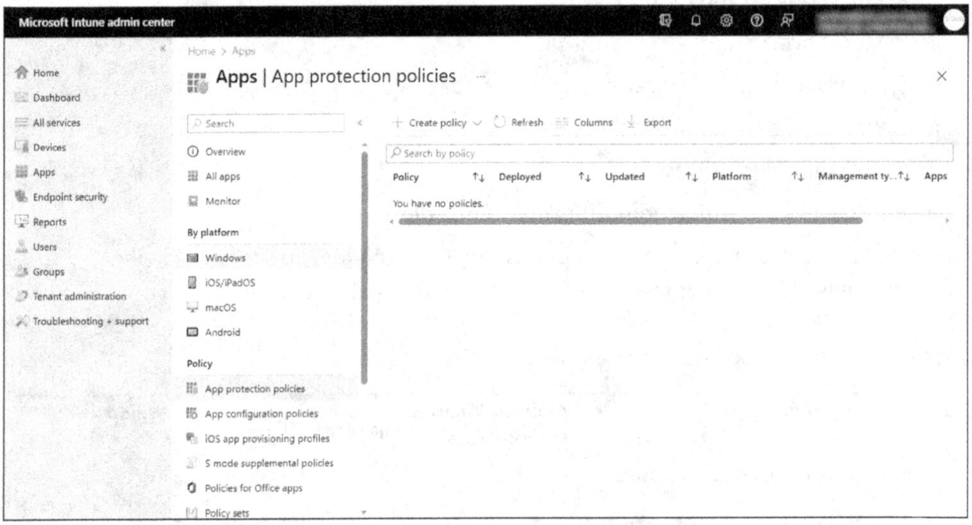

FIGURE 4-32 The Apps node in the Microsoft Intune admin center

The **App** blade provides the following functionality:

- **Overview**   View the tenant name, MDM authority, tenant location, account status, app installation status, and app protection policy status.
- **All apps**   Display a list of all available apps. Add additional apps to be managed. View the status of each app and app assignment status.
- **Monitor**   Display license status for apps by the following categories.
  - **App licenses**   View, assign, and monitor volume-purchased apps from the app stores.
  - **Discovered apps**   View apps assigned by Intune or installed on a device.
  - **App install status**   View the status of an app assignment you created. For more information, see Monitor app information and assignments with Microsoft Intune.
  - **App Protection Status**   View an app protection policy status for a user you select.
  - **App Configuration Status**   View app configuration status for a selected user.
- **By platform**   Select these platforms to view the available apps by platform.
  - Windows
  - iOS
  - macOS
  - Android

- Policy
    - **App protection policies**   Associate settings with an app to protect the company data it uses.
    - **App configuration policies**   Supply settings might be required when users run an app.
    - **iOS app provisioning profiles**   iOS apps include a provisioning profile and code signed by a certificate. Assign a new provisioning profile policy to devices with apps nearing expiration.
    - **S mode supplemental policies**   Select this option to authorize additional applications for your managed S-mode devices.
    - **Policies for Office apps**   Create mobile app management policies for Office mobile apps that connect to Microsoft 365 services.
    - **Policy sets**   Create an assignable collection of apps, policies, and other management objects.
- Other
    - **App selective wipe**   Remove only corporate data from a selected user's device.
    - **App categories**   Add, pin, and delete app category names.
    - **E-books**   Purchase multiple licenses for an app or books that you want to use in your company.
    - **Help and support**   Troubleshoot, request support, or view Intune status. All Intune customers have 24/7 technical support provided by Microsoft.
- Within the **Connectors and tokens** area of the **Tenant administration** you will find the following app-related functionality:
    - **Windows enterprise certificate**   Apply or view the status of code-signing certificates that are used to distribute line-of-business apps to your Windows devices.
    - **Microsoft Endpoint Configuration Manager**   Displays information about the Configuration Manager connector, including the recent synchronization status.
    - **Apple VPP Tokens**   Apply and view your Apple Business Manager iOS/iPadOS volume purchased licenses.
    - **Managed Google Play**   Access the Google enterprise app store, set scope tags, and sync the approved apps from the store to Intune.

Manage App Protection policies

In Intune, you can protect data stored in apps stored on devices that run Windows, iOS/iPadOS, and Android operating systems. You use Windows Information Protection (WIP) on enrolled devices when protecting Windows devices. Since July 2022, Microsoft began to deprecate WIP features though support for WIP will continue supported versions of Windows. As a replacement for WIP, Microsoft recommends using Microsoft Purview Information Protection and Microsoft Purview Data Loss Prevention. These topics are a focus of the Exam SC-400: Microsoft Information Protection Administrator certification, which can be found at *https://learn.microsoft.com/certifications/exams/SC-400.*

> **EXAM TIP**
>
> On the MD-102 exam, you can expect to see questions about managing protection on devices running iOS/iPadOS and Android operating systems rather than WIP.

Create an iOS app protection policy

Before creating an iOS app protection policy, you must ensure that the application supports policies that control the app behavior. Most modern and popular apps such as Word, OneDrive, and many third party apps support app protection policies. The app can be installed on an enrolled or are not enrolled in Intune (mam without enrollment).

To create an iOS app protection policy, use the following procedure:

1. Navigate to the Microsoft Intune admin center and sign in using your Global Administrator account.
2. In the navigation pane, select **Apps**.
3. In the **Apps** blade, under **Policy**, select **App protection policies.**
4. Select **Create policy**.
5. In the **Create policy** dropdown, select **iOS/iPadOS.**
6. On the **Basics** tab, enter the following information, and then select **Next**:
   - **Name**   Enter a name for your new policy.
   - **Description**   Enter an optional description.
7. On the **Apps** tab, configure the following information, and then select **Next.**
   - **Target policy to**   Choose **All Apps, All Microsoft Apps** or **Core Microsoft Apps** in the **Selected apps** dropdown.
   - **Public apps**   Select the **Select Public Apps** link, and on the **Select apps to target** blade, select one or more apps for protection, as shown in Figure 4-33, and then click **Select**.
   - **Custom apps**   Click the **Select Custom Apps** link, and on the **Select Apps To Target** blade, search for and select the custom apps by entering a **Bundle ID** and clicking **Select**. For example, to add a custom app from Contoso, enter the Bundle ID: **com.contoso.app**.

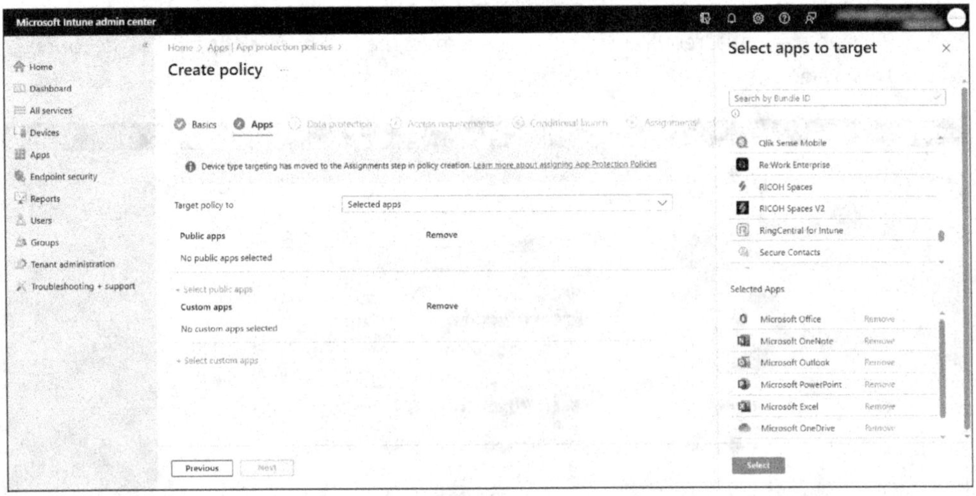

FIGURE 4-33 Specifying the apps to be protected in an app protection policy

8. Select **Next**, and then on the **Data protection** tab shown in Figure 4-34, configure the **Data Loss Prevention (DLP) controls like cut, copy, paste, and save as restrictions**. Settings include:

- **Data Transfer**   Controls whether users can send data from protected apps to other locations, such as iTunes and iCloud backups, and other specific apps. You can also control whether other apps can send data to the protected apps.

- **Encryption**   Enables you to specify whether organizational data must be encrypted.

- **Functionality**   Controls aspects of app usage with protected data, such as printing and synchronization.

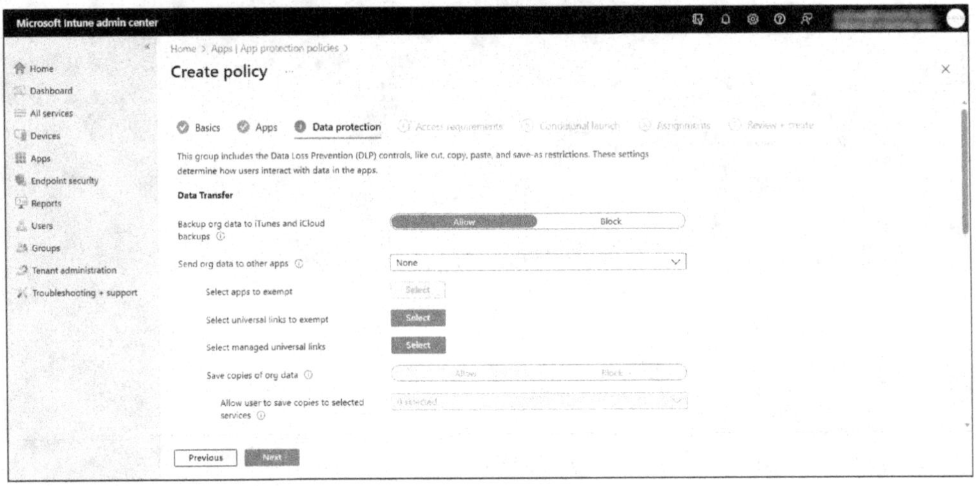

FIGURE 4-34 Configuring app protection policy data protection settings

9. Select **Next**, and on the **Access requirements** tab shown in Figure 4-35, configure the PIN and credential requirements that users must meet to access apps in a work context. Then select **Next**.

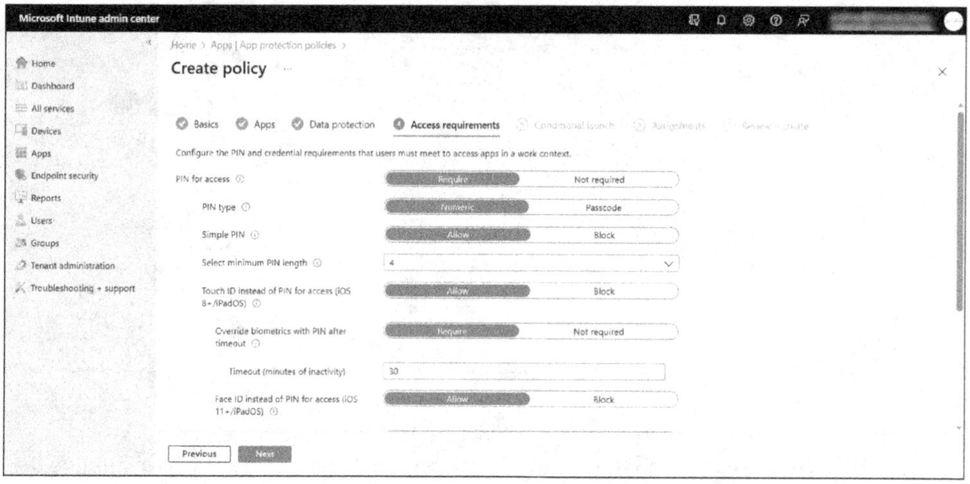

FIGURE 4-35 Configuring access requirements for an app protection policy

10. On the **Conditional launch** tab displayed in Figure 4-36, you can define the following:

- **App conditions** Defines actions taken when the maximum PIN attempts are reached or the action that is taken when a device is offline for more than a defined grace period. Actions include **Reset PIN**, **Block access**, and **Wipe data**.

- **Device conditions** Determines whether you'll allow devices to launch protected apps if they are rooted (also known as *jailbroken*).

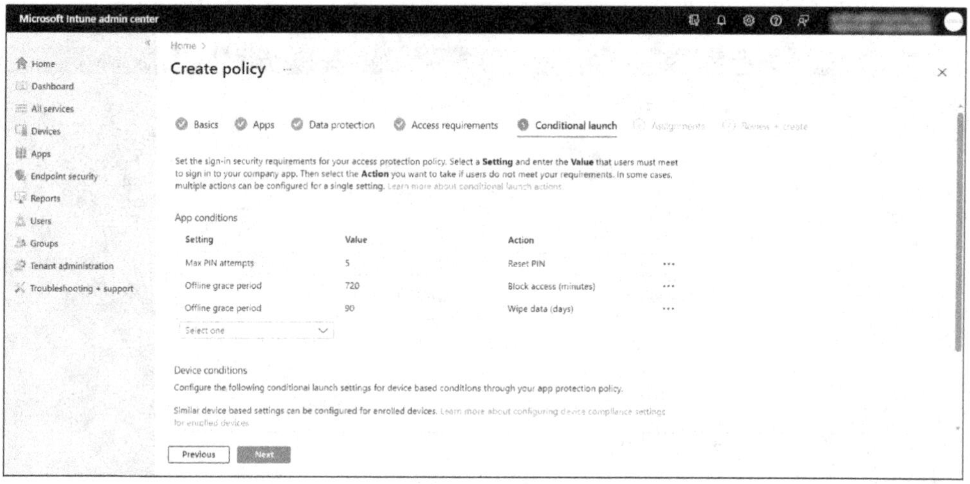

FIGURE 4-36 Defining the conditional launch setting in an app protection policy

11. Select **Next**. You must now assign the policy to group(s) to a group of users or a group of devices.

12. Select **Next**, review the settings on the **Review + create** page, and then select **Create**. The iOS/iPadOS app protection policy has been created and will appear on the list of app protection policies.

Create an Android app protection policy

To create an Android app protection policy, use the following procedure:

1. Navigate to the Microsoft Intune admin center and sign in using your Global Administrator account.

2. On the navigation pane, select **Apps**.

3. On the **Apps** blade, under **Policy**, select **App protection policies.**

4. Select **Create policy**.

5. In the **Create policy** dropdown, select **Android**.

6. On the **Basics** tab, enter the following information, and then select **Next**:
   - **Name** Enter a name for your new policy.
   - **Description** Enter an optional description.

7. On the **Apps** tab, configure the following information, and then select **Next**:
   - **Target policy to**
   - **Public Apps**
   - **Custom Apps**

8. On the **Data protection** tab, configure the DLP controls:
   - **Data transfer**
   - **Encryption**
   - **Functionality**

9. Select **Next**, and then, on the **Access requirements** tab, configure the PIN and credential requirements that users must meet to access apps in a work context. Then select **Next**.

10. On the **Conditional launch** tab, define the **App conditions** and **Device conditions**. Select **Next**.

11. Select **Next**. You must now assign the policy to group(s) to a group of users or a group of devices.

12. Select **Next**, and then review the settings on the **Review + create** page and then select **Create**.

The Android app protection policy has been created and will appear on the list of app protection policies.

Implement Conditional Access policies for app protection policies

Conditional Access is a capability Azure AD offers to add a layer of security to data, available on both enrolled and non-enrolled devices. When a user launches a managed app, Intune can assess app-based launch conditions that an organization has configured using app protection policies. Based on these policies, Intune can block the app from accessing company data or even wipe your company's corporate data from the end user's device.

You decide the compliance conditions to be implemented, and Intune enforces them. You can explicitly choose one or more actions, such as blocking access and wiping data.

App protection policy rules can be evaluated both explicitly and implicitly. For example, an app protection policy can be applied to Microsoft Outlook with a Conditional Access rule that adds Outlook to an approved list of apps that can access corporate email. Explicitly defining only, the Outlook app can be used to access Exchange Online will also implicitly block all built-in mail apps on an iOS/iPadOS and Android device from accessing corporate email.

Following are the prerequisites:

- Enterprise Mobility + Security (EMS) or an Azure AD Premium subscription.
- Users must have an EMS or Azure AD Premium license assigned.
- Azure AD Conditional Access supports the following device platforms:
  - Android
  - iOS
  - Windows
  - macOS
  - Linux

To create a Conditional Access policy

Use the following procedure to create an app protection policy using conditional launch actions (Conditional Access policy):

1. Sign in to the Microsoft Intune admin center as a Global Administrator.
2. Select **Endpoint security**, and under **Manage**, select **Conditional access**.
3. On the **Conditional access | Overview (Preview)** page, select **Create new policy**.

4. On the **New** page, enter a policy **Name**, and then under **Assignments**, select **Users** to apply the policy to users and groups. You can use the **Include** or **Exclude** options to refine the users and groups for the policy.

5. Select **Cloud apps or actions** and apply the policy to **Cloud apps** as shown in Figure 4-37. Use the **Include** or **Exclude** options to select the apps to protect. Choose **Select**.

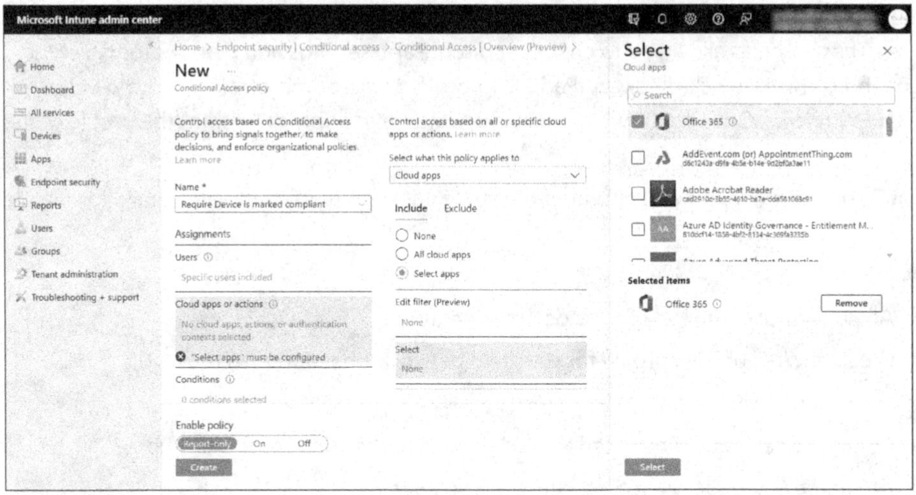

FIGURE 4-37 Configure Conditional Access app protection policy

6. Select **Conditions** and select **Client apps** to apply the policy to apps and browsers. Select **Done**.

7. Under **Access controls**, select **Grant** to apply control access enforcement based on a device compliance status. Once one or more controls have been defined, select **Select**.

8. Select and configure the **Session** option to create session-based restrictions for Office 365, SharePoint Online, and Exchange Online cloud apps.

9. Under **Enable policy**, select **Report-only**, **On**, or **Off** to define the policy.

10. Select **Create** to save your changes. By default, the Enable policy is set to Report-only.

11. Select Refresh on the **Conditional access | Overview (Preview)** page to view the policy overview pane with the policy summary displayed.

NOTE **DON'T GET LOCKED OUT**

Take care not to lock yourself or users out of your system. Blocking access is a powerful control that can have unintended side effects. You should ensure that you properly test and validate the block control's effects before enabling it at scale. You can use tools such as the Conditional Access report–only mode (*https://learn.microsoft.com/azure/active-directory/conditional-access/concept-conditional-access-report-only*) and the What If tool in Conditional Access (*https://learn.microsoft.com/azure/active-directory/conditional-access/what-if-tool*) to find out how app configuration policies will affect access to resources.

Plan and implement app configuration policies for managed apps and managed devices

You learned that Intune allows you to configure the security settings within Microsoft 365 apps to control the security settings within a corporate environment. Using the same process, you can configure the app's non-security settings on the device using Intune.

Intune allows you to create app configuration profiles that configure app settings and features. These profiles allow you to enable or disable app settings and features for different devices and platforms, including iOS/iPadOS, Android device administrator, Android Enterprise, and Windows. Once configured, you will use Intune to apply or "assign" the profile to the devices.

Mobile device management, provided by Intune, includes many templates that allow you to complete different app-related tasks.

Some profile examples include:

- Allow or disable the use of Bluetooth on the device.
- Create a Wi-Fi or VPN profile for specified networks that apps can use.
- Manage software updates.
- Configure devices as dedicated kiosk devices that can run one or many apps.
- Configure language or locale settings within apps.
- Branding, such as adding a company logo.

The app's supplier must allow this configuration for iOS and Android apps to be configured. The supplier normally publishes the configuration settings (keys and values), which you can specify using an **App Configuration** setting, or by providing an XML file containing the keys and values.

For Windows devices, you can further extend the capabilities of the built-in configuration profiles by using Administrative templates. These templates include hundreds of settings you can configure for apps, including Microsoft Edge, OneDrive, Remote Desktop, and Office apps. By using Administrative templates, you can apply settings like those found in group policy; they're 100 percent cloud-based.

> *NOTE* **GROUP POLICY ANALYTICS**
>
> If you use Group Policies to configure your apps and devices and need to migrate to the cloud, you can use a Microsoft Intune tool called Group Policy Analytics to analyze your on-premises GPOs. The tool shows the settings that Intune supports. You can use the Group Policy analytics tool to migrate your GPOs to a settings catalog policy that can be deployed to your Windows 10 and Windows 11 devices. To find out more about the Group Policy analytics tool, refer to the Microsoft website at *https://learn.microsoft.com/en-us/mem/intune/configuration/ group-policy-analytics*.

Manage App Configuration policies

Once you have identified the settings you want to apply, you will configure the settings on your iOS and Android devices using App Configuration policies.

Create an iOS app configuration policy

You can use iOS app configuration policies to configure selected apps on devices running iOS/iPadOS 8.0 and later. The app type needs to be a managed iOS/iPadOS store app from the app store or an App package for iOS.

To create an iOS app configuration policy, use the following procedure:

1. Navigate to the Microsoft Intune admin center and sign in using your Global Administrator account.

2. In the navigation pane, select **Apps**.

3. On the Apps blade, under **Policy**, select **App configuration policies**.

4. Select **Add**, and then in the **Add** dropdown, select **Managed devices**.

5. On the **Basics** tab, enter the following values:

   - **Name** Type a name for your new policy.

   - **Description** Type an optional description.

   - **Device enrollment type** This is set to **Managed devices** and cannot be changed.

   - **Platform** Select iOS/iPadOS.

   - **Targeted app** Choose **Select app** and choose the apps you want to configure, as displayed in Figure 4-38.

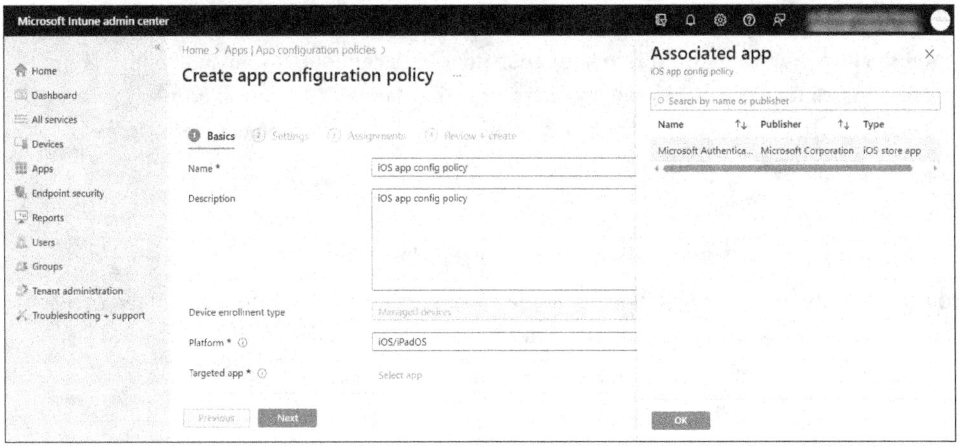

FIGURE 4-38 Selecting a managed app for an App configuration policy

6. Select **OK**, and then select **Next**.

7. On the Settings tab, in the **Configuration settings format** list, select either:

   - **Use configuration designer**   Enter the relevant configuration key, value type, and configuration values.
   - **Enter XML data**   Paste the values from an XML configuration file into the text box.

8. On the **Assignments** tab, assign the policy to your users and devices.

9. Select **Next**, and then review the settings on the **Review + create** page and then select **Create**.

> **NEED MORE REVIEW?**   **ADD APP CONFIGURATION POLICIES FOR MANAGED IOS DEVICES**
>
> To learn more about the configurable properties, including how to use the configuration designer and how to create an app configuration XML file, refer to the Microsoft website at *https://learn.microsoft.com/mem/intune/apps/app-configuration-policies-use-ios*.

Create an Android app configuration policy

You can use Intune to create app configuration policies on Managed Google Play apps on managed Android Enterprise devices. When the policy settings are enabled, the app checks for them and is configured the first time the app runs.

Intune supports Android 8.x or higher for managed devices' app configuration policies. For Intune app protection policies and app configuration delivered through Managed apps app configuration policies, Intune requires Android 9.0 or higher.

Creating an Android app configuration policy is nearly identical to the iOS process.

> **NOTE**   **DEPLOYING OUTLOOK FOR IOS AND ANDROID APP CONFIGURATION SETTINGS**
>
> You can find out how to use app configuration policies to configure a specific app (in this case, Outlook for iOS and Android) by referring to the Microsoft website at *https://docs.microsoft.com/exchange/clients-and-mobile-in-exchange-online/outlook-for-ios-and-android/outlook-for-ios-and-android-configuration-with-microsoft-intune*.

Create an Android app configuration policy

You can also create a managed app configuration policy by selecting the app instead of first choosing the device platform. Use the following procedure:

1. In the Microsoft Intune admin center, navigate to **Apps**.

2. On the **Apps** blade, select **App configuration policies.**

3. Select **Add**, and then in the **Add** dropdown, select **Managed apps**.

4. On the **Basics** tab, enter the following values:

   - **Name**   Type a name for your new policy.
   - **Description**   Type an optional description.

- **Device enrollment type**   This is set to **Managed apps** and cannot be changed.
- **Target policy to**   Select the appropriate app type: **All Apps**, **All Microsoft Apps**, or **Core Microsoft Apps**, and select **Next**.

On the **Settings** page, enter the configuration settings to configure your apps.

5.   Select **Next**, assign your policy, and select **Next**.

6.   Finally, on the **Review and create** page, select **Create**.

Chapter summary

- You can use Intune to deploy Store apps, Microsoft 365 apps, Web link apps, Built-in apps, Line-of-business apps, and Windows (Win32) apps.
- You can use the Office Deployment Toolkit and the Office Customization Tool to customize and configure bespoke installations of Microsoft 365 apps.
- After configuring an app for deployment, you must remember to assign the app to the appropriate user or device groups.
- You can customize the components of the Microsoft 365 apps that are available to your Windows 11 users.
- Using Administrative Template files for Microsoft Office allows you to manage Office apps with GPOs.
- You can use role assignments in the Microsoft Store to determine what designated users can do in the store.
- You must enable the Microsoft Store for Business Private Store before your organization's users can see and use it.
- To enable Intune to distribute Microsoft Store for Business apps, you must enable Intune as a management tool in the Microsoft Store for Business portal. Also, you must enable synchronization between Microsoft Store for Business and Intune from the Microsoft Intune admin center.
- Offline licensing in the Microsoft Store for Business enables you to distribute apps through Intune or your internal network infrastructure rather than relying on the Microsoft Store for Business storefront.
- When making apps available in the private Store in Microsoft Store for Business, you can choose to make an app visible to the following: No One, Everyone, or Specific Groups.
- Dynamic groups require Azure AD premium licensing.
- You can sideload LOB apps with Windows 11 by creating a provisioning package with Windows Configuration Designer and using that package to distribute the app.
- You can sideload apps directly into a Windows image using DISM.exe.
- App protection policies enable you to control corporate data when used in protected apps.

- You can layer conditional access on top of app protection policies to create app-based launch conditions.
- You can use app configuration policies to configure apps on devices to define settings that your apps will use.

Thought experiment

In this thought experiment, demonstrate your skills and knowledge of the topics covered in this chapter. You can find the answers in the section that follows.

Scenario 1

At Adatum, you want to be able to provide your users with several apps that are available in the Microsoft Store. However, you only want users to be able to view and install specific apps. Your organization has a Microsoft 365 subscription.

As a consultant for Adatum, answer the following questions.

1. How could you use the Microsoft Store for Business to help with this requirement?
2. How could you use Intune to help provide additional control over this solution?
3. You want the apps to be distributed using Intune. Apps are not synchronizing to Intune from the Microsoft Store for Business. What should you check?

Scenario 2

At Adatum, you are planning to migrate your app management from Group Policy to cloud management using Microsoft Intune. Adatum must retain the same level of security for the data that users access. Your organization has a Microsoft 365 subscription.

As a consultant for Adatum, answer the following questions.

1. How could you review whether Intune can implement the functionality provided by the existing GPO settings?
2. You implement several app protection settings within Intune. None of the users are receiving the settings. How would you troubleshoot to resolve the issue?
3. Users should only access corporate email using the Outlook app. How will you implement this?

Thought experiment answers

This section contains the solution to the thought experiment. Each answer explains why the answer choice is correct.

Scenario 1

1. You could acquire the apps from the Microsoft Store and then publish the apps to a Private Store in Microsoft Store for Business. Users can then browse the Private Store and access the desired apps.

2. You can use Intune to assign acquired apps by synchronizing the Microsoft Store for Business and Intune. The synced apps would show in the Microsoft Intune admin center in the Apps list. You can then assign the apps to specific groups of users or devices., meaning they wouldn't need to use the Store app at all.

3. You need to ensure that the Microsoft Store for Business is configured to use Microsoft Intune. Check the status and ensure that the status is activated. You will also need to check the status of the Microsoft Store for Business connector to ensure this is enabled. With both settings configured correctly, apps can be synchronized from the Microsoft Store for Business to Intune.

Scenario 2

1. You can use the analyzer tool to review existing GPOs and establish the equivalent settings within Intune that can be implemented.

2. As this is a new implementation, several issues could need troubleshooting. The following list is not exhaustive and includes:

    - Ensure users have been allocated an Intune license. Without an Intune license, the policies will not be available to users.

    - Check the assignment settings for the created policies. If they have been incorrectly assigned to users, they might not receive the settings.

    - Do the apps support configuration using Intune app protection settings? Only apps designed to be managed and configured using an MDM solution will support app protection policies.

    - Has sufficient time elapsed to ensure the Intune policies have been synchronized? Intune policies need some time to become effective for users.

    - Has the user launched the app? Only when the app is launched for the first time since the policies are enabled will the app be configured with the policy settings.

3. You would configure an app protection policy with a Conditional Access rule that adds Outlook to the approved list of apps that can access corporate email. This will implicitly deny access to corporate email using any other mail client. You would assign this policy to all users.

CHAPTER 5

MD-102 Endpoint Administrator exam updates

The purpose of this chapter

This chapter will be updated over time, and a PDF will be posted online so you can access the latest information about exam changes, even after purchasing this book.

Why do we need a chapter that updates over time? There are three reasons:

1. To add more technical content to the book before it is time to replace the current book edition with the next edition. This chapter will include additional technology content and possibly additional PDFs containing more content.

2. To communicate details about the next exam version, tell you about our publishing plans for that edition, and help you understand what that means to you.

3. To accurately map the current exam objectives to existing chapter content. While exam objectives evolve and products are renamed, much of the content in this book will remain accurate and relevant. In addition to covering any content gaps that appear through additions to the objectives, this chapter notes how the new objectives map to the current text.

After the initial publication of this book, supplemental updates will be provided as digital downloads for minor exam updates. We may announce a new edition if an exam has major changes or accumulates enough minor changes. We will do our best to provide any updates to you free of charge before we release a new edition. However, if the updates are significant enough between editions, we may release the updates as a low-priced standalone eBook.

If we produce a free updated version of this chapter, you can access it on the book's companion website. Simply visit the companion website page and see the "Exam updates" section.

If you have not yet accessed the companion website, follow these steps:

1. Browse to *microsoftpressstore.com/register*.

2. Enter the print book ISBN (even if you purchased an eBook).

3. After registering the book, go to your account page and select the **Registered Products** tab.

4. Click the **Access Bonus Content** link to access the companion website. Select the **Exam Updates** link or scroll down to that section to check for updates.

About possible exam updates

Microsoft reviews exam content periodically to ensure it aligns with the technology and job role associated with the exam. This includes, but is not limited to, incorporating functionality and features related to technology changes, changing skills needed for success within a job role, and revisions to product names. Microsoft updates the exam details page to notify candidates when changes occur. Once you register this book, you will be notified when updates are made, and the updated chapter is available.

Impact on you and your study plan

Microsoft's information helps you plan, but it also means that the exam might change before you pass the current exam. That impacts you, affecting how we deliver this book to you. This chapter gives us a way to communicate in detail about those changes as they occur, but you should watch the following sites for news:

- **Microsoft Learn**   Check the main source for up-to-date information: *microsoft.com/ learn*. Make sure to sign up for automatic notifications.
- **Microsoft Press**   Find information about products, offers, discounts, and free downloads: *microsoftpressstore.com*. Make sure to register your purchased products.

As changes to the MD-102 exam occur, we will publish an updated version of this chapter, which will likely include the following:

- **The content that has been removed**   If you plan to take the new exam version, you can ignore the removed content when studying for the exam.
- **New content planned per new exam topics**   This will tell you what's coming.

Exam objective updates

You can find the current study guide for exam MD-102 at *learn.microsoft.com/en-us/ certifications/resources/study-guides/md-102*.

It contains the most recent version of the exam objective domain.

Updated technical content

The current version of this chapter has no additional technical content.

Objective mapping

This *Exam Ref* is structured by the authors based on the topics and technologies covered on the exam and not based on the specific order of topics in the exam objectives. Table 5-1 maps the current version of the exam objectives to chapter content, allowing you to locate where a specific exam objective item has coverage without consulting the index.

TABLE 5.1 Exam Objectives mapped to chapters.

Exam objective	Chapter
Deploy Windows client	
Prepare for a Windows client deployment	1
■ Select a deployment tool based on requirements	
■ Choose between migrate and rebuild	
■ Choose an imaging and/or provisioning strategy	
■ Select a Windows edition based on requirements	
■ Implement subscription-based activation	
Plan and implement a Windows client deployment by using Windows Autopilot	1
■ Configure device registration for Autopilot	
■ Create, validate, and assign deployment profiles	
■ Set up the Enrollment Status Page (ESP)	
■ Deploy Windows devices by using Autopilot	
■ Troubleshoot an Autopilot deployment	
Plan and implement a Windows client deployment by using the Microsoft Deployment Toolkit (MDT)	1
■ Plan and implement an MDT deployment infrastructure	
■ Create, manage, and deploy images	
■ Monitor and troubleshoot a deployment	
■ Plan and configure user state migration	
Configure remote management	1
■ Configure Remote Help in Intune	
■ Configure Remote Desktop on a Windows client	
■ Configure the Windows Admin Center	
■ Configure PowerShell remoting and Windows Remote Management (WinRM)	
Manage identity and compliance	
Manage identity	2
■ Implement user authentication on Windows devices, including Windows Hello for Business, passwordless, and tokens	
■ Manage role-based access control (RBAC) for Intune	
■ Register devices in and join devices to Azure AD	
■ Implement the Intune Connector for Active Directory	
■ Manage the membership of local groups on Windows devices	
■ Implement and manage Local Administrative Passwords Solution (LAPS) for Azure AD	
Implement compliance policies for all supported device platforms by using Intune	2
■ Specify compliance policies to meet requirements	
■ Implement compliance policies	
■ Implement Conditional Access policies that require a compliance status	
■ Manage notifications for compliance policies	
■ Monitor device compliance	
■ Troubleshoot compliance policies	

Exam objective	Chapter
Manage, maintain, and protect devices	
Manage the device lifecycle in Intune	3
■ Configure enrollment settings ■ Configure automatic and bulk enrollment, including Windows, Apple, and Android ■ Configure policy sets ■ Restart, retire, or wipe devices	
Manage device configuration for all supported device platforms by using Intune	3
■ Specify configuration profiles to meet requirements ■ Implement configuration profiles ■ Monitor and troubleshoot configuration profiles ■ Configure and implement Windows kiosk mode ■ Configure and implement profiles on Android devices, including fully managed, dedicated, corporate owned, and work profile ■ Plan and implement Microsoft Tunnel for Intune	
Monitor devices	3
■ Monitor devices by using Intune ■ Monitor devices by using Azure Monitor ■ Analyze and respond to issues identified in Endpoint analytics and Adoption Score	
Manage device updates for all supported device platforms by using Intune	3
■ Plan for device updates ■ Create and manage update policies by using Intune ■ Manage Android updates by using configuration profiles ■ Monitor updates ■ Troubleshoot updates in Intune ■ Configure Windows client delivery optimization by using Intune ■ Create and manage update rings by using Intune	
Implement endpoint protection for all supported device platforms	3
■ Implement and manage security baselines in Intune ■ Create and manage configuration policies for Endpoint security including antivirus, encryption, firewall, endpoint detection and response (EDR), and attack surface reduction (ASR) ■ Onboard devices to Defender for Endpoint ■ Implement automated response capabilities in Defender for Endpoint ■ Review and respond to device issues identified in the Microsoft Defender Vulnerability Management dashboard	

Exam objective	Chapter
Manage applications	
Deploy and update apps for all supported device platforms	4
■ Deploy apps by using Intune	
■ Configure Microsoft 365 Apps deployment by using the Microsoft Office Deployment Tool or Office Customization Tool (OCT)	
■ Manage Microsoft 365 Apps by using the Microsoft 365 Apps admin center	
■ Deploy Microsoft 365 Apps by using Intune	
■ Configure policies for Office apps by using Group Policy or Intune	
■ Deploy apps to platform-specific app stores by using Intune	
Plan and implement app protection and app configuration policies	4
■ Plan and implement app protection policies for iOS and Android	
■ Manage app protection policies	
■ Implement Conditional Access policies for app protection policies	
■ Plan and implement app configuration policies for managed apps and managed devices	
■ Manage app configuration policies	

Index

A

access
   conditional access policies, apps, 296–297
   Controlled Folder Access, Microsoft Defender Exploit Guard, 224
   RBAC, 94
      Azure AD, 94–97
      configuring, 97
accounts
   domain accounts, 87
   local accounts, 87
   Microsoft 365 accounts, 86
   Microsoft accounts, 86
   Windows 11 accounts, 86–87
activating
   firmware-embedded activation keys, 28
   Windows 11, subscription-based activation, 21–28
AD (Active Directory), Intune Connector for Active Directory, 107–111
AD DS (Active Directory Domain Services), 84
   domain accounts, 87
   joining domains, 84–85
adding images to MDT, Windows client MDT deployments, 45–46
administration
   LAPS, 117–120
   Microsoft 365 Apps admin center, 255–257
   Microsoft Store for Business apps, 275–277
   PowerShell remoting, 74
      configuring, 74–76
      using, 76–77
   Windows Admin Center, 70
      authentication, 72
      installing, 71
      using, 72–74
administrative template profiles, 169–171
ADMX files, importing, 171

analytics
   Azure Log Analytics, 198–199
   Endpoint Analytics, 199–201
   Group Policy, 171–172
Android OS
   apps
      configuration policies, 300–301
      protection policies, 295–296
      store apps, adding to Intune, 271–272
   devices
      configuration profiles, 167–168, 186–187
      enrolling, 158–159
      updating with configuration profiles, 211
antivirus software, Microsoft Defender Antivirus, 229–230
apps (applications)
   adding to Microsoft Store, 279–281
   Android apps
      configuration policies, 300–301
      protection policies, 295–296
      store apps, adding to Intune, 271–272
   conditional access policies, 296–297
   deploying, 245–246
      deploying to specific app stores, 269–285
      with Intune, 246–251, 258–262
      Microsoft 365 apps, 251–255
      Microsoft Store app, 250–251
      to specific app stores, 269–285
   distributing with Intune, 282–283
   grouping, 283–285
   Intune
      adding Android store apps to Intune, 271–272
      adding iOS store apps to Intune, 273–274
      categories, 271
      distributing apps, 282–283
      grouping apps, 283–285

F

G

H

I

J - K - L

M

N

Network Protection, Microsoft Defender Exploit Guard, 224

noncompliant devices
    device management, 128–129
    retire lists, 130

non-Windows devices, enrolling, 158–160

notifications, compliance policies, 124–125

O

objective mapping, MD-102 Endpoint Administrator exam, 306–309

objective updates, MD-102 Endpoint Administrator exam, 306

ODT (Office Deployment Tool), deploying Microsoft 365 apps, 252–253, 258–262

Office app policies, configuring with
    Group Policy, 263–267
    Intune, 267–269

Office Customization Tool, deploying Microsoft 365 apps, 253–255

OOBE, device enrollments, 156–157

operating system images, Windows client MDT deployments, 43

P

passwords, LAPS, 117–120

permissions
    PowerShell scripts, 175
    Remote Help, configuring, 60–61

PIM (Privileged Identity Management), 95

PIN (Personal Identification Numbers), 90–92

planning device updates, 202–204

policy sets, configuring, 160–161

PowerShell
    deploying scripts from provisioning packages, 7
    remoting, 74
        configuring, 74–76
        using, 76–77
    scripts
        deploying from Intune, 172–175
        permissions, 175
        policy creation, 173–174
        runtime settings, 173

Private Store, Microsoft Store for Business apps, 277–278, 279–281

protection policies, apps, 288
    Android apps, 295–296
    iOS apps, 292–295
    MAM, 288–291

provisioning, dynamic, 3–4
    methods, 3
    provisioning packages, 4–5
        applying, 7–8
        creating, 5–6
        customizing, 6
        deploying PowerShell scripts, 7
        managing, 8
        troubleshooting, 9–10
        usage scenarios, 8–9

provisioning strategies, Windows client deployments, 11–16

PXE BOOT, 14–15

R

RBAC (Role-Based Access Control), 94
    Azure AD, 94–97
    configuring, 97

readiness data, Microsoft 365 apps, 261–262

rebuilding new computers, Windows client deployments, 10–11

recovery, BitLocker, 213–218

reference images, Windows client MDT deployments, 44–45

registering devices, Azure AD, 106

regulations and compliance policies, 121–122

Remote Desktop
    configuring, 64–65
        creating connections, 66–68
        customizing from command line, 68–70
        troubleshooting connections, 70
    enabling, 65–66

Remote Help
    configuring
        capabilities, 55–56
        free trial, 56
        network considerations, 56–57
        network endpoints, 57
        permissions, 60–61
        prerequisites, 56–57
        user role assignments, 61

X - Y - Z

Plug into learning at

MicrosoftPressStore.com

The Microsoft Press Store by Pearson offers:

- Free U.S. shipping

- Buy an eBook, get three formats – Includes PDF, EPUB, and MOBI to use with your computer, tablet, and mobile devices

- Print & eBook Best Value Packs

- eBook Deal of the Week – Save up to 50% on featured title

- Newsletter – Be the first to hear about new releases, announcements, special offers, and more

- Register your book – Find companion files, errata, and product updates, plus receive a special coupon* to save on your next purchase